ROMANTICISM AND THEATRICAL EXPERIENCE

Bringing together studies in theater history, print culture, and literature, this book offers a new consideration of Romantic-period writing in Britain. Recovering a wide range of theatrical criticism from newspapers and periodicals, some of it overlooked since its original publication in Regency London, Jonathan Mulrooney explores new contexts for the work of the actor Edmund Kean, essayist William Hazlitt, and poet John Keats. Kean's ongoing presence as a figure in the theatrical news presented readers with a provocative reimagining of personal subjectivity and a reworking of the British theatrical tradition. Hazlitt and Keats, in turn, imagined the essayist and the poet along similar theatrical lines, reframing Romantic prose and poetics. Taken together, these case studies illustrate not only theater's significance to early nineteenth-century Londoners but also the importance of theater's textual legacies for our own reassessment of "Romanticism" as a historical and cultural phenomenon.

JONATHAN MULROONEY is Professor of English at the College of the Holy Cross in Worcester, Massachusetts.

CAMBRIDGE STUDIES IN ROMANTICISM

Founding Editor
Marilyn Butler, University of Oxford

General Editor
James Chandler, University of Chicago

Editorial Board
John Barrell, University of York
Paul Hamilton, University of London
Mary Jacobus, University of Cambridge
Claudia Johnson, Princeton University
Alan Liu, University of California, Santa Barbara
Jerome McGann, University of Virginia
David Simpson, University of California, Davis

This series aims to foster the best new work in one of the most challenging fields within English literary studies. From the early 1780s to the early 1830s, a formidable array of talented men and women took to literary composition, not just in poetry, which some of them famously transformed, but in many modes of writing. The expansion of publishing created new opportunities for writers, and the political stakes of what they wrote were raised again by what Wordsworth called those 'great national events' that were 'almost daily taking place': the French Revolution, the Napoleonic and American wars, urbanization, industrialization, religious revival, an expanded empire abroad, and the reform movement at home. This was an enormous ambition, even when it pretended otherwise. The relations between science, philosophy, religion, and literature were reworked in texts such as Frankenstein and Biographia Literaria; gender relations in A Vindication of the Rights of Woman and Don Juan; journalism by Cobbett and Hazlitt; and poetic form, content, and style by the Lake School and the Cockney School. Outside Shakespeare studies, probably no body of writing has produced such a wealth of commentary or done so much to shape the responses of modern criticism. This indeed is the period that saw the emergence of those notions of literature and of literary history, especially national literary history, on which modern scholarship in English has been founded.

The categories produced by Romanticism have also been challenged by recent historicist arguments. The task of the series is to engage both with a challenging corpus of Romantic writings and with the changing field of criticism they have helped to shape. As with other literary series published by Cambridge University Press, this one will represent the work of both younger and more established scholars on either side of the Atlantic and elsewhere.

See the end of the book for a complete list of published titles.

ROMANTICISM AND THEATRICAL EXPERIENCE

Kean, Hazlitt, and Keats in the Age of Theatrical News

JONATHAN MULROONEY

College of the Holy Cross, Worcester Mass.

CAMBRIDGE
UNIVERSITY PRESS

University Printing House, Cambridge CB2 8BS, United Kingdom

One Liberty Plaza, 20th Floor, New York, NY 10006, USA

477 Williamstown Road, Port Melbourne, VIC 3207, Australia

314–321, 3rd Floor, Plot 3, Splendor Forum, Jasola District Centre,
New Delhi – 110025, India

79 Anson Road, #06–04/06, Singapore 079906

Cambridge University Press is part of the University of Cambridge.

It furthers the University's mission by disseminating knowledge in the pursuit of education, learning, and research at the highest international levels of excellence.

www.cambridge.org
Information on this title: www.cambridge.org/9781107183872
DOI: 10.1017/9781316874905

© Jonathan Mulrooney 2018

This publication is in copyright. Subject to statutory exception and to the provisions of relevant collective licensing agreements, no reproduction of any part may take place without the written permission of Cambridge University Press.

First published 2018

Printed in the United Kingdom by TJ International Ltd. Padstow Cornwall

A catalogue record for this publication is available from the British Library.

ISBN 978-1-107-18387-2 Hardback

Cambridge University Press has no responsibility for the persistence or accuracy of URLs for external or third-party internet websites referred to in this publication and does not guarantee that any content on such websites is, or will remain, accurate or appropriate.

For Grace and Anna

Contents

List of Figures	*page* viii
Acknowledgments	ix
Introduction	1
PART I THE MAKING OF BRITISH THEATER AUDIENCES	21
1 Theater and the Daily News	23
2 Britain's Theatrical Press, 1800–1830	57
PART II THEATER AND LATE ROMANTICISM	107
3 Edmund Kean's Controversy	109
4 Hazlitt's Romantic Occasionalism	152
5 Keats, Kean, and the Poetics of Interruption	191
Bibliography	236
Index	254

Figures

1. John Orlando Parry, *The Posterman* (1835); by permission of the Dunhill Archive. — page 4
2. Front page of *The Times* (Monday, September 4, 1809); by permission of the British Library. — 33
3. George Cruikshank, "Keen-ish Sport in Cox's Court!!: or Symptoms of Crim.Con. in Drury Lane" (Fairburn, 1824); by permission of Folger Shakespeare Library. — 126
4. "The Court of King's Bench turn'd into a Cock pit, or 800 Symptoms of Kean Sport" (Marks, 1825); by permission of Folger Shakespeare Library. — 126
5. "Mr. Kean as Richard The IIIrd, Act 5th, Scene 4th" (Marks, early c19); by permission of Folger Shakespeare Library. — 127
6. R. Cruikshank, "The Hostile Press; and the consequences of Crim.Con or Shakespeare in danger" (Fairburn, 1825); by permission of Folger Shakespeare Library. — 129

Jacket Illustration: Detail of John Orlando Parry, *The Posterman* (1835); by permission of the Dunhill Archive/Getty Images.

Acknowledgments

This book emerged from a desire to bring together two seemingly disparate early interests – performed theater and Romantic poems. It has been overlong in the making, with an extended hiatus in the middle in favor of other commitments, and consequently I have the pleasure of acknowledging those who offered much help and many favors along the way. Part of Chapter 1 was published in *Nineteenth-Century Contexts*, and part of Chapter 5 appeared previously in *Studies in Romanticism* (published by the Trustees of Boston University). I thank the journal editors for permission to reprint these materials. A passage from Chapter 4 appeared in different form in an essay in *The Fountain Light: Studies in Romanticism and Religion*, ed. J. Robert Barth (2002).

James Chandler believed in the project before I did and along with Linda Bree at Cambridge University Press exhibited long-standing patience and unstinting support even when I seemed to have lost the way. Kevin Gilmartin provided a first reading for the Press that was a model of rigor and collegiality, as well as a thorough reading of the revised manuscript. I am grateful as well for Gregory Dart's cogent and hugely helpful reader's report. Both readers' willingness to praise what was working and alert me to places I had gone amiss has greatly strengthened the final version. Alan Bewell, Miranda Burgess, Tom Crochunis, Mary Favret, Sonia Hofkosh, Jerrold Hogle, Jon Klancher, Paige Reynolds, Eliza Richards, Christopher Ricks, Charles Rzepka, David Wagenknecht, and James Winn read all or portions of the manuscript and offered vital corrections, suggestions, and enthusiasm.

Among the great joys of being a Romanticist is the company it enables one to keep. So many people have, whether they know it or not, helped me become a better scholar, teacher, and colleague. Indeed when I began compiling a list of those to thank personally, it quickly grew so long that the fear of omitting someone became debilitating. Instead, then, I will mention just a few of that company, beyond those I have already named, and further say that if you are reading this and can imagine yourself in any way as part of the circles in which I have moved, know that I am grateful for your presence and for the time we have spent together. Warm thanks, first, go to Jonathan Sachs and Andrew Stauffer, indispensable fellow travelers who have challenged me and celebrated with me in all the important moments. Jeff Cox, Greg Kucich, and Nicholas Roe have showed me in true Cockney fashion how sociability and intellectual work go hand in hand. I have grown up as a Romanticist alongside Miranda Burgess, Scott Hess, Jennifer Jones, Tilar Mazzeo, Brian McGrath, Emily Rohrbach, Emily Sun, and so many more whose intellectual gifts and human decency continually astound me. Matt Borushko, Carmen Faye Mathes, Anahid Nersessian, Michele Speitz, and others like them give me hope for the field, and I am lucky to call them friends. And the theater mafia (you know who you are, Terry Robinson et al.) will always remain a special cohort. I wish finally to give special mention to the ever-missed Jane Moody, without whose work on Romantic-period theater (and without whose personal encouragement) this book simply would never have existed.

Audiences at many lectures and presentations helped shaped the work, especially members of the North American Society for the Study of Romanticism (NASSR), the Keats-Shelley Association of America, and the Keats Foundation Hampstead Conference, whose regular activities are highlights on my calendar. The Boston Area Romanticist Colloquium (BARC), which a few of us formed in the wake of the NASSR 2013 conference, has provided a new venue for scholarly sociability. Research for the project was supported by funding from the National Endowment for the Humanities, the Keats-Shelley Association of America, and the College of the Holy Cross, and was conducted principally at the Harvard Theatre Collection and the Houghton Library, as well as on shorter voyages into the British Library. I thank the staffs at those archives for their acumen at finding often obscure and forgotten materials.

I am keenly aware of how lucky I am to work at the College of the Holy Cross, an institution willing to give its faculty time to develop as intellectuals in ways that do not always yield immediate professional benefits. Among the many English Department colleagues who have modeled for me the ideal of the teacher-scholar (not to mention teacher-scholar-parent), I am particularly pleased to share a hall with Debra Gettelman, Shawn Maurer, and Paige Reynolds. Maurice Géracht, James Kee, and Rich Matlak have been fine mentors over the years, and Melissa Schoenberger's arrival has reinvigorated the teaching of poetry at Holy Cross. Thanks also to Deans Timothy Austin and Margaret Freije, who supported me during my six years as Department

Chair trying to maintain an active scholarly life. It goes without saying how much my students continue to challenge and inspire me; I am thankful for their constant reminder of why I chose this profession. On the other side, my own teachers have at every stage showed me the best aspects of the intellectual life. Let Alan Bewell, John Howard S.J., Robin Jackson, Jon Klancher, John L. Mahoney, Mark O'Connor, John Paul Riquelme, Christopher Ricks, Charles Rzepka, Gabriele Schwab, Susan Stewart, and James Winn stand in for so many others who have improved my thinking and writing.

My parents, sisters, and extended family (both Mulrooneys and Hands) have given encouragement and good humor since the beginning and will no doubt be surprised when "the book" actually appears as a material object in the world. Most of all, I am grateful beyond telling for the dear friends within and outside academia who have helped and sustained me over the years. Deepest thanks to David and Karen Anderson, Miranda Burgess, Andrew Hartley, Heath Hightower, Dianne and Maarten Kraaijvanger, Paul and Rachel LaChance, Todd McGowan, Kirk Melnikoff, María José Sánchez Montes, Hilary Neroni, Paul Poth, David Puente, Paige Reynolds, Valerie Rohy, Prashant Watchmaker, Andrew Watson, Lisa White, and Lara Vetter.

Alicemarie Hand has provided sustaining love, support, and daily companionship. I can only offer that my ability to complete the book is just one small sign of how much she has given me. The first work on this project took place before my daughters Grace and Anna were born, and the book has grown in fits and starts even as they have flourished. Time was often stolen from it on their behalf, and sometimes the reverse was necessarily true. Both will be disappointed that there are no dragons or wizards to be found here, but perhaps one day they will read the book and find no less compelling figures to suit their imaginations. The girls are near to me as I write these words (one of them even asleep on the couch where I sit). As the book makes its way into the world, it carries the blessing that their presence, and their mother's, has been and will always remain.

Introduction

Writing to his friend and mentor Charles Cowden Clarke in March 1817, John Keats asked, "When shall we see each other again? In Heaven or in Hell, or in deep Places? In crooked Lane are we to meet or on Salisbury Plain? Or jumbled together at Drury Lane door?" (*Letters* 1.126). By way of *Macbeth*, Keats's joke encompasses a universe of experience – heaven, hell, London's crooked streets, the mythical English countryside, the textual Shakespeare, the performed Shakespeare – all held together conceptually by the notion of the theater. An intrepid playgoer, Keats knew what it was to visit the street carnival of the theater district, to be "jumbled up" with the crowds making their way down clogged byways to see Edmund Kean's latest impersonation of Shylock or Richard III. There, Keats implies, the metaphysical and the apocalyptic meet the bodily and the everyday on the threshold of the playhouse where his favorite actor reigns. Yet in a sense the letter imagines two Keatses at once: he is an actor parodying Shakespeare's lines even as he is a would-be audience member off to meet a friend. Both aspects give us a glimpse of how vital theatrical experience was to Keats's sense of himself as a social being. For him, theater was both an event to be attended and a naturalized sign of England's literary-cultural inheritance. Against the "binary assumptions" separating theater as literature from theater as performance – assumptions that have long governed our scholarly thinking – we see here a young man ensconced in the vivid and transgressive world of performance that Kean's Drury Lane embodied, and a poet for whom the act of writing and the act of theater-going were intimately connected.[1]

Keats's happy association of the theater with a distinctly English brand of sociable behavior is no rarity. As a wealth of recent scholarship has affirmed, theater was a central public experience in London and throughout Britain during the Romantic period. Some of that importance can be attributed to heightened public sensitivity, especially in the metropole, to the political theatricality the French Revolution had set in motion. In his

Reflections on the Revolution in France (1790), Edmund Burke had described events across the Channel as a theatrical spectacle run amok. Worse, the Revolution had aroused the degraded theatrical tastes of an English public: "Plots, massacres, assassinations, seem to some people a trivial price for obtaining a revolution. A cheap, bloodless reformation, a guiltless liberty, appear flat and vapid to their taste. There must be a great change of scene; there must be a magnificent stage effect; there must be a grand spectacle to rouze the imagination" (156). The implication of Burke's recourse to theatricality is, of course, that once theater is used to describe social revolution it threatens to occasion revolution. A public whose tastes for spectacle were indulged in the theater might seek similar satisfaction in the larger political and social spheres in which they lived and moved. For Burke, as for Wordsworth writing a decade later in his *Preface to Lyrical Ballads*, the line between news of the "great national events which are daily taking place" and the country's "theatrical exhibitions" had blurred dangerously, fomenting a "craving for extraordinary incident" among an increasingly urban populace (177). In the wake of the Revolution and the English reaction to its excesses, the city's playhouses rehearsed nightly the unsettled relations between lower and upper classes that would haunt the British polity throughout the next century. As theater grew more popular and theaters grew larger between 1789 and the first English Reform Bill in 1832, there was fear among some Britons that, in Jerome Christensen's words, "the proscenium would not hold" (*Romanticism at the End of History* 4).

Scholarship focused on the political and material aspects of the Romantic-period "theatrical revolution" continues to have great value (Moody, "Theatrical Revolution" 199). Daniel O'Quinn, Jane Moody, and Gillian Russell, among others, have explored the social effects of performance within Britain's national theaters, in a host of illegitimate venues that sprung up in the period, and throughout the wider culture of military and political spectacle that marshaled national sentiment on behalf of a nation at war.[2] In the 2000s, scholars expanded the historical and geographical range of inquiry to include the entirety of the British Empire and beyond, and they developed notions of "Romantic sociability" that transcended and complicated the (at times) monolithic notions of theatrical reception that had informed the work of earlier historians.[3] Where Burke and Wordsworth once perceived reasons for fear, current scholars have uncovered a complex set of cultural practices, the ideological dimensions of which vary markedly depending on the theater, national context, roster of actors, plays being performed, and other factors.

Introduction 3

Certainly theater's increased significance in Romantic-period Britain – as a site of symbolic contest no less than as a center of friendly sociability – occurred in part because of changes theater historians have already delineated well: the French Revolution, the expansion of London's Covent Garden and Drury Lane theaters in 1809 and 1811, developments in production technologies, the emergence of unlicensed playhouses and performances around the turn of the century, and the theatrical trajectories of Britain's public life.[4] *Romanticism and Theatrical Experience* aims to extend this work by arguing that a rapid expansion of Britain's periodical culture brought theater for the first time within the experiential compass of many who never even set foot inside a playhouse. Theater's continual presence both as advertisement and as reported event in commercial newspapers, and as the focus of a growing number of periodicals devoted principally and even solely to theatrical topics, rendered it part of the daily experience of a growing body of readers. Particularly after 1800, theater's impact began in new ways to reach beyond the restricted time and place of its performances because, quite simply, more and more people were writing and reading about theater on a regular basis. This expansion of periodical culture enabled theater to generate – and in turn be influenced by – written discussions about all manner of theatrical experiences: performances surely, but also the lives of actors on and off stage, the political and aesthetic significance of the plays performed, and accounts of audience members' attendance in the playhouses. What happened on stage and in the aisles of the city's playhouses came to symbolize, through a repeatable and reportable collective ritual, the happenings of the local and national communities with which readers' lives were bound up. No surprise, then, that Romantic-period theater became "the pre-eminent mode of public entertainment throughout Britain and the empire" (Russell, *Women, Sociability and Theatre* 12), and that people began, like Keats, to think of themselves and their communities in theatrical terms.[5]

John Orlando Parry's *The Posterman* conveys a sense of how theater's presence in Britain had by 1835 produced a new and unavoidable regime of signs that took on a life of its own, beyond their explicit connection to the particular events taking place in the playhouses (Figure 1). With its visual insistence on the accrual of theater's textual ephemera into a monolithic wall of signification, the painting emblematizes the subject of Part I of this book: the tension between theater's eventful impermanence and its lasting textual remainders. Presided over by a massive facade covered with the day's posted advertisements, more than half promote some form of theatrical

Figure 1: John Orlando Parry, *The Posterman* (1835)

entertainment, alongside travel postings, political ads, ads for consumer goods, and even a call to see a circus of "industrious fleas."[6] Theater is imbricated here with, and propels, the larger commercial and social movements of the city. Parry's street is not only a physical thoroughfare but also a venue for theatrical publicity that opens up myriad cultural experiences to passers-by, offering them imaginative transport beyond the everyday. Ads for the "ADELPHI/Robert Macaire/Tom and Jerry/The Christening!!!!/Every Evening," and for "The Destruction of Pompeii Every Evening" partially obscure others for "The Spectacular King Arthur" and for the "Native Tales" of "NOURJAHAD!" and "HERMANN!" The scene, in fact, lacks almost all sense of visual depth except that provided by the wall's commercial palimpsest, as the flatness of St. Paul's dome in the background confirms. Poster fragments can be seen four and five deep, and the building's support beams and fence are similarly covered. Torn bits of outdated ads lie scattered on the ground or hang loosely in the wind. Indeed, the human figures in the foreground are secondary in the picture to the advertisements presiding over them. Collected into two discrete groups – a soldier, two gentlemen, and a pickpocket on the left, and a series of street vendors on the right – the figures frame a central space where the posterman stands as he adds yet another poster to the wall's mighty collection.

Parry's scene conveys a public life outside the bounds of any kind of bourgeois public sphere, leaving little room for its viewer to imagine a culture defined by individuals coming together to engage in the "public use of their reason" (Habermas 27).[7] And yet the theater – its publicity, its performances, and most especially the textual afterlife it occasioned in newsprint and periodicals – played a crucial role in the continual reimagining of individual and collective experiences in Romantic-period England. My interest in how the theatrical press transformed daily events into readable texts extends the work of recent cultural historians of the eighteenth and nineteenth centuries who, in the words of Ann Bermingham, have begun "to explore the way in which the activity of consuming culture enables individuals to construct social identities" ("The Consumption of Culture" 9).[8] Such studies have deepened our understanding of the cultural choices available to consumers in the eighteenth and nineteenth centuries, as well as of the ways in which those choices came to be made by individual and collective agents. John Brewer's account is exemplary in its description of efforts "to create a culture that was polite, moderate, reasonable, morally instructive, decorous, and restrained" (341) in response to a perceived Rabelasian consumerist carnival "which undercut the claim that culture could and should be impartial, disinterested, dispassionate, and virtuous" (341). Against this attempted division of high from low or public from private, new historiographies have favored the particular experiences of individuals – men and women, rich, poor, and from the middle orders – in matters of writing, style, drawing, and other kinds of pastimes. Attention to such activities in their historical particularity – without recourse to the grand narrative of a "consumer revolution" offered by earlier scholars such as Neil McKendrick – has begun to yield insights into how our own enduring assumptions about culture and public life were profoundly shaped by the Romantic period. What Kathleen Wilson has called "localized contests for power" have now become a central concern of both historians and literary scholars as they attempt to understand more fully the roles that different kinds of people took in reframing notions of public and private experience (15).[9] Recovery of material contexts is of course central to this effort, but so too – especially among literary scholars – must be close attention to the textual forms through which people working and writing during that time expressed their experiences.

In dialogue with this scholarly conversation, *Romanticism and Theatrical Experience* seeks to elucidate how theatrical institutions – principally those in London – provided a prominent imaginative locus around which concerns about personal and collective cultural experience could coalesce. Rather than a historical account of early-nineteenth-century British theater that attends to the material conditions of theatrical production or to the economic factors surrounding periodical publication, I am interested in how those performances and institutions were mediated through the textual prisms of Britain's, and more specifically London's, newspapers and theatrical periodicals. Harriet Guest has argued that from the mid-eighteenth century on, British periodicals "can be understood to articulate and address the cultural nexus of instability formed by the complex of relations between the distinctions of public and private and of gender" (40). Nowhere is this articulation more evident than in London's theatrical press around the turn of the century. After the Old Price riots of 1809, in which audiences protested changes in pricing and seating at London's newly opened Covent Garden Theatre, Britain's theatrical press presented an ongoing conversation among varieties of people attempting to make sense of their engagements with performances in all manner of theatrical venues. On an almost daily basis, the writing I will consider in Chapters 1 and 2 manifested just the tension that Brewer describes, as theatrical critics and reviewers attempted to translate the unruly experiences theater provided into readable, consumable text. Accordingly, I will employ the term "theatrical experience" throughout the book to describe not primarily the encounters people had inside playhouse walls, but the ways in which reading, writing, and talking about theater facilitated reconsiderations of what it meant to be a person living in London in the first three decades of the nineteenth century.[10] Beyond enabling the evaluation of individual cases of theatrical experience, the totality of theater's print artifacts provides an important conceptual framework for understanding the emergence of aesthetic categories rooted in new modes of feeling, which have traditionally been marginalized and which Mary Jacobus argues "ought . . . to complicate any simple view between Enlightenment subjectivity and what comes to be called 'literature' during the period" (276).

My archival attention focuses on the early-nineteenth-century theatrical press because newspapers and theatrical periodicals constituted at that time a collective and repeated, even ritualized, effort to translate events into objects of readerly attention. The material text of the theatrical periodical offered a tangible (if usually) ephemeral artifact of a now-concluded performance, even as it provided for the reader a way of orienting the self toward the public world within which that event had taken place. The first two chapters of the book attempt to bring what Sean Latham and Robert

Scholes have called the approach of "periodical studies" together with accounts of cultural consumerism that, once attuned more to the consumption of objects rather than events, have begun to consider the social effects of various cultural practices on the formation of individual and collective subjectivities.[11] We can learn something, in other words, by considering how texts representing and occasioning theatrical experience set in motion new ways of thinking and writing beyond what might be strictly considered theatrical criticism. If, as Paige Reynolds has argued in a modernist context, "periodicals expose the productive tension between the emergence of mass print culture and the long-standing practices of poetic recitation and performance," the early-nineteenth-century theatrical press shaped the development of Romantic poetics no less dramatically, inaugurating, in fact, an ongoing textual negotiation between performance and poetry that Reynolds finds fully on display some nine decades later (120). Here, then, is a wide resource for imagining not only how people lived in and moved through what James Chandler and Kevin Gilmartin have called the "Romantic metropolis," – but more intimately how the effects of that living and moving shaped their literary writing. More than showing how preexisting subjects participated in the discursive activities of a stable public exchange, the archive of Romantic-period theatrical criticism exemplifies nothing less than a collaborative reimagining of cultural experience in Regency England.

Despite its significance, Romantic-period theater and its attendant print culture were largely forgotten for much of the twentieth century, as literary scholars fashioned a Romanticism presided over by poets who resisted contemporary political and social pressures by emphasizing personal interiority.[12] "Romantic drama," if considered at all, was explained as the curious by-product of an intensely lyrical age. As the new historicism began in the 1980s and 1990s to expand the canon of texts considered worthy of attention, renewed interest in Romantic-period drama manifested itself initially in two ways: first, in a commitment to challenge lyric poetry as the paradigmatic Romantic genre,[13] and second and more importantly, in a heightened awareness of theatricality in Romantic-period Britain's larger social world.[14] What is striking about the way these conversations developed is that even as scholars recovered forgotten texts, interrogated notions of Romantic canonicity, and rediscovered the material and political contexts of Romantic-period theatrical production, divisions between literary-minded and performance-minded scholars stubbornly endured.[15] To illustrate this point, I will turn briefly here to what is arguably the most significant work of 1990s theatrical historicism, Julie Carlson's *In the*

Theatre of Romanticism: Coleridge, Nationalism, Women, which was published in 1994. Among many important studies, Carlson's stands out for two reasons: first, because it considered Romantic drama as a textual genre in the context of counterrevolutionary England's performed theater, and second, because it exemplified how theatrical scholarship could begin to explore the social nature of "Romantic" literary writing. For Carlson, Romantic "antitheatricalism" is driven by a misogynist impulse to contain the threat of bodies, and particularly women's bodies, to a strictly defined performance space (2).[16] Arguing that Coleridge's playwriting in his "middle stage," between 1807 and 1816, is a systematic attempt to communicate anti-Jacobin political philosophy to popular audiences, Carlson posits a Romanticism in which theater must eventually give way to a highly textual literary culture.[17] Yet if Carlson's focus on Coleridge's sublimation of social tension into a paradigmatic antitheatricalism made a vivid case for how theatrical culture could help us rethink Romantic authorship, the full implications of that case remain even now, more than two decades later, relatively undeveloped when compared with the explosion of historicist studies focused on theater's wider political significances.[18] That is, despite the fact that some of our fundamental assumptions about Romantic-period theater and Romantic-period literary production have been overturned, we still need to understand more fully how Britain's late eighteenth- and early nineteenth-century theatrical world relates to the literature that came to constitute Romanticism generally, and Romantic poetry more specifically.

One salutary counter to this scholarly lacuna is the work of Michael Gamer, which explores how popular Gothic drama shaped writers' notions of cultural authority, genre, and literary history. As Gamer contends, "[T]he explosion of Gothic fiction and stage drama – especially a drama that depends on upon spectacle, and therefore upon the work of many hands, destabilizes notions of authorship and originality in the Romantic period" ("Authors in Effect" 833).[19] In this vein, Gamer's discussion of *Lyrical Ballads* in his book *Romanticism and the Gothic* (2000) remains the most significant attempt to date to describe theater's influence on Romantic lyric. Through an analysis of the textual venues and institutional contexts in which the Gothic genre was contested, Gamer situates *Lyrical Ballads* as an attempt to engage poetry readers' interest in Gothic while avoiding the taint of Gothic's "low" associations.[20] Still, given Gamer's focused attention to the Gothic and his formulation of a largely negative relation between Gothic and lyric, there remains a significant gap in current discourse about theater's relation to Romantic writing, a gap that our brief return to Carlson's study might begin to help bridge. Seizing on Carlson's concern not only with literary genre but also with the forms and rhetorical practices at work in Coleridge's dramas, *Romanticism and Theatrical Experience* asks some related but still unanswered questions: in contrast to the "antitheatrical" writers who came of age under the shadow of the guillotine, how might we account for a later generation's fascination with the centrality of theater to its own experience? And how might we come to understand that centrality to have influenced not simply that generation's efforts at dramatic authorship but also its more canonical poetic writings? How, in short, does literary and specifically poetic form represent and respond to Romantic writers' theatrical experience?

My interest in the so-called second generation of Romantic writers, principally Hazlitt and Keats, is prompted by a desire to move away from the well-explored theatrical aftermath of the French Revolution as well as by a recognition that the sustained production of theatrical periodicals between 1809 and 1830, an output that was unmatched in the century before or after, transformed how theater was written and read about. London is at the center of all of this, both because it was the theatrical capital of the nation and because the effects of the periodical culture I describe were felt there most fully. In this way, the figures I will consider in the book – Kean, Hazlitt, and Keats – can be taken as exemplars of a particular strain of second-generation, urban, Cockney Romanticism whose influence nonetheless reaches outward into the larger city and nation. Closely examined, the wide-ranging field of early nineteenth-century theatrical periodicals reveals a network of authors and readers continually remaking the relations between individual and community, private and public, cultural producer and cultural consumer. Reviews and advertisements in morning papers, daily theatrical gazettes reporting events of the stage, and moralistic weeklies railing against the commercialism of their competitors offered a growing range of choices for early nineteenth-century readers. Theatrical periodicals, that is, collectively constituted a social institution that not only, in Pierre Bourdieu's words, proved "indispensable to [the] consumption" of early nineteenth-century theater (*Rules of Art* 293), but also enabled writers and critics working in the field to respond to what they perceived as overly commercialized practices of cultural reception.[21] Examining a wide variety of these publications, many of them unread for the past two hundred years, I describe how reading audiences found in theatrical periodicals not simply new ways to encounter a rapidly expanding public world but also new ways to imagine what it mean to be an actor, a critic, and even a poet in that time and place. If many periodical reviewers displayed anxieties about the politically and aesthetically unsettling dimensions of theatrical performance, the figures who would preside over what came to be called late Romanticism took performance as an informing principle for their writing. Charting with increasing intimacy the ways in which witnessing a public performance could transform their sense of themselves as private individuals, theatrical critics like Leigh Hunt and William Hazlitt invited periodical readers – among them poets like Keats – to rethink their own positions between commercial and "high" culture, between their private lives and the public life represented and enacted by the theater.[22] My exploration of this phenomenon will also enable me to investigate why theatrical and lyric Romanticisms continue to be estranged, despite the nearly three decades of significant scholarly attention Romantic drama and theater have received. For even as rigorous historical work has provided us with new insights into late eighteenth- and early nineteenth-century theatrical production and its social effects, that work has often, if only by omission, reinforced the same generic divisions that first privileged Romantic-period poetry and later marked it as ideologically overburdened. *Romanticism and Theatrical Experience* will address this problem by drawing specific connections between the rise of theatrical experience and Keats's development of a new kind of Romantic prosody.

As Jon Klancher noted in 1987, gaining access to the forgotten archive of early nineteenth-century "text-making... means refusing any premature judgments of taste, since what is at issue is precisely the historical forming of taste as well as readers' interpretive modes" (*Making of English Reading Audiences* ix). This project is an attempt to chart a moment in Britain's cultural history when practices, and practitioners, of theatrical reception were beginning to display that formation in self-conscious ways, both physically in theaters and culturally in print, as journals and newspapers employed different formal strategies to cultivate distinct reading audiences. To that end, Part I, "The Making of British Theater Audiences," provides a field study of the period's theatrical writing, from reviews and advertisements in morning papers to daily theatrical gazettes to weekly and monthly journals. Chapter 1, "Theater and the Daily News*,*" analyzes how theater's appearance in daily newspapers' advertising and reporting discourses – as both play notices and as reviews – affected readers' perceptions of theater as a public experience. Chapter 2, "Britain's Theatrical Press, 1800–1830," charts the emergence of a range of new periodicals, in London principally but not exclusively, during the three decades after 1800. These publications differed widely in material quality, price, and look, and they employed diverse strategies to attract and maintain readerships. Although theatrical periodicals were all unavoidably engaged with the textual forms with which the daily newspaper presented its information, weeklies such as Thomas Dutton's *Dramatic Censor* often displayed a strain of anti-commercial commentary that attacked the daily press and aimed to enable the journal's readers to distinguish themselves from their news-reading counterparts. The emergence of what I call "playbill periodicals" will be of particular interest: chief among the wide range of periodicals, they attempted to construct diurnally what Gillian Russell has recently called "theater time" – an experience of theater that extended beyond the moment of performance ("Playbills" 244). The chapter concludes with a discussion of Leigh and John Hunt's periodical the *Examiner*. The unique position of the Hunts' weekly paper, which styled itself textually as a daily but refused to publish advertisements throughout its first decade, facilitated the development of what I call occasional modes of theatrical reviewing, which Hunt would pioneer and Hazlitt would come to epitomize. Part I's field study aims to contribute to the history of Regency public life Greg Kucich and Jeffrey Cox (xlvii) called for in 2003 and to extend the compelling 2009 claim made by Michael Gamer and Terry Robinson (220) that late eighteenth-century theater must be considered "as an identifiable collection of practices at once portable and applicable to other cultural arenas." Still, given the range of texts I consider, Part I is at times and by necessity expository, so some readers more interested in the effects of the periodical culture I describe may wish to move directly to the case studies offered in Part II.

After Part I describes a contest among writers trying to reconceptualize theatrical experience through the medium of print, Part II, "Theater and Late Romanticism," provides three case studies of how theatrical criticism's rise after 1809 transformed the theatrical experience of an actor, a critic, and a poet. Chapter 3, "Edmund Kean's Controversy," takes as its point of departure public reaction to Kean's January 1825 trial for "criminal conversation" with Charlotte Cox, the wife of London city alderman Robert Albion Cox, and his return to the Drury Lane stage the following week. I argue that the publicity Kean generated not only in 1825 but throughout his career – what I am calling Kean's "controversy" – marked a shift in the constitution of theatrical celebrity and illustrated the changing nature of theatrical experience in Britain. This shift displays distinct class and gender dimensions, in which Kean's low associations – manifested in his acting style and valued by the theater for the audience interest they generated – suggested to critics a looseness of moral and sexual identity. Fashioning himself as an interpreter rather than a straightforward orator of the dramatic text, Kean represented, in William Hazlitt's formulation, a "radical" departure from earlier actors' personifications of aristocratic cultural mastery. His nightly performances exhibited a vexed, deeply personal encounter with the nation's "legitimate" theater tradition. Responses to the 1825 trial, which included newspaper articles, journal reviews, court reports, literary travesties, and caricatures, display a British public's attempts to come to terms with this social and cultural shift and its effect on contemporary notions of class and gender. Representations of Kean caught *in flagrante* with Charlotte Cox exemplify in a theatrical vein, to use Harriet Guest's words, "the way problems about the morality of commercial culture come to be represented as anxieties about sexual difference" (Guest 23). A figure embodying the ongoing collision between 'high culture' and 'low company,' Kean inspired a generation of literary writers, Hazlitt and Keats chief among them, to experiment boldly with their own literary self-representations. In this, I suggest, Kean remains something of an overlooked catalyst for what Gregory Dart has called "the Cockney Moment" typically associated with Hunt and Keats (1).[23]

My broader goal in *Romanticism and Theatrical Experience* is more literary than materialist: I aim to reconsider theater's place in shaping the philosophical and historical content of "Romantic" – and specifically Cockney Romantic – writing as it occurs in Hazlitt's essays and Keats's poetry. Accordingly, the book's next two case studies argue that the aesthetic sensibilities of Romanticism's "second generation" were shaped by popular experiences of theater – as mediated by theatrical periodicals – to a far greater extent than has been previously noticed. Chapter 4, "Hazlitt's Romantic Occasionalism," examines how William Hazlitt's theatrical criticism represents to readers, in a variety of print venues, a critical subjectivity continually altered by periodic encounters with theatrical events in London and its environs.[24] Throughout his theatrical criticism, Hazlitt imagines a self contingent upon experience, where the occasion of public encounter can alter the identity of the observer irrevocably, and where the inscribing of that occasion into criticism enables the possibility of a transformative experience for the reader. In Edmund Kean, who debuted on the London stage the same month Hazlitt began writing theatrical reviews in 1814, Hazlitt found a model for how to represent publicly his own mobile subjectivity. Kean's performance of his character's conflicted affective relation to the situations of performed drama correlated for Hazlitt to the contemporary subject's vexed relation to the vagaries of London life. Hazlitt wrote as a parliamentary reporter, theater reviewer, and essayist for a variety of publications. His sensitivity to the exigencies of the periodical publishing world in which he worked enabled him to negotiate a critical path between the poles of elitism and commercialism the theatrical press comprised, even as he remained concerned with theatrical experience's ability to shape Britons' individual and communal life. Unlike much of the criticism I discuss in Part I, Hazlitt's writing imagines a discursive community defined not by a search for preexisting categories of taste but by a common interest among its participants in the occasion of the critic's encounter with the performances he reviews. The chapter concludes with discussions of Hazlitt's influential essays "The Fight" and "The Indian Jugglers," arguing that the critical voice Hazlitt imagined in theatrical reviews profoundly shaped the rest of his work.

Chapter 5, "Keats, Kean, and the Poetics of Interruption," connects John Keats's revisionary notions of poetry's expressive capacities to his theatrical experience. Keats is among a generation of poets who came of age after 1800 when theater and theater criticism were reaching their ascendancy. Attending, reading, and writing about theater were for this generation self-constitutive experiences. While acknowledging the common assumption that Hazlitt's *Lectures on the English Poets* (1818) was a formative text for Keats, I argue that the influence of Kean's public persona on Keats's notions of "negative capability" and the antiegotistical poet has been largely overlooked. Taking Keats's "negative capability" letter and his concurrent theatrical reviews for the *Champion* in 1817 as a point of departure, I offer close readings of several sonnets composed in early 1818 to demonstrate a crucial shift in Keats's understanding of the poet's role at that time. Beyond this, Keats's fascination with Kean's interruptive acting style – and with the mobile, imaginative, transgressive subject it imagined – shaped his poetry throughout *Lamia, Isabella, and The Eve of St. Agnes*, the 1820 volume upon which his canonical reputation rests. Contrasting Keats's representation of theatrical experience in *Lamia* to Frances Burney's more conservative containment of theatrical energies in her 1814 novel *The Wanderer*, I argue that Keats's poem both represents and enacts a scene of "Cockney interruption" that resists progressive notions of personal and national history. This Cockney resistance to narrative – fostered by Keats's attraction to Kean – in turn shapes the highly figural lyricism of the odes. The chapter, and the book, close with a reading of "Ode on a Grecian Urn" that claims the poem as a product of Keats's theatrical experience. Though the texts I consider in the chapter – the sonnets,

Lamia, and the odes – constitute the height of second-generation Romantic lyricism, they present a poet-speaker whose figural searching manifests theatrical experience's most enduring literary effect.

The thread connecting these essays is their focus on the textual mediation of theater, first in critical reviews and advertisements; then in journalistic essays and print caricatures; and, ultimately and most strikingly, in Keats's lyric poetry. Theater was offered to Britons as both a commodity to be consumed and as an institution cultivating and conveying the nation's cultural tradition. But theatrical periodicals deployed a variety of discursive tactics that by turns appropriated and resisted those seemingly disparate commitments. The forms of theatrical reviews found in newspapers and theatrical periodicals sought to attract readers habituated to the newspaper even as they offered anti-commercial statements as a sign of both writers' and readers' cultural distinction. After his debut in 1814, Kean became the most sensational focus of these new print institutions, an incorrigible public figure who flouted attempts to circumscribe his highly political, highly sexualized performance of personal celebrity. In turn, both Hazlitt and Keats produced works that demonstrated the continuing social agency of imaginative literature in a time when cultural experience was increasingly administered by commercially driven institutions. *Romanticism and Theatrical Experience* contributes to an ongoing scholarly formulation of British Romanticism as urban, middle and working class, and historically engaged. But it also seeks to follow more recent scholarship in widening the notion of what "the public" was by considering how individual agents both shaped and were themselves shaped by the act of reading and writing about theater. In this sense, though my focus on the theatrical engagements of three (arguably) Cockney figures can and should be viewed as a consideration of a subculture of second-generation Romanticism, it can also be taken as a way of teasing out the effects of theatrical experience more broadly. Balancing archival research and close attention to literary form, I aim to provide new rhetorical and social contexts within which notions of Romantic authorship, genre, and "the literary" can be reconceived, and to prompt work on theatrical figures the book does not consider (P. B. Shelley and Byron, most notably). Such an endeavor will enable us to understand better not only theater's significance to early nineteenth-century Londoners but also what engagement with its textual legacies can mean for our own ongoing reassessment of Romanticism as a historical and cultural phenomenon.

Notes

1. The phrase "binary assumptions" (6) and the sense of the division I mention are Jacky Bratton's. See *New Readings in Theatre History* 2–16.
2. Throughout his work, O'Quinn attends in unparalleled ways to the details of theatrical production and their consolidated ideological effect on audiences. See especially *Staging Governance* and, more recently, *Entertaining Crises*. Moody's *Illegitimate Theatre in London* is the definitive account of playgoing outside the national patent theaters. Russell's *The Theatres of War* moves further afield to explore the theatrical dimension of Britain's military culture.
3. Frederick Burwick's work has been indispensible in this effort. Burwick's *Romantic Drama: Acting and Reacting* provides the most comprehensive account of changes in dramatic writing, acting styles, the material conditions of performance, and audience practice in London theaters in the period, arguing that these factors came together to foster new communal and national identifications. Burwick's *Playing to the Crowd* offers a wider-ranging consideration of how managers and actors responded directly to changing ethnic and class demographics in London. Judith Pascoe's *The Sarah Siddons Audiofiles* presents a personal and provocative example of the degree to which the question of theatrical reception in the Romantic period is both unanswerable and irresistible.
4. For a history of Royal Theatre patents from the Restoration to the Romantic period, see Dewey Ganzel, "Patent Wrongs and Patent Theatres," 384–96. For a discussion of the impact of patent "legitimacy" on the wider London theatrical culture, see Jane Moody, *Illegitimate Theatre in London*, esp. 1–78.
5. David Worrall's assertion that "theatricality was a mode of public being, a representation of the self which was not confined to dramas performed in the playhouses" represents a common insight among recent theater historians (*Theatric Revolution* 2). Melynda Nuss has argued that the "public space" of theater enabled authors to imagine relationships with audiences, even when they were not strictly writing performance texts. For Nuss, theater enables "thinkers in the late eighteenth and early nineteenth centuries ... to think through the social relations created by a new mass culture" (12).
6. The visual variety of the "dead wall," Gillian Russell has shown recently, was in part made possible by developments in new typefaces and printing methods used in the production of playbills, rendering such spaces "a paradigmatic site of ephemerality and inscription in the late Georgian and Victorian city, the place at which the tide of commerce, including print culture and writing itself, washed up against the shores of obsolescence and loss" ("Playbills" 248).
7. Following Jerome McGann's insistence on the importance of the "socialized text" in the late 1970s and early 1980s, much work on Romanticism focused on the public circulation of texts as material objects rather than on the formation of publicly informed subjectivities. Paul Magnuson, for example, has resituated Romantic lyricism by arguing, "one cannot discover [poetry's] public nature by reading individual works of literature apart from the public discourse that

literature enters when it is published" (3). Andrew McCann's attempt "to discuss the different ways in which texts are implicated in the construction of community, imagined or otherwise" is closer to my approach (4).

8. For a discussion of the ways in which new forms of archival research have problematized "the conventional notion of separate spheres" of activity for women and men, for example, see Eger, Grant, Ó Gallchoir, and Warburton (3). Moving away from what Jean-Christophe Agnew has called a "pessimistic reading of consumer culture" presided over by the legacy of Marx and affirmed by Habermas ("Coming Up for Air" 22), scholars such as Ann Bermingham, Harriet Guest, and Jan de Vries have attended to the formative dimensions of a variety of cultural activities, from drawing to shopping. For early revisions of Habermas's position, see Bruce Robbins, ed., *The Phantom Public Sphere*; Craig Calhoun, ed., *Habermas and the Public Sphere*, esp. Nancy Fraser's essay "Rethinking the Public Sphere: A Contribution to the Critique of Actually Existing Democracy" (109–42); and Jon Klancher's introduction to the special issue of *Studies in Romanticism* entitled "Romanticism and Its Publics": 523–25. Russell similarly maintains Habermas's enduring importance for this sort of discussion. See *Women, Sociability and Theatre in Georgian London* 15–16.

9. Colin Campbell goes so far as to assert that historical scholarship of public engagement, and more particularly of consumerism, should take individual agents as its primary concern: "[T]he actual subjective meanings which prompt and guide action remain an indispensable ingredient in any successful theory of conduct and . . . the only proper place in which to search for such meaning is in the conscious minds of acting individuals" ("Understanding" 43).

10. My term echoes Oscar Negt and Alexander Kluge's notion of *Erfahrung* – itself a development of the notion used by Walter Benjamin – which expands the meaning of "public life" to include modes of expression and intersubjectivity that Habermas at least at times dismisses as uncritical. While I follow Loren Kruger's assertion that "a popular and specifically proletarian response to the national theatre may be more complicated than the resigned acquiescence of a passive and disenfranchised spectator" (7), it is certainly possible to employ Negt and Kluge's theorization of "experience" without accepting their now somewhat dated reliance on "proletariat" as a historically stable term.

11. See, for example, essays by Bermingham (art gallery viewing), Durning (The London Lyceum), and Manning (lecturing) in Chandler and Gilmartin, eds., *Romantic Metropolis*. Following Jon Klancher's *The Making of English Reading Audiences,* studies by Kevin Gilmartin (*Print Politics*), Mark Schoenfield (*British Periodicals*), and Kim Wheatley have propelled a renewed interest in Romantic-era periodical culture. Still, theatrical periodicals remain largely overlooked. Wheatley's introduction (1–19) provides a cogent overview of the early nineteenth-century British periodical field.

12. Harold Bloom's 1968 "The Internalization of the Quest Romance" epitomizes this approach (13–35).

13. Alan Richardson's *A Mental Theater: Poetic Drama and Consciousness in the Romantic Age* (1988) was the first attempt to consider Romantic drama as a legitimate genre rather than as the literary orphan of Romantic lyric. Daniel P. Watkins's *A Materialist Critique of English Romantic Drama* (1993) and Marjean Purinton's *Romantic Ideology Unmasked* (1994) advance the formal considerations of Richardson's work while considering "the sorts of social relations, anxieties, struggles, and so on that are constituent features of Romantic culture" (Watkins xi). Similarly, William Jewett's *Fatal Autonomy: Romantic Drama and the Rhetoric of Agency* (1997) considers the plays of the canonical poets as skeptical explorations of human political agency. In an encompassing study of the dramas of Byron and Shelley, Michael Simpson argued, "[T]he category of Romantic drama seems more appropriately an object of interrogation than a secure methodological given" (2).

14. Gillian Russell's *The Theatres of War: Performance, Politics, and Society 1793–1815* (1995) charts the theatrical presence of the armed forces in domestic British life throughout the Napoleonic wars. Kristina Straub's *Sexual Suspects: Eighteenth-Century Players and Sexual Ideology* (1992) discusses similar fears about theatrical spectacle by exploring growing social concerns over the representative power of players both on stage and as public figures in eighteenth-century English society. And Judith Pascoe's *Romantic Theatricality: Gender, Poetry, and Spectatorship* (1997) seeks to recast Romanticism by emphasizing its encouragement of performative social selves rather than (what have long been considered) poetic expressions of personal sincerity. In *Women, Nationalism and the Romantic Stage: Theatre and Politics in Britain 1770–1800* (2001), Betsey Bolton develops this discussion to focus on how late eighteenth-century theatrical production contested women's subordinate social roles. Melodrama has received significant attention as a nexus of performance and political anxieties in Britain especially. See Hays and Nikolopoulou's *Melodrama: The Cultural Emergence of a Genre*. Other important considerations of Romantic-period theater's political engagements include George Taylor, *The French Revolution and the London Stage 1789–1805* (2000) and David Worrall, *The Politics of Romantic Theatricality: 1787–1832: The Road to the Stage* (2002). Daniel O'Quinn's *Staging Governance: Theatrical Imperialism in London 1770–1800* (2005) provides the most thorough accounting of theater's response to (and shaping of) the wide-ranging social effects of Britain's economic and colonial expansion at the end of the eighteenth century. Propelled by Russell and Tuite's 2002 collection *Romantic Sociability: Social Networks and Literary Culture in Britain 1770–1840*, other studies have emphasized the influence theatrical "sociability" had in shaping British cultural experience. See for example David Worrall's *Theatric Revolution: Drama, Censorship and Romantic Period Subcultures 1773–1832* (2006), which focuses on "an essentially popular or plebian network of intricate intertextuality largely cut off from the heritage of English spoken drama as exemplified by Shakespeare" (1). Gillian Russell's *Women, Sociability*

and Theatre in Georgian London (2007) inverts the focus of this relationship by considering how venues for sociability in the larger city can provide a means to reinterpret the period's theatrical culture. For a discussion of the historical significance of "theatricality" as an interpretive concept, see Tracy Davis, "Theatricality and Civil Society" in Davis and Postlewait 90–126. Crisafulli and Liberto provide a recent compendium of approaches to the relations between theater's material history, dramatic writing, and the past two decades' editorial and recovery work.

15. Jeffrey Cox provides a thorough account of both these strains of criticism with his 2004 article "Re-viewing Romantic Drama." For another discussion of trends in the field, up to the early 2000s, see Mulrooney, "Reading Theatre, 1730–1830."

16. For Carlson, *Zapolya* and *Remorse* work out and display Coleridge's notion of the imagination before it develops into the elitist concept of a "National Clerisy." In these plays, Carlson argues, Coleridge's women are politically and physically active on stage as his men develop into contemplative imaginative beings upon whom the nation will renew itself. As Coleridge's middle stage progresses, imagination begins to lose strength as a politically mediating force – that is, Coleridge loses faith in the social benefits of live theater. Accordingly, Coleridge's later plays represent antitheatricalism as an ideal, until eventually he writes himself out of the genre. Like much of the work that immediately followed her study, such as Catherine Burroughs's *Closet Stages: Joanna Baillie and the Theater Theory of British Romantic Women Writers* (1997), Carlson finds in historical conditions of oppression an explanation for Romantic antitheatricalism. In some ways, this necessary and recuperative emphasis on gender has contributed to theatrical historicism's turning away from canonical Romanticism, as Burroughs's 2000 edited collection, *Women in British Romantic Theatre: Drama, Performance, and Society, 1790–1840* exemplifies, with its essays on Frances Burney, Anne Yearsley, Jane Scott, Joanna Baillie, and Elizabeth Inchbald, among others. Thomas Crochunis's and Michael Eberle-Sinatra's long-standing website *British Women Playwrights Around 1800* as well as much of Crochunis's written scholarship exhibit a similar focus. See for example Crochunis's "British Women Playwrights Around 1800: New Paradigms and Recoveries" and his "Women and Dramatic Writing in the British Romantic Era."

17. As Jane Moody asserted in her 1996 article "'Fine word, legitimate!' Towards a Theatrical History of Romanticism," the division of theater from Romantic literature – exemplified by Jerome McGann's claim that "the separation of the drama from the theatre is an index of Romanticism itself" (*Towards a Literature of Knowledge* 39) – continued to inform Romanticist scholarship well into the 1990s. McGann's comment is, of course, a version of the larger argument found in *The Romantic Ideology* that "the poetry of Romanticism is everywhere marked by extreme forms of displacement and poetic conceptualization whereby the actual human issues with which the poetry is concerned are resituated in a variety of idealized localities" (1).

18. Here the examples are too many to name, but the exemplary scholarship of Jacky Bratton, Frederick Burwick, Tracy Davis, Jane Moody, Melynda Nuss, Daniel O'Quinn, and Gillian Russell comes to mind.
19. See also Gamer's focus on the connection between hippodrama, satire, and questions of censorship in Byron's work ("A Matter of Turf").
20. See, for example, Gamer's claim that the structure of Wordsworth's "Hart-Leap Well" allows author and readers "first to indulge in the supernatural speculation of low and rustic characters and then to ally themselves with a more philosophical and chastened interpretation of the same events" (*Romanticism and the Gothic* 14).
21. I take the phrase from Bourdieu's assertion in *The Rules of Art* that "The history of the specific institutions which are indispensable to artistic production should be backed up with a history of the institutions which are indispensable to consumption, and hence to the production of consumers and particular, of *taste*, as disposition and as competence" (293). Bourdieu's relational model of cultural production will inform my examination of a field of competition and collision between various modes of theatrical criticism. See also *The Field of Cultural Production* 29–73. In later chapters, I will rely more generally on Bourdieu's concept of "field" – a structuring set of historical relations between, and exerting force on, social positions – to consider the import that theatrical criticism's formal gestures and qualities had for writers like Hazlitt and Keats.
22. Jane Moody remarks that British theater in the period stands always at the crossroads between event and history: "Amidst its transient and ephemeral wonders ... we find also a fervent excitement surrounding the description and judgement of theatrical performance and the relationships between theatre and modern society" ("Theatrical Revolution" 215).
23. Dart dates the beginning of the "Cockney moment" to Leigh Hunt's release from Surrey Gaol in February 1815. Kean debuted at Drury Lane thirteen months earlier.
24. Following the insights of Nicholas Roe's *Fiery Heart*, Gregory Dart has argued recently that, via Leigh Hunt's influence, the suburbs played an increasingly important role in the construction of the so-called Cockney aesthetic, as distinguished from the growing workaday neighborhoods closer to the city (40–53). In Chapter 4, I will consider Hazlitt's report, in "The Fight," of his attendance at an athletic event outside the city as one example of this shift.

PART I

The Making of British Theater Audiences

CHAPTER I

Theater and the Daily News

Charles Lamb could not do without the newspaper. On June 17, 1830, he wrote from Enfield, where he was living in a rented house with his sister Mary, to William Hone, "Coffee and Hotel Man" at Gracechurch Street, London: "I hereby impower Matilda Hone to superintend daily the putting into the twopenny post the *Times* newspaper of the day before, directed 'Mr. Lamb, Enfield,' which shall be held a *full and sufficient direction*: the said insertion to commence on Monday morning next." After promising to pay Hone the not inconsiderable "quarterly sum of £1" for delivery, Lamb closed the letter with an affectionate postscript, "Vivant Coffee! Coffee-pot-que!" (*Letters* 1.282). Neither Lamb's exuberance regarding so mundane a matter as newspaper delivery nor his association of the newspaper with the joys of the coffee house is surprising; he was, to say the least, an inveterate Londoner away from his favored environs. Tellingly, Lamb's financial situation at the time of this promissory writing was anything but secure, as he had confessed in a letter to Wordsworth some months before: "[I]f we ever do move, we have encumbrances the less to impede us: all our furniture has faded under the auctioneer's hammer . . . and we have only a spoon or two left to bless us. Clothed we came into Enfield, and naked we must go out of it" (*Letters* 1.244). Naked, it would seem, except for the *Times*.

Lamb's attachment to the *Times* marks him as one of many nineteenth-century British readers who imagined their relation to public life through the medium of newspapers. His request that the daily be sent through the post neatly collates two institutional frameworks around which the British social imaginary had formed, the newspaper and the post, its primary means of rapid geographical dissemination.[1] We discover in the letter to Wordsworth that the paper was important to Lamb not only for the information it contained but also for the manner of reading it enabled:

> From my den I return you condolence for your decaying sight, not for any thing there is to see in the country, but for the miss of the pleasure of reading a London newspaper. The poets are as well to listen to, any thing high may, nay must, be read out – you read it to yourself with an imaginary auditor – but the light paragraphs must be glid over by the proper eye, mouthing mumbles their gossamery substance. 'Tis these trifles I should mourn in fading sight. A newspaper is the single gleam of comfort I receive here, it comes from Cathay with tidings of mankind. Yet I could not attend to it read out by the most beloved voice. (*Letters* 1.242)

Freeing its reader from the imaginative exertion that poetry demands, in which an act of recitation requires at least the idea of an auditor, the *Times* offers a "gleam of comfort" because its "light paragraphs" illuminate a public world outside the bounds of Lamb's cloistered perception. While reading aloud defines the experience of poetry, newspaper consumption offers a sensation unrestricted by the temporality of the aural, as the eye moves effortlessly over the "gossamery substance" of the paper's printed matter. But the facility with which the newspaper is consumed masks its importance to a reader's psychological health. Lamb's fears for the even more remotely situated Wordsworth – loss not of the poetic faculty but of the simple necessity of orienting oneself to the daily world outside – reflect his sense of isolation living in Enfield away from the city's core, and his belief that the delivered newspaper could serve as an antidote to that isolation.

The daily newspaper remains a significant though still largely overlooked aspect of Romantic-period culture. Studies of the periodical press, Jon Klancher's and Kevin Gilmartin's most notably, have focused on review journals and radical publications largely to the exclusion of the commercial news.[2] Drawing on modern and contemporary sources to show how the newspaper continues to be understood incompletely as a social force in Romantic-period public life, this chapter examines the textual forms papers employed to maintain audience reading habits, and it discusses how those forms invited readers to engage London's theatrical culture. Until the Old Price riots of 1809 occasioned a Babel-like proliferation of theatrical periodicals – which will be the subject of Chapter 2 – theatrical criticism's most prominent vehicle of transmission was the daily press. Theater occurred as a textual sign and object of interest in both the advertising and the reporting discourses of the newspaper; in this, it was unlike any other public phenomenon. My aim is not to present a full history of the Romantic-period newspaper but rather to develop an understanding of the textual forms through which newspapers shaped Romantic-period readers' perceptions of theatrical culture. This will take us beyond theatrical criticism itself, but my discussion of advertisements, political commentary, and parliamentary reporting will help chart theater's presence in the newspaper's textual matrix and also serve as a prelude to Chapter 2's discussion of the more strictly focused theatrical press that emerged after 1800. A primary intention in this chapter will be to describe the techniques of sensation employed by the most popular Romantic-period daily newspapers (especially the *Times* itself), to which periodical theatrical criticism responded both in form and content. As I will argue in the book's later chapters, this periodical response to the news provided opportunities for writers such as Hazlitt and Keats to rethink the public representation of individual subjectivities.[3]

I   Free Press Ideology, Then and Now

Current assessments of the daily newspaper in late eighteenth- and early nineteenth-century Britain have displayed a continuing investment in the period's own descriptions of the press as an agent of democracy. For the past half century, historians have sought to assess the newspaper's influence in shaping the public opinion of an increasingly literate, and increasingly politically minded, national reading audience.[4] The governing aim of this attempt has been to establish as accurately as possible a date when commercial dailies gained "independence" from ministerial subsidies. Yet while historians differ with regard to such dating, most construct a developmental narrative in which advertising revenues eventually enabled "the emergence of a dynamic extra-parliamentary political culture" (Barker 3).[5] Such a view, exemplified here by Hannah Barker, is by no means restricted to the late twentieth century; indeed, it mirrors all too uncritically the eighteenth-century press's own ideologically inflected claims to legitimacy.[6]

Though the newspaper's power to initiate public discussion was a rallying point for radicals and a concern for reactionaries from the counterrevolutionary period of the 1790s through the agitation for parliamentary reform in the 1820s, the prevailing public idea of the press was on the whole uncompromisingly positive. John Wilkes's mid-eighteenth-century claims that press freedom was a distinctly English virtue would be echoed time and again in the Romantic period by radicals and conservatives alike (though what each group meant by freedom was a different thing altogether). In his *Speech in Defence of Jean Peltier*, delivered before the Court of King's Bench on February 21, 1803, James Mackintosh (no extremist, he) expressed concisely the developmental narrative that continues to inform histories of the British press two hundred years later:

> In the course of the eighteenth century, a great change took place in the state of political discussion in this country – I speak of the multiplication of newspapers ... it is very certain that the multiplication of these channels of popular information has produced a great change in the state of our domestic and foreign politics. At home, it has, in truth, produced a gradual revolution in our government. By increasing the number of those who exercise some sort of judgment on public affairs, it has created a substantial democracy, infinitely more important than those democratical forms which have been the subject of so much contest. (500–501)

"Gradual revolution" imagines a society defined by steady progress rather than violent upheaval; it is a useful phrase for an attorney defending a man accused, during a time of fragile peace with France, of libel before the court.[7] By invoking English freedom of the press and its "channels of popular information" as a conspicuous alternative to the French society that had "swallowed up all the asylums of free discussion on the Continent," Mackintosh situates Peltier as a man wronged by his native country (486). On English shores he is, by contrast, protected by a national recognition of the press as a preserver of democracy. In defense of a royalist client, Mackintosh imagines an England where rationality counters the forces that in France result in men like Peltier being "driven from their homes by the daggers of assassins" (484).

Mackintosh's distinction of the "gradual [English] revolution" from the violent French Revolution bespeaks the fears of many of his more conservative contemporaries, Burke and Coleridge chief among them, that England's social tensions would erupt violently as they had in France. Belief in the stabilizing effect of the press, along with other British institutions, would eventually allow those fears to give way to the more comfortable mid-century conservatisms of Thomas Carlyle and Thomas DeQuincey.[8] As Hannah Barker's position illustrates, this figuration of the near heroic role of the newspaper retained a strong currency throughout the twentieth century. Barker's brand of history, like Mackintosh's, is an exercise in political self-confirmation; for her, the newspaper's role in reforming Parliament serves as an inauguration of its modern function to check state power. Yet while nostalgia for the press of a purely democratic "public sphere" is understandable in our mediatized historical moment, it cannot explain the changing institutional status of Romantic-period newspapers, or the ways in which those newspapers shaped the everyday lives of readers. Our own ideological commitment to a developmental history describing the emergence of a "free press," a commitment Mackintosh marks in its adolescence, eclipses from view many of the newspaper's other, less easily narrated social effects.[9] Specifically, despite scrupulously detailing advertising's function as a source of revenue, twentieth-century historians largely ignored the degree to which advertisements shaped either the textual forms of the commercial newspaper or the reading habits those forms engendered.[10] Widening readerships required significant alterations in methods of reporting and textual presentation; newspapers responded to and in turn shaped new readerly expectations and desires. Bringing together advertisements and reports, the Romantic-period newspaper offered a textual form that presented the public world as completely intelligible to an emerging mass readership and encouraged the mode of "light" (which is not to say unsophisticated) reading Lamb's shrewd letter describes. What emerged in the Romantic period was a new genre of periodical publication situated at the center of mass reading activity and profoundly affecting readers' connections to the nation's collective public life and, as we shall see, to the theater at its center.

Hannah Barker recognizes that to be commercially successful, "newspapers needed to represent, or at least be seen to represent, the political nation" (73). But that effort was more about the process of manufacturing what Benedict Anderson has famously called an "imagined community" than about Barker's more easily imagined project, "articulating public opinion."[11] The task of the Romantic-period newspaper, as much as any other print publication in this time of uncertain and emerging readerships, was to "make" an audience for itself: inculcating reading habits and attitudes in a portion of the reading population, rather than simply giving voice to preexisting opinions or tastes. Unlike early nineteenth-century radical weeklies, which remained unapologetically polemical, and unlike interpretive quarterly reviews, commercial dailies needed to authorize themselves as objective conveyors not primarily of opinion but of information. Managed increasingly by professional editors and joint-stock companies geared toward profit, newspapers were no longer content to provide information tailored for a narrow segment of professionals or for an elite politically active class. Rather, they aimed to maintain a collective belief system that coalesced around the widespread habit of reading the daily news. Newspapers' sensational advertising and reporting conjured up and continually renovated for readers the idea of "Britain" as a network of social interactions necessarily facilitated by the daily periodical press. "In short, there is no disguising it," the *Edinburgh Review* could note in 1843, "the grand principle of modern existence is notoriety; we live and move and have our being in print" ("Advertising System" 2).

II News as Commodity, Commodities as News

The founding of the first daily newspaper in England, *The Daily Courant*, in 1702, inaugurated a century of rapid growth and diversification in the English periodical press.[12] Publications ranging from Daniel Defoe's *Weekly Review of the Affairs of France* to mid-century "advertisers" offered readers everything from philosophical meditations to "advertisements, together with the Prices of Stocks, Course of exchange, and Names and Descriptions of Persons becoming Bankrupts" (*Daily Advertiser* February 26, 1760).[13] Journals, from Defoe's through Addison's and Steele's and after, modeled the actions of the interpretive mind not only as a confirmation of the world's intelligibility but also as a performance of the reflective practices necessary for it to be properly encountered. The author served in these publications as a representative English cultural intermediary between his readers and the public events they sought to comprehend. To read such a journal was to mark oneself as part of the same privileged community of understanding the author exemplified. By contrast, daily newspapers, beginning with the *Courant*, presented no such conspicuous intermediary. Where the interpretive journal read events as signs of a greater social and historical order, the newspaper offered in its informational heterogeneity a seamless metonymy of the day's actual (reported) and potential (advertised) occurrences. With an encompassing illusion of immediacy, newspapers presented no event as unintelligible and required no special reading skills. At the same time, this very immediacy, and the daily printing that was its material result, connected readers to a British community of political and commercial mutuality. As Kathleen Wilson has argued, newspapers sought to be at once local and global: "[B]oth representing and verifying local experience, they functioned like imaginative literature in reproducing and refracting world events into socially meaningful categories and hierarchies of importance" (240). As I will argue, the sign of theater as both advertisement and as reported event was central to that effort.[14]

The Romantic period in England was, not unlike our own, an informational age enraptured by newly powerful media.[15] By the first decade of the nineteenth century, sixteen daily papers were published in London, eight each morning and eight each evening, with a collective circulation somewhere around 40,000 papers per day.[16] The Sunday press – geared more toward providing entertainment than information – had also begun to expand rapidly, with some estimates suggesting that more than 100,000 copies of various Sunday papers circulated in London each week ("Weekly Newspapers" 457).[17] Still, it was the morning dailies that became the nexus of what Hazlitt would call the city's "rage for conveying information in an easy and portable form" (Hazlitt 16.221).[18] Daily newspapers were things to be bought, borrowed, shared, read, and then (necessarily) replaced as the new day's number superseded the old.[19] An article in the Benthamite *Westminster Review* (1829) connected the expansion of London's daily news readership in the previous thirty years with the working class's shifting taste in daily beverages:

> We are not prepared to say exactly how this increase of readers has taken place, but a portion of it may fairly be attributed to the establishment of the little coffee houses or shops within which most of the daily papers are taken. Throughout the country, the number of places of this description being very great, it must have caused a considerable demand for newspapers; their object then was, to smoke and to drink, but now no man, or no man who can read (and how few there are of those who go into coffee-shops who cannot read), thinks of calling for his cup of coffee without at the same time asking for a newspaper. ("Weekly Newspapers" 476)

Of course this assessment prompts the question as to which historically came first: if there are few "who go into coffee-shops who cannot read," then does not the newspaper facilitate the sale of coffee rather than the reverse?[20] It is sufficient for our purposes, however, to recognize the *Review*'s strong association of the newspaper with an habitual act of consumption. And while this kind of daily reading has often been absorbed as a sign into the kind of free-press narrative I have described, closer attention to the newspapers' forms tells a different story. Considered historically, the commercialization of the English press – and more specifically its textual manifestation in newspaper advertisements and their interaction with the discourse of reporting – challenges traditional narratives of the newspaper's impact on English public life in the late eighteenth and early nineteenth centuries.

Romantic-period newspapers refined the textual strategies with which mid-century advertisers had sought to make themselves necessary commodities. Unlike the *Daily Courant,* which had introduced its advertising section a good month after its first number appeared, all three of the morning papers that would dominate early nineteenth-century London were founded with explicitly commercial aims. Yet these papers were more widely diverse in matter and ambition than the advertisers. John Walter's editorial apologia in the first edition of *The Daily Universal Register* (which in 1788 would become *The Times and Daily Universal Register* and later that year simply *The Times*), published on January 1, 1785, shows how the daily press's commercial interests responded to a new class of reader and facilitated the development of a new periodical form. Walter criticized the specialization of periodicals geared solely to "please the class of readers whose approbation their conductors are ambitious to deserve." Some papers "build their fame on the lengths and accuracy of parliamentary reports," others "are principally attentive to the politics of the day," and still others "deal almost solely in advertisements ... Thus it would seem that every News-Paper published in London is calculated for a particular set of readers only; so that if each set were to change its favourite publication for another, it would only produce disgust, and dissatisfaction to all" (*DUR* January 1, 1785).[21] The *Register* countered the possibility of such "disgust" by providing a balance of useful and entertaining printed matter, "steering clear of extremes." Bringing together miscellaneous features and informational reporting, the paper remade its genre to accommodate consumer desires for a daily dose of text that rendered the public world – in all its commercial and political dimensions – completely intelligible, and consumable *as* text: "A News-Paper conducted on the true and natural principles of such a publication, ought to be a Register of the times, and faithful recorder of every species of intelligence; it ought not be engrossed in any particular object: but like a well covered table, it should contain something suited to every palate" (*DUR* January 1, 1785).

Walter's attempt to make his paper a widely useful miscellany was not so much an innovation as a consolidation of trends that had been present in newspaper publishing since the early 1770s. Both the *Morning Chronicle* (founded 1769) and *The Morning Post* (1772) sought to strike a similar balance with their printed material, though each still claimed a unique focus on some aspect of public culture (the *Chronicle* on parliamentary intelligence and the *Post* on the world of fashion). Like these papers' editors, Walter was responding to competition from nightly and Sunday presses, which contained a wider range of features including poetry and sensational stories, even as he maintained a commitment to the informational mission required of a morning paper. The morning dailies' varied content does not alone render them historically or formally significant. What fundamentally changed the presentation of news was the manner in which the dailies combined discourses of report, entertainment, advertisement, and commentary into a single text. By 1824, *The Westminster Review* could assert the following:

> [T]he miscellaneous character of a newspaper makes it more valuable than if it contained political occurrences and political dissertations. The understandings of its readers are led on by degrees from the simplest domestic occurrences to those which affect their remotest interest, or appeal to their noblest sympathies: from the overturning of a coach to the overturning of an empire. ("Newspapers" 210)

Beyond educating a reading populace in the grammar of politics and economics, the daily newspaper's far more mammoth task was to facilitate its readers' daily interactions with the vast public world that comprised these fields of activity. In 1829, the same journal would go even further in its assessment: "The daily press ... has an omnipresent vision – there is nothing too high for its grasp – nothing too minute for its attention. It occupies itself with all public affairs – and with all private concerns as soon as they come within the circle of public interest" ("Newspaper Press" 216). The dailies were able to achieve this "vision" by constructing a periodical genre defined by the continual intersection of multiple strains of information: reporting of political and national events, sensationalist accounts of domestic troubles and gossip, occasional literary pieces, and advertisements.

III The Advertising System

More even than the narration of public events that was the ostensible purpose of a newspaper, advertisements were the daily's most prominent textual sign. As Walter recognized shrewdly in 1785, balancing an audience's desire for political information with the relentlessness of the English commercial spirit was crucial to the *Register*'s success. "The rage for parliamentary debates" caused many of London's morning papers to withhold publication to ensure that their renderings of the speeches were complete. These policies existed "to the great injury of trade" and "people interested in business" (*DUR* January 1, 1785). What was required was a paper particularly attentive to the needs of an emerging type of reader for whom connection to a community of financial and commercial interests was just as vital as an interest in the politics of the nation. Traditional methods of prioritizing and distributing information, Walter argued, had the following negative result:

> [P]arties interested in *sales* are essentially injured, as the advertisements, inviting the public to attend them at *ten* or *twelve* o'clock, do not appear, on account of a late publication, till some hours later. – From the same source flows another inconvenience; it is sometimes necessary to *defer* sales, after

they have been advertised for a particular day; but the notice of putting them off not appearing early enough, on account of the late hour at which the papers containing it are published, numbers of people, acting under the impression of former advertisements, are unnecessarily put to the trouble of attending. (DUR January 1, 1785)

Walter promised to give the substance rather than the details of parliamentary activity, enabling him to bring his paper out "*regularly* every morning at six o'clock." Time once measured in weeks or days was now measured down to a regimented hour of the clock. Given the staggeringly ambitious mission of Walter's *Register*, such regimentation is understandably necessary: "[T]he great objects of [the *Register*] will be to facilitate the *commercial* intercourse between the different parts of the community, through the channel of *Advertisements*, to record the principal occurrences of the times; and to abridge the account of debates during the sitting of Parliament." Facilitate – record – abridge: this would become an unstated mantra for many Romantic-period newspaper editors working in the field of periodical publishing over which the *Times* would eventually come to preside. It would also serve as a motto for theater critics writing in theatrical dailies.

Advertisements were every daily newspaper's primary means of "facilitat[ing] the commercial intercourse." By the early nineteenth century, advertisements usually occupied eight or nine of a typical morning paper's sixteen columns of space; sometimes they amounted to more than 75 percent of its text altogether. Front pages were no exception. Our modern "headlines" were still a thing of the distant future. (The *Times* resisted their placement on the front page well into the twentieth century.) Instead, the typical front page of the *Times* or the *Morning Chronicle* presented to its reader a well-ordered but vastly various network of possibilities for commercial, political, and cultural interaction – far more diverse than that offered by the typical eighteenth-century advertiser (Figure 2). Content of the ads ranged from the standard "shipping news" (which detailed departures, arrivals, cargoes, tonnage, and crew needs) to theater notices, to goods for sale (books and quack medicines were the two most popular type of items), to lotteries, to people seeking or offering positions of employment, to announcements for political meetings, to all manner of highly personal concerns. A quick study of the front pages of the *Times* over the same four-week period in 1790, 1800, and 1810 reveals that advertisements became shorter and more numerous, even as the size of the paper's pages remained fairly constant. In 1790, the front page averaged 23 advertisements over four weeks, with a high of 27; in 1800, the average

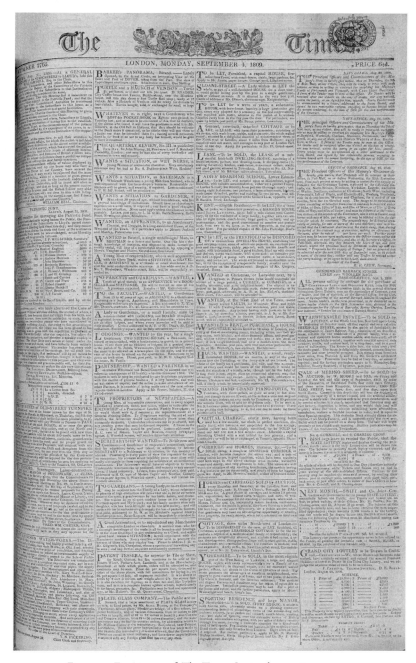

Figure 2: Front page of *The Times*, September 4, 1809, page 1

was 49, with a high of 82; and in 1810, the average was 78, with a high of 91. As Ivon Asquith has noted in a similar examination of the *Morning Chronicle*, "[T]he fact that the number of advertisements in the *Chronicle* increased at a much faster rate than the amount of space they comprised shows that they did get notably smaller" (713).[22] The 1790s saw a crucial shift not only in the size of ads but in the type of ads that earned prominence of place. Matters of individual and domestic interest came to outnumber corporate interests and their longer advertisements.[23] The two most common types of advertisements, shipping news and theater notices, which in the 1780s often dominated front page space, were now frequently relegated to page two or even page three.

These facts show not simply that the dailies were becoming more commercially oriented, but that there was a significant change in the textual forms through which they represented the public world to their readers. Reflecting back from a distance of forty years on his role as editor of the *Morning Post*, Daniel Stuart commented that both the small size and varied content of advertisements were crucial factors in attracting and shaping turn-of-the-century reading habits:

> I encouraged the small miscellaneous advertisements in the front page, preferring them to any others, upon the rule that the more numerous the customers, the more independent and permanent the custom. Besides, numerous and various advertisements interest numerous and various readers, looking out for employment, servants, sales, and purchases, &c., &c. Advertisements act and re-act. They attract readers, promote circulation, and circulation attracts advertisements. (25)[24]

James Perry, editor of the *Morning Chronicle*, who similarly encouraged more individually directed notices, claimed that in addition to enabling him to better support his enterprise because they produced more revenue, such advertisements formed "a kind of local history of the manners of the age" (*Morning Chronicle* May 3, 1792).[25] Like his fellow editors Stuart and Walter, Perry realized that the community represented by his paper's daily collection of advertisements was in itself a selling point to readers.[26]

A few examples of typical Romantic-period advertisements will fill in the picture for which Stuart's and Perry's comments provide an outline. These are taken from the front page of *The Times*, September 4, 1809:

> WHATEVER is, is right, says a Gentleman who LOST his POCKET-BOOK on Egham race ground, on Tuesday last, and so much is he convinced of this, that he declares, if the person who found it will have the goodness to send it to Mr. Gilbert's, at the Old Bell, in Holborn, that they should be welcome to the Bank notes it

III The Advertising System

contained, as he thinks they will put them to a better use than he intended them for; having several memorandums in the book of no use to anybody but himself, would be glad to have it restored.[27]

WANTS a SITUATION as a WET NURSE, a young woman of undeniable character. Very satisfactory references may be had at no. 8 Durham Place, West, Hackney-road.

LEASE. – To be SOLD, the LEASE of a substantial, brick-built DWELLING-HOUSE, consisting of a breakfast-room, parlour, and drawing-room, 8 sleeping rooms (including the attic), kitchen, wash-house, convenient cellars, stable, and good garden, situated in Tottenham. Enquire at No. 25, Norfolk St., or of Mr. Edridge, tallow-chandler, Tottenham.

THE QUARTERLY-REVIEW, No. III. is published This day, for John Murray, 32, Fleet-street, and J. Hatchard, Piccadilly, London; and may be had also of every bookseller and newsman in town and country.

WANTED, an APPRENTICE, to an Apothecary, Chemist, and Druggist, in a long-established House, at the West end of Town. For particulars apply to Messrs. Jackson and Manley, Paternoster-row.

Accompanying these ads were scores of others, including the sale of linen and woolen rags; an official ordnance offering the exchange of stable dung for forage to feed government horses; solicitations for contributions to various charity funds, including one for "a distressed Widow with four children, the second of whom, a boy of five years old, has been an ideot and cripple from his birth"; a used piano for sale; and a large number of employment opportunities. Each of these advertisements follows a standard pattern of direct address and description typical of "miscellaneous advertisements" at the time. Capitalized words at the beginning of the lines announce the advertisement's subject: a "LOST ... POCKET BOOK," a woman who "WANTS a SITUATION as a WET NURSE," a "DWELLING HOUSE" for "LEASE." Such eye-catching tags are followed by instructions as to how the reader can respond: "Very satisfactory references may be found at no. 8 Durham place" for the potential wet nurse. The *Quarterly Review* "may be had ... of every bookseller in town and country." And, perhaps most interestingly, the good soul who returns the lost pocket-book to "Mr. Gilbert's, at the Old Bell, in Holborn ... should be welcome to the Bank notes it contained." The advertisements all call for a personal exchange of one sort or another; indeed, some of them offer the advertiser's very body for sale as a commodity.[28] If Perry's claim is right, and newspaper advertisements of the period do present some sort of local history, it is a history that was renewed actively every day not only in the symbolic form of the paper's text but also in the myriad interactions that the text both anticipated and represented.

Until the mid-1790s, when the crucial shift in the form and number of advertisements occurred, theatrical advertisements dominated the front pages of the *Times*, *Morning Chronicle*, and *Morning Post*. They were, in short, the day's most pressing news. Well into the 1790s, such ads were charged only a small duty by the paper's editors, "such was their news value, particularly when they contained cast lists" (Asquith 719). Almost invariably theatrical ads were the largest on the page and occupied much of the first (or sometimes fourth) column. The Saturday, January 7, 1792, issue of *The Times* contained three major theatrical ads: for the "King's Theatre, Pantheon," which offered "La Pastorella Nobile" and several inter-actes; for the Drury-Lane Company at King's Theatre, Haymarket, and its production of an "Opera, in five Acts (7th time) called CYMON"; and for the "Theatre Royal, Covent Garden," which was showing "ARTAXERXES." Principal cast members were listed along with the plays' titles and intermission entertainments. Especially before 1800, it was often difficult to tell where advertisements left off and reviews began. Brief and more informational than evaluative, reviews of the 1780s and early 1790s were the product of a system of favors and patronage between the institutions of the theater and the press. While not as blatantly biased as the typical puffing that characterized much eighteenth-century theatrical reviewing, these criticisms were hardly comprehensive and made little pretensions to "objectivity." As on Tuesday, August 3, 1795, in the *Times*:

HAYMARKET THEATRE

Mrs. Kemble's Night[29]

> The motives which induced Mr. Kemble and Mrs. Siddons to appear Saturday evening, in the characters of *Douglas* and *Lady Randolph*, should not be passed over in silence. In this age every tribute to *domestic affections* should be peculiarly marked.
>
> The FAIR CALEDONIAN was brought from *Edinburgh* to *London*, to gratify her "*Scottish friends*." It is *National* but pretty; one hit at fashion was strongly applauded: – "If we may judge of them by this sample – *Lords* have no more *honour* than *Ladies* have *waists*."

The audience was an immense one, and grateful it was to see *public favour* so warmly patronizing *private worth*.

This is the extent of the review – somewhat less than a quarter of the size of the show's advertisement.

As portrayed in the daily newspapers, theater offered a new kind of cultural experience, a place where readers could immerse themselves in the great and small currents of history for the price of admission. By the turn of the century, theater advertisements were distinguished in the *Times* by a particular iconography that always stood at their head: under the prominent image of a clock was an open book with the words "The Times" printed on its pages; the book was flanked by two others, one on the left, opened, entitled "Past Times" and one on the right, closed, with the title "Future." Theater ads were the only ones distinguished by this emblem, as they would be throughout the nineteenth century. As the paper's forms became more devoted to smaller, more personal advertisements, however, theater advertisements lost some of their prominence, often relegated to page two or three of both the *Times* and the *Morning Chronicle*. This change does not so much indicate the diminishing importance of theater as suggest that the reader's experience of theater – as a textual sign and as a cultural event – must be considered in the context of the changing forms of textual publicity the paper offered. Theater was at the very center of the lived "history" James Perry imagined. It had become, by 1800, one form of cultural exchange among many.

IV Toward "Objectivity"

Advertising was not the newspapers' only business, nor the only element of their publication that focused readers' perceptions of theater. Meticulously detailed reports of public events were also a central part of the daily and particularly the morning paper's textual form. Like the *Courant* before them, Romantic-period commercial newspapers oriented readers toward the world at large by presenting national – and theatrical – events as matters of universal concern. The typical newspaper brought together under its presiding title and date information from a variety of assumedly reliable sources: intercepted letters, official correspondents, excerpts from foreign newspapers, and direct publications of official documents. As the range of coverage grew, so necessarily did the methods of acquiring information. The same issue of the *Times* (September 4, 1809) published letters on page two from the following sources:

> From the LONDON GAZETTE, Saturday Sept 2.
>
> Downing-Street, September 2, 1809
>
> a dispatch of which the following is a copy, was, on the 30th ult. received at the office of Lord Viscount Castlereagh, one of his Majesties Principal Secretaries of State, from Lieutenant-General Lord Viscount Wellington, dated Deleytosa, 8th August 1809.
>
> ****
>
> Downing-Street, September 2
>
> a dispatch of which the following is a copy, was yesterday morning received at the Office of Lord Viscount Castlereagh, one of his Majesties Principal Secretaries of State, from Lieut.-General the Earl of Chatham, dated Head-quarters, Batz, August 29, 1809.
>
> ****
>
> ADMIRALTY-OFFICE, September 2
>
> *Extract of a Letter from Rear-Admiral Sir Richard John Strachan, Bart. K.B. to the Honourable William Wellesley Pole, dated on board His Majesty's Ship the St. Domingo, off Batz, the 27th of August 1809.*
>
> ****
>
> ADMIRALTY-OFFICE, September 2, 1809
>
> Rear Admiral Sir Alexander Cochrane has transmitted to the Hon, William Wellesley Pole, a letter from Capt. Pigot, of his Majesty's Ship the Latona, giving an account of his having, on the 18th of June last, captured La Felicite, a French frigate . . .
>
> ****

These letters all contain information on troop movements from men in the action of the Peninsular War. Wellington's, for example, begins:

> I apprised your Lordship on the 1st instant of the advance of a French corps towards Puerto de Baños, and of the probable embarrassments to the operations of the army, which its arrival at Placencia would occasion; and these embarrassments having existed to a degree so considerable, as to oblige

IV Toward "Objectivity"

us to fall back, and to take up a defensive position on the Tagus, I am induced to trouble you more at length with an account of what passed on this subject.

Wellington goes on to provide a narrative approaching two thousand words that not only details the movements of the English and Spanish allies against the French, but also offers assessments of the strength of enemy forces; he even describes the reasons behind his several decisions to advance and to retreat finally to his current position on the Tagus. Chatham's dispatch provides a similarly bleak story of withdrawal to Batz.[30] Official, dated documents complement the letters on page two with information about military promotions, new baronets, and recent bankruptcies. In the fourth column, just under the day's half column of theater notices, the paper's anthology of reports from foreign newspapers begins; on this day reports principally from the Spanish, German, and Dutch occupied most of page three. Page four is filled almost entirely with advertisements, adjacent to small blocks of text informing the reader of local marriages, deaths, and court proceedings.

While the September 4, 1809, issue of the *Times* is typical in presenting itself as a compendium of information gathered from sources not initially produced for the paper, it also evinces a powerful yet subtle editorial presence that organizes those sources even while it naturalizes its own presence. The editorial voice of the paper functions as an unobtrusive mediating device for the reader, implicitly manifesting the structuring principle behind the paper's form: to integrate texts of disparate informational content. On this day, the editorial voice in one place amounts only to headings denoting sources ("We insert to-day copies of the German papers ... the contents of which are interesting, though they contain no one fact of leading importance"), while in another place it provides opinions on reports and the events they describe:

> From Lord Wellington and Lord Chatham the accounts are equally afflicting; but with this difference in our manner of bearing the double disgrace that pours in upon us – that in the one case we have luckily ourselves to blame; and amidst its mortification vanity finds relief, by assigning to itself all the merit of whatever temporary advantages may have been gained, and heaping upon the Spaniards the exclusive reproach of ultimate defeat. But what have we to say in relation to the projected attack upon Antwerp? We have no Spaniards to accuse here.

The unifying rhetoric of the passage – in which first-person plural pronouns stand in collectively for editors and readers together, and in which comment is rendered as if it too were reported fact – structures audience response in such a way that the reader perceives the communicated knowledge of events as entirely unmediated. By assuming the reader's assent, that is, the newspaper manufactures it without resorting to the elaborate philosophical justifications attractive to a more self-conscious class of reader. Raymond Williams has asserted, "The daily newspapers ordinarily abstained from political comment, not because comment was thought unnecessary but because this could obviously be more conveniently done in periodical publications" (*Long Revolution* 204). But such abstention involved commercial strategy as much as convenience; editors sought to shape the reader's perceptions of the world without appearing in view, preserving the illusion of immediate intelligibility that was the newspaper's primary appeal.

Nowhere is the daily newspaper's commitment to intelligibility more evident than in its development of a discourse of report characterized by supposed objectivity and attention to detail. Increasingly papers offered descriptions of public happenings not through the publicized privacy of dispatches, but through a language that reported events as professionally observed. A process in which several parties took notes and then passed them on to a writer for composition resulted in highly standardized language, essentially the third-person perspective that, before the advent of Internet blogging, defined twentieth-century newspapers. Changes in parliamentary reports are exemplary in this sense because the proximity and predictability of Parliament as an ongoing public occurrence enabled correspondents assigned to the venue to produce regular informational narratives.[31] Parliamentary reporting thus stands as a kind of forerunner to the theatrical reviews that would develop both in papers and in theatrical periodicals after the turn of the nineteenth century. Nurturing a growing "cult of Parliament," reporters monitored the debate as much for its spectacle as for its content. Parliament took on special importance not only because it was the body within which governmental policy was formed but also because it was an arena in which the upper classes could publicize themselves in ways increasingly necessary for the maintenance of aristocratic prestige; that is, they could show themselves as active members of the nation's no longer intimate political sphere (Colley 48–50). When Parliament was in session, the *Chronicle* offered substantive daily descriptions of the debates. Special reports sometimes occupied more than three of the paper's four pages.

In the 1770s and 1780s, the famous William "Memory" Woodfall revolutionized the *Morning Chronicle*'s reporting with his uncanny ability to remember almost verbatim entire debates in the House of Commons, where note-taking was forbidden, and reporters were forced to sit in the dark confines of the "Strangers' Gallery." His technique was a far cry from the ways of that other sometime journalist, Dr. Johnson, a generation before, whose reports consisted of rhetorically complicated speeches he surreptitiously composed himself. John Nichols's 1812 *Literary Anecdotes of the Eighteenth Century* remarks of Woodfall's influence:

> Before his time a very short sketch of the debate was all that the newspapers attempted to give on the same night, and the more detailed reports were deferred to some subsequent day. Without taking notes to assist his memory, without the use of an amanuensis to ease his labour, he has been known to write sixteen columns after having sat in a crowded gallery for as many hours without an interval of rest. (303)

In fact, until Woodfall most regular reporting on debates could be found in digest form in monthly magazines rather than newspapers (Thomas 623). His retentive memory made him something of a cult figure around town. But if Woodfall was a recognizable anomaly in the 1780s, his very human reporter's skill was soon overshadowed by rapid improvements in information technology that rendered daily reports a necessary commonplace when Parliament was in session. In the decades following Woodfall's retirement, the parliamentary reporting systems of the *Morning Chronicle*, *Morning Post*, and the *Times* would divide and specialize their labor. By the time William Hazlitt was hired at the *Chronicle* as a parliamentary reporter in 1812, two other reporters on the staff were already responsible for parliamentary coverage.

The typical parliamentary report consisted of a third-person narrative of various speakers in their turn. In late November and December 1812, about the time Hazlitt began work for the *Morning Chronicle* and would have composed his first reports, Parliament was engaged in strenuous debate regarding the Peninsular War against France. Much of the paper was devoted to long, if standard, reports of the proceedings. Two short excerpts follow from the paper's account of the new session:

> A great number of Members were present at about a quarter to three o' clock, when the Usher of the Black Rod arrived, and desired their attendance at the Bar of the House of Lords, to hear the Commission read for assembling the present Parliament. On their return they proceeded, as usual, to elect a Speaker, when SIR JOHN NICHOLL rose and observed, that their first duty was to exercise their antient and undoubted privilege in the election of the Speaker to the Chair of that House. The proper cognizance of this privilege, he considered as of the highest importance, not only

> to the House itself, but to the rights and liberties of the people, and consequently to the happiness and welfare of this extensive empire.
>
> Mr. Abbott having then been conducted to the Chair in the usual manner, proceeded to address the House from it. He entertained a deep sense of the arduous duties which every person who filled that Chair was called upon to fulfill; and so long as he discharged these duties, to the best of his judgment and ability, he hoped he should receive the support of the House. He begged leave to assure the House, that he was entirely devoted to its service. *(Hear, hear, hear!).* (*The Morning Chronicle* November 25, 1812)

The language of this report differs from that of Wellington's letter from the 1809 *Times*. The characteristic voice of parliamentary reporting – anticipated by Woodfall and perfected by his paper – enables the reader to imagine witnessing firsthand the events described. With its seamless change in perspective, from "Mr. Abbot ... proceeded to address the House" to "He entertained a deep sense of the arduous duties which every person who filled that Chair was called upon to fulfill," the second passage shifts, without any alteration in tense, from description to an implicit appropriation of Abbott's voice. The language borders on a kind of free indirect style, in which a narrative voice relates a character's thoughts by taking on the rhetorical qualities of the character's imagined interior discourse. As Mr. Abbott's thoughts are transformed from an observed fact into an experience seemingly unmediated by the distanced language of report, the reader connects with the debate not only as a past event but also as a psychological drama concurrent with the act of reading. Eventually, this standardized "objective" style becomes the norm over dispatches and correspondences in all areas of nineteenth-century reporting. That the older informational genres endured for some time due to the difficulty of establishing regular information channels merely highlights areas of report where early innovation was more conveniently possible, principally in parliamentary and theatrical reporting. With the emergence of the professionally reported event, the concept of publicity itself underwent a major shift. The newspaper no longer relied for information on what were, in effect, overheard communications between private parties. Instead, it generated its own narration of a much larger sphere of activity that was recognized as public *because it was reported*. The letters of Wellington and Chatham spoke of their individual perspectives to a restricted audience and were only subsequently published, but the anonymous reporter spoke in the present moment from an expansive public arena to an unnamed and unbounded, yet distinctly English, audience.[32]

Parliamentary intelligence was one of two major kinds of reporting to manifest this new notion of publicness; theatrical reviewing was the other. At about the same time that the theatrical advertisement became one type among many in the daily paper, enmeshed in a discourse that emphasized the more accessible aspects of English communal life, theater performance became the focus of a more scrupulous commitment to objective and detailed reporting. James Perry, editor of the *Chronicle*, which since Woodfall's time had maintained a close relationship with the theater establishment, began in the late 1790s to professionalize his paper's reviewing by discouraging free advertising and puffing. On April 30, 1808, Perry wrote to Thomas Sheridan, manager of Covent Garden, informing him that the free admission his reviewers received would be put to an end once and for all:

> I for one certainly do not use the cards that were presented to me six times in a Season; and yet almost every night I have an advertisement sent to me from the Theatre, not only to be inserted gratis, but which also compromises the character of the paper about everything that is brought out. It will be essentially better for both of us to put an end to this pitiful arrangement, and resolve in future to pay for admission to each other's premises.[33]

As the role of the reviewer altered from sometime advertiser to independent reporter, reviews began to lengthen and became more substantive. Much like the parliamentary reports that were their model, theatrical criticisms attended increasingly to performances as public events. Though the reviewer ostensibly had the dual task of evaluating a performance with regard to abstract cultural standards and of reporting it as an occurrence in the most conspicuously public space in the city, reporterly detail often took precedence over aesthetic evaluation. A review from the Tuesday, September 30, 1806, *Times* exemplifies this imbalance:

> Last night the Tragedy of *King Richard the Third* was performed, with the Farce of *The Adopted Child*. Mr. Cooke came forward as *Richard*, it being his first appearance on a London Stage after his strange and abrupt manner of withdrawing himself last season. When he advanced to the front of the stage, he appeared for a moment doubtful of the reception he was likely to meet, but he was soon welcomed by the loudest and most general applause, often repeated; his former disrespect of the audience appeared now to be forgiven and forgot.

The reviewer considers the performance as a public event, emphasizing Cooke's celebrity presence before an audience that bestows its favor upon him. Star status trumps the impersonation of character. And even as the *Times* reviewer does begin to evaluate the performance loosely on aesthetic grounds, the evening's status as a communal occurrence outweighs any larger philosophical or cultural concern: "The principal novelty of the night was the début of a new actress, a Mrs. Makins, who appeared in the character of the *Queen Dowager*, King Edward's widow. She is uncommonly tall, and her person (although on a very large scale), is good. Her voice is also naturally good, and well adapted to pathetic expressions" (*Times* September 30, 1806). More detailed than those common to the 1790s *Times*, and ostensibly more objective, the review reinforces the reader's experience of theater as a comfortably ritualized but pleasingly unpredictable brand of news.

The third week of September 1809 would bear out theater's unique status at the center of England's news-driven commercial and cultural life. During the "Old Price" (or "O. P.") riots at the new Covent Garden, theatrical coverage came to dominate the pages of all the major London dailies. For weeks the theatrical columns of the papers were expanded to narrate a nightly audience uproar against the theater's new price scales. The September 19, 1809, *Times* began, "The New theatre opened last night. It is certainly very elegant. Its shape has been before described ... The Theatre was crowded the instant the doors were open, and though on the steps of the portico the mob were hissing and exclaiming against the advance prices." The report went on for three whole columns. And similarly, in the September 19 *Chronicle*: "Last night this Theatre, the first stone of which was formally laid in December, was opened to the public with the Tragedy of Macbeth under circumstances which made it impossible to hear a syllable that was uttered." The expansive coverage continued daily until the crisis subsided when a compromise was reached between management and audience. No other cultural event seized the attention of the commercial newspapers in the same way. As I will demonstrate in Chapter 2, the publicity surrounding the Old Price riots was unparalleled and occasioned a new interest in reading about theatrical events (in the theater and out). And this in turn spurred the growth of an already rapidly expanding field of theatrical periodical production.

V   Theatrical Sensation

The shift in the nature of textual publicity occasioned by the Romantic-period newspaper affected not only those areas of reporting where regular correspondents could be situated: its influence could be seen in all the discourses that the daily newspaper comprised. At times the rhetorical divide between reports and advertisements is difficult to discern because each sought to focus readers' interests in similar ways. Advertisements aspired to the truth content and sensational quality of reporters' voices, even when what they were offering to the reader was nothing more than a quack medical remedy; reports sought the sense of immediate connection to readers' everyday lives that well-crafted advertisements conveyed. Sensationalist – indeed theatrical – details were the common factor in both kinds of text. On the morning of August 19, 1789, just around the time when details of the summer's events in France were flowing into London, readers of the *Times* met with the following capital headings at the top of page one's second column: "THE ASSAULT of the BASTILE ... Surrender of the Governor, and his Detachment – The Release of the Prisoners ... " Looking down the column a few more inches, their eyes would be caught by "The FRENCH REVOLUTION ... PARIS IN AN UPROAR!" What accompanied these lines was not a detailed correspondent's account of events in France, or even an editorially sanctioned essay of political commentary, but a description of the "most Extraordinary and Accurate MODEL of PARIS ... 50 feet by 85" that was being advertised: "Displaying one of the grandest and most extraordinary Entertainments that ever appeared, grounded on authentic facts." The panorama was complemented by a new dance called "La Coquette," which served as the pre-show, and "music compiled from the French." Similar ads appeared any time major political events occurred, seeking to capitalize on an audience's publicly sensitized fascinations. Headings like "Fatal Catastrophe" or "Extraordinary Case" were equally likely to be followed by a sales testimonial for skin clarifier as by the blood and guts stories that peppered newspapers amid more conventional reports. News stories cultivated the same appetites for narrative sensation that was used to sell both durable and cultural products. The *Times* of August 30, 1809, for example, reported that a man was found in the Dublin road alive, with "the whole surface of his body covered with worms ... His eyes were dissolved, and the cavities, as well as those of his ears, mouth, and nose, were filled with a white moving mass, more horrid and disgusting than it is possible for the imagination to conceive." Another such report, published on January 15,

1829, kept readers attuned for two days of sequential narrative. It described the "mysterious disappearance" of a young tradesman's wife, suspicions of whom were aroused because "a plot of ground behind the house was overgrown with weeds, with the exception of two spots, which appeared to have been recently disturbed." The wife's return the next day fortunately solved the mystery.

These are not simply examples of "melodramatic tactics" newspapers used to hold a reader's attention (Hadley). Taken together, they emphasize editors' attempts to make many such devices cohere into a single text, appealing to an audience larger than any that could be brought together by one type of information. While the interplay of objectivity and sensationalism characterized the detailed language of many reports and ads, it also served as a structuring principle for the paper as a whole. The allure of these various narratives – borrowing as they did from the sensational language of theatrical ads – was consolidated into an eye-catching text that interspersed reports and advertisements of all sorts throughout the paper's pages. With its multiply divided textual space, the paper declared itself a miscellany to the reader's eye even before its informational content could be assessed. Clearly printed lines divided columns and blocks of text, presenting an appearance of regulated diversity. Looking quickly across the page of virtually any daily paper, a reader could encounter as many (or more) different kinds of information as there were columns of text. Page three of the August 29, 1809, *Times* offers an easily found example: in column one a correspondent's description of the French surrender of Flushing to the English dated August 25, in column two a series of official proclamations along with the day's theater review, in column three a report on an episode of fatal domestic violence from North Carolina, in column four a series of advertisements for the lease of assorted properties.

Theater criticisms were presented in the matrix of the paper's pages alongside such sensational reports and offered similar kinds of details, providing a lower-order version of the "associationist literary strategies" John Strachan sees linking culture and advertisement in the period (46). The second page of the Tuesday, October 7, 1806, *Times* contains a daily theater advertisement in column two and a review of the previous night's entertainment at Covent Garden in column four: "Last night Mr. Bellamy made his first appearance on the London boards, in the character of *Robin Hood*. He has a manly figure, and a deep and full toned voice; is by no means deficient in science, but appears to want compass." Turning the page, column one presents the reader with an extensive description of an "*AFFRAY:*" "A bloody and desperate battle was fought on Saturday afternoon last, in Angel Gardens, Ratcliff Highway, between a number of Lascars and Chinese men, lately arrived in this country, which was attended with serious consequences." And one more column brings the police report of an "ASSAULT" in which "a woman named *Elizabeth Hodson*, who attended several days last week, again appeared to complain against *Isaac Lyons*, a young Jew dealer, for a most violent assault upon her person." The generic blurring of all these discourses, through the reporterly rhetoric, the detailed language they share, and their juxtaposition in the bricolage of the paper's pages, has larger ramifications for the Romantic-period newspaper's social function and for theater's position at the center of the commercialized reader's daily experience.[34] Newspapers continually fulfilled and maintained readers' consumerist desires not only for useful political and commercial information but also for the repeatable, daily, dated activity of reading a text that reminded them of the world's intelligibility and of their place in it. Alan Liu has commented that the popular picturesque served at this time as an "enclosure act of the eye" by domesticating rugged nature into the consumable commodity of framed pictures (728). In a related way, the newspaper enclosed the events of the day in a framed text that that could be "glid over by the proper eye" of its reader (Lamb, *Letters* I.242). And it was the reader's impulse toward a communal experience of sensation – exemplified most readily by theatrical ads and reports – that taught that eye what to search for, and where to alight.

VI Signs of the *Times*

James Chandler has described the emergence after Waterloo of a collective historical consciousness in which "the massive influence of the press and the grand scale of the assemblies for public speeches gave verbally talented young men and women the impression that they could do anything" (*England in 1819* 432). But while attempts to contest the future through literary and political writing were certainly expressions of a new sense of contemporaneity between author and audience, the daily popular press had created, renovated, and maintained the foundation of that sense long before Napoleon's final defeat in 1815. In the English newspaper, "accounts appear side-by-side for no other reason than that the occurrences they chronicle are supposed to have coincided in a given duration" (Chandler, *England in 1819* 103).[35] Yet this is just why the paper was so valuable for individuals attempting to make sense of the world of events around them. In contrast to the public of revolutionary France, where in Lynn Hunt's words "the mythic present was inherently undatable" (27), the English commercial press reenacted its datedness each day, invoking the papers of the day and week and year before, and giving implicit assurance that a new number would arrive tomorrow, making the world intelligible all over again.[36] If the large spectrum of periodicals that scholars such as Jon Klancher and Kevin Gilmartin have charted – from the elite philosophizing of Francis Jeffery's *Edinburgh Review* to the polemical interventions of William Cobbett's *Political Register* – enabled readers to imagine connections to like-minded audiences, the newspaper offered itself as at once local and universal, a means to connect not merely to a discrete community but to a world.[37] To rely on Benedict Anderson's still apt formulation, "The idea of a sociological organism moving calendrically through homogeneous, empty time is a precise analogue of the idea of the nation, which also is conceived as a solid community moving steadily down (or up) history" (Anderson 26).[38] The newspaper does not provide or interpret the signs of the times; that is, it offers itself *as* a master sign of the times. Its datable present was a representation of continuity in English life, whereby the grand events of politics would proceed apace, but not without the more immediately lived conditions of local interaction signified by the paper's advertisements.[39]

I return finally to the image with which this chapter began: Charles Lamb, habitual newspaper reader. I do not mean to suggest that a man like Lamb, who was a great if vexed lover of the theater, was exclusively conditioned in his understanding of public life by the daily newspaper. Nor do I argue that those individuals who read newspapers avoided other periodicals. Publicly oriented newspaper reading certainly coexisted with other forms of reading like the middle-class review journal and the novel. But if review periodicals, like the novels they often treated, manifested, and perpetuated the imaginative orientations of an increasingly private middle-class reader, the newspaper's textual forms invited reader's individuated consciousness to reengage with a world of commerce and political events.[40] With its metonymic textual structure, the newspaper provided a psychologically manageable compendium of the world for its readers by encompassing past and future, great and small, in an ordered, readable text. Its long, almost endless, axes were both geographical and temporal. Together, newspaper representations of advertisement and report comprised textually a nexus of imagined events within which the reader could refashion herself daily, *by reading*, as a public and historical subject. Charles Lamb's gliding eye, at once a facile means of perusal and a deeply felt method of connecting to an imagined English community, was the newspaper's concomitant mode of consumption. "Reading [newspapers],"

Linda Colley has commented, Englishmen "would be constantly reminded that their private lives were bounded by a wider context, that whether they liked it or not they were caught up in decisions taken by men in London, or in battles fought on the other side of the world" (41). But this way of describing the newspaper's role relies on a traditional privileging of one kind of historical event over another. The Romantic-period daily newspaper – with theater among its central concerns – demanded a new set of reading practices from its audience. As a consequence, the imaginative connection Colley speaks of can be described differently: newspaper readers came to see the sweeping narratives of history as an ongoing serial that complemented interactions closer to and within the domestic and microeconomic spheres of their daily lives. Because it compressed the larger events of nationhood (battles, diplomacy, politics) into text that stood side-by-side on the page with text manifesting readers' more immediate personal concerns (the buying and selling of books and quack medicines, lost articles or runaway servants, the search for employment), the daily newspaper presented a world in which the English were by definition mutually – commercially and politically – interdependent. The living and dying population encompassed by the newspaper – the historical subjects of which it spoke – could be imagined by those who read the news each day as forming a community bounded by nothing but English shores and the steady forward march of England's time.

The political and cultural importance of Romantic-period theater was shaped as much by this textual afterlife as by theatrical performances themselves. Theater was a unique early-nineteenth-century institution because it was the single public phenomenon to occur as a textual sign in both the informational and advertising discourses of the daily newspapers – which is to say that for readers of the daily press, theater was everywhere. The development both of middle-class review culture – to which theatrical periodicals were important contributors – and of the cultural standards the reviews disseminated are part of a wider discursive field that the daily press bounded and defined. The newspapers' presentation of theater can therefore serve as the basis for a more developed study of theatrical criticism in other kinds of publications, which responded continually to newspapers in both form and content. In Chapter 2, I will argue that as the discourse of theatrical reviewing changed, so too did the public's sense of theater's social function, and of their own theatrical experience. And that shift enabled the emergence of a strain of Romantic writing that transformed literary work in nineteenth-century Britain.

Notes

1. For an account of the distribution of newspapers in the period, see *The History of "The Times"* 1.33–8. See also Cranfield 152–77.
2. See Klancher, *The Making of English Reading Audiences*; Kevin Gilmartin, *Print Politics*. See also the collection edited by Stephen Behrendt, *Romanticism, Radicalism, and the Press*; and Michael Scrivener's *Poetry and Reform: Periodical Verse from the English Democratic Press*.
3. Some work has begun to address this issue more fully. For a discussion of the newspaper's "teeming presentness" (77) and its effect on lyric poetry, see Kevis Goodman, *Georgic Modernity and British Romanticism*. Arguing that newspapers provide a new context for the imagination of individual subjectivities in the late eighteenth century, Goodman's account is consonant with my own. Her emphasis on how William Cowper's poetry represents a "georgic attempt to offer a rival medium of information" (101), however, describes a more conservative response to that culture than I find in second-generation writers such as Hazlitt and Keats. See also Nikki Hessell's "The Opposite of News: Rethinking the 1800 *Lyrical Ballads* and the Mass Media," which situates Wordsworth and Coleridge's aesthetic project as a similar kind of response to the expanding culture of news.
4. Hannah Barker's *Newspapers, Politics, and Public Opinion in Late Eighteenth-Century England* (1998) analyzes the financial records of a variety of newspapers in London and the provinces and argues that increasing commercialism enabled newspapers to align themselves freely in the ongoing controversy of English partisan politics. Barker's work revises that of earlier historians, such as Arthur Aspinall and Lucyle Werkmeister. In his *Politics and the Press 1780–1850* (1949), Aspinall describes a complex network of party alliances governing English newspaper production. In Aspinall's view, newspapers "were not independent and responsible organs of public opinion" in the late eighteenth century (v). Similarly, Werkmeister's *The London Daily Press: 1772–1792* (1963) details the deep political corruption of the press, dating its beginnings even earlier than Aspinall's study, to the 1770s and the "age of the scandal sheet" (4). For Werkmeister, "the history of the daily press from 1784 on is largely an account of the cat-and-mouse game played by George Rose and Richard Brinsley Sheridan" (13). Robert Rea, also writing in 1963, argues to the contrary that the newspaper "came of age" in the years 1760–1774 as an extraparliamentary organ of public opinion. Despite their differences, these studies all consider the press's explicit attention to politics as its defining property.
5. The lone exception I have found is Jeremy Black's *The English Press in the Eighteenth Century* (1987), which is more skeptical about the press's social function. Black considers advertising, political alliances, news sources, and paper distribution as fundamental to assessing the press as a social institution; he argues that newspapers were far less influential in shaping public opinion than most historians contend.

6. See, among myriad examples, the letter to the editor printed on page 1 of the January 4, 1785, *Daily Universal Register*: "the free press affords an uncommon share of room for the display of patriotic abilities, it being not only a chief supporter of our liberties, but also from its great operation in refining the savage barbarity of mankind, and meliorating the tempers and dispositions."
7. Peltier was an exiled French Royalist who had several times attacked the "French First Consul" (i.e., Bonaparte) in print. He was brought to trial during the Peace of Amiens as a conciliatory gesture by the British government. Though Mackintosh failed in his defense, Peltier ultimately escaped punishment because of renewed hostilities between the countries.
8. For a discussion of the ways that in DeQuincey and Carlyle "the 'French Revolution' cannot mean something distinct from the English 'reaction' to the French Revolution," see Jon Klancher, "Romantic Criticism and the Meanings of the French Revolution" (470–71). See also Terry Eagleton's related discussion of the nostalgic nineteenth-century "man of letters" in *The Function of Criticism* 45–50.
9. The continuing influence of this "free-press" line of thought can be seen in the work of both James Chandler and Jerome Christensen. See Chandler, *England in 1819* 100–106, and Christensen 1–8.
10. Newly examined revenue records, for example, indicating that government subsidies were quickly losing ground to public advertising as a major source of newspaper income, have been offered by Barker and others as evidence that the press was free to facilitate the formation of an ever-widening, and evermore-inclusive, sphere of public discussion. See Barker, esp. 1–8. John Strachan's *Advertising and Satirical Culture in the Romantic Period* offers a notable correction to this assessment. For an alternative history of the role of the press in revolutionary politics, see Lynn Hunt, *Politics, Culture and Class in the French Revolution*.
11. For a cogent summary of the historical conditions that enabled the development of the national "imagined community," see Anderson 36. As Linda Colley notes in the introduction to *Britons*, "Britishness was superimposed over an array of internal differences in response to contact with the Other, and above all in response to conflict with the Other" of the French nation (6). For a discussion of the role newspapers had in accomplishing that superimposition, see Colley 40–42. Following Colley's observation that the terms "England" and "English" could increasingly be taken to mean "Britain" and "British," I have used them virtually interchangeably throughout the book, with the awareness that each carries a slightly different emphasis.
12. Factual aspects of this historical narrative are gleaned from Bourne, Morison, Harris, and from original sources. For much of the seventeenth century – first under Charles I and again, despite a brief respite, during the Commonwealth – censorship limited the development of the press. And the Restoration brought little relief from restrictions imposed by Cromwell's

major generals. Yet after the Glorious Revolution in 1688 and the subsequent lapse of the restrictive print licensing act in 1695, a host of news purveyors began to ply their wares, seeking wider reading audiences by employing a variety of printing strategies and formats, from pamphlets to single-leaf layouts. In the four years between 1695 and 1699, *The Post Boy*, *The Flying-Post or Post-Master*, *The London Post*, and *The Post Man* were published for the first time, each imitating the others' textual layouts and claiming to have the most up-to-date information on domestic and continental happenings. Morison 53–70 provides an illustrated account of these eighteenth-century posts. Still, as Jeremy Black points out, "[T]he lapsing of the Act did not signal the end of all interest in press censorship" (9). Efforts were made to renew the act at the time and in the years leading up to final passage of a new scheme of taxation in 1712. But lack of consensus in Parliament led to legal ambiguities surrounding the printing of papers and pamphlets. By 1705, twenty papers were available in London, most on a twice- or three-times weekly basis. *The Daily Courant* was the lone daily. For a related discussion, see Harris 83.

13. The field of eighteenth-century periodical publication is so wide ranging that it would be impossible in a study of this nature to address it in all its complexity. Certainly any number of review-like texts, of which Steele's *Tatler* would be a famous early and the *Edinburgh Review* a late example, had commercial interests. Further, government attempts to regulate the press often encouraged one publication or the other to adopt formal aspects normally not its own. For example, the 1712 government tax on papers up to one whole sheet (which folded into a four-page half sheet paper) resulted in many dailies adopting six- or eight-page formats, filling the additional space with essay-like commentaries. And there are, of course, eighteenth-century review publications that did not display such interpretive practices – often reviews, even as late as *The Monthly Review* (1749) and the *Critical Review* (1756), were largely collections of abstracts of current publications. Yet as John Clive argues, even these periodicals demonstrated larger social commitments (to political parties, for example), which steadily widened their scope (Clive 31). Still, the distinction between commercial and interpretive publications is a useful one because it is borne out by the increasingly radical differences in textual presentation between daily newspapers and less frequently published journals.

14. As the primary advertising and informational vehicle of the eighteenth century, and as commodities that necessitated a daily ritual of consumption, newspapers like *The Times*, *The Morning Post*, and *The Morning Chronicle* operated at the very center of the eighteenth-century "consumer revolution" famously described by Neil McKendrick. Revisions of McKendrick's position have stressed, however, that emergent consumerism not only altered the way that goods were made, produced, and sold; it also occasioned major shifts in how individuals imagined relations to the public arenas within which commodity exchanges took place, creating a newly coherent system of relations but with a continually obtaining "problematic of exchange" (Agnew 9).

The daily newspaper is a textual embodiment of these negotiations, for it is at once the most significant contemporary representation of a multitude of specific material consumer needs and a consumable commodity itself. The transformation of the eighteenth-century press occurs not only when news becomes a commodity, as Habermas asserts, but also when commodities, and their exchanges actual and potential, become news. Colin Campbell, for example, has written that the central task of historical inquiry into the development of modern consumer culture is to determine how subjectivities are shaped as "individuals manage to develop a regular and endless programme of wanting in relation to new goods and services" (58). Campbell's strained connection between (1) the Romantic artist's empowerment of readers as consumerist "re-creators" of cultural products and (2) the "autonomous, self-illusory hedonism which underlies modern consumer behavior" notwithstanding, his critique of Veblen's thesis of social emulation as a satisfactory explanation of consumer behavior is compelling (200). See especially the early chapters of *The Romantic Ethic and the Spirit of Modern Consumerism*.

15. Clifford Siskin has focused on the social effects of new writing technologies in the eighteenth century. For Siskin's suggestive connections between that time and ours, see *The Work of Writing* 1–5.

16. This estimation is from Bourne, 354–55. The number would fluctuate somewhat throughout the period: *The Westminster Review* counted the number at thirteen in 1829. See "Newspaper Press" 216.

17. Such a huge circulation would seem to support Raymond Williams's claim that "the real history of the nineteenth-century popular press has to be centered in the development of the *Sunday* paper" ("The Press and Popular Culture" 41). But the *Review* goes on to assert that "within the last four or five years there has been a good demand for the daily papers, without any material decrease in the sale of the Sunday papers; and we are able to assert that the number of readers has very considerably increased within the last six years" ("Weekly Newspapers" 474–75). The alternative history Williams would construct is not at odds with my focus on daily readership.

18. All parenthetical citations to Hazlitt's work are to the P. P. Howe edition, with volume and page number.

19. As Michael Harris points out, comprehensive histories of the English press of any period are difficult due to "wastage of copies, lack of associated manuscript material, and far-flung and isolated library holdings" (Harris 82). Yet this begs the question as to why early newspapers were less rigorously archived than other kinds of periodicals. Clearly, the mode of consumption they encouraged should be viewed as a factor in the "wastage of copies."

20. The historical emergence of the eighteenth-century English coffee house has been well documented. See Habermas; Aytoun Ellis, *The Penny Universities*; and Bryant Lillywhite, *London Coffee Houses*.

21. *The Daily Universal Register*. Cited parenthetically in the text as *DUR*.

22. More specifically, Asquith observes of the *Chronicle* that "Advertisements increased by nearly 50 per cent from 1798 (22,869) to 1806 (33, 428), whereas

the amount of paper filled with advertisements increased from 50 per cent in 1798 to only 53 per cent in 1807" (713).

23. Warren's Blacking was, in the 1820s, the first household product to be advertised on a large scale in papers throughout the nation. See Walker 125.

24. Letter by Stuart published as "Anecdotes of Public Newspapers," *Gentleman's Magazine* (July 1838): 25. The letter is in response to one from Hartley Nelson Coleridge, nephew of Samuel Taylor Coleridge, who had according to Stuart overestimated the importance of S. T. Coleridge's essays in boosting the turn-of-the-century *Post*'s circulation.

25. Quoted in Asquith 717. Perry's comment echoes Dr. Johnson's ironic question in *Idler*, no. 40: "When these collections [of advertisements] shall be read in another century ... how shall fame be possibly distributed among the tailors and bodice-makers of the present age?" (*Works* 2.128–29). Parties who preferred long advertisements, particularly booksellers who often monopolized as much of the paper's space as they could, became so disconcerted by policies that disadvantaged their products that on occasion they even founded their own papers. This is true of the *Post*, which Stuart altered greatly from the time when founder "John Bell regarded [it] as the advertising department of his bookselling business" (Hindle 9). On the founding of the booksellers' paper *The British Press*, see Hindle 84. More often than not, these papers quickly disappeared.

26. Anecdotal evidence, both factual and fictional, supports Stuart's assertion that most readers perused the paper's advertisements. I provide one example of each: in a letter to John Hamilton Reynolds on November 22, 1817, Keats comments, "I see there is an advertizement in the chronicle to Poets – he is so overloaded with poems on the late Princess" (*Letters* 1.190). And in Austen's *Mansfield Park*, Edmund Bertram amuses himself, while Crawford courts Fanny, by taking up a newspaper, "earnestly trying to bury every sound of the business from himself in murmurs of his own, over the various advertisements of 'a most desirable estate in South Wales' – 'To Parents and Guardians' – and a 'Capital season'd hunter'" (Austen 310).

27. The ad, of course, quotes Pope's *An Essay on Man, Epistle I* (289). For a discussion of the relation between advertisement and satire in Romantic-period news, see Strachan.

28. The degree to which the personal and the commercial were imbricated is nowhere more evident than in this single advertisement, taken from *The Morning Chronicle*, December 2, 1812:

> ADVANTAGEOUS OFFER to Ladies and Gentlemen – A Gentleman of good family and connections, wishes to borrow EIGHT HUNDRED POUNDS, to be employed in a novel and lucrative speculation, which cannot fail to be very beneficial to the Public and to the Advertiser, who will give his bond or promissory note for double the sum, payable in twelve months. Should a Lady advance this sum, and prefer the hand of the Advertiser, he is not averse to

matrimony, and his age, his person and manners, will not be found unpleasing. None but principals need apply, and such as are seriously inclined to advance the necessary sum immediately. – Direct in post-paid letters to R.I.M. at Stafford-row, Buckingham-gate.

29. Traditionally, actors were allowed by their contracts certain nights, known as "benefits," on which portions of the house proceeds – often gratuities beyond the ticket price – went to supplement their salaried incomes. The actor who was benefiting was responsible for gathering fellow performers to participate without monetary recompense. This was done commonly as a professional courtesy. For a concise description of benefit performances, see Nicoll, *The Garrick Stage* 91–95.
30. Both Wellington's and Chatham's dispatches were published in London's other major dailies on that same day.
31. For a definitive recent account of these changes, see Hessell, *Literary Authors, Parliamentary Reporters*.
32. Nikki Hessell describes how Hazlitt's parliamentary reporting exemplified the practices of the day and highlights the difference between his parliamentary reporting and his rhetorical accounts in *The Eloquence of the British Senate*. Recording speeches in notes (with varying degrees of accuracy, depending on his interest in or approval of the speech), Hazlitt produced a standardized narrative discourse for the paper; the account was then supplemented or redacted by a second correspondent or editor. Hazlitt's participation in this collective form of authorship and editorial practice evinces his "thorough integration into the parliamentary corps" (*Literary Authors* 124). For another account of Hazlitt's time as a parliamentary reporter, see Wu 144–46.
33. British Museum, add. MSS 42,720, fo. 121 (quoted in Asquith 719).
34. That this sensational language accompanies, in both cases, narratives involving racialized or gendered violence is worth noting. For a discussion of the representation of such violence on stage, see O'Quinn, *Staging Governance*. Gamer and Robinson present Mary Robinson's public career as an example of the ways in which newspaper culture blurred the lines between theatrical performance, news, and advertising.
35. As with most assessments of the press, Chandler's focuses largely on the newspaper's reporting function, but the argument is only strengthened if it is enlarged to consider the textual presence of advertisements as potential occurrences.
36. An example of conspicuous dating: aside from its own date of September 4, 1809 – and excluding those occurring in advertisements or in the bodies of reports – I count more than forty separate datings in the four pages of the *Times* (five dates at the head of Wellington's letter alone).
37. As Klancher has noted, middle-class journals such as the *Edinburgh Review* and *Quarterly Review* attempted to cultivate audiences more narrowly defined by a desire for philosophical consistency and cultural distinction. Their

reflective and even overwrought prose manifested, in Klancher's words, "the activated interpretive mind in its power to reincarnate everyday life: to form a 'philosophy' of one's encounter with the street and the city, with fashion, with social class, with intellectual systems and the mind's own unpredictable acts" (51). Gilmartin, in a related way, describes how radicals like Richard Carlile and Cobbett worked to construct a "counter system" of linguistic usage that enabled readers to see beyond the veil of corrupted governmental and informational systems (*Print Politics* 1).

38. As Chandler points out, Anderson's is a sequential rendering of Walter Benjamin's oppositional concepts, "messianic" and "homogeneous, empty time" (Chandler 100–106; Benjamin 264). For Benjamin, the newspaper's chronicling strips events of their potentially transformative effect: "[T]he intention of the press [is] to isolate what happens from the realm in which it could affect the experience [*Erfahrung*] of the reader" (158). For a discussion of the potential of modern media to create rather than dull "experience," see Negt and Kluge.

39. Mark Parker has argued that current studies of the early-nineteenth-century periodical have overlooked the impact that conspicuous "periodicity" had on the rhetoric of the magazine's literary criticism. But any consideration of readers' literary experiences should likewise account for the maintenance of the concept of the "period" in commercial publications. See Parker 10.

40. In presenting the newspaper as text that encouraged reading practices dissimilar but complementary to those encouraged by the novel, I revise Ian Watt's contention that both forms provided alleviation from the psychological individuation occasioned by the rise of market capitalism. See Watt 71.

CHAPTER 2

Britain's Theatrical Press, 1800–1830

By the third decade of the nineteenth century, the theater critic was a sufficiently recognizable social type to warrant self-parody:

> Full of our critical importance and self-created dignity attendant on our new avocation, we dined full two hours earlier than usual, that we might be thereby enabled to procure an enviable seat on the critics bench, in that fiery ordeal of players or playwriters; employed our friseur half an hour extra in powdering our *cranium* and then put our glass almost out of countenance by *our reflections* of which was the fittest expression to assume on this momentous occasion, we at length screwed up our features into what we considered the very epitome of criticism. Armed with a memorandum book of the most elegant quality, a Bramah pen and patent inkstand; we sallied forth, determined to take the town by storm, or batter its places of amusements about the ears and shew our voice as "Double as Dukes."[1]

Taken from the short-lived *Theatrical Mince Pie*'s first issue of January 1, 1825, this passage mocks the day's play-going conventions even as its writer celebrates his participation in them. Calling attention to his "critical importance," he details a preparatory routine of dining, dressing, and equipping himself that precedes his attending the play and composing a review. Readers are invited to enter the theater alongside him not as aesthetic judges, but as companions in the lobby and pit:

> On arriving at our destination we took our station near the door, and in a very few minutes after "a pretty considerable d – d number" of persons arrived till we began to "groan and sweat" beneath this accumulating pressure and continual monotonous cry of "take care of your pockets," which sent our neighbours elbows into our sides, by their endeavors to ascertain whether what was theirs still belonged to them. At length the door opened, and we were carried to the pay place, where there was the "devil to pay," some poor uniformed individuals having rushed on without remembering they ought to have taken a tin-check, or they would find a *wooden* one. Once seated we began to review *ourselves* and found the whole economy of our dress considerably deranged; our hat with the crush had assumed the

clerical form, the knot of our handkerchief had got under our left ear, which caused a disagreeable sensation, as it was sometime before we could assume the composite order in which we set out. Amidst catcalls, whistling, "Tom where are you," "Love Sarah, &c." the curtain rose and discovered Mrs. Bunn and Mr. Mercer in the characters of Elvira and Valverde.

Half a century on from Richard Brinsley Sheridan's 1779 decorous satire *The Critic*, the *Mince Pie* reviewer makes his interaction with the theatrical crowd the principal object of his critical writing. Waiting in Drury Lane's jostling throng, purchasing a ticket, and finding a seat provide the setting within which the critic "reviews" his inability to maintain "the composite order in which we set out." Only after this evaluation does he attend to the performance of *Pizarro* on stage: "Mrs. W. West aims too much at point making and the pleasure of the Gods [of the gallery] to please us ... The Rolla of Mr. Wallack is a very unequal performance."

Narrating the difficult circumstances of its composition and deploying cool irony in the face of social chaos, the *Mince Pie* review depicts a turbulent theatrical experience at the intersection of public and private worlds, an experience that exemplifies Romantic-period theatergoing and marks much of its theatrical criticism.[2] If, as Gillian Russell has asserted, the eighteenth-century theater offered an "alternative representative assembly" to the conspicuously limited representation found in the British Parliament ("Theatre" 223), the *Mince Pie* reviewer presents himself as part of a crowd whose methods of interaction were far more unruly.[3] Much like the newspapers whose "free press" commitments were inflected through a commercial discourse of information and exchange, Drury Lane's idealized national standing as a "Theatre Royal" gives way in this account to the particularities of an embodied, urban, even intimate interaction with fellow Londoners. To the *Mince Pie* reviewer, his fellow audience members are a "pretty considerable d – d number of persons" who elbow him, "derange" his attire, and attempt to steal his money. The crowd threatens not only his physical comfort but also the "self-created dignity" his critical office is supposed to provide. A Bramah pen and elegant memorandum book are hardly sufficient defense against the pit's human crush.[4]

Over the past two decades, historians have explored the complexities of Romantic-period theatergoing, and to that end have recovered many reviews and other material remainders of theatrical performance. Still, the daily practices of reading and writing about theater in periodicals remain largely unconsidered as a cultural practice that was in dialogue with, and influenced by, other kinds of writing.[5] As I argue in Chapter 1, beginning in the 1770s newspapers presided over a change in the way theater was represented textually to a growing commercially oriented readership. Around the turn of the century, though, a periodical culture devoted largely to theater began to emerge, expanding the ways in which theater was to be accounted for in, and translated into, text. Numbers tell part of the story: from Richard Steele's *The Theatre*, first published in 1720, to 1799, thirty-two periodicals devoted solely or primarily to theatrical topics were published for the first time in Britain, an average of less than one every two years, with no single year seeing the launch of more than three. By contrast, between 1800 and 1832, there were 182 new theatrical periodicals published, an average of between five and six per year. And the twelve years alone from 1821 to 1832 saw the new publication of approximately ten per year, with a high of sixteen in 1828.[6] The number drops off considerably after 1832, marking the first three decades of the nineteenth century as a time of sustained production for theatrical periodicals unmatched again until the early 1900s. Yet while I take this increase as a compelling sign of the period's importance in the development of theatrical criticism, my central concern in this chapter will be to examine the textual forms that these new periodicals exhibited.

After a brief consideration of how the conflict between "legitimate" theater's legislated role at the center of British culture and its increased commercialization altered the conditions of theatrical reception in the Romantic period, the central sections of the chapter describe a wide range of theatrical periodicals published after 1800, analyzing the different textual strategies they employed to attract and maintain readerships. There was, of course, no uniform critical voice among theatrical periodical writers. Publications ranged from daily pamphlet-like reprints of playbills to weekly journals of performances to substantive monthly magazines offering colored engravings and actors' biographies. The frequency of a periodical's publication had a significant impact on its size, look, and feel. Yet while their textual presentations and critical methodologies could be very different, these publications all attempted to shape readers' encounters with the theatrical world through the medium of the regularly issued text. Although all manner of theatrical periodicals were in their textual forms and concerns engaged with theater as it appeared in the daily newspaper press, I find particularly in the weeklies and monthlies between 1800 and 1830 a shifting deployment of anti-commercial commentary. Around the turn of the century, anti-commercial rhetoric offers a direct protest to the moral decline of theater as a national cultural institution. After the Old Price (O. P.) riots of 1809, however, such rhetoric begins to appear as one facet of a refigured critical discourse. Realizing the insufficiency of moralistic critique, critics tend to adopt a more subtle resistance to what they see as the commercialization of theatrical experience.

The chapter concludes with a discussion of the most innovative periodical to publish theatrical criticism in the Romantic-period, Leigh and John Hunt's *Examiner*. Founded in 1808 as a newspaper that refused advertisement, the *Examiner* negotiated the complex discursive terrain between daily information and cultural evaluation by styling itself an independent interpretive organ even as it exploited the reading practices encouraged by the *Times* and other newspapers. Representing theater in its pages as a public experience equal to politics and commerce, the *Examiner* provided writers with a philosophical and stylistic freedom that propelled the emergence of what I will call occasional modes of theatrical reviewing. My discussion of the *Examiner* will in turn provide an opening for the case studies found in Part II of the book, which show how such criticism became a constitutive element of second-generation Romantic literary writing.

I   1809 and After

As theater historians have documented, developments in production technology, theater financing, and playhouse architecture changed the British theatergoing experience markedly during the eighteenth century. With the Licensing Act of 1737, Parliament had formally recognized the two theater patents granted by Charles II at the Restoration, held at the time of the Act by the proprietors of Drury Lane and Covent Garden. During the Romantic period, these patent theaters would be the only houses legally allowed to perform the spoken genres of tragedy and comedy. With exclusive rights to the performance of Shakespeare and other major figures, they claimed stewardship of a national literary tradition. Yet as Jane Moody has shown, even as such claims and the legislation that empowered them posited "an absolute opposition between authentic and spurious theatrical forms" (*Illegitimate Theatre* 12), they created a cultural domain that was, by definition, beyond the law's purview. Further attempts to regulate performance, such as the Act of 1752, in fact spurred the proliferation of theatrical venues in and around London that emphasized physicality, spectacle, and generic innovation, indicating "the declining political and cultural authority of the fashionable 'town', identified with Westminster and the West End of the city, and the rise of the more socially and politically heterogeneous metropolis" (Russell, "Theatre" 224).[7] Audiences came to see new forms of musical pantomime, burletta, and melodrama, and their ways of thinking and writing about theater shifted to accommodate the new experiences these performances provided.

Increased competition with minor theaters in the late eighteenth century ensured that material changes occurred inside the patent theaters as well, though these had been slow to come. The sharp delineation between stage and house that emerged in continental theaters early in the 1700s was delayed in England for decades by architectural designs honoring a fundamentally different notion of theater's public function. Christopher Wren's 1674 plan for Drury Lane, in which the performance area extended well beyond what would eventually become a proscenium arch, discouraged innovations in lighting and scenery that in French and German theaters had darkened the house and lit the stage for more spectacular viewing.[8] This traditional English layout helped maintain the idea that theater was a space not only of cultural encounter but also of social exchange, for it "established a rapport between the spectators and the actors that occasioned a frequent interchange . . . of suggestions, criticisms, [and] commendations" (Hogan, *Critical Introduction* lii). With the coming of David Garrick to Drury Lane in mid-century, however, a standard of commercial concern previously unseen in English theater began to take hold. Garrick's shift in acting style accompanied his more professional management of the theater. He made numerous changes in Drury Lane's modes of production, many of which chastened the carnivelesque atmosphere of the playhouse by separating events on stage from activity in the pit, boxes, and galleries. Garrick resisted the tradition of actors' benefit performances in favor of a more stable, professionalized company structure; helped abolish the practice of allowing gentlemen backstage to mingle with the actors during performances; and, after his visit to the Comédie Française in 1761, improved English lighting and scene technologies to the continental standard. The arrival of the great French artistic director Philip de Loutherbourg at Drury Lane in 1771 ushered in an age of further innovation, in which audiences were treated to elaborate spectacles of illumination and scenic perspective. "Rapport" between spectators and actors gave way to a theatergoing experience designed, in the words of Allardyce Nicoll, "to ravish the spectators' gaze by swift changes and transformation [of] scenes" (*History* 34).

The last two decades of the century also brought drastic changes to the patent theaters' architecture, at once expanding their commercial base of ticket buyers and enhancing the notion of the theaters as an encompassing political assembly. Drury Lane was demolished in 1791, rebuilt in 1794, destroyed by fire in 1804, and rebuilt again in 1811. Covent Garden was reconstructed in 1784, renovated in 1792, burnt down in 1808, rebuilt and reopened in 1809. By the early nineteenth century, both theaters had capacities of more than three thousand spectators.[9] Behind the scenes, mechanisms were installed to facilitate the movement and presentation of scenery and to improve the position of lighting. Boxes took up more space in the new buildings and were rendered more conspicuously private by changes in their position and by the dimming of their illumination. The galleries, traditionally costing two shillings for the lower tier and a single shilling for the upper, were moved up and back from the stage with each reconstruction, until finally they came to be known derisively as "pigeon-holes."

Taken together, these changes presented conditions that helped occasion the theatrical riots of 1809 and – more important for our purposes – the press reaction to those riots: by that time, the newspaper had ensured that Romantic-period theater had become an imaginative locus around which competing vocabularies of national and personal identity could coalesce.[10] Although there had been disturbances or "riots" at patent theaters throughout the eighteenth century, most occurred within the context of expected patterns of crowd behavior. What E. P. Thompson has called "the moral economy of the English crowd" was exercised as a "highly-complex form of direct popular action, disciplined and with clear objectives," in which "the men and women in the crowd were informed by the belief that they were defending traditional rights or customs" ("Moral Economy" 78).[11] Despite the intensity of such demonstrations, most theater historians agree that they posed little threat to the established social order; on the contrary, they almost invariably acted to preserve it, because the rioters asserted themselves according to the logic of traditional social hierarchies.[12] Theater was throughout the century seen by many Britons as an inherited right under their constitution; any infringement on that right would be met with organized resistance. With the rise of spectacular productions, the darkening of the house, the physical division of the audience, the construction of a stage immensely distant from many viewers, and the representation of theater in the daily news as both commodity and cultural experience, those old codes for acceptable audience behavior came into tension with a growing conception of theater as part of the world of political and commercial interactions the newspaper represented.[13] The patent theaters were in a particularly precarious position with respect to this tension because the redistribution of cultural prestige occasioned by the rise of the "heterogeneous metropolis" had begun to erode their claims to a constitutionally sacralized position and had begun to encourage in their managers an increased concern for profit. This, even as much of their audience still believed – in the words of one pamphleteer – that "the amusements of the public are in a degree, *the right of the public.*"[14]

The London theatrical disturbances that occurred in 1809 differed from eighteenth-century riots in part because the outcome of the dispute was less clear to the participants, but also because the riots were so widely reported in the theatrical presses that they became constitutive public events rather than limited and focused exercises of existing rights. On September 18, 1809, a newly constructed Covent Garden theater opened its doors for the first time. The scheduled performance was John Philip Kemble, actor but also the theater's manager, in his signature role of Macbeth. A preemptive pamphlet war had informed the public of management's attempt to privatize boxes and raise prices for most of the theater's seating. The audience, however, was not prepared to endorse the changes. From the beginning of the prologue, in which Kemble exclaimed "Strong our building, heavy our expense;/We rest our claim on your munificence," his voice was drowned out by hisses and catcalls. When magistrates arrived to quell the disturbance by reading the riot act on stage, the crowd grew even more antagonistic until, the entire performance suspended, they sang "God Save the King" and "Rule Britannia!" at two o'clock in the morning, and left the theater.[15] Similar disturbances occurred for months, with audience members bringing signs protesting the rise in prices, allocation of private boxes, and the hiring of an Italian singer to suit the tastes of the upper classes. In December, a negotiated settlement, complete with a signed contract between Kemble and the riot leaders, was agreed upon at London's Crown & Anchor tavern. Tensions would erupt again in the next season's opening month when management reneged on its contractual promise to open a number of the private boxes to the public.

Most studies of the O. P. riots have focused on how the crowd resisted changes in their theatrical experience by invoking the terms of "deferential" economy against management's invocation of exclusive property rights and commercial profit.[16] The middling and lower orders resented the private isolation of the new theater's boxes because it exempted those seated there from participation in theater's traditional performance of class interaction. As Leigh Hunt commented in the *Examiner*, the managers "consulted little but the accommodation of the higher orders. The people seem to have felt this immediately."[17] The aristocracy's conspicuous presence in the eighteenth-century theatrical audience had given way to the monied classes' conspicuous absence within the nineteenth-century theater. Print responses to the riots, though, complicate the picture of a crowd relying exclusively on traditional vocabularies of resistance. A widely read pamphleteer complained that a major cause of the riots was

> the depriving of the people of those parts of the house to which they have formerly been accustomed, for the purpose of accommodating a few Noblemen and opulent Commoners, who are too aristocratical in their notions to mingle with the British public. We cannot sufficiently express our indignation at this separation from what these purse-proud Peers term, the *vulgar herd*. Every principle of our Constitution is at variance with this distinction, which at once reflects on the cupidity of the Managers of the Theatre, and on the weak and despicable ideas of the Proprietors of these *snug retreats*. (*Remarks on the Causes of the Dispute*)

This criticism displays a complex interarticulation of deferential and market-oriented terms. The essence of the complaint is that monied audience members, be they "Nobleman" or "Opulent Commoners," have set aside their duties as members of the theatergoing public in favor of private interests and privately consumed pleasures afforded by "snug retreats."[18] This is equally true of the theater managers, whose greed has driven them to forsake "every principle" of their constitutional obligations:

> Much has been spoken of the right, which, under the present circumstances, the managers of Covent Garden Theatre, have to advance their prices of admission. In this right we think they are defective. A private tradesman may at any time augment the price of his articles, but the case here is essentially different. – The tradesman is not supposed to be the only one in his line, there are other similar, to whose shops the public may resort. They, therefore, are not under the necessity of purchasing of him unless they choose. It has, however, been observed, "you are under no obligation to go to the Theatre." "If you do not like the prices of admission why do you go?" This argument is founded on an erroneous idea. The amusements of the public are in a degree, *the right of the public*, and in all countries have been so considered. As such they are here placed, under the superintendence of the King, who, in fact, is the trustee of the public. The monopoly is granted by him under an implied condition, that the prices of admission shall be such as the public can conveniently afford to pay. (*Remarks on the Causes of the Dispute*)

The stridency of this claim to public "right," however, reveals the degree to which, by 1809, such a claim needed to be reaffirmed before a theater whose institutional structures and textual presence in the commercial news had begun to compromise such logic. As Cheryl Wanko has recently asserted, the shift from a patronage to a consumerist economy in eighteenth-century British theater gave rise to the prerogatives of "fans" who believed it their right to mediate performances in print (223). Yet the rights the pamphleteer is now at pains to claim might have been assumed in the time of Garrick and Johnson, even if the degree to which management had met them was in dispute. His expressed contrast of "private tradesmen" with the "public" responsibility that theater managers had as stewards of theatrical tradition attempts to reestablish a division that has already collapsed or indeed may never have existed.[19]

As the conflicted rhetoric of this account reveals, during 1809 and 1810 theater became not only a center of crisis in the physical and symbolic interaction between classes and between theatrical audiences and performers, it became the center of a discursive contest seeking to recast the nature of those public interactions.[20] The O. P. riots thus mark a decisive moment in the mediation of theater – via print – to reading audiences.[21] Publicly playing out a contest about what the national theater's responsibilities were, the events in and around Covent Garden occasioned a proliferation of print responses over two decades that sought to assign new meanings to Britain's theatrical experience. Spectators *qua* readers were aware that the dispute's outcome would be negotiated, beyond any printed contract or settlement, in the pages of newspapers, pamphlets, and theatrical periodicals. Even though, as Elaine Hadley asserts, the protests made by the O. P. audiences hearkened back to a deferential economy and a deferential mode of class interaction, the institutional settings within which they did so, both in the theater and in theatrical periodicals, had already begun a transition toward a more commercial model of interaction. While managers and theatergoers alike paid continual homage to the theater as an ideal public space, constituted to develop national virtue and maintain the people's "rights," the actual experience of theater – including the riots themselves – was occurring in new kinds of spaces, both physical and psychological, built to indulge national pastime and to sustain consumer desire.

II The New Periodicals

During the eighteenth century, theatrical criticism struggled to keep up with the technological and stylistic innovations occurring in English playhouses.[22] Following Richard Steele's almost single-handed founding of professional theatrical journalism in the early 1700s, when he wrote for the *Tatler*, *Spectator*, *Guardian*, and ultimately in 1720 his own *The Theatre*, most criticism produced throughout the century focused on how best to preserve public morality.[23] Questions of genre, acting style, and theatrical management were all raised in this context, with the result that innovative approaches to character and audience reception were painfully slow to emerge. Many early pamphleteers relied on neoclassical aesthetic standards, resulting in the condemnation of plays like John Gay's *The Beggar's Opera* (1728), for which there was little generic precedent. Regular production of theatrically concerned periodicals was rare; when they did survive more than a season or two, it was generally because they were engaged with philosophical issues most interesting to elite readers. In 1770, Francis Gentleman's *The Dramatic Censor, or Critical Companion*, a two-volume collection focusing on Shakespeare's plays, still thought an explicit disavowal of the neoclassical standard necessary. Gentleman's approach provides a counter to the enduring classicism of his contemporary, Samuel Johnson. "To pursue all the nice and intricate distinctions of classical criticism," Gentleman wrote in his preface, "would occasion prolixity; appeal only to the judgments of learned readers, and therefore be totally incompatible with our design" (2). The *Censor* not only examines the structures of dramas but also discusses at length their potential effect on audiences in matters of pacing and actors' characterizations. Gentleman's belief that theatrical – and dramatic – standards are negotiated through direct contact with audiences, and that commentary should serve as a "critical companion" to those audiences, anticipates the early-nineteenth-century theatrical writing boom. New theatrical periodicals – dailies, weeklies, and monthlies – all aimed like the *Censor* to reach audiences larger than those composed by "learned readers." Unlike Gentleman, however, the new periodical writers had to seek their audiences from a much larger body of readers already habituated to reading newspapers, miscellaneous magazines, radical journals, and quarterly reviews.

Theatrical periodicals' strategies for attracting and keeping readers became, after the turn of the century and especially after 1809, far more varied and complicated than those of even their late-eighteenth-century counterparts. While some publications sought to develop readerships in concert with the modes of reception encouraged by newspapers, others displayed in their reviews a sustained reaction against commercialism – even as their textual layouts revealed the influence of the commercial press. The print cycle of a given periodical was a significant factor in determining the means by which it would cultivate its audience. Daily theatrical periodicals tended to present themselves as enmeshed in the commercial system of publication that newspapers embodied, while weeklies and monthlies displayed a more dramatic strain of anti-commercial rhetoric that explicitly attacked newspapers. After 1809, the rhetorical polarization of commercial publications and moralistic anti-commercial theatrical journals began to spur the emergence of periodicals for which moral critique became a means of cultural distinction rather than social intervention. While many periodicals demonstrate later in the period a consistent strain of anti-commercial criticism, that criticism speaks increasingly to a class of readers that even as they wish to distinguish themselves from vulgar consumers also seek to remain engaged with the undeniable allures of commercial entertainments.[24] The explicit address to privileged audiences characterizing turn-of-the-century journals becomes more rare as the mainstream theatrical press develops new ways to satisfy changed reading audiences. In the sections that follow, I present a brief field study of the kinds of theatrical periodicals most commonly published in Britain between 1809 and 1830.[25] While recognizing the limits of the taxonomies I offer, such an overview will provide an understanding of the publishing contexts from which Leigh and John Hunt's influential *Examiner* emerged, as well as of the realm of theatrical experience within which Hazlitt and Keats wrote and published their work.

A Observers *and* Gazettes: *Playbill Periodicals and the Dailies*

Daily theatrical periodicals emerged in Britain after 1809 and emulated commercial newspapers in both textual form and writing style. As a relatively new phenomenon in the publishing field, however, they were constantly at pains to display their value. Like newspapers, their mission was to cultivate readerships committed to the habitual purchase of each day's issue. Implied by newspaper-like fonts and dated headings adorning their front pages, that mission was made explicit to potential buyers in many an issue's content. The *Covent Garden Theatrical Gazette*'s advertisement "To the Public" typifies the self-promotion of theatrical dailies. Reprinted on page two (the verso of the title page) of most issues of the *Gazette*, the advertisement states frankly that "The Theatrical Gazette will be published daily, and will contain a complete Analysis of the whole of the Evening's Entertainments, with the names of the Characters, performers, &c., &c. on Eight pages of closely printed letter-Press."[26] Tellingly, the advertisement goes on at length to justify why such dailiness is useful. "The advantages of this Publication must be obvious to every one at first sight," it asserts – though not obvious enough to preclude their being listed explicitly:

[T]he Public have here, for a mere trifle, a complete account of each evening's performance, which, at the same time that it serves to fill up the tedious vacuum that occurs before the commencement and between the acts of the Pieces, and to prepare the mind for what is about to be presented, will most admirably refresh the memory at any time afterwards.

Almost every theatrical daily in the period made similar claims, emphasizing as virtues its regular publication and quick, cheap conveyance of information. Dublin's *The Drama* (1821) emphasized, "[W]e have made our plans that the Drama shall be delivered to our Subscribers every morning regularly, at nine o'clock precisely."[27] London's *Theatrical Observer* (1821) promised to present to readers "at a trifling expense [the] full and authentic particulars respecting the performances to take place, which, from the early hour of publication, may be procured through the Newsman for the Breakfast Table."[28] And the *Edinburgh Dramatic Review* (1822), "published each morning, containing a Critique on the previous Night's Performance, [and] a Biographical Account of the Play for the present Evening, with a Correct Copy of the Play-Bill," argued that "the utility of an independent Work of this description, few, we believe, will dispute, in any city, but more particularly so where no daily journal exists; and where consequently the Public can have but seldom opportunity of reading the opinions of Public writers as to the merits and demerits of their theatrical amusements."[29]

Like the *Edinburgh Dramatic Review*, most theatrical dailies had as a major feature the reproduction of playbills for the upcoming night's performances. Playbills were single sheets, in the mid-eighteenth century, usually about 15 cm by 25 cm, and by the early nineteenth century 23 cm by 33 cm, that contained the title of the play and its afterpieces, and often cast listings. For many years, they could be found posted almost anywhere in the city and were as ephemeral as what passed upon the stage. According to Charles Beecher Hogan, although "the playbills of all the theatres were drawn up by the prompter on the night preceding the performance ... the better part of the printing occurred on the day of the performance" (*Critical Introduction*, cxxxix, cxli). Often the morning run of bills heralded late changes to the coming night's scheduled acts. Billposting restrictions passed in the late eighteenth century, however, left less space available for display in the city. A curious consequence of these restrictions was that bills began to be treated as commodities themselves. They were distributed frequently through commercial channels, offered for a fee by newsvendors or in shops, and sold to theatergoers in and around the playhouses by "orange women" (women who sold oranges and were often prostitutes)

II The New Periodicals

who plied playbills along with their other wares.[30] Early-nineteenth-century shopkeepers were commonly paid to hang bills in their store windows, and newspaper editors were paid to print playbill information – or at least forgave the theater's advertising fee. To call the bills "advertisements" in the modern sense is therefore not entirely accurate. Playgoers perceived them as a necessary part of an evening at the theater. As Leigh Hunt commented in 1830, "without a play-bill, no true play-goer can be comfortable."[31]

While some theatrical dailies merely reprinted information from the playbills, as the newspapers did, others went further by reproducing the fonts and typefaces of the bills as closely as possible in their pages, sometimes to the exclusion of space for other features.[32] The first of what I will call the "playbill periodicals" to include such reprints seems to have been the short-lived *Theatrical Gazette*, published during the 1815–1816 season and focused alternately each day on Covent Garden and Drury Lane. The evening's playbill reproduction occupied two-thirds of the *Gazette's* 12 cm by 21 cm front page. Though published for only one season, variations on its style would typify theatrical dailies for much of the next twenty years. Most prominent among playbill periodicals was London's *Theatrical Observer*, published first in September 1821 and then continuously until August 1876. The popular success of the compact *Theatrical Observer* format, two pages of brief performance criticism and two full pages of playbill reproduction, is confirmed by the fact that after 1815 similar playbill periodicals emerged in every major city in Britain and Ireland including Dublin, Edinburgh, Birmingham, Liverpool, Surrey, Sheffield, and Manchester.[33] A statement "To Those That Can Read" in the July 24, 1823 *Theatrical Examiner* reveals the ways in which the struggle for readers' attention caused confusing formal imitations between publications – and resulted in more strident efforts by each to achieve distinction:

> At the commencement of this Publication, we told our Contemporaries, "*The world was wide, there was room for us all,*" that we wished them every success their merits justly entitled them to, and we now repeat it most sincerely. Still, they will not be quiet, they caution the public in buying ours in mistake for theirs, which is very unnecessary; although there may be a likeness in the play bills, the CRITICAL REMARKS are as like ours as a *horsechesnut* is to a *chesnut horse*. There are, no doubt, some folks like PETER PINDAR, who make *razors* for sale, not for shaving; ours are of a different texture, as it is pretty well known they can cut one day's growth within the skin, so that none but an F.R.S. or *fellow remarkably stupid*, can be so blind as to mistake one Publication for the other!![34]

The allusion to Sterne's Uncle Toby and his kindly mantra notwithstanding, the rest of the passage reveals that the world was not quite wide enough. And in case the quality of its criticism was not sufficient to distinguish the *Theatrical Examiner* from its competitors, the paper's heading each day displayed the icon of a hand pointing to the phrase "*When going to the play, ask for the Theatrical Examiner.*" The intensity of this competition indicates both the popularity of daily theatrical periodicals and the frenetic publishing climate within which their forms developed.

Playbill periodicals were more than advertising devices; they were inexpensive sources of entertainment (usually costing only 1*d.* or 2*d.*) that filled the "tedious vacuum" of time before performances – which is to say that they relied for their attractiveness on an ability to satisfy consumer desire for informational reading. Because of their brevity and their short print cycle, such periodicals had little recourse to the philosophical reflection favored by weekly or monthly journals. The printing of playbills by theatrical dailies was not, however, a simple act of reproduction; if consumers wanted playbills, they could simply purchase them. In the playbill periodical, the playbills' information was recast in the context of a reading act provided by a daily publication. Again, Leigh Hunt (here in his post-*Examiner* days) provides a cogent justification for the "union of a paper with a play-bill":

> A *Tatler*, we allow, costs two-pence, whereas the common play-bill is a penny. But if the latter be worth what it costs, will it be too great a stretch of modesty to suppose that our new play-bill is worth it also? Our criticisms, we will be sworn, have, at all events, a relish in them: they are larger; and then there is the rest of the matter, in the other pages, to vary the chat between the acts.[35]

This utility, argued Hunt, will make "*Tatlers* . . . frequent and full in the pit and boxes."[36]

David Gowen has pointed to the ways in which the informational mission of playbills announcing entertainments at the legitimate theaters influenced the public's perception of those plays. Although bills were designed to inform potential audience members of the planned entertainments, they "withheld explanatory notes concerning the dramatised action on all but their pantomime bills, maintaining the primacy of the spoken expository word over its printed equivalent yet furnishing exhaustive descriptions of every cast member and afterpiece" (159). The typical playbill supported with its textual form a legislated cultural hierarchy privileging traditional drama over the genres of melodrama, burletta, or pantomime. Lower dramatic forms were explainable with text, whereas traditional drama was an experience properly restricted to the moment of performance. Playbill *periodicals*, though, held an ambivalent position with respect to these hierarchies because the periodical's criticism supplemented the bill's restricted information; this leveled distinctions by translating all theatrical entertainments equally into textual signs to be consumed through the medium of the periodical. Not surprisingly, commentary that accompanied bill reproductions varied from publication to publication, as the *Theatrical Examiner*'s (albeit self-interested) statement points out. But as a brief examination will show, most of these commentaries aimed to reproduce the commercial press's popular informational discourse, relying on its seeming immediacy to connect the reader imaginatively to reported events. By appropriating the existing reading habits of newspaper audiences, theatrical dailies attempted to establish their own indispensability to theatrical experience just as newspapers had with readers in the larger public world.

After page one's bold proclamation of the evening's plays and casts, the *Covent Garden Theatrical Gazette* usually offered three to four pages of "Descriptive Analysis." Though this analysis did little more than summarize the events of the drama, it still aimed to shape substantively readers' perceptions of what occurred on stage. On March 3, 1817, Junius Brutus Booth played Richard III, and the *Gazette*'s analysis began as follows:

> ACT I. A garden near the tower – the lieutenant of the Tower and an officer enter. The lieutenant gives the latter orders, not to let any stranger into the garden, when the latter is walking there. The Lord Stanley arrives, he brings an account of Edward's victory, at Tewksbury. "This will be news to Henry's ear," cries the lieutenant, that "Ere he left the field, a proclamation from the king was made, in search of Edward – Henry's son, – offering a reward to those who should discover him, and him his life if he'd surrender." The lieutenant comments on the spirit of "that brave young prince"; and of King Henry's resignation.[37]

The narrative continues for more than two thousand words, describing scene changes and occasionally offering substantive quotations from the play. The final moments of Act V, when "the scene then changes to Bosworth field," are rendered in this way:

> Richard ... encounters Richmond – they fight – Richard is killed. Richmond's party is triumphant, and he is proclaimed Henry VII, King of England. News is brought, that the queen and her daughter, the fair Elizabeth, are at hand. Richmond resolves on a union with her, to twine the red and white roses together, and end, for ever, England's civil wars.

This synopsizing transforms the play's action into a prose narrative that, with its chronologically ordered cause-and-effect construction, resembles the reporting discourse of the commercial newspaper. The difference, of course, is that the *Gazette* text is anticipatory, serving to "prepare the mind for what is about to be presented."[38] Yet like the anticipatory personal advertisements on the front page of the *Times*, the *Gazette* helps define the reader's relation to an arena of public behavior, the theatrical event, by enabling an empowered spectatorial relation to the stage action: the playgoer subsequently witnesses with her own eyes the events about which she has already read. More even than the newspapers with which she is familiar, the *Gazette* assures an understanding of what has just happened, is happening, will happen in front of her.

Other theatrical dailies focused their reports more squarely on the behavior of the audience and the effect performances had on theatergoers. This was especially true when the evening's entertainment included new plays or spectacles that stood outside the canon of spoken drama – plays, in other words, that would not easily allow the pre-scripted encapsulation exemplified by the *Gazette*'s account of *Richard III*. Witness the *Theatrical Observer* for December 27, 1821:

> The entertainments last night were *Virginius* and the long expected Christmas festival. The galleries and pit were at *first* price crowded: the upper tiers of the boxes were very well attended, but the dress circle *indifferently* so. The latter circumstance was such as is generally the case on the *first* night of a new pantomime; on which occasion the higher classes of theatrical persons prefer restraining their curiosity; the probability of incurring a head ache for the two following days and such a precaution was, we assure them, last night not unnecessary. On the performance of the play it would be absurd to offer a remark, for the noise of the galleries quite excluded the possibility of paying that attention to different parts of the acting, which would enable us with confidence to offer our opinion of them.

Though this description has a wider scope than that found in the *Gazette*, its purpose is similar: to provide the reader with a coherent sense of the action inside the playhouse. The reading habits engendered by the daily theatrical periodical provided an exemplary exercise in public engagement. Just as newspapers transformed the past and future events of Britain's public life into informational narratives, theatrical dailies distilled the night's events into a narration that enabled readers to believe that their experiences had a coherent structure. Even those who were not at the performance could, by reading such an account, imagine that they had been spectators.

Beyond their role as catalyst for an evening's cultural event, playbill periodicals' collective presence day after day offered readers a sense of the theatrical history only fractionally represented by a single performance. London's *Theatrical Observer* claimed to provide "a constant record of past Theatrical representations."[39] Similarly, the *Covent Garden Theatrical Gazette* stated that its pages could in the future become a material aid to "refresh the memory" of the night's events and even "if preserved and bound up, will form a complete *Catalogue Raisonée* of the performances of every season, and a much more perfect Dramatic Record of the pieces and players, than can be found from any other source."[40] The perspective presented to readers on daily events widened when one evening's issue took its place in a volume marking the passage of many such evenings. The weekly and monthly periodicals with which the dailies competed could not rival the evocative power of the text that had been in the playgoer's hands during the show. Nor could the reprinted theatrical information or criticisms found in the miscellaneous pages of the daily newspapers be preserved for posterity like those of the *Gazette*, the *Observer*, and others of their genre. The text of the theatrical daily was easily carried around on the night of the performance and easily saved afterwards. (The *Gazette*, which was physically one of the larger daily periodicals, measured only 12.5 cm by 21 cm.) When bound in a permanent volume, the most common *Observer*-type textual layout allowed the previous day's playbill reproduction to face the next issue's commentary on the advertised performance. Archival evidence suggests that a small but significant percentage of readers did save and bind playbill periodicals in this way. Forming a privately possessed sign of theater's ongoing public presence, collected dailies in turn provided a weighty context of permanence to each of their individual numbers.[41] The march of history encapsulated by newspapers found its cultural correlative in theatrical dailies.

This is not to say that playbill periodicals were only interested in reporting or memorializing cultural events. The rapid informational capacities and material compactness that made them indispensable companions for most theatergoers simultaneously empowered them to render aesthetic judgments they hoped would have a lasting effect on repertory canons. Like many eighteenth-century critics, the writers for early nineteenth-century theatrical dailies claimed their task was to safeguard the integrity of Britain's theatrical institutions. London's *Thespian Sentinel* asserted that "the theatre should be a scene of rational amusement, and moral instruction ... and should [management] be found wandering from their oath of duty, it is the business of the press, like faithful beacons, to warn them back."[42] Yet along with this moralizing, the dailies' critical language displayed, like their textual design, the unmistakable marks of commercialization. This was the case on Wednesday, October 11, 1821, even as London's *Theatrical Observer* railed against the continued performance of "melodrame, spectacle and farce" at Drury Lane. Because the summer season had come to an end, the critic argued that Drury Lane should replace its "light and shewy pieces" with traditional spoken drama, but "the managers here are inclined to rest their fame – hem! – *profits* we should say, on their powers of attracting great and little babies":

> [A]lthough we do not relish a cold collation when October warns us of the approach of December, yet we would rather sit down even to one of Dibdin's lean joints, served up by Harley, Munden, &c. &c., than have placed before us an eternal *tureen* of monstrosity, glitter, and balderdash ... The treasury of the Theatre may benefit for a time, but will eventually suffer from the extension of a well-found disgust at the utter want of intellectual attraction. The *price* of a seat in the Theatre is, in these times, considered as no light sum, and before it is paid, the merits of the evening's bill of fare is well canvassed. Public criticism and private report are referred to, and operate powerfully on the decision. Will it, then, be said, that a Theatre can maintain its interests by an utter neglect of all that can satisfy cultivated taste, or common understanding? – certainly not. Opinion will follow the rules of plain sense, modified as they may be, and the result will exhibit empty benches to the House which neglects to allure John Bull with *solid* entertainment.[43]

We see in this passage the commercial vocabulary of consumption figured as literal digestion and superimposed on an underlying belief in theater's traditional social function. Though the writer claims to speak on behalf of a populace who would still have theater function as a stabilizing, "cultivated" institution, his demand for better entertainment and his proposed solution to theater's excesses are those of the theatergoer accustomed to thinking about theater attendance as a commercial exchange.

Powerful because they were theatergoers' most immediate textual connection to theater, daily theatrical periodicals produced a criticism that on many occasions explicitly disdained commercialism. By doing so, they posited an ideal standard of theatrical production against which real productions could be found lacking. But the repeated recourse to such a standard was not designed so much to damn performances as it was to demonstrate the value of daily criticism itself. Explicit association with a moral theatrical ideal was an attempt to resist the charge, levied principally by the weekly and monthly journals, to which I will now turn, that daily criticism was too much like that found in newspapers to be worthwhile. Still, the empowered spectatorial position theatrical dailies offered their readers was complemented by an equally forceful sense of cultural empowerment. Even as theatergoers participated in the rituals of commercialized reception, they could have faith that the critics guiding them were protecting their moral and social interests and connecting them with theater's traditional prestige. Daily theatrical criticism put itself forward as the defender of an ideal theatrical tradition, the dissolution of which it helped occasion.

B   Censors *and* Mirrors: *Weekly Reviews and Monthly Magazines*

Theatrical periodicals issued at weekly and monthly intervals were larger and formally more diverse than the typical four-page daily. Monthlies, costing anywhere from 6*d.* to 1*s.* 6*d.*, were the most miscellaneous of theatrical publications; they provided for audiences a host of features including theatrical reviews, "green room chit-chat," colored portraits of performers, extended dissertations on the history of the drama, and actors' biographies. The growth of the *Monthly Magazine* and the *Monthly Review*, with circulations of approximately 5,000 each by 1807, testifies to the popularity of general interest cultural magazines, at least among the ranks that could afford them.[44] These magazines, along with such others as the *Monthly Mirror*, first published in 1795, were distinguished by their fine printing style, colorful "embellishments," and organized presentation of information. The *Mirror*, for example, was divided into departments titled "The Stage," "Biography," "Novels," "Miscellany," "Review," "Poetry," and "Record of Events." Theatrical monthlies that followed, such as Thomas Holcroft's *Theatrical Recorder* (1805), the *Theatrical Inquisitor* (1812), *The Monthly Theatrical Review* (1829), and the immaculately printed *Dramatic Magazine* (1829), mimicked the magazine format with increasing ornateness and expense.[45] Like their daily counterparts, theatrical magazines were constantly developing new ways to attract audiences. In some instances, the quest for novelty and distinction led them to resemble more general publications. At the beginning of its publishing run, *The Drama, or Theatrical Pocket Magazine* (1821) seized upon one such effort and criticized the *Theatrical Inquisitor* for straying too far from theatrical interests. "'The Theatrical Inquisitor' would have been a work of *standard value*, had it been *entirely confined*, as it is *intended this work shall be*, to DRAMATIC SUBJECTS ALONE."[46] Usually comprising forty to sixty pages of closely printed text and illustrations, a theatrical magazine's self-described role, according to *Oxberry's Theatrical Inquisitor*, was to "make our pages as full of entertainment and intelligence as possible."[47]

Weeklies displayed in form and content the influence of both magazines and daily newspapers. They varied in size and price from the likes of the *Plymouth Theatrical Spy* (1828) at eight 10 cm by 17 cm pages, costing 2*d*., to London's thirty-two page *Dramatic Censor* (1800), twenty-page *Theatrical Repertory, or Weekly Rosciad* (1802), to the large, three-columned 22 cm by 27 cm eight-page *Opera Glass* (1827), at 6*d*. Some simply offered reprints of criticisms found in companion daily publications. *The Weekly Dramatic Register*, founded in 1825, was "compiled from the *Theatrical Observer*" and served as that daily's compact digest.[48] Others, such as the *Theatrical Repertory*, printed along with criticisms a full week's worth of Drury Lane and Covent Garden playbills. *The Dramatic Correspondent, and Amateur's Place Book* (1828) focused extensively on amateur and private theatricals in London. And *The National Omnibus and Entertaining Advertiser* (1831), published biweekly, aimed to capture the attention of the vast audience of theatrically interested readers who had emerged in the previous three decades. It was filled with ads for literary publications, magazines, and play performances; theatrical criticism and reviews took up only a small part of its pages.

The primary textual component of most weeklies, however, was the review and evaluation of performances, principally those taking place in the city's patent theaters. By virtue of its size, scope, and publication interval, the typical journal provided a venue where daily reporting and reflective evaluation intersected more fully than in other periodical forms. For this reason, these publications are the most complex of the new theatrical periodicals, displaying textually their editors' attempts to capture a newspaper reading audience, even as they attempted to chasten the commercial expectations of such readers with substantive aesthetic commentaries. Most such theatrical journals were distributed along the same channels as quarterly reviews, magazines, and books, but the issues' higher cost might have prevented them from regularly reaching the hands of many common readers. Instead of being "procured through the Newsmen" like playbill periodicals,[49] weeklies could "be had of all the Booksellers."[50] Yet as Robert Altick comments, weekly and monthly publications alike sought to reach a significant number of readers beyond those who owned individual copies: "They were publications distinctly intended for the drawing-room in town and country, and for the subscription reading-rooms whose very existence was evidence that many readers on the cultural level to which these periodicals appealed could not afford to buy them outright" (*English Common Reader* 319). Still, the journals' different means of distribution parallels the ways in which they cultivated among their readers a sense of distinction from more ephemeral periodicals. While the theatrical dailies' economic success and social position was predicated on an ability to facilitate the growth of theatrical consumerism, many weekly and monthly publications worked explicitly, at least early in the century, to counter commercialism's effects on the production and reception of theater. In 1800, Thomas Dutton's weekly *Dramatic Censor* asserted the following in no uncertain terms:

> If ever, in the annals of British dramatic Literature, the intervention of BOLD and UPRIGHT criticism was wanted to check the progress of false taste, to rescue Genius from oppression, the Stage from prostitution, and the national literary character from infamy, *at home*, and merited opprobrium, *abroad* . . . the present is avowedly the crisis, when such intervention is most peremptorily demanded by imperious necessity.[51]

For Dutton and many other reviewers, theater was perceived as the front line of a greater battle for the cultural soul of the Briton, and it was described as a public institution in need of protection from the pressures of economic self-interest. The coming together of people habituated to newspaper reading and sensational theatrical production had, in the early nineteenth century, begun to shift British theatrical experience away from the old models of interaction Dutton valued. Critics sensed that the relationship between audiences and theatrical producers was no longer a friendly negotiation in which, as Samuel Johnson wrote in his famous prologue for David Garrick in 1747, "the drama's laws the drama's patrons give" (*Poems* 6.89).

Journals and magazines were filled with expressions of concern over this phenomenon. Bath's *Theatrical Review* argued that the shift in theatrical entertainments toward illegitimate forms of spectacle was caused by the growing inability of audiences to respond to "higher objects" presented on stage. Many contemporary theatergoers lacked the education or vigilance to demand more than sensation from the nation's theaters, the *Review* asserted, and managers chose to satisfy those audiences rather than instruct them. It was the "system of the old school of scenic representation to solicit patronage from consideration of real merit, to represent virtue as amiable, and to render vice contemptible . . . but these notions are now exploded." Instead of "the sublimity of poetic imagination," theaters now offer "the more interesting effusions of fashionable debauchery" to satisfy audience desire.⁵² Dutton's *Dramatic Censor* evinces even more vividly the degree to which early nineteenth-century critics believed Britain's systems of theatrical production had been corrupted. The pitch of his anti-commercial rhetoric echoes that of contemporary radical journalists seeking to expose government corruption. Like William Cobbett's and Richard Carlile's prophetic styles, Dutton's prose exhibits formal disruptions as he conspicuously substitutes raillery for aesthetic evaluation: "Upstart pretenders, hireling compilers, shameless plagiarists, and conceited scribblers of the lowest order, have, by dint of servility, temporizing cunning, and the sacrifice of principle into sordid interest, unhappily succeeded in obtaining complete possession of the Stage, over which they rule and domineer with more than Oriental despotism."⁵³ Dutton's staccato phrasing and copious taxonomy of offenders relate the urgency, even desperation, of his critical stance. At stake was far more than a way of seeing plays, for theater's effects reached out into the larger public world. *The Theatrical Rod!* cautioned similarly as follows:

> [The] present age has occasioned a remarkable revolution in the nature of every thing: in many instances aggravated circumstances have vitiated the minds of men, and obliterated their better sentiments; while on the other hand, the really worthless portion of mankind, have made this change the foundation of their own fortunes and the establishment of despotism. Such is now the case with the *great* men of the Drama! Such is the system of tyranny they have erected over their fellows in the profession. They have but one idea of interest, and that is centered in the word *self!*⁵⁴

For editors of the *Censor*, the *Rod!*, and others like them, theater's commercial corruption not only compromised its stewardship of England's cultural and moral value systems; it also indicated greater degenerations at basic levels of human interaction. The life-world of everyday commercial society had "vitiated the minds of men, and obliterated their better sentiments," making room for the cooptation of culture by barbarians. The *Rod!*'s critique, part of an attack on theater managers' attempts to underpay actors, imagines a world where a political economy of self-interest governs every individual action and every collective association. A vicious circle of theatrical production geared toward profit and theatrical reception bent on unreflective sensory satisfaction empower the most ambitiously self-interested men, "the really worthless portion of mankind," to ascend over those beaten down by the "aggravated circumstances" of the time.

Of course critics had throughout the eighteenth century railed in similar fashion against what they saw as theater's increasing neglect of its ordained social function. What changed at the beginning of the nineteenth century, with the threatening rise of the middling and lower ranks, was a demonstrated concern for the ways in which commercialized criticism itself damaged common modes of theatrical experience. Publications that did not foster sophisticated reception were considered suspect, unable to fulfill their moral duty, and indeed more responsible for the general decline of the theatergoing public than performances themselves. The issue was not simply that theater-goers were missing out on the experience of "higher objects"; it was that Britain's entire cultural landscape had become clouded by the sensational and the banal. Newspapers were a particular object of attack among publications with longer print cycles, which claimed that the papers, in league with the theaters' profit-seeking managers, had poisoned the public's theatrical reception by commercializing its taste. Explicitly disdaining not only the mercantile interests of theater and the sensational desires of its audiences but also the commercialism of daily theatrical criticism, journal and magazine editors claimed to renovate the channels through which the public's everyday theatrical experience was conducted. The monthly *Dramatic Censor*, not to be confused with Dutton's weekly, asserted in 1811, "Our Newspapers are so civilly undiscriminating, that they beplaister all alike with the broad towel of flattery, until the point and force of honest praise is lost in the sweeping encomium."[55] In the same year, the *Irish Dramatic Censor*, another monthly, complained, "[Too] long have our dramatic criticisms submitted to the servile control of managerial influence – been warped by the private interest of individual performers – or prostituted by the abominable rancor of malicious and mercenary writers. – An impartial Theatric Comment has long been wanting."[56] When impartiality did "occasionally, burst forth in the columns of a News-paper or the pages of a Magazine, every art was exerted to corrupt it by bribe, or silence it by legal terror."[57]

Not uncommon in monthlies, such attacks are unrelenting in weeklies. Weekly periodicals, closer in structure, style, and print cycle to corrupting newspapers and dailies, displayed a more pressing need to counter the modes of reception those publications encouraged; more accurately, they had to distinguish themselves from the dailies so as not to be associated too closely with them. In January 1800, Dutton's weekly *Dramatic Censor* asserted the following:

> The diurnal prints, instead of exercising a wholesome check upon these illicit proceedings, have, for the major-part, become accessaries [sic] to the

deed, and lend their countenance to this traffic in literary prostitution. Fallen, many of them, into the hands of illiterate proprietors, and conducted by editors, as unqualified and uninformed as their employers, they are vilely bungled and put together by persons, who possess neither the faculty of sound judgment, nor the virtue of critical integrity. Hence the system of *toad-eating* opens a ready path to panegyric, and the dullest trash, that ever was engendered in the human brain, may safely reckon on *Newspaper* support, on the usual terms of degraded venality.[58]

Because newspapers are run by professionals committed to "wantonness and tyranny," they are incapable of fulfilling criticism's moral mission. The *Dramatic Censor* would often point to factual errors and descriptive inaccuracies in the newspapers' theatrical reports as evidence of their incompetence. In the first issue, for example, Dutton cites a *Morning Herald* review of the December 24, 1799 new pantomime at Drury Lane as "a flagrant instance of how little faith is to be placed in the reports of these superficial journalists." The *Herald* describes "a skittle-ground scene, in which the pins rise up of their own accord, as fast as they are knocked down." But the paper, says Dutton, fails to fulfill the very task upon which its claims to utility rest: "This is evidently a *critique* sent to that paper from the Theatre, no such scene having taken place in the course of the pantomime. We would recommend to the editor, as a necessary preliminary towards *criticising* a piece, to *witness* its representation."[59]

The *Censor*'s dismissive attitude toward daily criticism was by no means simply the product of Dutton's personal moralism. The reviewing style common to newspapers and the commercialism occasionally denounced but implicitly embraced by theatrical dailies were continual targets for many weekly periodicals both in London and the provinces. Weekly journals repeatedly contrasted the commercial degradation of daily criticism with their own objectivity, claiming an ability to supersede newspapers because, while the "recording pen of the theatrical critic" could attend to current events of the theater, longer print cycles provided an opportunity for reflection and review (as well as, one might add, the publication of such attractive commercial features as theatrical biography, dissertations on acting style, and historical considerations on the state of the English drama).[60] *The Plymouth Theatrical Spy* claimed that it would attempt "by endeavoring through the medium of strict and impartial criticisms on the Performances at the PLYMOUTH THEATRE, and observations on every subject connected with the establishment, to correct many abuses which partiality or supineness of the Newspaper Press has hitherto suffered to prevail unnoticed."[61] The *Lincoln Dramatic Censor* "disclaim[ed] every motive of private enmity or interest."[62] And Bath's *Theatrical Review* asserted that its reviewers were "free and independent critics." Describing how independence was especially foreign "to the printers of newspapers," the *Review* asserted that "to those gentlemen we should observe, that false praise is rank falsehood, and suppressing the truth in a matter of public amusement (of which they ought to be the guardians) is as palpable a corruption as supporting the venal tool of power, or oppressing the unfortunate."[63]

A diatribe in London's *The Stage; or, Theatrical Touchstone* was even more severe. "When that species of Criticism which we read in all the newspapers," the journal commented on July 20, 1805, "is of itself a delusion and chicane, at once false and hostile to common sense, we cannot too soon endeavor to put an end to a practice so pernicious, and so destructive in its consequences." The newspaper's institutional affiliation with the theater renders it incapable of producing impartial criticism: newspaper critics "are all acquainted with the actors; they often meet and spend convivial hours together, and many of the performers in the higher walks of the Drama do invite and entertain these *gentlemen* in their own houses. Hence the bond of union is more firmly cemented, and hence the Public is deprived of the exercise of its free and unbiased voice."[64] Not only, according to the *Stage*, does the reporting function of the newspaper compromise its ability to evaluate performances, reviewers intentionally use reporting to divert readers from the possibility of higher discourse: "[T]hese gentlemen writers cram their papers with long details of the performances, deciding on their merits in such a way as in a certain degree to preclude all other comment and remark." Consumption of information takes the place of genuine, reflective cultural reception – a shift that has repercussions beyond an individual's encounter with any single theatrical event. Newspapers deaden readers' aesthetic sensibilities and damage interactions between theatergoers even after the performance is over:

> The injury done by the Newspaper criticisms goes a great way farther. If a man has a situation at a Theatre in London, he begins gradually to despise the barn in which he made his first *entré*. He fills many parts much to *his own* satisfaction, but probably *not* to the entertainment of the judicious. Conversation is excited, but all remarks are cut short by a statement that the actor must *certainly be right*, as the papers lavish unqualified praise upon his performances.[65]

Daily criticism, according to the typical periodical review, cannot engender fruitful discussion among its readers or criticize theater properly because it inhabits the same commercial system designed to puff actors and draw in audiences. Such criticism produces an absent-minded public that in the words of the same *Stage*, "has no opinion of its own."

My aim in describing the anti-commercial discourse of the weekly and monthly theatrical press is not to suggest that newspapers and theatrical dailies served a commercial reading public while reviews and magazines did not. On the contrary, these publications, weeklies especially, emphasized differences between themselves and the dailies precisely because they were part of the commercial system the dailies fostered. Still, where dailies made gestures of anti-commercialism to authorize their critical judgments, weeklies offered a continual barrage of anti-commercial reviews, prefaces, and commentaries, even as they appropriated the dailies' textual strategies to attract commercialized readers. Considered in the context of the wider newspaper field I have described, and of theater's central role as a focus of that field, vehement resistance to incursions of the popular appear in theatrical journals as a strategy of cultural distinction. That is, critics not only reacted against the commercialization of theatrical pursuits and the rise of newspaper reading, they also conspicuously performed that reaction in an effort to display distinctive reading practices, rendering themselves more valuable to self-styled theatrical connoisseurs.[66]

C   Harlequins *and* Opera Glasses: *Theatrical connoisseurship*

These were the seemingly contradictory aims of theatrical periodical criticism in early nineteenth-century Britain: first, a resistance to theater's growing commercialism and to the habits of reading modeled by newspapers and encouraged by theatrical dailies; second, the necessity of continual engagement on the level of both form and content with commercial publications that maintained the daily connection between readers and theater. Weeklies and monthlies needed to resist, or at least appear to resist, the "mercenary motives" to which newspaper writers succumbed, while maintaining a close enough connection to the commercialized theater to be viable as textual commodities.[67] Consequently, the project of cultural distinction undertaken by theatrical journals and magazines shifted its rhetoric as the nineteenth century lengthened. The moral outrage prominent among turn-of-the-century critics steadily gave way to a criticism registering the necessity of participation with the commercial system of publication and reading.[68] Comparing the criticism and textual forms of some early and late journals – weeklies in particular – reveals that reviewing after 1809 began to take on the properties of what might be called theatrical connoisseurship.[69] Unlike their earlier counterparts, who performed rhetorically a belief that theater's moral and aesthetic dimensions were inseparable, and a belief that their readers shared that assumption, theatrical critics later in the Romantic period faced the more difficult task of shaping the reception of readers whose theatrical experience had become far more varied.

Again, it is Thomas Dutton's *Dramatic Censor* that provides the best example of how pre-1809 periodicals attempted to transform public opinion as a whole, deploying moralistic critique as a means of countering the commercial system of production and reception. A January 18, 1800 review of Morton's *A Cure for the Heart-Ache* at Covent Garden praises the play's moral strength and ability to educe the rational faculties of viewers:

> If to blend instruction with delight be, as most unquestionably it is, the true aim and object of the stage, Mr. Morton (though we cannot pronounce his pieces faultless, and invulnerable to the shafts of criticism) may, however, justly lay claim to the merit of having furnished the public, in the play now under construction, with no mean stock of *rational* amusement, accompanied with, and forcibly impressing upon the mind, the most wholesome and weighty moral lesson.

Here the logical progression of Morton's plot and the play's regularity in not attempting to overwhelm its viewers with sensation render it an effective impetus to rational thought, despite its weak and unnatural characterizations. As the review continues, Dutton congratulates himself on his open-mindedness in finding such positive qualities in a drama new to the English stage:

> As little bigoted to arbitrary rules of faith, we shall never lend our suffrage and cooperation to enslave genius in the trammels of scholastic prescription; nor seek to restrict the sallies of fancy to the narrow limits, which pedants would fain assign. As long as there is a visible connexion of the several parts of the fable; as long as the plot is consistently managed, and the final object in view, or *denouement*, is effected by a regular train of incidents, naturally originating out of, and mutually promoting, each other; – as long as these essential requisites are duly complied with, we can easily pardon a few eccentricities, and occasional *extravagances*, which, if brought to the test of rigid criticism, would, it must be confessed, rank rather as *Farce* than legitimate *Comedy* ... The grand excellence of dramatic writing consists in the perfect *preservation* of character, which must be a true transcript of Nature, in every varied and contrasted situation.[70]

Few critics of the day were as invested in traditional aesthetic standards as the editor of the *Censor*. But even in Dutton's work, as his disdain for newspaper criticism has already shown, we can see a recognition that the reviewer must assert those standards in a field of criticism increasingly threatened by new kinds of performance and new kinds of reading.

For Dutton, the critic's job is to remind his audience of the proper production and reception of theater; yet he must do so without seeming classically archaic and therefore socially irrelevant. He is, he assures, "little bigoted to arbitrary rules" and able to recognize a coherence in the new piece even though it does not meet his standards for portraying characters that are the "true transcript of nature." Dutton finally contrasts Morton's play with the growing penchant among managers and audiences for sensation and spectacle:

> In the *Cure for the Heart-Ache*, there is no attempt to benumb the mental faculties, by fascinating the senses: – no tawdry scenes, no unmeaning sing-song, no heterogeneous jumble of pantomime and tragedy, usurp the place of incident, and regular development of the plot. It possesses sufficient comic force to exercise the risible propensities, and the moral it inculcates is of the purest and most impressive nature.[71]

The review points to the play's possible social benefit and confirms criticism's role in elucidating that possibility for readers. The superimposition of aesthetic on moral vocabulary is palpable here: scenes are "tawdry" and "unmeaning" because they are a "heterogeneous jumble" of aesthetically inferior genres. Because Dutton's criticism relies ultimately on a moral standard of judgment, however, he finally demonizes that "heterogeneous jumble," using it as a foil against which dramas that "inculcate" a "moral" are judged superior.

The threat of spectacle "benumb[ing] the mental faculties, by fascinating the senses" is the primary concern throughout Dutton's *Censor* reviews – as it was for Wordsworth at this time, writing his *Preface to Lyrical Ballads*.[72] Repeatedly, Dutton's reports of individual performances give way to descriptions of the degraded state of the public mind. A week before the *Cure for the Heart-Ache* review, the *Censor* published a review of Hoadley's *The Suspicious Husband*, performed at Covent Garden on January 8, 1800, that explicitly recognizes two competing modes of theatrical reception. "We consider it," Dutton writes, "as an irrefragable proof of the prevalence of false taste, that this lively and busy comedy, ranks at present in the list of what are *technically* denominated *Box-plays*."[73] Plays that appeal to the upper ranks of theatergoers, seated in the boxes, have little attraction for the lower ranks in the pit and galleries, where "false taste" prevails. Though "lively and busy," *The Suspicious Husband*'s excellences go unrecognized by those who dismiss it as entertainment not made for them:

> Replete with incident; well (And even at times, high) seasoned with humour, repartee, and *equivoques*, of, very palpable allusion; yet, inculcating withal, a weighty moral, of general utility, by exposing the self-tormenting folly of jealousy, on the one hand; and the evils of libertine principles, on the other; we should have hoped, that a play of this description might command a good house; especially, when we see the Theaters overflowing, night after night, with the crude abortions of *Kotzebue*, and the still more senseless productions of our own native *play-botchers*, who succeed but too well in cramming their vile trash down the public throat, by the help of a little *sing-song*, a little attention to the whim of the day; and above all, by an equally consummate degree of impudence, meanness, and conceit.

Again, the *Censor*'s evaluation of a single night's performance occasions a more extensive diatribe against the corruption of London's systems of theatrical production, and the "prevalent" modes of cultural consumption speeding that corruption. Soon, Dutton has lost entirely his focus on the play:

> When an audience can once bring their stomachs to digest such nauseous fare, as *Turnpike-gate* and *Embarkation-mongers* dish up for them; when they can patiently witness the representation of pieces patched together by writers, who neither possess genius, nor education – writers, who are equally destitute of ideas, and the power of expressing ideas (if they were capable of forming any,) in appropriate language; when once the taste of the town is debauched to so hopeless a degree as this, legitimate drama must look for a very cool and forbidding reception. Then is the time for your *Fr – l – ns,* your *D – s*; your *C – s*; your *L – s*; and the whole *et cetera* of this vile herd of illiterate *play-mongers* to watch their opportunity, and gather in the harvest of associated dullness and impudence.[74]

This Popean rant (though significantly lacking Pope's stylistic discipline), which Dutton subsequently styles a "digression," does finally cede to an "immediate discussion of the play itself," where actors are once again congratulated for their portrayals being the "true transcript of nature." Like the review of *A Cure for the Heart-Ache*, Dutton's criticism of *The Suspicious Husband* displays both an adherence to moral standards and a recognition of the threat posed to moral criticism by theater's commercialization. Again we see the language of gluttonous digestion employed to deride the commercialized theatrical experience. The abruptness of Dutton's style – its haphazard shifts from aesthetic criticism to moral outrage and back – evinces his difficulty in responding productively to the changing nature of theatrical experience.[75] These rhetorical fractures stand in Dutton's work as signs of a collapsing world view. In writers like Leigh Hunt and, even more dramatically William Hazlitt, they will signal an imaginative mobility open to the transformative possibilities that new forms of theater enabled.

Though Dutton's philosophical assumptions differ radically from those of many of the periodical critics who followed him, his anxiety over the growing divide between the critic's view and that of most theatergoers exhibits the pressures that emerging commercialism was exerting on the practice of reviewing. Critical attitudes toward audience reaction were not always as dismissive as Dutton's, nor as fraught with irony as that of the *Mince Pie* reviewer. Some theatrical periodicals, particularly in the beginning stages of their publication run, demonstrated a hope that their interventions would renovate theater's public reception. Birmingham's *Theatrical Looker-On* was particularly sanguine about its ability to shape the experience of consumers during the 1823 summer season: "The approach of the dramatic season finds us once again 'labouring in our vocation,' and the LOOKER-ON returns to delight and instruct mankind. Drake's shop is once more the resort of anxious crowds, and eager excitement and intense curiosity are at their topmost height."[76] Because the "theatrical campaign will now give a new impulse to conversation," the public will have an opportunity to exercise and develop its taste, directed, of course, by the *Looker-On*. In a June review of *Kenilworth*, the *Looker-On* congratulated the audience for the consistency with which it supported a fine performance, and the assiduity with which it heeded the periodical's judgment:

> The performance of this play, by its continued attraction, puts us a little in spirits – we feel that things are coming around again – that good taste has not died away, but has merely been taking breath, "while grosser things held sway" and we will neither so far satirize our fellow townsmen, or the influence they have allowed our work to have over their judgments, as not to suppose that, after they have tolerated an interregnum of horses and asses, they will return with renewed delight to the reign of men and manners.[77]

Manchester's *Townsman* noted in similar fashion how its admonitions to a certain actor for importing patriotic sentiment into his lines had swayed the opinion of the town against him: "Great therefore is my delight to find that the call which I have made upon your judgement, has been answered in a truly spirited manner."[78] But attention to audience reception was not always, or even mostly, positive. Most critics, like the intrepid *Mince Pie* reviewer himself, believed that they were continually working against theatergoers' tendency to engage in vulgar and facile modes of theatrical experience.

By the 1820s, periodical writers who believed, like Dutton, that their interventions could stem a rising tide of commercialized reception were outnumbered by those who catered to more discrete audiences. Between 1800 and 1830, anti-commercialism was deployed increasingly as a rhetorical strategy of cultural distinction rather than as an explicit attempt to resist the changes the decades had wrought in theatrical experience. The formal qualities of weeklies, in particular, bear witness to this change: their complexity increased significantly between 1800 and 1830. Rather than emphasizing their critical role with plain-fronted pages and prominent placement of philosophical criticism as one might find in Dutton's *Censor*, later journals and magazines bolstered their appeal with features more commonly found in the larger and more ornate publications.[79] As the pocket-sized *Dramatic Correspondent, and Amateur's Place Book* (1828) declared, "This work will contain Theatrical Biography, original essays on subjects connected with the Stage, Poetry, Anecdotes, and Bon-Mots of Performers, descriptions of all places of amusement ... Accounts of New Plays, Operas, &c., with their plots, and critical remarks thereon."[80] An 1821 effort entitled *Thalia's Tablet and Melpomene's Memorandum Book*, of which only one number survives, boasted as its alternative title the "Album of All Sorts":

> Being a collective, selective Medley of *Odd, Laughable, Funny, Droll, Tragical, Comical, Poetical, Prosaical, Elegaical, Whimsical, Satirical, Critical, Biographical, Theatrical, and Piratical*, Songs, Duets, Glees, Chorusses, Orations, Recitations, Lucubrations, Translations, *Prologues, Epilogues, Monologues, Dialogues*, TALES, MEMOIRS, HISTORIES, FRAGMENTS, **Flights of Fancy**, FUGITIVE PIECES, SCRAPS, &c. &c. &c. gathered from Tragedies, Comedies, Operas, Plays, Farces, Burlettas, Operettas, Farcettas, Melodramas, Pantomimes, NEWSPAPERS, NOVELS, MAGAZINES, & ROMANCES.[81]

Before 1820, a commitment to miscellany this far-reaching would rarely, if ever, have been found in a weekly theatrical journal. Certainly it would not have been explicitly championed. After that time, however, even weeklies began yoking together disparate kinds of information, such as reporting and biographical features. The result was a hybrid type of journal that, though unapologetically enlisting commercial reading practices, packaged itself for a discriminating theatrical connoisseur.

The Opera Glass ("for peeping into the microcosm of the fine arts, and more especially the drama"),[82] first published in 1826 and more successful than *Thalia's Tablet*, presented a newspaper-like front page with bold headings and three full columns of type, but it also included *Behind the Curtain*, a compendium of gossip, theatrical anecdotes, and brief information, and *Our Scissors*, which compiled information from various city papers "to preserve the many floating theatrical paragraphs which are scattered throughout the Daily Papers." Just as theatrical dailies brought playbills into the context provided by their reports, later weeklies such as the *Opera Glass* captured theatrical discourse "floating" in the newspaper to ground it for readers in the context of a more acceptable high-end publication. By 1829 the weekly *Harlequin, A Journal of the Drama* was virtually indistinguishable from a monthly theatrical magazine. Its front page was always adorned with a picture of one of the kingdom's theaters, and its text was divided into a multitude of departments, including "anecdotiana," gossip, and reports of events in the provincial as well as foreign theaters. A chief imitator, the 1829 *Columbine*, further developed the *Harlequin*'s miscellaneous form, including short stories and poems along with information on London's "minor" entertainments.[83]

This shift in the typical weekly's textual layout and topical focus indicates a change in the ways that those publications attempted to engage their audiences, a shift that is also reflected in the structure and style of their reviews. Thomas Dutton's writing reveals that as late as 1800 and beyond, some critics attempted to assert theater's moral dimension as a way to convert a degraded and commercialized public.[84] As the century lengthened, however, more reviewers began to recognize the insufficient efficacy of an aesthetic standard strictly tied to public morality. Again, this is not to say that moral concern for theater disappears from criticism between 1800 and 1830. The eighteenth-century standard endured, at least as an ideal. But what had once been an assumed connection based on a mutual acceptance of criticism's mandate to evaluate theater as a realm of instruction and entertainment became instead a way for certain writers and certain readers to distinguish themselves from wider readerships for whom such questions were no longer primary. Recognizing the crisis in reception brought on by the commercialization of theatrical experience, reviewers eventually and repeatedly confirmed the division between an elite, if still commercialized, group of connoisseurs and an absent-minded consumerist public. This confirmation enabled critics to maintain a measure of cultural prestige without cutting themselves off from the audiences who sustained them.

What had been in Thomas Dutton's reviews an uncontained anxiety over commercialized modes of reception was transformed, by the 1820s, into a sign of critics' and readers' cultural sophistication. In 1826, *The Opera Glass* claimed that amid the many theatrical periodicals then available, "no adequate vehicle for Dramatic Criticism exists."[85] Steering a middle course between the compromised criticisms of the dailies and the keepsake hauteur of more general monthly magazines, *The Opera Glass* took as its "jurisdiction" "dramatic concerns of all kinds." And though the weekly "claim[ed] dominion over them only as far as they belong to the public," still the editors distinguished themselves from the popular discourse – not with a superior sense of morality but with a superior sense of taste: "If we cannot command success by the fair means of taste and literature, we shall never stoop to look for it from the filthy resources of scandal and calumny."[86] *The Opera Glass*'s style of review differed radically from that of Dutton and his counterparts, as a February 1827 account of Howard Payne's *Brutus* reveals:

> There was a very crowded house this evening, and the play, altogether, went off exceedingly well. Kean performed many of those passages to which the decrease of his physical powers did not disenable him from giving their utmost effect, better than we have ever seen him do them. In the early scenes, his utterance of several points was admirable . . . but the call upon the multitude for revenge, and the whole of the previous scene with Collatinus, Lucretius, and Valerius, had not the force for which they were formerly remarkable. Indeed it may be observed generally, that it was only in parts where great energy was not required to assist his expression, that he accomplished as much as he once did; in those he did more. All the last act was exquisitely performed, – so much so, that in one of its most trying situations a lady in a private box shrieked, and was borne out fainting.[87]

The massive crush of audience members that confronted the *Mince Pie* reviewer and conspicuously distracted his critical attentions and the constant "digressions" and rants against audience behavior that disrupted Dutton's reviews give way in *The Opera Glass* to a steady consideration of the actor's ability to represent his part *to* that audience. Spectator behavior has been integrated here into the review's organized structure, as a comment on performance. The critically unwieldy phenomenon of the crowd's collective response to the play is replaced by the gracefully described shriek of a symbolic "lady" in a "private box." There is no "considerable d – d number of persons" to present the reviewer with the risk of being "shouldered or pushed about by men."[88] Rather, the lady's outburst confirms the effectiveness of Kean's emotive style. It is her response, the response of those like her, and the response of those who *would be* like her, that now interest the critic and his reader.

The comfortable tone of the typical late Romantic-period review, coupled with the change in textual format within which these reviews were presented, indicates a gradual capitulation to the idea that theatergoing audiences were becoming more specialized. That is, the descriptions of audience behavior and response, placed in high-end weeklies such as the *Opera Glass* and the *Harlequin*, were not necessarily intended for the people being described. Rather, the narratives of theatrical events were consumed by readers who saw the behavior of "the multitude . . . who are at all times caught by show and surprise" as itself a phenomenon to be considered and reviewed.[89] By the third decade of the nineteenth century, many weeklies were at ease with describing plays' popular appeal and the ability of actors to engage the sympathetic faculties of the audience, simply because reviewers no longer saw the commercialization of theatrical experience as a political or social threat to their existence. Critics focused, instead, on maintaining standards of reception among their distinct audiences, and common theatergoers' theatrical experience became a foil against which the reflective criticism of later Romantic-period theatrical periodicals distinguished itself.

What the *Opera Glass* offered, along with similar types of weeklies like the *Harlequin, a Journal of the Drama* and the *Columbine and Weekly Review*, was a publication geared to satisfy readers conditioned by, but wishing to distinguish themselves from, the habits of a wider, commercialized theatergoing public. With an "endeavor to give more variety . . . [and] to encourage a gentler and more analytical style of criticism than has prevailed for some years," the journal addressed readers who, rather than rallying to repeated cries about the degraded state of the commercial stage, sought a cultivated, which is to say legitimate, way to consume its productions.[90] Straightforward moralism gave way in the 1820s to the dictates of a new group of theatrical connoisseurs and their critics. By 1827, the *Hull Dramatic Censor* could assert unapologetically that by offering "opinions . . . which are seldom or never in accordance with the general voice," it addressed a restricted and elite "dramatic public."[91] As weeklies altered in structure and style from the prophetic moralism of the *Dramatic Censor* to the frenetic concern of the *Theatrical Mince Pie* to the confident rhetoric of distinction and the commercial miscellany of the *Opera Glass*, the possibility of a critic imagining that he could transform theatrical experience for the commercialized nineteenth-century reader virtually disappeared.

III *The Examiner*

In 1808, some months before the O. P. riots, Leigh and John Hunt established *The Examiner*, a weekly paper that, in its own words, sought the "cultivation of common reason." Leigh Hunt, the paper's editor, explicitly situated his publication at the center of the early-nineteenth-century periodical field, disdaining the "petty and prejudiced manner of journal writing" found in newspapers corrupted by party bias. "Freedom from party-spirit," he resolved, "is nothing but the love of looking abroad upon men and things, and this leads to universality, which is the great study of philosophy, so that the true love of enquiry and the love of one's country move in a circle."[92] Like other critics before him, Hunt saw the press's lack of institutional independence as a central cause of decline in critical discourse, because "the ignorance and corruption of the journals naturally produced a correspondent style" that either coddled or alienated readers:

> There is very little political writing in the daily papers; and their articles are read throughout, because they are short, as well as of daily and party interest: but I have ever remarked, that in the political essays of the weekly prints, the interest of the reader has been proportioned to the manner as well as matter of the writing. It is much the same in Theatrical Criticism, a department which none of the papers seem inclined to dispute with a person fond of the subject, the daily ones for want of independence, and the weekly for want of care.[93]

For Hunt, the dailies were incapable of producing effective theatrical criticism, and criticism that did transcend the boundaries of typical puffing or casual consideration was shackled by adherence to outdated aesthetic rules and institutional affiliations. This left room for something new.

Between 1805 and 1807, Hunt had served as theatrical critic for *The News*, a paper also published by his brother John. Reflecting in his *Autobiography* from the distance of a half-century, Hunt remembers his disdain, as he took up the mantle of the paper's "theatricals," for the theatrical press's commercial commitments:

> It was the custom at that time for editors of papers to be intimate with actors and dramatists ... The newspaper man had consequence in the green-room, and plenty of tickets for his friends; and he dined at amusing tables. The dramatist secured a good-natured critique in his journal, sometimes got it written himself, or, according to Mr. Reynolds, was even himself the author of it. The actor, if he was of any eminence, stood upon the same ground of reciprocity ... Puffing and plenty of tickets [were] the system of

the day. It was an interchange of amenities over the dinner table ... and what the public took for criticism on a play, was a draft upon the box-office. (*Autobiography* 181–82)

The Hunt brothers sought to counter this corruption with their fledgling paper by sticking to a resolute "independence in theatrical criticism ... We announced it, and nobody believed us: we stuck to it, and the town believed everything we said" (*Autobiography* 181). For Hunt himself, this independence meant that "to know an actor personally appeared to me a vice not to be thought of; and I would as lief have taken poison as accepted a ticket from the theaters" (*Autobiography* 182). In his May 25, 1806 publication for *The News*, Hunt presented a satiric set of rules that theater critics should follow. Including such injunctions as "Never take any notice of the authors of a play or of the play itself" (14) and "Indulge an acquaintance with every dramatic writer and with every actor, and you will have a noble opportunity of showing your fine feelings and your philanthropy" (15), Hunt listed a series of key phrases critics should employ, complete with their real meanings. The list is worth quoting in its entirety in the accompanying table.

A crowded house	– a theatre on the night of performance, when all the back seats and upper boxes are empty.
An amusing author	– an author whose very seriousness makes him laugh in spite of himself.
A successful author	– an author who has been damned only four times out of five.
A good author	– the general term for an author who gives good dinners.
A respectable actor	– an insipid actor; one who in general is neither hissed nor applauded: a DECAMP, a BRUNTON.
A fine actor	– one who makes a great noise; a tatter-demalion of passions; a clap-trapper; one intended by nature for a town-crier. This appellation may on all occasions be given to Mr POPE, who has the finest lungs of any man on stage.
A good actor	– the general term for an actor who gives good dinners.
A charming play	– a play full of dancing, music, and scenery; a play in which the less the author has to do, the better.
Great applause	– applause mixed with the hisses of the gallery and the pit.
Unbounded and universal applause	– applause mixed with the hisses of the pit only. The phrase is frequently to be found at the bottom of play-house bills in declaring the reception a new piece has met with. The plays announced in these bills are generally praised in red-ink, an emblem, no doubt, of the modesty with which they speak of themselves.

With this lexicon, Hunt addresses not only the rhetorical excesses of theatrical critics but also the habits of specific actors and audiences, as well as the untruths that plague the commercial marketing of performances. His almost prophetic project of cultural demystification echoes the accusatory rhetorical tactics that Kevin Gilmartin finds characterizing turn of the century radical writers, and anticipates by 140 years the similar list of hyperbolic keywords George Orwell would deploy in "Politics and the English Language." More than candor or a widening in critical attention to encompass all aspects of theatrical production, Hunt offers here, and throughout *The News's* theatrical columns, a template for the theatrical critic's responsibility to reclaim public language from the excesses of commercially beholden cant.

As H. R. Fox Bourne points out, the *Examiner* "was a speedy consequence of the success that attended the first venture of the brothers in newspaper work, and a bold attempt to apply to the discussion of political and social affairs ... the same independence which had appeared in Leigh Hunt's notices of the performances" (336).[94] The independence Hunt demonstrated in his early theatrical criticism, that is, authorized more ambitious interventions into the commercial system of news production. If the daily newspapers displayed their objective reporting principally in parliamentary coverage, the Hunts' papers likewise sought first to declare independence in the cultural realm. In the "Prospectus" that accompanied the *Examiner*'s first number, Hunt described his position with respect to newspapers, commenting that the typical daily was "very mean in it's subservience to the follies of the day, very miserably merry in it's puns and it's stories, extremely furious in politics, and quite feeble in criticism."[95] He proposed instead, with the *Examiner*, a weekly that would appeal to an equally wide audience but would remove itself from the commercial and political subservience that sullied other newspapers' chances at objectivity. Hunt imagines for the critic a social position far less precarious than that of the *Mince Pie* reviewer: "[A] crowd is no place for steady observation. The *Examiner* has escaped from the throng and bustle, but he will seat himself by the way-side and contemplate the moving multitude as they wrangle and wrestle along" (7). Though the *Examiner* was a paper whose authorial perspective was *removed from* the crowd, it both *concerned itself with* and *spoke to* readers who were part of that crowd. As such, it demonstrated the kind of rhetorical hybridity – engaged yet removed, colloquial yet discriminating, learned yet accessible – that Gregory Dart argues characterizes the "Cockney Moment" of the Regency period (1). Indeed, the *Examiner,* authorized at the outset by Hunt's standing as a respected theater critic, provided the public platform that enabled Hunt to become the Cockney School's prime mover upon his release from Surrey Gaol in February 1815 after a two-year sentence for libeling the Prince Regent in the journal's pages.

Uniquely among review journals with longer periodical cycles, both the *Examiner*'s content and its textual layout unapologetically showed the influence of the commercial daily press. With sixteen pages of two-columned type, subdivided into topical categories and heavily dated, its material properties were strikingly similar to those of the newspapers it derided. The journal's major sections, such as "The Political Examiner," "Fine Arts," and the "Theatrical Examiner," were subdivided into departments that included "Miscellaneous Sketches," "Law," "Police," "Bankrupts," "Marriages," "Deaths," "Provincial Intelligence," "Foreign Intelligence," and digests from a host of gazette reports. Yet despite the *Examiner*'s all-encompassing, newspaper-like perspective, and its textual similarity to the dailies' layouts, the Hunts chose to avoid one major component of the commercial news. Crucial to the *Examiner*'s unique position in the field of periodical publication was its refusal to accept advertisements of any kind. Hunt commented at length in the "Prospectus" about advertisements' detrimental effect on the newspaper's ability to shape the nation's cultural life. The *Examiner* was declared an ad-free zone, enabling readers to engage the events of the day without the possibility of being drawn into commercial interaction:

> Advertisements ... shall neither come staring in the first page at the breakfast table to deprive the reader of a whole page of entertainment, nor shall they win their silent way into the recesses of the paper under the mask of general Paragraph to filch even a few lines: the public shall neither be tempted to listen to somebody in the shape of a wit who turns out to be a lottery-keeper, nor seduced to hear a magnificent oration which finishes by retreating into a peruke or rolling off into a blacking-ball. (7)

The separation between entertainment and commercialism Hunt implies here registers the *Examiner* as a unique publication in the London periodical field. It was, with its newspaper-like layout, its weekly print cycle, its refusal of advertisements, and its equal emphasis on theatrical and political experience, what might be called London's preeminent cultural newspaper.[96] Not surprisingly, theater criticism was a major component of the *Examiner* from 1808 on; one of the chief draws of the new paper was Hunt's success with *The News*, as well as with the 1807 publication of some of those theatrical essays in a single volume entitled *Critical Essays on the Performers of the*

London Theatre.[97] If, as Michael Eberle-Sinatra has argued, Hunt posits with the publication of *Critical Essays* "that theater reviewing as a literary form (or at least his own theater reviewing) is deserving of serious attention" (13), the *Examiner* consolidated that argument by returning reviews to their rightful home in the pages of a periodical publication. The "Theatrical Examiner" was among the paper's most prominent sections each week, placing it on par with the political discussions, international reports, and legal information that also filled the weekly's pages. While the daily press situated culture as one facet of a world that was commercial before it was political or cultural, the *Examiner* took cultural experience as a paradigmatic way of relating to the world. During the 1809 O. P. riots, several editorial sections at once were attuned to happenings in the theater. With its equal division between major political and cultural departments, the *Examiner*'s layout did more than strike a different symbolic balance between theater and other events than that found in the typical commercial daily, where theater was a significant but not determining part of public life. It actually undermined the notion of such divisions at all, providing testimony that for Hunt "the aesthetic is not reduced to the political but united with it" (Kucich and Cox xxxviii).[98] The Hunts' paper indicated to readers the primary role theater had in constituting public experience as a whole.

Despite his dismissal of the discourses of commercial reviewing, Hunt's theatrical criticism in the *Examiner* continued the middle-way of critique that he initiated during his years at *The News*, equally resisting the high moralism and exclusionary rhetoric of many contemporaries in journals and magazines. As he comments in the "Preface" to the *Examiner*'s first number, the best theatrical critic is, on the contrary, a new kind of philosopher, attentive to the fact that

> the treatment of the passions ... both in actors and dramatists, demands a greater portion of what the schools call Humanity, than any other subject of the day; and I am never so afraid of the criticism of my readers, as when my endeavors to separate the thousand niceties of human feeling may render me liable to the charge of wordiness.

Hunt's style, like his attention to the play, would be plain rather than high, correct rather than classical; in short, it would engage readers in dialogue, not preach to them. Hunt aimed to refashion the critical office so that "every body might be able to read me" and "every body might wish to read me ... I would not," he remarked, "willingly quote Greek and Latin to the actors, and certainly not to the modern dramatists."[99]

Hunt's criticism in the "Theatrical Examiner" was true to the promise of the "Preface" – colloquial and direct. Eschewing traditional use of the critical "we," Hunt offered opinions as an individual subject encountering performances without political or personal predisposition. A review from November 1809 provides an example of his approach:

> The various and delightful comedy of *Much ado about* Nothing, on Monday night introduced Mrs. Edwin to us as *Beatrice*. I have already criticized at large this play and the comparative merits of Lewis and Elliston in *Benedick*. (No I. p. II.) There is but one fresh remark that suggests itself to me now. Dr. Johnson objects to the similarity of contrivances practised on the two wits of the piece; and Mr. Steevens, too, wishes "that some other method had been found to entrap *Beatrice* than that very one which before had been successfully practiced on *Benedick*." The uniformity of the case however appears to me to be a great beauty.[100]

Demonstrating conversational ease and comfortable knowledge of fellow critics' attitudes, both past and contemporary, Hunt allows the reader to witness his thought process, as "one fresh remark ... suggests itself to me" even as the play's "uniformity of the case ... appears to me to be a great beauty."[101] The construction not only juxtaposes subjective reaction ("I"/"me") with wider claims about "uniformity" and "beauty"; it also suggests that individual experience must be the ground upon which such abstractions are conceived. This kind of theatrical casuistry, which Hazlitt would later develop more fully, is present in the criticism not as self-indulgence but as testament to the fact that Hunt's assessment is based on his own personal, and therefore genuine, engagement with the play. The *Examiner* resisted the pseudonymity and corporate authorial presence Mark Schoenfield argues promoted "a philosophical skepticism about identity" in the periodical culture of the day (*British Periodicals* 3), reasserting instead an individual imagining in the face of such rhetorical-editorial consolidations. Unlike many early-nineteenth-century reviewers who maintained, or attempted to maintain, a critical voice authorized by connection to traditional systems of aesthetic evaluation, Hunt authorizes his opinions by naturalizing the encounter between the subject-viewer and the performance and, in turn, between the reviewer and his reader. His comments later in the review regarding Mrs. Edwin's "figure," "countenance," and "voice" therefore sound differently in the reader's ear than similar observations made by a critic like Thomas Dutton. For Hunt, the assessment of reception – an assessment educed from personal experience – replaces moral surveillance or puffery as the critic's defining activity, cultivating what he called "a peculiar intimacy" between periodical writer and audience that would lead to "lasting" acquaintance based on "the greater variety of subject and opinion" the writer's shifts of opinion and demeanor could manifest.[102]

The *Examiner*'s position in the nineteenth-century periodical field enabled its writers, Hunt first but Hazlitt preeminently, to engage topics of cultural interest, especially theater, with a freedom unavailable to critics working for typical review periodicals or commercial newspapers. *Examiner* critics were able to attend to theatrical performance without resorting to moralism or traditional aesthetic norms to authorize their judgments, instead making theatrical experience itself the subject of their accounts. As a consequence, their criticism could be more wide ranging and, finally, more subjective than that of their counterparts in other journals. Jane Moody has commented that Hunt's "significance as a theatre critic is partly in his comic demystification of the patent institution, as well as his persuasive championing of certain productions at the minor theatres" ("Fine Word" 230). This is certainly true, as far as it goes; but attention to illegitimate performance, coupled with Hunt's reliance on personal reaction as the basis for reviewing, evinces a more fundamental shift in his figuration of theatrical experience. Entertainments typically considered illegitimate or unworthy of serious consideration were valuable to Hunt *because* they could impact the spectator in unexpected ways. And the reviews that communicated that impact imagined a readership able to hear and understand Hunt's intimate voice. The *Examiner* emphasized the occasional nature of both the theatrical event and the critic's response to it, rooting critical authority in the demonstration of individual imagination and feeling rather than preexisting standards of evaluation.

Presenting something of a hybrid between the unified diversity of commercial publications and the straightforward philosophical discourse of review journals, the *Examiner* became the principal vehicle through which Hunt and his circle attempted "to infuse the sometimes alienating medium of print with the communal values of coterie production" (Cox, *Poetry and Politics* 64).[103] With the colloquial style and subjective reactions of its theatrical criticism, and its testament of independence from advertising's commercial system, the paper invoked the pre-commercial coterie publications of the eighteenth century, even as its newspaper-like form registered a resistance to elitism by addressing a wider audience.[104] As Hunt was to recall nostalgically four decades later in his *Autobiography*, the *Examiner* imagined theater as an extra-commercial cultural experience in which audiences were not collections of individuated consumers, and theatrical critics were neither hirelings at their service nor moralists ranting at their depravity.[105] Centrally locating discussions of theater in the paper's pages, and unabashedly engaging performances on intimate subjective terms, Hunt and the *Examiner* critics who followed him "presented theatre as an ideal public sphere" precisely because the discussion of theater the paper imagined was not divorced from its reader's everyday experiences (Moody, *Illegitimate Theatre* 174). Even as the *Examiner*'s gestured toward independence from commercial corruption, its content and textual form imagined an audience deeply engaged with the everyday realities of English public life. As such, its reviews collectively presented a manifesto of the Cockney response to London's theatrical world.

The *Examiner*'s commitment to independence from, yet engagement with, the commercial discourse of news rendered it a crucial vehicle for the development of a new kind of theatrical criticism. Its reviewers were not only self-conscious of their changing social function, they also called attention to that change with their candor and subjective style. Hunt's success as both editor and critic gave momentum to a shift in which the personal experience of the critic came to replace codified aesthetic standards as both the measure of theatrical events and the means by which audiences could connect to them. Because it was something of a genre unto itself, the *Examiner* was not limited by readers' strict generic expectations. This fact, when considered with regard to the emergence after the turn of the century of a weekly theatrical criticism designed to demonstrate cultural distinction, indicates why the *Examiner* played a crucial role in reshaping how readers perceived theater's public function. By maintaining a connection between everyday events inside and outside the theater, a connection unseen in the same way in any other journal, the *Examiner* embedded its consideration of plays and actors into a larger social context created by the commercial daily news. And yet it took its position self-consciously in a periodical field that had already become commercialized, so that paradoxically "the 'commercial state of the press' became a cause for optimism about the future, the presumed necessary consequence of a 'diffusion of knowledge' that would soon liberate readers and writers from the marketplace" (Gilmartin, *Print Politics* 206). The *Examiner* took seriously commercialism's creation of cultural experiences never before imaginable in theater and in reading. Hunt's critical voice was at once a response to his own changing theatrical experience and a rhetorical self-presentation designed to engage readers who were attuned to commercial representations of theater yet uninterested in moralistic critique. Using the tools of commercialism, the *Examiner* sought to counter commercialism's reduction of theatrical experience to a habitual consumer's act by emphasizing the occasional, mobile, and imaginative nature of theatrical experience. Like the example of Hunt before him, Hazlitt's formulation of a theatrical criticism propelled by this mode of writing would, in turn, have generic and philosophical impact well beyond theatrical criticism.

Notes

1. *Theatrical Mince Pie* 1.1 (January 1, 1825): 2. Due to the extensive information necessary to specify editions of theatrical periodicals, coupled with their oftentimes confusing pagination, citations of such texts will appear in the chapter's footnotes rather than parenthetically in the text.
2. Here the "torrid partnership of confessional author and curious reader" that Tom Mole sees flourishing in Romantic-period print publicity takes a self-conscious turn (2).
3. Gillian Russell details how theater enabled people of various political opinions to "legitimately confront each other" (*Theatres of War* 112).
4. In one sense, then, the review could be seen to qualify Ann Bermingham's notion that in the eighteenth century, consumption was gendered female and judgment male, for the reviewer offers as much cautionary tale about his displacement as he does a recommendation of the play ("Elegant Females" 489).
5. Nicoletta Caputo's "Theatrical Periodicals and the Ethics of Theatre" describes how after 1800, "Theatrical magazines provided endless opportunities for discussion and debate in which everybody could join" (44) and argues that while some critics did "not always appear qualified for their task," on the whole theatrical periodicals "relentlessly endeavored to refine the taste of the audience and, even more, to create an ideal theatre, peopled by ideal actors and ideal spectators" (53). My reading extends and qualifies Caputo's observation by attending to the differences in style and political aims various kinds of periodicals displayed.
6. For an overview of these changes, see Stratman 124. Following Stratman, Caputo has provided a similar account of these changes, noting that "Between 1800 and 1830 one hundred and sixty periodicals wholly concerned with drama and the theatre appeared throughout Great Britain" (43).
7. For the most encompassing history of theatrical entertainments in the nineteenth century, see Richard Altick, *The Shows of London*.
8. For an illustrated description of the eighteenth-century playhouse, see Nicoll, *The Garrick Stage* 35–77. See also Lynch 199–207 and Hogan, *Critical Introduction* xx–xciii.
9. For a concise description of alterations in the physical layout of both theaters, see Mander and Mitchenson, especially 52–59, 64–68.
10. For a reconsideration of the nineteenth-century crowd and its effect on literature, see John Plotz. For a more recent discussion of the controversial

political significance of the discourse of sympathy with respect to crowds in the Romantic period, see Fairclough.

11. This was true of the 1747 "Kelley riot" in Dublin's Smock Alley Theatre, where audience members protested their exclusion from the backstage area; in the 1755 disturbances, precipitated by the Seven Years' War, against shows at Drury Lane conceived by the Frenchman Jean-Georges Noverre; and in the infamous 1763 "Fitzgiggio riots," where demonstrators rejected management's attempt to eliminate half-price admission for spectators only wishing to see the afterpieces. Elsewhere, Thompson has remarked that the "plebian culture" that accompanied paternalist notions of class relations "was not, to be sure, a revolutionary nor even a proto-revolutionary culture (in the sense of fostering ulterior objectives which called in question the social order); but one should not describe it as a deferential culture either. It bred riots but not rebellions: direct actions but not democratic organizations" ("Patrician Society, Plebian Culture" 397).

12. Ian Christie argues that such social actions helped maintain a balance between "stress and stability" in eighteenth-century Britain. Marc Baer extends Christie's notion to the Old Price riots, citing "the paradoxically stabilizing influence of disorder" (10). But Baer overstates the socially conservative undercurrent of the riots, which were more threatening in the nineteenth century than in the eighteenth because of the changes in theatrical culture I detail. For a wider discussion of "the politics of riot" in Britain between 1790 and 1810, and the development of "riotous bargaining," see Bohstedt (207). For a comprehensive account of the riots and public reaction to them, see Terry Robinson.

13. Marc Baer has argued that theater's "social importance lay in the fact that it was one of the few urban areas – perhaps the only one – where a variety of social orders heard and saw national virtues demonstrated, and could therefore learn together how to be English" (193). But the early nineteenth century brought with it an upheaval in those "orders" and in their interactions with one another. What passed for "national" and for "virtue" – or for that matter "demonstration" – was becoming less clear.

14. *Remarks on the Causes of the Dispute between the Public and Managers of the Theatre Royal, Covent Garden, by John Bull.* [pamphlet] London: John Fairburn, 1809.

15. Details of this brief narrative are taken from principally from contemporary newspaper accounts and pamphlets, and from Baer, Hadley, and Russell ("Playing at Revolution").

16. The term "deferential" is used extensively by Elaine Hadley. For E. P. Thompson's discussion of the term's historical limitations, see his "Patrician Society, Plebian Culture."

17. "Theatrical Examiner 52," *Examiner* 91 (September 24, 1809): 618.

18. Prostitution and sexual activity in the darkened boxes were an important issue in the riots. See Baer 206–9.

19. The *Remarks on the Causes of the Dispute* pamphleteer continues by attacking management's reliance on new notions of private property to justify theater's commercialization:

> Theatrical property is therefore not of the nature of other property. It is held from Government under a tacit tenure, for the benefit, amusement, and instruction of the people. It has been properly observed, than when a Parliament grants an exclusive right to build a bridge, or make a private road, it limits the amount of the toll to be exacted from the public for using them. And though, in this case, the prices of admission are not expressed in the patent, it is exactly similar, and should be subject to the same construction.

20. As I noted in Chapter 1, newspapers covered the events at Covent Garden with extensive daily reports. In addition to these multiple accounts of the riots, theatrical periodicals provided their own narratives and analysis of the events. The January 1811 issue of the monthly *Dramatic Censor*, for example, provided a twenty-two-page summary of the "extraordinary and important events" that happened at the season's opening the previous autumn.

21. In *Idler* 60 and 61 (1759), Samuel Johnson had told the tale of *Dick Minim*, theatrical critic:

> Mr. Minim had now advanced himself to the zenith of critical reputation; when he was in the pit, every eye in the boxes was fixed upon him, when he entered his coffee-house, he was surrounded by circles of candidates, who passed their noviciate of literature under his tuition; his opinion was asked by all who had no opinion of their own, and yet loved to debate and decide. (*Works* 2.189–90)

By 1809, Mr. Minim's oral coterie had become a textually constituted community, as critics attempted quite literally to make sense, in print, of what they were seeing in the theater.

22. As Charles Harold Gray noted in 1931, "A good deal of the entertainment offered in theatres from the very opening of the period was of kinds which could not be approached with any of the accepted modes of criticism" (20).

23. This is true of the most prominent of eighteenth-century theatrical periodicals, Aaron Hill's *The Prompter* (1734–1736). For an example of Hill's anti-commercialism, see *The Prompter* 30 (February 21, 1735).

24. For a discussion of the political alignments (Whig vs. Tory) of commercialized performances in popular scientific culture, see Schaffer 489–94.

25. While recognizing significant differences in regional and national contexts, and keeping a principal focus on periodicals published in and around London, I do include provincial theaters in Britain and Ireland in this discussion because the periodicals from those cities are almost identical in their rhetorical and textual properties as those found in London.

26. Among other printings of this message, see *Covent Garden Theatrical Gazette* 130 (March 3, 1817): 2.

27. *The Drama* [Dublin] (January 18, 1822): 129.
28. *The Theatrical Observer* [London] (November 3, 1821): 1.
29. *The Edinburgh Dramatic Review* (October 7, 1822): 2.
30. For a description of these and other practices pertaining to the distribution of playbills, see Gowen, esp. 47–68.
31. *The Tatler* (September 17, 1830). rpt. *Leigh Hunt's Dramatic Criticism* 222.
32. Gillian Russell describes "the smaller handbill form of the playbill, sold both outside and inside the playhouse" as "the most widespread and enduring form of theater publicity" leading up to and into the nineteenth century ("Playbills" 243).
33. Intracity rivalries were fierce. In Dublin there were two playbill periodicals with the title *Theatrical Observer* for much of 1821. That December, one editor changed his title to the *Original Theatrical Observer*; his competitor followed suit by becoming *Nolan's Theatrical Observer* in January 1822. A few months later, an *Independent Theatrical Observer* emerged, claiming to supersede the *Original Theatrical Observer* – which did not, however, disappear. And 1823 saw the arrival in Dublin of the *Genuine Theatrical Observer*. Other cities were no less competitive. Edinburgh's *Theatrical Observer* (1824) contended with the *Edinburgh Dramatic Review* (1822) and the *Edinburgh Dramatic Tete-a-tete* (1828). And in London, besides the playbill dailies already described, readers could choose from, among others, the *Theatrical Examiner* (1823), the *Dramatic Observer and Musical Review* (1823), the *Thespian Sentinel* (1825), and the *Theatrical Mirror* (1827).
34. *Theatrical Examiner* (July 24, 1823).
35. *The Tatler* (September 17, 1830); rpt. *Dramatic Criticism of Leigh Hunt* 233–34.
36. *The Tatler* (September 17, 1830); rpt. *Dramatic Criticism of Leigh Hunt* 232.
37. *Covent Garden Theatrical Gazette* (March 3, 1817).
38. *Covent Garden Theatrical Gazette* (March 3, 1817): "Advertisement."
39. *Theatrical Observer* [London] (November 3,1821): 1.
40. *Covent Garden Theatrical Gazette* (March 3, 1817): "Advertisement."
41. This capacity to represent at once the culture of the day and, ultimately, the greater course of theatrical history was not lost on the dailies' editors. In the words of the *Covent Garden Gazette* advertisement, its complementary immediacy and collectability would "render the work, independent of its utility, an amusing and instructive companion to the theatrical world, and the public in general, at all times."
42. *Thespian Sentinel* (October 28, 1825).
43. *Theatrical Observer* [London] (October 11, 1821): 1.
44. For a listing of circulations for these and other magazines in the period, see Altick, *The English Common Reader* 391–96.
45. Also popular were "pocket magazines," which reduced the larger publications' miscellaneous material to forty or fifty small pages, about 9 cm by 14 cm.
46. *The Drama, or Theatrical Pocket Magazine* (May 1821).
47. *Oxberry's Theatrical Inquisitor* (February 1828).

48. *The Weekly Dramatic Register, A Concise History of the London Stage for 1825.* London: E. Thomas, 1825.
49. *The Theatrical Observer* [London] (November 3, 1821).
50. Among myriad examples of such references, see the title pages of any of the following: *The Stage, or Theatrical Touchstone* [London], 1805; *The Censor* [London], 1828; *The Stage, or Theatrical inquisitor* [London], 1828. The dailies, of course, were also available at "the Booksellers," in addition to being sold on the street.
51. *The Dramatic Censor* (January 4, 1800): 1.
52. *The Theatrical Review* [Bath], I.6 (November 23, 1822): 21. This periodical was published somewhat irregularly, up to four times in one week, or with intervals with no number up to a month.
53. *The Dramatic Censor* (January 4, 1800): 2. For a discussion of the radical styles of Cobbett and Carlile, among other radical publishers, see Gilmartin, *Print Politics*.
54. *The Theatrical Rod!* 2 (1831 – no dates given): 2.
55. "Advertisement." *The Dramatic Censor, or Critical and Biographical Illustration of the British Stage* [monthly], J. M. Williams, Ed., London: G. Brimmer, 1811.
56. *Irish Dramatic Censor* [Dublin] (1811, numbers not dated).
57. *Irish Dramatic Censor* [Dublin] (1811).
58. *The Dramatic Censor* [weekly] (January 4, 1800): 3.
59. *The Dramatic Censor* [weekly] (January 4, 1800): 16.
60. "Dedication." *The Theatrical Repertory, or Weekly Rosciad* [London], 1802.
61. *The Plymouth Theatrical Spy* (January 5, 1828): 1.
62. *Lincoln Dramatic Censor* (October 21, 1809). For a similar protestation of impartiality on the part of a monthly, see "Address to the Public." *The Theatrical Inquisitor*. London: Sherwood, Neely, and Jones, 1812.
63. *The Theatrical Review* [Bath] 1.11 (December 4, 1822); 1.19 (January 30, 1823). An earlier article in the *Theatrical Review* 1.7 (November 25, 1822) had attacked theatrical dailies as similarly corrupt:

> We cannot, however, attribute any ... discrimination to the *Gazette* critics, whose appetite for excellence is so easily gratified, that when assailed by the promise of favour, or the hope of remuneration, they can very conveniently banish every particle of that judgment they were once supposed to possess, and acknowledge every thing as good, delightful, admirable, grand, striking, forcible, and (by way of a climax) excellent.

64. *The Stage; or, Theatrical Touchstone* (July 20, 1805).
65. *The Stage; or, Theatrical Touchstone* (July 20, 1805).
66. Pierre Bourdieu asserts, "[E]xplicit aesthetic choices are in fact often constituted in opposition to the choices of the groups closest in social space, with whom the competition is most direct and most immediate, and more precisely, no doubt, in relation to those choices most clearly marked by the

intention (perceived as pretension) of marking distinction vis-à-vis lower groups" (*Distinction* 60).
67. On October 2, 1826, the *Opera Glass* claimed that these advantages made the *weekly* in particular the only type of theatrical periodical able to produce worthwhile criticism. After commenting on "the inadequacy of our newspapers for performing this duty," the editors stated that "magazines come out at periods too distant to be of much use towards chronicling the rapid movements of the drama, even if three or four periodicals worth reading attended seriously to dramatic affairs, which some of them do not even notice" ("Advertisement," October 2, 1826). Theatrical weeklies, even more than most monthly magazines, voice a philosophically detailed, consistently anti-commercial message while attempting to cultivate audiences accustomed to intimately commercial publications. The weeklies, that is, were where the daily's descriptions of performance and the monthlies' attractive miscellaneous features met with a discourse that imagined a public sphere where rational discussion of theater prevailed over absent-minded consumerism. For this reason, it is the weeklies that display most clearly the tensions that conflicting reading publics wrought on the production of theatrical criticism.
68. This shift evinces one facet of what Jon Klancher has called the "cosmopolitical struggles" of discrimination that took their origin in the 1790s but came to fruition in Romanticism's second generation ("Discriminations" 67).
69. Typically, connoisseurship and scholarship of connoisseurship have focused more readily on visual art. With the term I mean to describe the distinction that particular practitioners make in assigning a thoughtful or polite dimension to their modes of reception, as distinguished from the vulgar or absent-minded consumption of larger audiences. For a helpful discussion of the "polite" dimensions of artistic activity in eighteenth- and nineteenth-century England, see Ann Bermingham's *Learning to Draw*, esp. 96–181.
70. *The Dramatic Censor* [weekly] (January 18, 1800): 75–77.
71. *The Dramatic Censor* [weekly] (January 18, 1800): 77–78.
72. Among the causes "now acting to blunt the discriminating powers of the mind," Wordsworth cites the following:

> [T]he encreasing accumulation of men in cities, where the uniformity of their occupations produces a craving for extraordinary incident which the rapid communication of intelligence hourly gratifies. To this tendency of life and manners the literature and theatrical exhibitions of the country have conformed themselves. The invaluable works of our elder writers, I had almost said the works of Shakespear and Milton, are driven into neglect by frantic novels, sickly and stupid German Tragedies, and deluges of idle extravagant stories in verse. (*Lyrical Ballads* 177)

73. *The Dramatic Censor* [weekly] (January 11, 1800): 52–53.
74. *The Dramatic Censor* [weekly] (January 18, 1800): 53–54. Presumably, Dutton refers to Andrew Franklin, author of *The Embarkation*; Charles Dibdin,

songwriter and author of *The Deserter* and *Poor Vulcan*; George Colman the younger, manager of the Haymarket Theatre and author of *Blue-Beard, The Iron Chest*, and *Inkle and Yarico*; and Matthew "Monk" Lewis, author of the wildly popular *The Castle Spectre*. See Hogan, *The London Stage* part 5, volume 3 for specific performances of these plays.

75. In Dutton's criticism, when the language of consumption emerges, it is always accompanied by a sneer of derision. A review of Sheridan's *Pizarro* in the same week's issue implicates the audience's "infatuation (it deserves no other name)" for the play's "splendid spectacle," arguing, "as long as the town chooses to be *gulled* with repetition upon repetition, the manager may persist in physiking them, even to *nausea*." *The Dramatic Censor* [weekly] (January 11, 1800): 47.
76. *Theatrical Looker-On* [Birmingham] (May 10, 1823).
77. *Theatrical Looker-On* [Birmingham] (June 23, 1823).
78. *The Townsman* [Manchester] (December 23, 1803).
79. A look at the front pages alone of a number of late weeklies demonstrates their increasingly ornate presentation. See for example *The Opera Glass* (1826), *The Harlequin* (1829), and *The Columbine* (1829).
80. *The Dramatic Correspondent, and Amateur's Place Book* (July 26, 1828).
81. *Thalia's Tablet* [London] (December 8, 1821).
82. This subtitle was present on each issue's front page.
83. The titles of these journals alone indicate the influence of illegitimate modes of production: Harlequin and Columbine were prominent characters in unspoken pantomimes. See David Mayer, *Harlequin in His Element*.
84. Thomas Dutton, who had given up the weekly *Dramatic Censor* in mid-1800, returned in 1814 with a new journal. Tellingly, though he renewed his mission "to emancipate the stage from the tyranny, and sinister influence of News-paper-criticism," he did so with a monthly publication, *The Monthly Theatrical Reporter*.
85. *The Opera Glass* 1 (October 2, 1826): "Advertisement."
86. *The Opera Glass* 1 (October 2, 1826): "Advertisement."
87. *Opera Glass* 20 (February 10, 1827): 42.
88. *Theatrical Mince Pie* (January 1, 1825); *The Townsman* [Manchester] 2 (undated, December 1803).
89. *The Monthly Theatrical Reporter* (January 1815). For a discussion of the transformation of the crowd as a sign in other kinds of periodical literature, see Klancher, *The Making of English Reading Audiences* 76–97.
90. *The Opera Glass* (January 6, 1827): "Advertisement."
91. *The Hull Dramatic Censor*. Hull: W. S. Allen, 1827: "Preface."
92. "Preface," *The Examiner* 1 (January 3, 1808).
93. "Preface," *The Examiner* 1 (January 3, 1808).
94. Michael Eberle-Sinatra has argued similarly that the *News* criticisms "laid the foundation for many of [Hunt's] later views on drama and acting" (10).
95. "Prospectus," *The Examiner* 1 (January 3, 1808): 6.

96. As both Eberle-Sinatra (27) and Kucich and Cox (xxxvi) report, the *Examiner*'s circulation reached 2200 by late 1808 but spiked after 1809 to reach between 7000 and 8000 copies weekly in 1812. This popularity rivaled that of the *Edinburgh Review* (12,000) and the *Times* (8000), making it "as an organ of political and cultural commentary ... a key journal of its day" (Kucich and Cox xxxv).
97. Nicholas Roe offers a discussion of the largely positive reception of Hunt's *Critical Essays* (*Fiery Heart* 82–83).
98. Seen in this light, Hunt's later turn toward less obviously political topics after his release from prison in 1815 "is not a retreat from the public sphere but a fierce engagement in the culture wars of the day" (Kucich and Cox, "Introduction" l).
99. "Preface," *The Examiner* 1 (January 3, 1808).
100. "Theatrical Examiner, No. 57," *Examiner* 98 (November 12, 1809): 728.
101. This rhetorical self-presentation is, of course, similar to Defoe's a century earlier. But Hunt's candor does not occur within a scene of philosophical instruction such as that Defoe constructed in his *Review*. The relationship to the reader established by such familiarity is therefore quite different.
102. "On Periodical Essays," *Examiner* 1 (January 10, 1808).
103. Kevin Gilmartin has similarly asserted that the *Examiner* "aligned [Hunt] with a radical effort to resist specialization in periodical discourse, and recuperate a sphere of unalienated labor" (*Print Politics* 205). For a history of Hunt's editorship of the paper, see Blunden 3–122.
104. In Jon Klancher's assessment, the "*Examiner* formed a small audience of liberal reformers whom Hazlitt and Shelley addressed, a readership parallel to the radical artisan public" (*Making of English Reading Audiences* 101).
105. Hunt writes in his *Autobiography*: "Forty or fifty years ago, people of all times of life were much greater play-goers than they are now. They dined earlier; they had not so many newspapers, clubs, and piano-fortes; the French Revolution only tended at first to endear the nation to its own habits; it had not yet opened a thousand new channels of thought and interest; nor had railroads conspired to carry people, bodily as well as mentally, into as many analogous directions. Every thing was more concentrated, and the various classes of society felt a greater concern in the same amusements" (1. 162).

PART II
Theater and Late Romanticism

CHAPTER 3

Edmund Kean's Controversy

Edmund Kean was a creature of the nineteenth-century theatrical press, who in turn propelled new modes of theatrical experience following his London debut in 1814. Narrated, evaluated, and judged almost daily in newspapers and theatrical periodicals, the Regency actor's life on- and offstage challenged the boundaries with which editors and writers attempted to define their textual and discursive fields. Because he refused the illusion of rhetorical mastery embodied so effectively by his predecessor John Philip Kemble, Kean invited theatergoers to encounter the actor onstage – and the text he represented – in new ways.[1] Presenting a barrage of verbal and physical starts and stops, a pantomimic style that Coleridge compared to "reading Shakespeare by flashes of lighting," Kean's emotionally charged acting signaled his connection to London's illegitimate theaters and challenged the patent theaters' claims to exclusive guardianship of Britain's national drama.[2] No longer was drama in general and Shakespeare in particular a script for Kemble's senatorial oration or Garrick's bourgeois naturalism. Nor was the actor an authoritative voice transmitting the playwright's words to an audience who, despite their diverse class interests, could imagine themselves a unified community in the playhouse's idealized public space.[3] Rather, Kean was a harlequin from the provinces whose unmistakable class status and conspicuously vexed encounter with the written play-text emblematized the increasing uncertainty of theater's social function. The most visible and controversial figure in London theater for nearly two decades – a "metropolitan sensation" almost from the moment of his 1814 Drury Lane debut until his death in 1833 (Moody, *Illegitimate Theatre* 229) – Kean became the focus of an ongoing public discussion that moved through the era's shifting periodical channels, reshaping them as it went. His case is therefore exemplary for exploring how theatrical experience was imagined and narrated in print during the second half of the Romantic period.

In this chapter, I focus on public reaction to Kean's January 1825 trial for "criminal conversation" with Charlotte Cox, the wife of London city alderman Robert Albion Cox, and his return to the Drury Lane stage the following week. With a view toward the theatrical press described in Chapters 1 and 2, I argue that the publicity Kean generated not only in 1825 but throughout his career – what I am calling Kean's "controversy" – marked a radical shift in the constitution of theatrical celebrity and illustrated the changing nature of theatrical experience in Britain. Lawrence Klein has asserted that eighteenth-century consumer culture generated a sense, particularly among the middling and lower classes, that "identity is not an essence but rather a set of skills adapted to a range of environments." In such a condition "multiplicity and even inconsistency become the self's natural consistency" (377). Kean's departure from acting convention suggested in just this way a personality without internal consistency and offered spectators what Leigh Woods has called an "interpretive latitude" in assessing his performances (96). Such latitude in turn disconcerted reviewers who sought consistent evaluative standards to distinguish their voices from one another's in a competitive periodical field. If, as I note in Chapter 2, the subjectivity of the theatrical reviewer was typically gendered male, Kean's presence as an object of criticism challenged that privileged spectatorial position for both theatrical critic and reader. The presence of Mrs. Cox alongside Kean in both visual and narrative accounts of the 1825 trial associated Kean with an effeminized subject position and aligned his acting with a dangerously uncontrolled, which is to say feminine, sensibility. Kean embodied a kind of theatrical bad taste, a mobile, sexually ambiguous, working-class and even Cockney subject that threatened the "drive for virtuous independence" Harriet Guest sees characterizing masculine professionalism in the late eighteenth century (301). His acting style, and audience responses to it, refused to exhibit what Guest has called "the ability of consumers smoothly to assimilate the goods they purchase preserving their own personalities from becoming dissipated in the variety of objects they desire" (26). Responses to the 1825 trial – which included newspaper articles, journal reviews, court reports, literary travesties, and caricatures – display the British public's attempts to come to terms with how Kean presented destabilizing mobility as the *sine qua non* of theatrical experience.[4] Rather than merely illustrating how the publication of one man's private conduct altered the public's assessment of him, then, Kean's controversy reveals how changes in print culture – specifically the expansion of the theatrical press – reframed the conditions under which categories such as privacy and gender could be imagined at all.[5] Ostensibly a debate about sexual morality, press reaction to *Cox* v. *Kean* evinces more fundamentally how theatrical experience was transforming public life in Regency Britain.

In an insightful discussion of the institutional forces influencing Kean's late career, Jacky Bratton has argued that Kean played a crucial role in shaping how "the emergent modern self was literally as well as symbolically theatricalised" ("Celebrity" 90).[6] Caught between the decline of the patent theater system and the rise of newspaper-formed public opinion, Kean's fame was, according to Bratton, "the creation of middle-class esteem, and completely vulnerable to its withdrawal" (91). At the outset of Kean's career, *The Times* had lent the actor a measure of critical support. But in 1825, the paper and its editor, Thomas Barnes – once a theatrical critic for Leigh Hunt's *Examiner* – responded to *Cox* v. *Kean* with relentless attacks on Kean's moral character, even as the *Times* claimed to represent public opinion with the kind of generalized "objectivity" I describe in Chapter 1. *Cox* v. *Kean* elicited an outrage that, in Bratton's account, revealed theater's post-1809 decline as a civically unifying institution. Theatergoers who had in 1809 produced a nearly unanimous voice protesting Kemble's managerial and architectural changes to Covent Garden had by 1825 begun to fracture into discrete groups manifesting divergent class interests: "Between the O.P riots and the Cox vs. Kean affair the invocation of class antagonisms, the mishandling and ossification of ancient customary practices, the loss of consensus about cultural values, all harden and widen into fissures in the institution" (101). The *Times* attacks were, in Bratton's words, an attempt to bridge those fissures, enlisting theater as a tool in the newspaper's reconsolidation of "the hegemonic ascendancy of the newly self-aware British public" (92), which Kean's sexual indiscretions and overhasty return to the stage had brazenly challenged.

But the *Times* was far from the only periodical to pass judgment on Kean, nor was *Cox* v. *Kean* the actor's first, or last, controversy. As Bratton's attention to the newspaper suggests, the threat Kean posed was produced not simply by his actions with Mrs. Cox, nor even by the adultery trial itself, but also by theatergoers and members of the press who disputed among themselves the significance of those events. The moral authority to which the *Times* aspired in its 1825 condemnations of Kean, which Bratton rightly sees as the harbinger of an eventually triumphant Victorian Britishness, was still one attempt among many to shape the public's opinion of the actor.

The *Times* attacks elicited pointed replies from other periodicals, most notably the theatrical dailies. What is striking about the ongoing exchange between the *Times* and the publications I will discuss, though, is not simply the heated discussion about Kean himself, but the fiercely self-conscious debate the case prompted, first about the nature of public opinion and the press's role in shaping it and, second, about the relationship between private and public life that Kean's celebrity persona signified. Kean's role in *Cox v. Kean* was finally intolerable to his critics not only, or even most significantly, on moral grounds but because it revealed starkly the erosion between traditional notions of public performance and private authenticity that his performances had long been indicating. Itself a construction of London's great engines of print publicity, Kean's celebrity served in the 1825 affair as a conduit through which the most domestic of spaces – the lady's bedchamber – became public property. But the implicit challenge Kean posed to traditional notions of privacy had been on display in the way even his earliest performances resisted Kemble's regal masculine persona and the cultural authority it embodied. From the start of his London career, Kean offered himself as a creature of that larger public realm of exchanges and interactions where most of his audiences now lived and moved, a world presided over textually by the commercial press. Like his audiences, he emerged from a rapidly shifting life-world whose social boundaries and norms were increasingly difficult to define and within which gender and class had become more fluid concepts. With this in mind, the controversy surrounding *Cox* v. *Kean* takes on the qualities of what Kathleen Wilson has called "localized contests for power," the microhistories of which can illuminate how class and gender knowledge were formed (15).

If Kean's celebrity was primarily generated by his ability to elicit controversy, the question must be asked as to why he was so relentlessly and enduringly controversial. An answer can be gathered in part from the ways in which his offstage associations brought commercialism to bear on the sacralized texts of British drama, Shakespeare in particular. Several scholars, Jane Moody most notably, have described how Kean's acting altered the British understanding of Shakespeare by replacing Kemble's aristocratic characterizations with politically and socially "radical" interpretations.[7] I am interested here in extending that work to show how Kean's controversy – manifested by both his acting style and the discursive reactions it engendered – reimagined even more fundamentally the reading and theatergoing subject who encounters Shakespeare. Inasmuch as his stage technique revealed the actor as a subject born out of a turbulent collision between legitimate and illegitimate modes of theatrical representation, Kean challenged audience idealizations of the playtexts and playwrights he enacted. The 1825 contest to assign meaning to the actor mirrored the controversy that had been staged both in the press and more immediately in Drury Lane's house for many years, as partisan spectators translated their affection for or opposition to Kean's acting into vocal cultural evaluations. The vulnerability of his fame to the "withdrawal" of middle-class esteem therefore invites further examination, because with Kean esteem and derision were always inextricably linked. From one perspective, even, the outcry against him in 1825 can be viewed without hyperbole as adulation by other means: Kean's pillorying by the most powerful periodical in the city produced equally strident praise from many other corners of the press. Certainly public reaction to *Cox* v. *Kean* extended the concerns of 1809 to comprise, in Bratton's words, a debate over "the patent, and the special, publicly owned space created by the patent" (93). But more was at stake: while newspapers initially followed expected partisan lines in their attitudes toward the case, with the *Times* attacking Kean and the *Morning Chronicle* defending him, debate shifted rapidly to focus on the unsettling power the commercial press was developing to shape the nation's social and cultural values. Kean's voice and body emblematized this debate on stage, presenting by night and eliciting by day a distinctly British crisis that reverberated far beyond the theater itself.

What I aim to show by exploring the range of press reactions to Kean is that the modern, metropolitan subject he embodied and helped create was in fact defined by its ability to elicit just such a contradictory response. The Keanian persona, that is, was born from and defined itself as a *subject of controversy*, constantly eliciting intense discussion about its own nature and significance, and revealing in the process the impossibility of imagining a wholly unified British public or British cultural tradition. Seizing the stage as a forum for a personal, literally "controversial," encounter with the words of the playtext, Kean's earliest Drury Lane performances anticipated the print response he would receive in reviews and, ultimately, as a result of *Cox* v. *Kean*. The integral private self that both Kean's attackers and defenders posited for him – by turns depraved or heroic – was a construct designed to seal off a more dangerous possibility: Kean could not be assigned permanently to either condition. Such indeterminacy made him an exemplary object of, and catalyst for, discussion in the contemporary periodical field. Kean's celebrity therefore has broader implications not only for how we understand Romantic-period theater and print culture but also for how we might rethink the era's theatrical experience as a whole – and with it the writing of prose and poetry in

Romanticism's second generation. For Hazlitt, Keats, and other writers whose careers developed in the shadows of London's Regency theaters, Kean's case – a case that culminated with the publicity surrounding *Cox v. Kean* but which began as early as his first performances – modeled radical changes in the way that a private individual could imagine himself in relation, or more accurately could be imagined as a relation, to Britain's public world. Signifying a subject relentlessly open to and constructed by theatrical experience, Kean enabled the remaking of Romantic writing.

I Criminalizing Shakespeare

In the winter of 1825, John Fairburn of Ludgate Hill published a seventy-six-page quarto-sized volume, the title matter of which read as follows:

> *Cox versus Kean.* **Fairburn's Edition** of the **TRIAL** between Robert Albion Cox, Esq. and Edmund Kean, Defendant, for Criminal Conversation With the Plaintiff's Wife, including the *Evidence, Speeches of Counsel* and all the Curious Love Letters, &c. &c. *Tried in the Court of King's Bench, Guildhall, January the 17th, 1825, before the Lord Chief Justice Abbott and a Special Jury* to which is added A MEMOIR containing ECCENTRIC ANECDOTES Of the Defendant in the Case, and also of LITTLE BREECHES.

An epigraph at the bottom of the page provided a quote from those "curious love letters": "'I will hold my darling in my heart, and sleep in spite of thunder' – KEAN." Turning the leaf, readers found on the verso an advertisement for a slightly less exalted volume, also published by Fairburn: "***Cox and Cuckoldum!!!*** This day is published, in Demy Octavo, price Threepence, ORIGINAL SONGS ON KEEN, COCKS, and LITTLE BREECHES, containing" such favorites as "An Alderman's Wife, she bother'd me so," "The old Cocks, the Keen Bantam Cock, or the Frail Hen," "Avoid Crim.Con.; or Keen, Cocks, and Little Breeches," and "Keen's Consolation for his Friend Cocks on the Loss of his Charlotte." The song list is followed by the words of Lear:

> Blow winds and crack your cheeks,
> Rage, blow – your cataracts and hurricanes spout,
> Till ye have drench'd the steeples,
> drown'd the cocks   – SHAKESPEARE

On the facing page appeared yet another advertisement for a "New Caricature. Keen-ish Sport in Cox's Court!!: or Symptoms of Crim.Con in Drury Lane."

1   Criminalizing Shakespeare

The case to which all of these publications attended was another in a string of "criminal conversation" trials that had inundated the courts since the middle of the eighteenth century.[8] "Criminal conversation," the legal term for the seduction of a married woman, could bring substantial damages; Alderman Robert Cox sought £2000 from Edmund Kean as compensation for Kean's adulterous affair with Cox's wife.[9] These trials, in which a typical defense was to argue the husband's complicity in his wife's violation – turning him into a bawd – were easy fodder for newspapers eager to provide readers with sensational stories.[10] As Elizabeth Fay has shown, though, "crim con" trials were also publicized by quickly produced tracts whose narratives intermixed "literal" reports of argument and summation with "dramatic" renderings of witness testimony (408).[11] For Fay, who is concerned with Mary Robinson's autobiographical defense against continual charges of sexual impropriety, criminal conversation narratives were a particularly powerful tool limiting the subject positions available to women in the late eighteenth and early nineteenth centuries. Just as the woman's adulterous body becomes in the court case a violated legal property for which the husband can be awarded damages, so the woman's public – and in Robinson's instance authorial – identity becomes the site of a discursive contest over moral value systems. For a woman implicated in criminal conversation, to publish was to "implicitly accept the charge of impropriety" (399), because by violating the confines of the domestic sphere the female subject engaged in yet another kind of illegitimate behavior. Robinson's attempts to influence the public determination of her character were therefore destined to fail, read inevitably and always "through the lens of scandalous gossip" that elicited them in the first place (420).

Failure, though, is in the eye of the beholder. As Michael Gamer and Terry Robinson's account of Mary Robinson's public career in the 1780s shows, her cultivation of, even curacy of, fashionable talk and gossip was a powerful means to combat such silencing.[12] Robinson's defiant self-fashioning thus provides a compelling precursor to Kean's position at the center of one of the Romantic period's most famous criminal conversation trials. For if Robinson was in some way silenced by her gender – her exonerating publicity made impossible by virtue of the subject position she as woman inhabited – Kean's typical method of self-publication, the talent for which he had become famous, *depended* on his lack of a stable personal identity. Neither Robinson nor Kean could embody the authoritative subjectivity necessary to redeem themselves morally in public discussion.[13] Yet Robinson's ongoing ability to remain an object of public fascination, which included but was not restricted to her published counterattacks, presented their author as a public agent who, like the "accomplished" women Ann Bermingham describes, demonstrated skills to "mitigate [the] brazen solicitation of vulgar gazing" that woman's public presence elicited ("Elegant Females" 489). Seeking a reading audience for herself, Robinson indicted the idealized notion of a public sphere constituted only by genderless, ideologically neutral subjects.[14] By contrast, Kean rarely makes any attempt to speak for himself and as such embodies even more purely than Robinson a subject made by the theatrical celebrity the periodical press provided. At least in the minds of the audience, "Kean" was constructed first at the violent point of contact between actor and script and then by the critics' published evaluation of his performance. He therefore became a dangerous subject whose variable personae – generated by but not restricted to the stage – challenged even more fundamentally than Robinson's the ways in which gender and class could be used to limit individual identities and, consequently, to constitute public communities.

The Fairburn volume resists the explicit moralizing Fay finds in many criminal conversation accounts of the time, instead relying on a pretense of journalistic integrity to evaluate Kean's character. Suggesting that its recounting of the trial is not driven by voyeuristic desire, or even a concern for public morality, the narrative assumes a reporterly authority that ostensibly transcends sensationalism. However, with language that evokes both the constructed objectivity that characterizes early-nineteenth-century newspapers, as well as the self-conscious connoisseurship found in theatrical periodicals, the author's negotiation of competing informational discourses quickly becomes evident:

> Trial for Crim Con
> Cox versus Kean

> *Court of King's Bench, Guildhall, Jan 17th, 1825*

> The powerful interest excited by this extraordinary case was beyond all precedent; and it being generally understood that it would be brought forward on Monday last, at an early hour in the morning crowds began to assemble adjacent to the court where the trial was to be heard, and among them were observed several members of the theatrical profession. As soon as the doors were opened, a rush was made, and the body of the court nearly filled, when the doorkeepers had a difficult task in their duty, by keeping out those who attended merely out of curiosity; and in the performance of which they were obliged to put up with the impertinent threats of students, who never studied the law, *reporters* who never reported, and witnesses who never gave evidence; and it being impossible for them to be acquainted with

1 Criminalizing Shakespeare 117

all, many unprivileged persons gained excellent situations, while others, who were actually engaged to perform their important duties for the press, &c. found it impossible to obtain convenient places in the court for the purposes of hearing evidence. Prior to the commencement of the trial, Messrs. Elliston, Cooper, Hughes, and several other actors, took their seats, and we also noticed many persons of distinction in the court.

The correspondent authorizes himself as a professional both explicitly – presumably he is one of those "actually engaged to perform their important duties for the press" – and implicitly through the narrative's reporterly diction. Duly noting the presence of some of London's most significant theatrical personages, the report then recounts testimony and evidence, including love letters between Kean and Mrs. Cox that had been read into the court record. Like the accounts of the *Times* I will discuss shortly, the narrative encases the sensational in a reporterly guise, appealing to both readers' taste for dramatic scandal and their desire to distinguish themselves as dispassionate consumers of information.

Though it was by no means the only narrative published in the weeks that followed the January 1825 decision against Kean, Fairburn's *Cox v. Kean* is audacious in presenting its putatively objective narrative as one component of an otherwise entirely sensationalized approach to the trial. With an allusive conflation of literature and news, the edition's opening pages not only represent a wide range of textual reactions to Kean's conduct; they also suggest the deleterious cultural consequences the affair might produce. Even before the trial account begins, Kean's infamy has transformed high Shakespearean tragedy into low comic device. Macbeth's claim that he will rid himself of MacDuff and "sleep in spite of thunder" and Lear's ranting from the heath would have been well known to Fairburn's audience, yet both passages are altered and associated with degraded sexuality: Macbeth's tragic defiance becomes an expression of illicit love, while Lear's sympathetic "our steeples" and "our cocks" become the sexually evocative "*the* steeples" and "*the* cocks." These misquotations exemplify one form of cultural appropriation Jonathan Bate has described occurring frequently in the Romantic period, during which Shakespeare's words and symbolic figure became tools in an ideological contest to determine Britain's social and cultural values.[15] Here, though, the appropriation is commercial before it is political: the poet's lines are transformed into an advertising tag amid other ads for bawdy songs and caricatures. Given in this context, which contrasts vividly with the seriousness of the tragic scenes from which they are taken, the quotations can be recognized by the reader as illegitimate appropriations – that is, as incomplete or in bad taste. More than indicating Shakespeare's criminalization, the lines' illegitimacy produces a comic effect designed to sell publications: Kean has deprived Shakespeare of his rightful cultural context, but the publisher and reader can distance themselves from that transgression through the derisive laughter Fairburn's account elicits.

Because the Fairburn volume's bowdlerized Shakespearian epigraph is attributed to Kean's love letters, it recalls – along with the advertisement's travesty of *Lear* – Kean's practice of quoting Shakespeare when writing to Mrs. Cox. First published as part of the *Times* report on the trial on January 18, 1825, the letters between the two are rife with Shakespearean diction and allusion. One letter purportedly written while Kean was in America offers Hamlet's doggerel verses as an affectionate conclusion: "Doubt that the stars are fire,/Doubt that the sun doth move,/Doubt truth to be a liar,/But never doubt I love." (That the address has the apparently unironic intention of putting Charlotte in the position of Ophelia further heightens the reader's sense of the lines' misappropriation.) These stolen Shakespearean verses in turn served as the epigraph for other trial-related publications, most notably *The Poetic Epistles of Edmund*, one of many republications of the letters.[16] In letters attributed to Mrs. Cox by Reed's Cheap Edition of *Secrets Worth Knowing: Suppressed Letters Cox v. Kean*, Kean's paramour reinforced his Shakespearean self-identification, calling him a "crook-back'd tyrant" whose body compares favorably with "the heap of senseless clay that lay by my side," and later urging him to express his love forcefully: "Let Richard be himself again – in love, as well as in war, strike deep."[17] Whether or not these letters are authentic is beside the point: their publication reflects the prevailing sense that quotation from (and indeed identification with) Shakespeare had become in the relationship a tool of mutual seduction. After echoing Juliet's "Three words, dear Romeo, and good night indeed" in another letter, Mrs. Cox acknowledges as much: "Have I not read Shakespeare, with some purpose, to write thus; I have changed a few words, 'tis true, they suit my humour best." Between the two lovers, reading the national poet's work is accomplished always with an eye toward its future bawdy uses.

Most of the anti-Kean publicity surrounding the trial seized on the case's lurid details to suggest that Kean's immoral conduct and his misappropriation of Shakespeare made him unfit to embody Shakespearean characters. The *Epistles of Edmund* volume concludes with a poem that asks:

> – Who dares insult the name of Shakespeare?
> Who is the Mortal that, with tongue profane,
> Deeply polluted by disgraceful vice,
> Would speak the nervous language of the page
> Where Avon's bard, with Nature's glowing pen,
> Recorded all the feelings of his heart
> And all the breathings of his mighty mind?
> O let not him whose dark degraded soul
> Delights in profligate and impious deeds
> Of lawless Passion, e'er presume to tread
> The Stage once honor'd by the Bard himself! (1–11)

This is a typical condemnation, but the attack then takes a step beyond the age-old critique of actors' low morals. In stark contrast to Shakespeare's "glowing pen," which contains no artifice in recording "all the feelings of his heart," Kean's "outward show of grace" is a dissemblance that lacks "the inward fire,/The inward glow, that Nature gives to him/Whose conscious virtue pacifies his mind" (*Epistles* 46–47). Kean's illegitimate acting – physical and vocal movement governed by passionate, seemingly spontaneous displays of feeling – is generated by the same "lawless passion" that drives Kean to dishonor Mrs. Cox. According to the poet's logic, Kean should be barred from enacting Shakespeare not simply because he is an immoral man but because his acting takes its source from, and evokes, illegitimate desire.

A miscellany of report, review, and satire, Fairburn's account of *Cox v. Kean* stands at the center of a field of theatrical publicity that by 1825 was composed of everything from newspaper reviews to literary travesties. Evoking larger questions about the relationship between the actor's private life and his public role on the national stage, the volume's first few pages vividly display various logics of allusion and intertextuality that mix factual reporting, advertising, and satiric caricature. The edition therefore necessarily speaks to the wider field of which it is a part, its signifying gestures only made possible by the conflicted and disputatious theatrical press then thriving in the city. The trial elicited responses from different corners of that field: trial accounts and theatrical reviews published in the *Times* were countered by stinging rebukes of the paper in the *Theatrical Observer*, London's most prominent theatrical daily. Considering these publications together, I aim to show that the breakdown of barriers between high and low, public and private that Fairburn's text represents for comic effect was in fact the fundamental condition of theatrical experience in the late Romantic period. What was at stake in the *Cox* v. *Kean* debate was not simply the social role of the patent theatres or even the constitution of a public Shakespeare, but the changing understanding of how theatrical performance, and more pointedly public writing about theatrical performance, could reshape the imagination of personal identity.

II A New Short Cut to Sublimity

A brief consideration of reviews from earlier in Kean's career confirms that the attacks of 1825 were extending long-existing fears about the social implications of his acting. From January 1814, when he debuted in the role of Shylock at Drury Lane, Kean's departure from typical patent house acting challenged the sufficiency of conventional critical vocabularies. He was an actor who imagined a new idea of intimacy both between himself and the playtext and between himself and his spectators. An 1822 review of Kean's Henry VIII reveals the endurance of this effect through the actor's first seven years at Drury Lane, remarking that "this singular being is always turning to naught the most grounded expectations, succeeding and failing on principles that are not easily understood."[18] Kean's contradiction of established tradition registered with some, William Hazlitt not least, as a politically radical indictment of the aristocratic personae Kemble and his contemporaries had envisaged with their characters.[19] As Tracy Davis has shown, the perception of Kean's radicalism was likely enhanced because his eschewal of Kemble's monumental gestures and swelling oration made him an actor best seen close up – that is, from the pit frequented by lower classes of theatergoers. Kean's voice, by most accounts far weaker than Kemble's, would not have easily reached those sitting in the more distant boxes or the upper reaches of Drury Lane's vast house.[20] But architectural and technical conditions were not the only factors shaping how Kean's celebrity transformed British theatrical experience. Beyond the house, the theatrical press created and shaped Kean's public figure, continually considering his performances in light of his offstage life even as his appearances in London society became extensions of his roles.[21] While the major actors of the previous century, David Garrick most notably, were certainly objects of popular interest, the engines of publicity with which they contended were neither as vast nor as complex as those operating in Kean's day. Because theatergoers would simply not have had as much information about the private lives of their stars, for Garrick or even Kemble and Sarah Siddons, the stage was still the primary avenue from which their celebrity issued. They were known first as actors, and their private actions were for the most part considered only through that lens. By the time Kean debuted in 1814, the commercial press had begun to dismantle that practice in ways his case would highlight. As the first celebrity actor to emerge in the post-1809 theatrical world, Kean was both the product of and the test case for a press that had become increasingly interested in treating a night at the theater as a newsworthy public event. Kean's offstage behavior and political associations were of continual interest for their own sake, but also because they were the background against which his dramatic characterizations could be understood. Similarly, because his controversial performance style catered to readers' craving for extraordinary incident, reviews were influenced by Kean's status as an object in the daily exchanges of information and goods that newspapers such as the *Times* enabled. Thomas Crochunis has suggested astutely that onstage "Kean does not serve the play, but exploits its central character's differences from his public persona" ("Radical Acting"). Yet the relation Crochunis imagines need not only be one of difference. Bouts of public drunkenness, association with fans in a raucous group called the "Wolves Club," the alleged overturning of his chaise in the early morning hours resulting in a dislocated shoulder and cancelled appearance: these were typical accounts that informed how Kean's performances would be assessed.[22] Devoid of established character, a subject whose increasingly transparent offstage existence was evoked by his acting, Kean's performances were exercises in a kind of self-publicity that would have been inconceivable even a decade before his debut.

Many early reviews noted Kean's small stature and weak voice – measuring him against the strengths of Kemble, his most prominent predecessor, and marking him as an actor who could not have reached the patent stage but for his success as an illegitimate pantomimist. In contrast to Kemble's steadiness, Kean's embodiment of characters' psychological states seemed to lack a consistency that traditional reviewers found reassuring. As Leigh Woods has suggested, "Kean's acting carried implications most commentators found disturbing, particularly when it challenged prevailing notions of personality as cohesive and tragic characterization as dignified and sustained" (77–78). The most famous of these critics was, of course, Coleridge, who in his 1817 *Biographia Literaria* found in Kean's enactment of Charles Maturin's *Bertram* an example of degraded, overly sensational modern tragedy.[23] But periodical reviewers had anticipated Coleridge's position in the years leading up to the *Biographia*. An April 1815 review of Kean's Richard II refers to the actor's "feebleness – his want of great powers, and of that easy energy which accompanies them" and chastens him for "his attempts to supply this deficiency by bustling violence and fidgety activity – his excessive fondness for petty contrasts." While some critics saw Kean's energetic style as evidence of his originality, this early assessment goes on to argue that he uses sensation to hide the fact that he cannot act properly:

> A remark of a Brother Critic most particularly falls in with our idea of Mr. KEAN's acting. "It is to be estimated according to the number of *hits* he makes; for he has no general truth and purity of style." This is precisely the case. It is a piece of patch-work; of various contrasted colours, producing a good deal of effect: but there is no pervading harmony – no relieving back ground. As we have said before, it is all in the petty and the detail. It is by hits and points and little contrasts, that Mr. KEAN supplies the place of bold employing and powerful expression, And many of the noblest passages of Shakespeare he converts in something neat and pointed and epigrammatic, which, if it was not for the egregious affront to good taste, we would certainly admire, as we do the feats of the Indian Jugglers, or any other kind of manual dexterity.[24]

Equating Kean to a street performer, the reviewer reduces his acting to little more than an athletic achievement lacking in real thought or aesthetic judgment. Shakespeare becomes a ball thrown into the air by a circus performer, transformed by Kean into an object of casual delight that has no real substance. Another review of Kean's Shylock found similar weaknesses in Kean's "judgment," arguing that "Mr. Kean has too much of the school boy rant in his principal speeches – in endeavoring to give effect to them, his voice rises and falls in a manner which, not merely renders his efforts unsuccessful, but goes to the extent of depriving his audience of comprehending what he says."[25] And an October 1815 review criticized Kean's "vulgar conception" of Richard III's character, whose "body and soul are wound up to one intense occupation ... Not so Mr. Kean: in him we in vain look for any unity of purpose – this absorption of intellect – this self-wrapped abstraction – He bustles about the attainment of his golden prize with a considerable degree of confused activity."[26]

Even supporters expressed concerns about how Kean's characterizations undermined stable notions of personal identity. The liberal *Champion* defended Kean's impersonation of Richard III, arguing that despite the fact that "his person ... is small," his depiction of Richard's variability revealed that the actor "has thought for himself, and discovered that the common practice" of presenting a singularly focused Richard "is wrong." But its consideration of his Othello offered only qualified enthusiasm, noting, "Those characters whose leading features are uniform though lofty ... who are too impetuous in their feelings to use finesse, and too grand in their thoughts to be pointed in their expressions – those are the characters in which Mr. Kean must appear to last advantage."[27] The *Chronicle*, similarly, praised Kean's Hamlet "in the easy, natural conversations of life, such as the scenes with Horatio and the players" but found that "even here, though he has much graceful action ... he wants a dignity which is necessary to complete the fascination of Hamlet's exalted character ... an easy, habitual dignity of deportment." Vested in physical sensation as Kean's acting was, it lacked "some external symbol of the noble lofty spirit which animates the frame of Hamlet."[28] Hazlitt, too, notes Kean's lack of consistently noble qualities in his famous review of Kean's Coriolanus, though as I discuss in the next chapter, Hazlitt will turn the class distinction on its head by interrogating how Kean's portrayal questioned readers' own class sympathies. The point here is that both positive and negative reviews implied that Kean's changeability did violence to the playtext's construction of unified characters. Still, we can take this intensity to indicate not weakness but rather a refusal to suspend his private self or subordinate it to the rhetorical unity of the passages he was uttering. By using his new kind of public celebrity as a tool in shaping the reception of his performances, Kean became the first British actor to embody what Joseph Roach has called "public intimacy" (15). Primarily the product of a filmic age and the advent of the close-up, a star actor's reception is for Roach invariably predicated upon the audience's knowledge of the details of an actor's private life. Personal faults and failings – what Roach calls "stigmata" – paradoxically bolster the actor's appeal – "charismata" – in a given character because audiences can identify with that character more readily. Performance becomes a representation of the star's human encounter with the part, an embodiment that, even as it transcends everyday experience, both is and is not "him."

Kean's mode of self-representation raised serious concerns about how a publicly intimate star might alter the reception of the cultural texts he enacted onstage. An 1815 review of Kean's Macbeth expresses explicitly the potential danger of his approach:

> Mr. Kean is always a step below Shakespeare – He never rises to the full rich sublimity of his conceptions; but he is a sort of go-between – a kind of mediating chorus between the Poet and the Audience, who compromises the dignity of the former, to make all plain and smooth, and levelled to the meanest capacity. In short, it seems that his object is to familiarize *Macbeth*, as he did *Richard*, with the homespun feelings of every man in the Pit and Gallery; and these gentlemen, many of whom from the

> deficiencies we specified, had probably found themselves unable completely to fathom some of the sublime mysterious depths of the Poet, rejoice to find in Mr. Kean a man who unlocks an undiscovered door, and thereby opens a new short cut to sublimity, so smooth, so easy, so practicable, that they begin to wonder they never entered into Shakespeare before ... The excellence of the actor is in raising his audience to the height of the Poet's conception, not in debasing the Poet to the level of ordinary every day feelings of common minds, which it is the very business of scenic delusion to dispel.[29]

The reviewer claims that Kean's "short cut to sublimity" is an attempt to evacuate theater's long-standing social role in favor a politically suspect imaginative enfranchisement of the lower orders. Compromised as they are by Kean's worldly style, theater's "scenic delusions" can no longer provide an aesthetic antidote to the "business" of everyday life. Made "so smooth, so easy, so practicable," Shakespeare becomes a consumer's delight. A slightly later review of Kean's Timon, from November 1816, complains in the same way that Kean "never rises to Shakespeare, but he pulls Shakespeare down to him. Shakespeare, passing through Mr. Kean's medium, comes out so unlike himself, that we are puzzled to know him again."[30] Kean's shifts between various psychological states indicated the irreducibility of the historical moment in which the performance was taking place by reminding spectators of his illegitimate celebrity and of the theatrical and press institutions that had produced it. By emphasizing rather than eliding these connections, Kean threatened to puncture the idealized rendering of Britain's national poet that the patent theaters cultivated, and that critics such as Charles Lamb sought to commit to the private experience of solitary readers ("On the Tragedies"). Embodied as he is, Kean's "*Timon* is no longer *Timon* of Athens. He is *Timon* of Drury-lane, – of the new school of 1816, – bustling, fidgety, tricky, sneering, pedantic, quaint, full of quiddits and conceits."

Far from limiting his engagement with the Shakespearean text in its fullness, as critics often claimed, Kean's acting posited that theatrical experience could become a means to imagine a different kind of human personality.[31] Tracy Davis has argued, for example, that "Kean's galvanizing physicality constituted a new distinctly masculinized school of acting" (937). But the *Cox* v. *Kean* furor would highlight in Kean something closer to the threatening "sexual contradictariness" Peter Holland finds over a century later in Laurence Olivier. The ultimate effect of Kean's publicly intimate acting style was to undercut traditional notions of masculine authority, replacing them with a sexually dangerous subject that, as Jeffrey Kahan has noted, had politically revolutionary, even French, associations.[32] The publicity surrounding the trial merely imagined Kean more widely as his acting had already done: he was a conduit through which the realms of private and public experience could conspicuously and continually achieve uninterrupted contact. Even as Kean's publicized transgression with Mrs. Cox dismantled imagined boundaries that had long enabled the domestic and sexual privileges of bourgeois privacy, it also prevented the theatrical establishment from maintaining the illusion that the patent theaters were an ideal public space where the business of that daily life could be transcended.

Visual representations of Kean in 1825 illustrate the ways in which his star power had begun to threaten these assumptions. In caricatures and illustrative plates, even those that purport to represent Kean in his private capacity, he is almost always pictured in the theatrical costume of his most prominent role, Richard III. The most famous early example of this was published four months after his debut, in May 1814, and pictures a crookback'd Kean supporting the Drury Lane edifice on his shoulders while standing on a book labeled "Shakespeare." As Jane Moody has discussed, the plate illustrates both Kean's commercial associations and the manner in which they shaped the popular reception of Shakespeare. By the time of *Cox* v. *Kean*, it is difficult to find a visual representation of Kean out of costume. The George Cruikshank caricature advertised in the Fairburn's edition, "Keen-ish Sport in Cox's Court!!: or Symptoms of Crim.Con. in Drury Lane" presents a costumed Kean whose commercialization of the theater has extended its influence to the most intimate of human experiences (Figure 3). While Mrs. Cox sits on a couch in Kean's dressing room with the actor on her lap, a horned Cox looks on through the window, holding a letter from Kean advising Cox to keep a "<u>Keen</u> eye on your wife" as he cries "Fire! Fury! and *Gold Dust!!!* What do I see? K – kissing my wife! – My Head swims, and my *Horns* stand erect!! – But, Damages, Damages, damme!!" Kean's reply to Charlotte's "O Romeo, I would thy love were as pure as the driven snow" seems as much a response to Cox's exclamation as to his mistress's advances: "By Heaven 'tis as pure as ever lover felt in the parlour of Drury, pure as refined Gold, as ever was seen in Great or Little Britain, dearest Juliet!" Here the exchange of affection carries the taint of commercialism, and the position of the lovers, with the man seated on the woman's lap, suggests Kean's disregard for traditional gender roles.[33]

Another caricature, "The Court of King's Bench turn'd into a Cock pit, or 800 Symptoms of Kean Sport" depicts even more vividly the ways in

Figure 3: George Cruikshank, *Keen-ish Sport in Cox's Court!!: or Symptoms of Crim.Con. in Drury Lane* (1824)

Figure 4: *The Court of King's Bench turn'd into a Cock pit, or 800 Symptoms of Kean Sport* (1825)

II   *A New Short Cut to Sublimity* 127

Figure 5: *Mr. Kean as Richard The IIIrd, Act 5th, Scene 4th*

which treatment of the trial was influenced by Kean's theatricality. Kean is pictured as a prostrate Richard, lying before the court bench in an almost identical pose to that which he assumed during his death scene in the play (Figures 4 and 5). As a scantily clad Charlotte and five court magistrates look on, the cuckolded Cox stands over Kean, exulting in his victory and promising to "hasten home/And assay the purity of that Gold/This day hath drawn reluctant from thy purse." He castigates Kean in Shakespearean terms: "Croak on Prostrate Richard, or rise if thou wilt,/ For now I have branded the [sic] th'ungrateful guest/And never more shall thou in triumph cry/Richards himself again! Go storm and fret/Thy brief hour on the stage!" Kean's defiant response to Cox is a version of Richard's final speech, which he would have delivered hundreds of times at Drury Lane.[34] But Kean also counters Cox's jumbled echo of Richmond and Macbeth with a satiric allusion to *As You Like It*, turning the world into a stage for his irrepressible self-fashioning:

> Perdition catch thy arm! the chance is thine!
> But oh! The vast renown thou hast acquired
> In conquering Edmund does afflict him more
> Than even did Charlotte's mutation in love.
> Now, let the world in future be my Stage,
> To feed lewd vengeance in a lingering act:
> And let one Spirit of this first born lust
> Reign in all bosoms: that each heart being set
> On Crim Con actions, the rude scene may end,
> And lawyers be the burier of the dead!

While Cox consorts with his gold and retires into damaged domesticity, presumably without the love of his unfaithful wife, Kean goes beyond the stage and courtroom into "the world," spreading the moral contagion of "lewd vengeance" and "lust." That he does so in a Shakespearean mode suggests again that the actor's private conduct has compromised his public role as a cultural ambassador.

Nor was it only Kean's opponents or those who sought to mock him who relied on the image of Kean's onstage roles to communicate their positions. Not to miss a trick, Fairburn published a pro-Kean caricature entitled "The Hostile Press; and the consequences of Crim. Con or Shakespeare in danger" (Figure 6). The plate depicts Kean standing on stage holding a volume of Shakespeare's plays in one hand and an unsheathed sword in the other as he is stalked by fire-breathing serpents named "Old Times" and "New Times" that breathe out "Gall, Spite, Venom, Hypocrisy, Cant, Envy, Slander, and Malice." Recalling and inverting the critique of the 1814 Cruikshank caricature, which satirizes Drury Lane's commercial reliance on Kean, "The Hostile Press" fashions Kean as the defender of a culture the press has profaned by refusing to allow him to act in his public capacity.[35] As with textual accounts of Kean, these

Figure 6: R. Cruikshank *The Hostile Press; and the Consequences of Crim.Con or Shakespeare in danger* (1825)

depictions conflate theatrical, civil, and domestic spaces. Kean is shown time and again as a man whose private character cannot be considered apart from his public role as a Shakespearean actor. He transforms the court into a theater, the theater into a court; the actor's dressing room becomes a bedroom, and the bedroom a scene for public display. Following *Cox* v. *Kean*, outraged critics imagined Kean wearing his theatrical garb everywhere, it seems, except the legitimate stage. Chief among those critics was the *Times* that, for all its own reshaping of privacy as a function of the commercial world, could not abide Kean's brazen embodiment of that growing reality.

III The *Times*'s Kean

Daily commercial newspapers were the catalysts of the *Cox* v. *Kean* debate, and it is to them that most other representations of the trial explicitly responded. In this contest about cultural values, as in many others in the Romantic period, the *Times* played a central role. Its attacks on Kean titillated a commercial readership even as the paper cloaked itself in outrage over Kean's conduct, setting the tone for a blitz of publicity that endured well into the winter's theatrical season. From the outset, the stakes were higher than simply Kean's reputation. Jacky Bratton has described Thomas Barnes's employment of "a discourse of sexual purity" to defend the female modesty Kean's transgressions had threatened, concluding, "The Cox/Kean affair and *The Times'* construction of it could be said to mark the end of ... a pragmatically open view of the sex trade in the theatre" ("Celebrity" 99). But there is an added dimension to the debate that becomes clearer when the *Times* reviews are considered in the context of London's wider theatrical press. As Fairburn's *Cox* v. *Kean* illustrates, the nature of the case – in which theatrical, informational, intimate, and legal discourses intersected – elicited trial accounts that likewise employed all of these genres. This was particularly true for the city's commercial dailies, which sought to attract the largest number of readers with their wide-ranging approach to the day's events. On January 18, the *Times* published a report of more than twenty thousand words on the *Cox* v. *Kean* court proceedings. Commenting briefly on "the curiosity excited by this case," the report begins with a prelude much like that found in the Fairburn edition: "Soon after the opening of the doors, the spacious area was crowded, and many who were enabled to obtain admission to the places set apart for attornies and counsel filled them. At half-past nine precisely, the Lord Chief Justice took his seat, and the case was called on for trial." The account then shifts rapidly into the kind of indirect narrative style typical of parliamentary reporting I describe in Chapter 1. While retaining a third-person address, the reporter communicates the trial participants' words without employing explicit quotations. This technique positions the reader as an eyewitness to the speeches being delivered:

> The Common Sergeant then addressed the jury. It was his painful duty to bring before their attention that inquiry for which the plaintiff sought redress at their hands: and when he had done so, and established these facts in evidence, he was sure they would be of opinion that of all the cases of this nature of which they had ever heard, this was one most destitute of excuse and most aggravated by the violation of a long and steady friendship.

The ensuing narrative occupies more than half of the paper's space – nine of its sixteen columns. Where the Fairburn edition could revel in its miscellaneous nature, the *Times* evinces the pressure the case exerts on its claim to represent an ideologically neutral public opinion. Describing the cross-examination of Alice Humber, a servant who testified about Kean's illicit presence in the Cox home, the account shifts instantly out of the indirect style found in the previous passage to a more removed informational commentary:

> Cross examined by Mr. Scarlett. – I live with Mr. Cox now. At the time of these affairs, I was a servant of all work ... Eight years ago my master and mistress went with Mr. Kean to Tamworth –
> Here the noise, which had been for some time increasing in this gallery, and which exactly resembled that of an over-crowded pit of the theatre, became so great, that it was impossible for the witness or the counsel to be heard.

Encouraging spectatorial distance, the interjectory voice ("Here the noise ... ") attempts to achieve a dispassionate authority that the reenactment of the trial's speechmaking had destabilized for the sake of sensation. This oscillation between report and commentary requires a shifting orientation toward the reported events, asking readers to imagine themselves at once in the position of Alice Humber and of the reporter who attends to the events of the wider courtroom.

Courting the reader's contradictory alliances, this interarticulation of informational discourses also provides a dramatic frame for the most sensational aspect of the *Times* account: twenty-two love letters that were read into evidence by the prosecution, which the paper published verbatim. Because they displayed Kean's variable emotional states and his relentless duplicity in arranging secret meetings between the lovers, the letters stood out from the rest of the narrative so vividly that they were excerpted and republished independently in numerous cheap editions. They became, in a way, the story of the trial. Chief among these were the "Twin Letters" sent to Mr. and to Mrs. Cox simultaneously but under separate cover. They are worth quoting in full as the *Times* published them:

> (Post mark) Exeter, Jan. 6, 1823

> Dear little imprudent girl – Your incantation has been very near bringing our acquaintance to the most lamentable crisis: of course he will show you the letter I have written him; appear to countenance it, and let him think we are never to meet again, and in so doing he has lost a friend: leave all further arrangements to me. My aunt desires her best wishes to you, notwithstanding her anger, she says, of your conduct before him. Love shields the object of its wishes, not exposes it. All shall be shortly as you wish.
>
> Mrs. Simpson care of Mrs. Matthews, 12, Tavistock-row

Covent-garden, London

(Post mark) Exeter, Jan. 6, 1823

My dear Cox – I have been seriously considering the mass of nonsense uttered by us the two last nights at Salisbury. I must own likewise that they have given me great uneasiness. If I have paid more attention to your family than any other of my acquaintances, the simple motive was, to show the world that I value my friends as much in adversity as when I shared their hospitality in their prosperity. I am sorry my conduct has been misconstrued, as the inference is unworthy of yourself, me, and a being, whose conduct, I am sure, is unimpeachable. To remove all doubts upon the subject, and to counteract the effects of insidious men, I shall beg leave to withdraw a friendship, rendered unworthy by suspicion.

I must be the worst of villains, if I could take that man by the hand while meditating towards him an act of injustice. You do not know me, Cox; mine are follies – not vices. It has been my text to do all the good I could in the world; and when I am called to a superior bourne, my memory may be blamed, but not despised. Wishing you and your family every blessing the world can give you, believe me nothing less than,

Your's most sincerely

EDMUND KEAN

R.A. Cox, Esq. 6, Wellington-street
Waterloo-bridge, London

The publication of the letters complete with postmark, date, and address further complicates the *Times* account, situating the reader – by turns eyewitness and dispassionate judge – now as a voyeur with seemingly immediate access to the intimate communications between lovers. Yet the letters' positioning within the paper's larger evidentiary narrative questions in turn the authenticity of the intimate feelings they express and enables readers a critical distance on the affect on display. Almost every subsequent publication printed the letters as they appeared in the *Times*, with Kean's letter to Mrs. Cox first, an arrangement that accentuates his lack of internal consistency. In the first letter, Kean directs a scene of deception, and his subsequent communication with the husband becomes merely a prop in that scene: "of course he will show you the letter I have written him; appear to countenance it and let him think we are never to meet again." Kean's frank solicitude in the second letter about his "great uneasiness" and his desire "to do all the good I could in the world" stands in this context as evidence of a highly refined ability to deceive. Further, the elevated, almost Shakespearean diction – "when I am called to a superior bourne, my memory may be blamed" – taints with private insincerity Kean's function as a cultural steward of Shakespeare. Ironically, Kean's ability to dissemble in private life makes him an incapable actor, or at least one who should not in the *Times*'s view be accepted by the British public.

The publication of the exchange between Kean and Charlotte Cox presents, to echo Mary Jacobus's formulation of Mary Wollstonecraft's dangerous epistolarity in *Letters to Imlay*, "an intra-psychic realm that can no longer be described by the terms 'public' or 'private'" (277). And yet the *Times* embeds the expression of intimacies in a larger narrative that seeks to confirm rather than destabilize the discrimination of private and public experience.[36] In its subsequently published theatrical reviews, which began one week to the day after the trial decision, the *Times* continued to espouse this paradoxical position. In lieu of conventional critical appraisals of Kean's acting, the crowd again becomes the story, old antagonisms resurface, and the class prejudices that accompanied Kean's debut ten years earlier are redeployed with new fervor. The *Times* opened its January 25 review with a rhetorical conflation of trial and performance that would inform its treatment of the case throughout the debate:

> Richard the Third was last night performed. The crook-back'd tyrant was performed by Mr. Kean: who on this occasion, made his first theatrical appearance this season; but most unfortunately, he had made, on Monday week, a very extraordinary first appearance on another stage – the Court of King's Bench – where he had seen rather a loss in money and reputation.

What is at stake here for the *Times* is not simply Kean's fitness as an actor but the constitution of a British public that would, or should, refuse to receive him. Yet the paper's attempt to represent that public voice is complicated by its ideologically inflected account of the dissension evident in the Drury Lane house: "The audience was one dark, dingy mass of combatants – many applauding him who had betrayed and dishonoured his friend." Kean's support is described as coming almost entirely from the lower orders: "We cannot speak very decidedly about the company in the Pit (although from the numerous quarrels and fights, incited by the 'Kean-for-ever-boys,' we can guess at their respectability) but of the audience which filled the two shilling galleries we must say that they gave us the most perfect idea of Falstaff's 'ragged regiment.'" Among those in the boxes, "a portion of them viewed the scene in sullen silence; another vociferated the praises of Kean; while a third amused themselves with an imperfect rehearsal of the 'hark follow' chorus from *Die Freischutz*, occasionally interspersed with exclamations (which we will not repeat) gleaned from Mr. Kean's unpublished letters." This discord, in which the love letters are translated into racy epigrams and recirculated verbally as disruptive noise, turns Kean's acting into "dumb show" and prevents him from addressing the audience directly. Still, the *Times* imagines itself rescuing from the din a representative British voice, cautioning Kean near the review's end not to "imagine that he has achieved a victory over public opinion." Shortly thereafter, the review makes the paper's central concern explicit:

> It is said, that his conduct is altogether a matter of a private nature, and we are reminded of many impurities that are alleged to have been committed by various persons connected with the scenic profession. We deny that Mr. Kean's offence is of a private nature. It has been brought before the public through the medium of a court of justice. The other cases are matter of whispers. Here there is an infamous certainty, and here the great court of public opinion will exercise its right.

More than an actor to be reviewed, Kean becomes here the focus of a larger discussion about the public's right to maintain proper boundaries between public and private experience.

A few days later, on Saturday, January 29, 1825, the *Times* described the Drury Lane house directly as a kind of representative public sphere. This review approached 2200 words, occupying a full column of page two. Beginning with a comment that Kean's Othello was not "sufficient to command attention," the reviewer immediately shifts to a polemical defense of his own critical task: "In spite of all the shallow aphorisms which have been advanced, for the purpose of proving that the public have no right to interfere on this occasion, they still persist in their determination not to spare a great moral delinquent." What follows is a point-by-point refutation of various defenses of Kean – some of which had been submitted to the paper and some that had been published elsewhere. The review then fashions a "public" opinion by positing an implied majority who presumably parallel the paper's readership and whose silence in (or absence from) the theater suggests support for the *Times*'s position. In this rendering of the event, mannered theatergoers refuse to take part in the vulgar contention arising in parts of the house. "Ladies" in particular have refused to attend, while those women seated outside the dress circle become nondescript "females" unworthy of attention:

> The house last night was not by any means so full as it was on Monday last. The pit was thronged: but even at half price there was abundance of room in the boxes. In the dress-circle there was not a single lady – there were a few females in the pit and the other parts of the house. The audience in the dress-circle took very little part in the dispute; neither were the galleries very active. The great scene of contention was in the pit; and a good deal of partisanship was displayed in the upper tiers of boxes. The appearance of Mr. Kean on the stage was the signal for one general shout, which lasted, without intermission, from the beginning to the end of each of his scenes.

As the review attempts to consolidate the evening's events into a coherent narrative, its description of disturbances from different parts of the house again emphasizes a fracturing of theatrical experience along class, gender, and political lines. "Placards" express contending opinions against and for Richard Elliston, the theater's manager, and of course Kean himself ("Who has outraged public decency? – Elliston"; "Down with *The Times*!"; "No cant! – No Hypocrisy! – Kean for ever!"). When Kean finally addresses the audience, he attempts to reframe the debate as a civilly conducted dispute that has been unfairly sensationalized, relying on familiar address even as he encourages the crowd to separate his personal from his public conduct:

> If you expect from me a vindication of my own private conduct, I am certainly unable to satisfy you (Applause and disapprobation.) I stand before you as the representative of Shakespeare's heroes. (Much contention between the parties favouring and disapproving Mr. Kean.) The errors I have committed have been scanned before a public tribunal; and – (here the uproar was so great that we could not collect the termination of the sentence).

Claiming that he had withheld evidence in his defense "from delicacy," Kean suggests, "It appears at this moment that I am a professional victim. (Laughter.) If this is the work of a hostile press, I shall endeavor with firmness to withstand it; but if it proceeds from your verdict and decision, I will at once bow to it." Like the *Times* itself, Kean rallies "the public" to his cause by separating its interests from the interests of a minority inflamed by the "hostile press." This self-defense is extraordinary, even as rendered by the *Times,* because Kean's explicit request that the audience separate his private conduct from his performance confirms the conflation that the *Times* fears: he speaks as himself yet from the stage and in costume.

Though occasioned by the events of *Cox* v. *Kean,* the tumultuous reaction depicted in the *Times*'s January 29 review represents in a more general way the effect that Kean's celebrity had on British theatrical experience from the beginning of his career. He was the subject, always, of widely divergent assessments because the nature and technique of his stage representations could never be separated from the dangerous instability of his relentlessly publicized offstage identity. The review emblematizes the larger situation in which the *Times* found itself as a commercial newspaper covering Kean's controversy – necessarily reporting on theater as a politically volatile public event while attempting to maintain an approach to reviewing that confirmed theater's, and the reviewers', cohesive social role. Because *Cox* v. *Kean* had elicited impassioned responses from theatergoers within the house and from reviewers without, the tension between those opposed ideological commitments strains the rhetoric of the paper's reporting. The *Times* was, in the end, forced to defend explicitly its claims of political and class disinterest. The result was a zero-sum game for the paper, as its increasing stridency inhibited reviewers' ability to claim their position as representatives of an assumed "public" norm. By February 4, even civility had slipped away: Kean was simply a "baboon" and Elliston a "showman," neither of whom "can have any sense of decency, any respect for morals, or any regard for that public by the favour of which they live." The next day, Saturday, February 5, two reviews of Kean's Macbeth were preceded by an extraordinary bracketed preface: "[In order to secure a correct narrative of what passed last night at Drury-lane, we desired two gentlemen to attend, who have written the subjoined accounts without communication with each other: –]." The first review referred to Kean's "unblushing assurance" and "brutish impudence" while describing a house that was "ill-attended, until the period of half-price." Describing a series of placards "exhibited in front of the second circle of boxes, and of the two-shilling gallery," including one that referred to "The Obscene Times," the reviewer took it upon himself to answer their charges:

> A second placard Bore the words, "What Kean wrote, the newspapers published. Which is worse?" This does not apply to us. We did not, and would not, publish the filthy part of his correspondence. A third placard set forth "One of the dearest rights of Englishmen is, not to be tried twice for the same offence." Mr. Kean has, it is true, been punished for his offence, so far as the individual injured is concerned. But, we contend, that the public, an offence having been committed, *contra bonos mores*, (most flagrantly so), have a right to express their opinion, when the guilty individual is, night after night, placed before them. A fourth placard ran thus: – "Let not animosity reign in the bosoms of Englishmen." Mr. Kean has to thank himself, or that "honourable gentleman" Mr. Elliston, for any animosity that does exist.

This description has a dual effect. By incorporating the evening's events into a standard kind of report, the review translates one night's furious contention into a readable element of the paper's commercialized informational discourse. On the other hand, by engaging the placards as forms of legitimate argument, contending with them point by point, the reviewer situates the paper as one contending voice among many, one segment of a public decidedly at odds with itself. The publication of a second review on the same page further undermines the paper's claims toward objectivity: theatrical experience had become in the wake of *Cox* v. *Kean* larger and more unwieldy than even the multifarious *Times* could encompass.[37] The trial exposed that commercial newspapers, like the Drury Lane house, had become a forum for competing signs rather than a consumable amalgamation of them.

If the publicity surrounding Kean reveals that theatrical experience had pressured traditional boundaries between public and private modes of experience by the time he debuted, his celebrity was largely a product of the very newspaper culture that would in 1825 upbraid him on moral grounds. Both the actor's behavior and the newspaper's condemnation of it mark a shift in which individual privacy becomes in the paper's account a function of a new kind of commercialized dailiness. This is true not simply because of the frequency with which the papers reported on Kean's performances but also because of the ways in which Kean's self-presentation resonated with the newspaper's larger commercial mission. Just as Kean's acting brought Shakespeare into contact with the sensational, consumer-oriented productions of London's illegitimate theaters, the *Times* presented its cultural criticism within a discursive framework whose primary function was to facilitate commercial exchange. As the most bankable actor on London's stages and in the press, Kean was the cultural dream commercialism imagined for itself. Yet that very quality also made Kean a threat to the newspaper's ideological construction of British objectivity. The *Times*'s response to attacks on its disinterestedness in the wake of *Cox* v. *Kean* compromised its grand pretense to speak for an idealized British public. In 1825, the newspaper's veneer of objectivity and its capacity to fashion the public's theatrical experience on its own terms broke down in the face of Kean's controversy.

IV Richard's Himself Again

Given the vibrant and contentious field of theatrical criticism that developed in London between 1809 and 1830, it is not surprising that the theatrical press's defense of Kean focused squarely on newspapers, specifically the *Times* and its growing power to influence public opinion. As I argue in Chapter 2, many theatrical periodicals were like the newspapers they criticized, beholden both to commercialism and to an elite discourse of cultural evaluation that, at least on its face, resisted commercialism. Keeping this tension in mind, I will now consider the *Theatrical Observer*'s ongoing commentary on *Cox* v. *Kean* during the first six weeks of 1825. Among London's most prominent theatrical dailies, the *Observer*'s initial criticism and subsequent support of Kean not only provides an alternative view of the trial's contemporary significance, it also illustrates how the *Times*'s claim to be the voice of "public opinion" concerned journal editors far more than any of Kean's moral indiscretions. If Kean's presence on the most important stage in the nation could never be read apart from the scandal of his offstage conduct, as the *Times* suggested, any traditional understanding of how London's legitimate theater preserved the nation's cultural tradition could also be called into question. As the *Theatrical Observer* would come to suggest, the *Times*, for all its vitriol toward Kean, had enabled that threat by advancing the breakdown of eighteenth-century notions of privacy.

What emerges when we view the *Theatrical Observer*'s coverage of *Cox* v. *Kean* alongside that of the *Times* is the picture of a theatrical press at odds with itself, particularly as it attempted to reconceive theatrical experience in light of the illegitimate and transgressive enactments Kean embodied. As I have argued, many theatrical periodicals resisted the newspapers' saleable universalism even as those publications sought to cull audiences from the readership the newspapers were fostering. Like many other theatrical journals, the *Theatrical Observer*'s coverage of *Cox* v. *Kean* employed residual cultural assumptions – in this case a belief in the separable coexistence of public and private modes of experience – to distinguish itself from the commercial press. While the *Times* conflated Kean's private and public personae, bemoaning the fact that the actor had compromised his responsibilities as a steward of British theatrical tradition, the *Observer* sought to relegate the private and the public to discrete spheres of experience, revealing in the process a conservatism that complicated – even contradicted – its expressed alliance with Kean. Kean's private conduct, the journal argued, need not occasion a crisis in how Britons imagined their theatrical experience because it had little to do with his capabilities as an actor. Ostensibly defending him against the *Times*, the *Observer* and its allies were in reality defending themselves against the sea change in theatrical experience Kean's acting had wrought.

The *Observer*'s coverage of the trial began in earnest on January 18, 1825, the day after *Cox* v. *Kean* reached the Court of King's Bench. While similar to the reports published that same day in the *Times*, the journal's account opens with the distinctive ring of a theatrical review:

> Mr. Kean – Yesterday this far-famed tragedian appeared in the character of *Defendant* in a *Piece* which was represented at the Court of King's Bench under the title of *Crim Con*. The plot of this unhappy affair lies in small compass. The Plaintiff, Alderman Cox, was the Defendant's friend, and had a wife whose attractions made the latter a traitor to friendship. The consequences were a scandalous intimacy between the Defendant and the lady, for which a jury gave the Plaintiff £800 damages, of which £2000 at which they were laid. We are very sorry to say that Mr. Kean appeared to the worst advantage in this affair; and it is our sincere hope that he will never resume the part. The following are some specimens of the epistolary style of the fond swain.

Kean is evaluated as an actor who has failed in his stage impersonation, appearing "to the worst of advantage in this affair." He has enacted a part the journal hopes he will "never resume." Beneath the review, the *Observer* excerpted a dozen letters from the court transcript and, two days later, offered readers a look at the "Twin Letters" the *Times* had published on January 18. On Saturday, January 22, the *Observer* expanded its coverage to include letters from two readers who differed in their assessments of the case's significance. In the first, "Titus D" decried the *Times*'s reviling of Kean, concluding "I would ask two questions. Whether a man's private character has anything to do with his appearance before the public? – if it has we might shut the Theatres. 2nd. – Has The Times any right to *try* to prejudice the public against Mr. Kean on Monday next?" As if in reply to this position, "John Brown" resisted in the second letter the liberal *Morning Chronicle*'s attempt "to question the right of the public to point at him and dwell upon his conduct with deserved severity." According to "Brown," the *Chronicle*'s "folly" was its inability to recognize that "*public characters are public property*, and when a servant of the public chooses to outrage the best feelings of society, he must expect that the disapprobation of the respectable part of it will be expressed *publicly* as it ought to be." Titus contends that Kean's domestic affairs are irrelevant to his acting and, further, that the newspaper has no province to influence audiences against Kean based on those affairs. For John Brown, however, Kean can commit no act that is not immediately public: his position as an actor in the patent theaters renders him a public subject for whom private experience is an impossibility.

The *Observer* vetted these opposing positions with a cautionary editorial tone, imagining private and public realms of experience as neither entirely divided nor entirely joined: "We cannot say we go the length of our correspondent John Brown, in considering 'public characters as public property' – for *private* character in every station is without the proper range of *public* criticism." Yet the impact of Kean's private conduct must be recognized, given that his return occurred so quickly after the trial's conclusion: "It would be impossible, we think, for the British public to withhold their reprobation of a Person who being previously proved to have committed a gross outrage on every proper feeling, should *immediately* afterwards return to seek their approval in a public manner." The *Observer*'s assessment concluded, "*Time is a healer of many evils*; and we should be happy to find it resorted to by more than one individual, to soften down the remembrance of certain events. – (Ed.)" Presenting the case in this manner, the journal authoritatively mediates the public's disputatious conversation by maintaining a pose of thoughtful moderation. On Monday, January 24, just a few hours before the actor's anticipated return in the character of Richard III, the *Observer* replied to "correspondents" by emphasizing that in Kean's

> intending to appear on the stage within *a few days after* [the decision against him], there was a tacit declaration of utter disregard for the feeling of the best portion of society, and of a boastful reliance on his professional fame to bear him through in triumph against the few, who might think it an act of justice to the national character, to express their disgust at the *individual* when he appeared as the *actor*. We trust that it is not yet too late for Mr. Kean to retire form the storm.

According to the *Observer*, Kean mistakenly sets one form of publicity against another, believing that his fame as a tragedian will offset his infamy as an adulterer. Because his private offense is so recent, however, he cannot appear before audiences as an actor without their calling to mind his identity as an individual. Though the *Observer* would shift from this position over the next several days, becoming quickly a staunch supporter of Kean, it maintained throughout all its commentary the same clear distinction between private and public spheres of experience, a distinction that the *Times* steadfastly refused to allow.

On January 25, the day after Kean's return, the journal urged that the vocal resistance he had encountered from the house during his performance should be sufficient punishment for his crimes. After describing the "immense" crowd "around every avenue to the theatre" and the "dreadful sense of riot and confusion" that necessitated Kean acting "in perfect dumb shew," the reviewer moves swiftly to consider the night's greater significance: "Thus has Mr. Kean's very ill-judged attempt to disregard *public opinion of private character*, terminated in a manner that every one who knew the nature of Englishmen, must have expected: in truth an English public contains abundance of good materials." Kean's "chastisement" has illustrated "an effective lesson" of the public's intolerance for immorality, but that lesson "being shewn, we think the task of chastisement should now terminate. We trust, that no further scenes, of the nature of that of last night will again occur." Urging Kean to amend his private life and "move respected through his circle of society," the journal promises that it feels "no inclination to return to Mr. Kean's past private conduct." Significantly, the reviewer seems aware that his refusal to condemn Kean any further will be viewed as a partisan capitulation to the power of celebrity:

> Perhaps the wretches who last night bawled out *"no canting,"* may call *this* canting; but it is then the *canting,* not of conventicle groaners, but of men who love their country's reputation, and who feel the blessings of a virtuous and happy fire-side. The drunkards, the bullies, the wolves, may bellow as they please in favor of any idol – they will find, as they did last night, that there are plenty of young men of better principles than they possess, ready to muster in a *good cause.*

Refusing to align himself with the "cant" of "drunkards, the bullies, and the wolves" – a reference to Kean's vocal and sometimes violent fan organization, the "Wolves Club" – the reviewer claims instead the universal authority of "better principles": of patriotism and British domesticity and the "blessings of a virtuous and happy fire-side." Having paid for his crimes, Kean can now be welcomed back into a public sphere constituted by its connection to the circle of Britain's idealized private life.[38]

The *Theatrical Observer*'s initial response to the trial was to recognize the public impact of Kean's private transgression even as the journal attempted to shore up the border between the two realms of experience the incident had threatened. As the *Times* attacks intensified, however, the *Observer*'s editors became less concerned with Kean's improprieties and more focused on the newspaper itself. Whether or not "The Times has any right to *try* to prejudice the public against Mr. Kean," as Titus put it, fast became the *Observer*'s primary anxiety. After several days of repeating its initial call for forgiveness, including one review that described Kean's emotional attempt to address the audience from the stage ("here Mr. Kean appeared affected, and applied his handkerchief to his eyes … "), the journal published on January 31 an extended reflection worth quoting at length. Kean was no longer the central culprit:

> Mr. Kean appears tonight as *Sir Giles Overreach*, a character in which he stands unrivalled. The line of conduct adopted by *The Times* newspaper towards him, must strike every one as most unnecessarily harsh. On Saturday, the Report in it of the proceedings at Drury Lane Theatre of the proceeding [sic] night, and also an article under the leading head, were cruelly severe on Mr. Kean. What does *The Times* propose to effect by this harshness? Does it wish to drive Kean from the stage? If so, we were convinced it never more miscalculated the influence it possesses over Public Opinion.

Recognizing that "we felt, in common with every one of right feeling, who had read the proceedings, that it was necessary to convince Mr. Kean of his mistake," the *Observer* contends that the *Times* has begun "carrying antipathy beyond due bounds," committing "an act of positive injustice." More importantly, the newspaper has abrogated its responsibility as a conduit of authentic publicity:

> How does the case stand? Why, a Court of Justice forces into partial notice certain letters intended alone to suit the vitiated taste of a shameless wanton – the knowledge of these is widely extended through the medium of the press; and, then, the fact of their being general known is made the foundation of a charge by that press, against an actor for coming forward before that public whom it has, for the immediate time, rendered inimical to his performances! What *right* had the press first to inform all the world of a man's errors, and then blame him for walking abroad, as an act of indecency? *The Times* may answer this by saying that common rumour would soon spread the news of the proceedings of a Trial like the one in question – Indeed! Then, pray, what is the use of *Newspapers*, if common rumour can herald events so well? The fact is, the power of making any event *thoroughly known* is vested in the press; and we do say the press has *not* the *right*, after *using* this power, in a matter of the present nature, to turn against a *professional* man a stigma of *private character*, (disseminated by itself) on the very ground of its being extensively known.

Here the *Times*'s power has in effect become the story. According to the *Observer*'s counter-narrative, the *Times* creates a sensation by publishing Kean's private letters and then condemns him for bringing the taint of that sensation to the legitimate stage. Aligning itself with "the correct part of the public" that resisted Kean's hasty return but then accepted his public apology, the *Observer* contends that the *Times*'s hypocrisy in manufacturing an ongoing scandal negates its claims to speak for a universal "Public Opinion." Still, the *Observer*'s position overlooks the journal's own role in publicizing the case: given the rampant publicity of which the journal's reports were a part, the editor's contention that "For our part we see Mr. Kean in no other point of view but as a talented actor; and as an actor alone" must ring somewhat hollow. *Cox* v. *Kean* made it impossible for even sympathetic theatergoers to ignore the effect that Kean's controversy had on his enactment of his most famous characters.

The reviews and commentaries that followed this crucial counterattack, both in the *Theatrical Observer* and in other journals and occasional publications, manifest vividly the strategies of audience making that had come to define the field of theatrical criticism after 1809. The *Observer*, in particular, increasingly framed the debate as one in which those who opposed Kean were unreasonably partisan, an unruly subculture that had isolated itself from the larger British public. Kean's antagonists – for whom the *Times* claimed to speak in universal terms – become in the pages of the *Observer* a new generation of "O. P.ers" whose goal is merely to disrupt the proceedings of the national theaters for their own partisan ends. "O. P.," a term used in 1809 to describe the large segment of the theatergoing public whose disruptions had challenged Kemble's management of Covent Garden, has sixteen years later become a way to mark an outsider, someone who does not belong to "the correct part of the public." Describing in its February 1 issue a performance from the previous night, the *Observer* claimed that the tide of public opinion had shifted in Kean's favor. Against a backdrop of largely favorable signs and placards ("Let every man have his desert, who shall escape a whipping," "Forget and Forgive," etc.), the review cannily reduces the size and shifts the class associations of the anti-Kean force, segregating from the rest of the audience those "few O. P.s" who had come to the theater "for the express purpose of opposing Kean." The group begins as "a knot of some half dozen" in the pit: "upon their shewing their intentions," they are met with universal derision among their peers who "almost to a man, rose, and as with one voice, called for their being ejected from the Theatre." That threat dismissed, the opposition diminishes into a single "O. P.-ist" in the boxes. Vocally denouncing Kean, he is met with "groans and hootings" and then a shower of orange peels from the "groundlings" beneath him in the pit. More importantly, as he continues his disruption, the members of his own middle class – who were presumably those most offended by Kean's presence on the stage – turn on him: "At length the noisy O.P. was attacked in his own quarters, and being dragged to the lobby a scuffle ensued." Remarkably, the impulses of the lower orders become the source from which middle-class opinion against the O. P. is derived, and Kean is deemed once again suitable to perform.

Many occasional publications that entered the fray set the terms of the debate in similar ways, both by explicitly resisting the *Times* and by anathematizing Kean's antagonists.[39] In Reed's Cheap Edition of *Kean Vindicated, or the Truth Discovered with his Flattering Reception on Monday Evening*, a one-penny tract published in January 1825, the author presents his audience with a distinction akin to that offered in the *Observer*, contending, "[I]t has been shewn that the private life of an Actor is distinct from his public one." *Kean Vindicated* goes further, accusing the *Times* of using its position to prosecute private vendettas. Reminding readers that the "pompous and immaculate" newspaper was once "the most enthusiastic admirer of Mr. Kean," the tract purports to expose a personal agenda that drives the *Times*: "although all may not perceive the 'wheel within the wheel' that puts its venomous works in motion; Be it known then that there exists an old Grudge on the part of this consistent and Leading Journal and the indefatigable manager of D.L.T." This language echoes rhetoric Kevin Gilmartin finds in radical writers like Richard Carlile and William Cobbett, who positioned themselves as prophets working within but against a fundamentally corrupt public sphere.[40] Just as Carlile and Cobbett attacked governmental institutions for their false claims of ideological disinterest, the author of *Kean Vindicated* discredits the newspaper's objectivity, claiming that the attacks on Kean reveal the *Times* as a malicious instigator of incivility among "partisans, dependents, and hangers-on":

> As it was anticipated, an ineffectual attempt was made by the partisans, dependents and hangers-on of that part of the Press which has degraded itself by its endeavors to excite unnecessary odium upon Mr. Kean, to create a disturbance and an uproar; but it was suddenly seen through, and their hisses drowned in the applause of the reasonable and forgiving part of the Audience, which was as TEN TO ONE in favour of Mr. Kean. That Gentleman it seems was desirous to say something from himself, but the friends of the Drama – those who came to be amused by the Play, forbade it, and rendered futile the endeavors of those who hoped to have their insignificance flattered by an Address. (*Kean Vindicated*)

In this account, the public majority will not allow Kean to speak in his own defense because to do so would be to acknowledge the relevance of his accusers. Forbidding his attempt to step out of character and give voice to his private persona, the audience demands that he maintain his professional identity while on the stage. Yet in forgiving him and restricting him to his scripted performance, Kean's supporters paradoxically limit the power that his celebrity persona has to question theater's connection to the larger public world. By the end of Reed's tract, Kean's private individuality disappears entirely behind the mask of his most famous Shakespearean part:

> Mr. Kean stands as he did stand, like a rock against which the Cantwells may level their thunder, and against which the surges of calumny and illiberality may dash without sapping its foundation ... Let us look forward to those nights when we shall again behold the stirling Drama supported by the first Tragedian of the Boards, and reflect with pleasure that "RICHARD'S HIMSELF AGAIN." (*Kean Vindicated*)

In a sense, these anti-*Times* accounts of the trial attempted to redeem Kean by reclaiming for him a notion of privacy that had long been eroding, and which the publicity surrounding *Cox* v. *Kean* had shown was for many Britons in its final death throes. Many of the theatrical periodicals and occasional publications that responded to the trial attempted to inoculate Britain's theater culture from Kean's personal indiscretions by refusing to collapse private and public modes of experience. Yet in doing so they resisted changes that had from the first enabled Kean's celebrity and his power as an actor. Though the relentless antagonism toward the *Times* that these publications display is, on its face, a straightforward defense of a popular actor, the critiques constitute a more fundamental attempt to maintain practices of cultural consumption that Kean's own acting had begun to dismantle. Kean himself was as much a threat to their notions of theatrical experience as he was to any moral standard the *Times* advocated.

V   No Actor

Writing the week of Kean's January 1825 return to the stage, an "English Gentleman" offered the following assessment:

> Mr. Edmund Kean has two performances to sustain, one in his own character, with which play going folks have nothing to do, and another with which they have. That people pay money to see him in the latter character, and go of their own accord; and to go, therefore, *to injure him*, when his acting is good and excellent, is a tort. Moreover, the *English Gentleman* further finds, by his verdict, that the Letters of Mr. Edmund Kean conclude him to be *no actor*, but a real Richard, and further he findeth not.[41]

Like the critic in the *Theatrical Observer*, this reviewer attempts to render private and public conduct distinct but acknowledges despite himself that the power of Kean's performance comes from its connection to his offstage life. If Kean was "no actor, but a real Richard" in his private life, there could be no privacy apart from his stage persona, and no stage performance apart from that of the "real" Kean. Here the implications of Kean's controversy are neatly expressed: privacy and publicity have become mutually constitutive; trials have become dramas, dramas trials; bedrooms have become stages, stages confessionals. Given these stakes – and especially in the absence of Lord Byron, who had died in April 1824 – it is no surprise that in 1825 Kean became with renewed intensity a lightning rod for press attention.[42] The product of a one-man news machine, Kean's acting – and his acting out – raised the very questions about contemporary life that the press was attempting to resolve on a daily basis.

Ironically, it was Thomas Barnes who read the signs of the times more accurately than the critics of the *Theatrical Observer*. For even as the *Times* decried the advent of Kean's new brand of celebrity, Barnes's paper was offering its miscellaneous layouts that exhibited the imbrication of commercial and cultural life. Against this encompassing program, the *Observer*'s attempt to maintain a discrete notion of privacy appears yet another strategy of cultural distinction, recasting the journal's readers as part of a more judicious, less sensation-minded public than that imagined by the *Times*. Rather than indicating his decline, the "removal" of middle-class favor from Kean that the *Cox* v. *Kean* debate enacted in fact confirmed his continuing significance. In disgrace, Kean was a subject who continued to remake British theatrical experience, who emerged from the commercialized theatrical culture that the *Times* and other papers facilitated and against which the *Observer* rallied. Kean's so-called downfall, much like Byron's before him, radiated publicity's triumph. If Kean was commercialism's cultural dream of itself, he was for just this reason an incorrigible subject for which neither newspaper nor periodical criticism had any kind of ready answer. It would take William Hazlitt to craft an approach to theater that could accommodate the full scope of Kean's theatrical revolution.

Notes

Several of the reviews quoted in this chapter are taken from page clippings found in extra-illustrated books at the Houghton Library. Dating on these reviews tends to be fairly accurate, but in some cases I have not found the original periodical source. In these instances, I have cited the clippings' position in the extra-illustrated book.

1. Remarking that "dignity, grandeur and majesty were the hallmarks of Kemble's Shakespeare," Jane Moody provides a concise assessment of Kemble's style in "Romantic Shakespeare" 41–49.

2. The original quote was first reported in Coleridge's *Table Talk* (14.41):

> Kean is original; but he copies from himself. His rapid descents from the hyper-tragic to the infra-colloquial, though sometimes productive of great effect, are often unreasonable. To see him act, is like reading Shakspeare by flashes of lightning. I do not think him thorough-bred gentleman enough to play Othello.

For a discussion of the derisive quality of the comment, and its possible connection to Kean's consumption of alcohol and lower-class behavior more generally, see Tracy Davis, "'Reading Shakespeare by flashes of Lightning:' Challenging the Foundations of Romantic Acting Theory." See also Simon Schaffer's account of the politicized nature of electricity and its connection to theatrical spectacle, in which he argues, "Secrecy, surprise, wondermongering and commerce were ... an intimate accompaniment of electrical culture" ("The Consuming Flame" 493). In Joseph Donohue's words, "the spasmodic nature of Kean's gesture and utterance would always draw attention, especially because, to many commentators, it called into question the whole relationship between artistic convention and life" (*Theatre in the Age of Kean* 59). For examples of contemporary derision of Kean, see for example the *Theatrical Inquisitor* (February 1814): 122–24 and the *Drama, or Theatrical Pocket Magazine* (May 1821): 1–5. For other more positive reviews, see *The Monthly Theatrical Reporter* (February 1815), and *The British Stage* (January 1817). Hillebrand (104–36) and Playfair (50–54) provide summaries of Kean's initial emergence on the London stage and critical reactions to him. Gillian Russell has more recently reaffirmed Kean's status as "the Regency actor par excellence" because of his status as a "bastard product of theatre, trained by itinerant showmen" ("Keats, Popular Culture, and the Sociability of Theatre" 197).

3. For a discussion of how Kean's acting subordinates verbal articulation to "sensual and tortuous" expression, see Leigh Woods 83.

4. With this discussion, I of course touch upon two decades of revisions to Jurgen Habermas's notion of the "bourgeois public sphere," particularly those accounts that contend with the notion that the private subject precedes its entrance into the public realm. For example, while Nancy Fraser's well-known formulation of a "counter-public sphere" challenges the exclusionary nature of Habermas's model, arguing instead for an ongoing contest between a number of smaller discursive communities, Fraser follows Habermas in assuming the preexistence of subjects whose collaboration constitutes a given public. See Fraser, "Rethinking the Public Sphere" in Calhoun 109–42. By contrast, Miranda Burgess's discussion of early-eighteenth-century women's writing calls for "an account of gender as a by-product of the discourses producing privacy and publicity in particular material and historical contexts – and as cognate with the production of individual identity itself" ("Bearing Witness" 396). Burgess provides a thorough accounting of revisions of the idealist Habermasian project. See "Bearing Witness" 393–99.

5. I here echo Joan Scott's injunction that historical work must become "not just an attempt to correct or supplement an incomplete record of the past but a way of critically acknowledging how history operates as a site of the production of gender knowledge" (10).
6. For Bratton, Kean's acting innovation is secondary to the politics that accompanied his celebrity. If Kean's move toward a more "natural" style was another example of the way in which "the western acting tradition, posited on revealing truth, renews itself regularly by such re-concealments of its artifice," still his post-1789 "return to nature was read as an aspect of political and philosophical revolution" unlike that of any actor before him ("Celebrity" 90).
7. See Moody, "Romantic Shakespeare," esp. 50–56 and Davis, "Reading Shakespeare." Thomas Crochunis also addressed this issue in a conference paper entitled "Edmund Kean's 'Radical' Acting" delivered at the Association for Theatre in Higher Education Conference in Chicago, IL, July 1994. I thank the author for sharing his unpublished manuscript.
8. For a cogent review of criminal conversation trials beginning with the conviction and execution of Mervyn Lord Audley in 1631, see Fay 411–13. Audley's case established the precedent that a husband found complicit in his wife's violation could collect no damages. Laurence Stone details the vast increase in adultery cases after 1740, as legal damages replaced dueling as the primary means of communicating reparations for adulterous behavior. See Stone, quoted in Fay 398.
9. The jury found for Cox but awarded him £800 rather than full damages.
10. This was in fact a significant part of Kean's defense. According to the narrative, one of his attorneys argued that "Not only was the alderman culpably indifferent to his wife's honour, but he became instrumental himself in a great degree to her dishonour" (Fairburn *Cox* v. *Kean*, 36).
11. The ostensible purpose of these accounts, often written by law students or clerks, was to maintain public morals and prevent similar incidents from recurring. Part of their process of moral correction was the silencing of the offending parties: during the trial and subsequent publication, the accused subordinated their voices to "the restrictions set by legal practice, and guided by the conventions of legal discourse" (Fay 408). For an account that describes criminal conversation cases as themselves a "battle of genres" within the courtroom, see Korobkin 5.
12. Gamer and Robinson focus on Mary Robinson's "comeback" from her romantic entanglements with the Prince of Wales in 1781–1782. Through various means of self-publication in fashionable circles (e.g., publicized appearances) and the newspaper press, "Robinson in those years embodied the figure of desire and loss that was 'Perdita'" (241). This self-fashioning eventually enabled Robinson's return to London literary society later in the decade. In other words, the legal "silencing" that Fay describes enabled alternative publicities that could, eventually, be converted into literary authority.

13. For a discussion of the "masculinist conception" of Habermas's public sphere, see Fraser 117–18. Extending Fraser's work, Shawn Maurer has argued that endorsing traditional separation between domestic and public spheres limits our understanding of how gender functioned as a social construct in the eighteenth century. For Maurer, the traditionally feminine domestic sphere extends from public authorizations of masculinity in eighteenth-century print culture. See *Proposing Men*, esp. 6–33.
14. Caroline Gonda contrasts the cases of fallen women – put into scripted roles beyond their making – with aristocratic ladies for whom public display is a dutiful obligation (66–68). In this context, Robinson's professionalism would be read as a further indictment of her public character.
15. See Bate, *Shakespearean Constitutions*.
16. *The Poetic Epistles of Edmund, with Notes, Illustrations, and Reflections.* London: Effingham Wilson, 1825. Another version of the lines published at the time went as follows:

> "Doubt that the stars are fire
> "Doubt truth to be a liar – "
> As great as I am now – a sort of fox, fox, fox;
> "Doubt that the sun doth move,
> "But never doubt I love,"
> Both you, my dear, and worthy Mr. Cox, Cox, Cox,
> Both you and my good patron, Mr. Cox.

See Hawkins, F. W., *Life of Edmund Kean*, extra-illustrated book, Harry Elkins Widener Collection, Houghton Library, HEW 14.9.2.
17. *Secrets Worth Knowing: Suppressed Letters, Cox v. Kean.* London: T. Reed, 1825.
18. *The Museum, or Record of Literature* (June 1822).
19. Jane Moody describes the methodical intent behind Kean's seemingly spontaneous style: "Far from being a wild, unstudied genius, Kean's theatrical revolution was the work of an iconoclastic actor who defined himself in opposition to the traditions of legitimate performance" (*Illegitimate Theatre* 230).
20. According to Davis, Kean's technique anticipated by several years the introduction of gaslight to London theaters, which would transform spectator's perceptions of the bodies on stage before them by rendering facial expression more readable. See "Reading Shakespeare," 934–36.
21. Tom Mole has noted that shifts in print culture during the Romantic period heightened the possibility for such conflation, "so that neither self nor celebrity can be conceptually quarantined from the other" (3). For a discussion of Romantic figures, including Kean, around whom a new apparatus of publicity coalesced to enable a "hermeneutic of intimacy," see Mole 1–27.
22. The chaise accident was probably concocted as a cover for Kean's absence from the theater due to drunkenness on March 12, 1816. See Hawkins.

Accounts of Kean's late night forays can be found throughout newspapers and reviews from the early part of his career.
23. For Coleridge's criticism of the tragedy, see chap. 23 of *Biographia Literaria* (207–33).
24. See the extra-illustrated copy of F. W. Hawkins's *Life of Edmund Kean* (Evert Jansen Wendell Collection) #TS 941.3 (vol. 1, p. 452).
25. See the extra-illustrated copy of F. W. Hawkins's *Life of Edmund Kean* (Evert Jansen Wendell Collection) #TS 941.3 (vol. 1, p. 192).
26. See the extra-illustrated copy of F. W. Hawkins's *Life of Edmund Kean* (Evert Jansen Wendell Collection) #TS 941.3 (vol. 2, p. 7).
27. *Champion* February 10, 1814.
28. See the extra-illustrated copy of F. W. Hawkins's *Life of Edmund Kean* (Evert Jansen Wendell Collection) #TS 941.3 (vol. 1, p. 280).
29. See the extra-illustrated copy of F. W. Hawkins's *Life of Edmund Kean* (Evert Jansen Wendell Collection) #TS 941.3 (vol. 1, p. 404).
30. See the extra-illustrated copy of F. W. Hawkins's *Life of Edmund Kean* (Evert Jansen Wendell Collection) #TS 941.3 (vol. 2, p. 163).
31. Kathryn Pratt has described the ways in which Kean's being honored by the Huron tribe of North America in 1820 can be viewed as an attempt to reclaim the "human" subject from Anglo-American commodity culture. See Pratt, "The Indian as Human Commodity."
32. For a wide-ranging discussion of the politics of Kean's sexual escapades, see Kahan 64–86.
33. Other caricatures emphasized this point as well. "A Theatrical Dressing Room, or Trunks and Leggings" pictures Mr. Cox sitting on a couch observing as Mrs. Cox, standing next to a partially clad Kean, tries on the actor's pants.
34. In Colley Cibber's adaptation of the play, which Kean would have performed hundreds of times, the opening line of Richard's final speech is "Perdition catch thy arm – the Chance is thine" (Cibber 138). Cibber's adaptation alludes to Othello's "Perdition catch my soul." See *Othello* 3.3.98.
35. At times, the same images were used both to attack and to defend Kean. For example, the *Defence of Kean against the Unmanly attacks of "The Times"* fronted its pages with a woodcut of Kean's portrait as Richard – the same woodcut that had graced the front page of the anti-Kean *Secrets Worth Knowing*.
36. The *Times* accounts exemplify the ways in which, in Michael McKeon's assessment, "modern knowledge," particularly in its production of the categories of domesticity and the public, "is defined precisely by its explanatory ambition to separate itself from its object of knowledge sufficiently to fulfill the epistemological demand that what is known must be divided from the process by which it is known" (xix).
37. The second review in large measure confirmed the opinions of the first by commenting derisively on Kean's "publishing himself, for the fourth time, at Drury-lane theatre."

38. Kean himself would hold this same line. His repeated apologies and attempt to separate the private and the personal contradicted the relationship between publicity and privacy that his acting imagined.
39. Notable among these defenses were *The Wind-Up; or, Candour versus The Times* (London, 1825) and *Complete Defence of Kean against the Unmanly Attacks of "The Times"* (London: W. Mason, 1825).
40. See Gilmartin, *Print Politics*, 65–113.
41. See the extra-illustrated copy of F. W. Hawkins's *Life of Edmund Kean* (Harry Elkins Widener Collection) #HEW 15.9.3.
42. For a consideration of the relationship between Byron's aristocratic prestige and the early-nineteenth-century commercialization of literary culture, see Jerome Christensen's *Lord Byron's Strength*. More recently, Nicholas Mason has described the emergence of Byron as a commodified cultural "brand." My contention is that Byron's unique status as an icon of British commercial culture was paralleled by Kean's rise, and Byron's death only heightened Kean's position as the focus of the commercial press.

CHAPTER 4

Hazlitt's Romantic Occasionalism

> We have become a nation of politicians and newsmongers; our inquiries in the streets are no less than after the health of Europe; and in men's faces, we may see strange matters written, – the rise of stocks, the loss of battles, the fall of kingdoms, and the death of kings.
> William Hazlitt, "The Drama, No. IV." *London Magazine*, April 1820

William Hazlitt shaped theatrical experience in Britain more than any other prose writer in the Romantic period. In 1814, the year of Edmund Kean's debut at Drury Lane, Hazlitt had just begun working as a theatrical critic for *The Morning Chronicle* newspaper and for Leigh and John Hunt's weekly *The Examiner*. Over the next eight years, between 1814 and 1822, he would publish hundreds of theatrical reviews, almost as many periodical essays, and several full-length volumes, including *The Round Table* (1817), *Characters of Shakespear's Plays* (1817), *Lectures on the English Poets* (1818), *A View of the English Stage* (1818), *Lectures on the English Comic Writers* (1819), and *Table Talk* (1821). This is a crucial body of work in the development of theatrical criticism – and criticism as such – not simply because of its stylistic and philosophical innovation but because in the face of a rapidly changing periodical culture it envisions for criticism a new social function altogether. Hazlitt's reviews authorize the critic not as an arbiter of essential cultural value to a confirmed elite, nor as an interpreter of events for a nascent radical community, nor finally as a communicator of information to a newspaper-reading public. Rather, with a mode of criticism committed to the irreducible particularities – the specific occasions – of his own attendance at the theater, Hazlitt imagines an audience that intersects and overlaps all these readerships. His personal style resists both the homogenization of experience effected by the commercial press and the fracturing of readerships that responded to newspaper commercialism.

In an 1820 contribution to the *London Magazine* on the subject of "The Drama," Hazlitt decried the French Revolution's transformation of even the most particular human experiences into a function of global politics. Overwhelmed by the newspapers' daily representation of "the large vicissitudes of human affairs" (18.305), local and individual identities had begun to disappear:

> What is an individual man to a nation? Or what is a nation to an abstract principle? The affairs of the world are spread out before us, as in a map; we sit with our newspaper, and a pair of compasses in our hand, to measure out provinces, and to dispose of thrones; we "look abroad into universality," feel in circles of longitude and latitude, and cannot contract the grasp of our minds to scan with nice scrutiny particular foibles, or to be engrossed by any singular suffering. What we gain in extent, we lose in force and depth ... We are become public creatures.[1] (18.304)

In such a world even men's faces, met on the street, become merely signs to be read like the newspapers that inform their looks. "[L]iterature and civilization" – themselves now products of a globalized consciousness – "have abstracted man from himself so far that his existence is no longer *dramatic*; and the press has been the ruin of the stage, unless we are greatly deceived" (18.305). Courting an audience whose experience had been administered by the commercial press's universalizing gestures, the stage can no longer produce the vital and unique characters so common to previous ages.[2] Hazlitt responds to this "bias to abstraction," which he marks as "the reigning spirit of the age," by imagining theater as a catalyst for what I will call "Romantic occasionalism."[3] Because the best drama is "essentially individual and concrete, both in form and power" (18.305), attending to those "particular foibles" and "individual sufferings" elided by contemporary discourse, it refuses claims to universality. The writer of tragedy "can only deliver the sentiments of given persons, placed in given circumstances," for "within the circle of dramatic character and natural passion, each individual is to feel as keenly, as profoundly, as rapidly as possible, but he is not to feel beyond it, for others or for the whole" (18.305). By providing scenes of interaction, drama reveals its characters' particularity, so that "each ... must be a kind of centre of repulsion to the rest" (18.305). In the midst of a dehumanizing politics, drama – and as we shall see in Hazlitt's reviews of Edmund Kean's acting, theater – asks audiences to attend once again to the personal.[4]

The testimony against universal figures that begins in Hazlitt's theatrical criticism undergirds his most famous mature work. Published in 1825, *The Spirit of the Age* "refuses," in the words of James Chandler, "either to capture 'the spirit of the age' in a single portrait that could stand as its total representation *or* to select from among the 'spirits of the age' a single" representative portrait (185, emphasis Chandler's). This refusal, which

Chandler claims inheres throughout Hazlitt's familiar style, is to my mind a product of Hazlitt's closeness to the nightly life of London's theaters. By translating theatrical performances into conversational prose, Hazlitt calls forth a community bound, through the critic's persona, to undeniably particular experiences.[5] Hazlitt's criticism thus participates in what Chandler calls a Romantic casuistry both in its attention to an actor's particular responses to changing dramatic situations and in its representation of the critic's reaction to the occasion of performance. As Hazlitt wrote in *On Actors and Acting* in January 1817, "The merits of a new play, or of a new actor, are always among the first topics of polite conversation. One way in which public exhibitions contribute to refine and humanise mankind, is by supplying them with ideas and subjects of conversation and interest in common. The progress of civilisation is in proportion to the number of common-places current in society" (4.154). Here the "civilisation" that reading, writing, and talking about theater take on is a humanizing rather than a dehumanizing tenor. The best actors present their audiences with particular *cases*, studies in human behavior from which new modes of experience may be imagined. The coming together of men and women in theater's urban and unruly space is for Hazlitt, and consequently for his readers, nothing less than an ongoing reconception of Britain's public life along experiential rather than "abstracted" lines.

As Julie Carlson has shown, Hazlitt along with Charles Lamb and Leigh Hunt "evince a sea-change in cultural defences of theatre, valuing it explicitly not on moral grounds but for its capacity to unite people, humanize them, reconcile their conflicting interests and give them something to talk about" ("Hazlitt" 146). Even as Hazlitt's critical voice courts a post-revolutionary despondency – a loneliness born of broken idealism – he finds in that loneliness an impetus toward communal renewal. His theatrical reviews engender a cultural conversation that, in Carlson's words, "handles some of the fall-out from the failure of revolutionary friendship and its dream of disinterested relations between people" ("Hazlitt" 162). Yet if this sociability stands, for Carlson, as the "last defense of the revolutionary effectiveness of theatre on rationalist grounds" ("Hazlitt" 149), it also marks Hazlitt's response to the commercial periodical culture within which he worked. Hazlitt's itinerancy – both professional and rhetorical – refuses to situate the critic as a stable repository of moral truth, but it also does more than assign to him the role of conversational catalyst. Hazlitt's criticism, like the acting of the performers he encounters, offers itself to readers as a new model of cultural negotiation, an imagining of what it means to be a human being in an age when the most radical of idealisms has failed and in which the

British response to that trauma has begun to elide individual and local identities. This is an exemplary Romantic occasionalism, ill at ease with its own desire to idealize or generalize. Yet it is that ill at easeness that Hazlitt sees as a solution to the numbing comforts of self-abstraction. If, as Mary Fairclough has argued, Hazlitt distrusts the "unruly crowd" as imposing a tyrannical "collective sympathy" on individual acts of imagination and argument, still it is by engaging that crowd that the possibility of "individual autonomy," to employ Fairclough's phrase, can be found (8). In this, Hazlitt's work participates in what Paul Hamilton has called a "metaromantic" project. Refusing idealism as a solution to history's traumas, still it looks "for ways to redeploy an aesthetic grasp of the self whose utopian potential is too powerful to be justifiably abandoned" (2).[6]

My focus on Hazlitt's occasionalism begins with a brief speculation on how early employment as a parliamentary reporter at the *Morning Chronicle* honed his sense of the reporter's role. Situating Hazlitt at the center of a burgeoning periodical culture, I then argue that his reviews of Edmund Kean provided him with a new way to imagine theatrical experience. The periodical contests I have described in Chapters 1 and 2 made possible the emergence of a theatrical figure – a case – like Kean's, and Hazlitt seized the opportunity offered by Kean's iconoclastic acting to transform theatrical reviewing itself, substituting for exhausted models of reception a vital enactment of the critic's own subjectivity. For Hazlitt, criticism must refuse a universalizing aesthetic just as Kean's performances had refused universalizing modes of acting. And Hazlitt's writing seeks to renovate not only theatrical criticism but also more largely a press that had, to his mind, been co-opted by commercialism. Going beyond the innovative occasionalism even of Hunt's *Examiner* reviews, Hazlitt crafts a writing subject that is not only sociable in Carlson's terms but also provides readers an occasion for their own subjective reorientations. Even as he refuses to moralize, Hazlitt resists the prevailing commercial representation of theater newspapers continually offered in their pages, as well as the consumerist modes of engagement theatrical dailies encouraged. To understand Hazlitt's influence on Cockney Romanticism, and particularly his influence on Keats, we must recognize that this modeling of the theatrically experienced subject has implications beyond theater criticism itself. Accordingly, in the last section of the chapter, I move beyond Hazlitt's strictly theatrical writing to offer readings of two essays, "The Indian Jugglers" and "The Fight." These essays, published in 1819 and 1822, respectively, widen the scope of Hazlitt's reviews, inaugurating a cultural criticism that imagines the critic as both creature and creator of an ongoing local conversation. While essays such as

"On Londoners and Country People," "The Free Admission," and "On the Feeling of Immortality in Youth" – and more explicitly dramatic writings such as *Liber Amoris* or *Conversations of James Northcote* – evince Hazlitt's keen understanding of the theatricality of everyday life, I choose "The Indian Jugglers" and "The Fight" because each of them explicitly situates itself in a larger field of conversation made possible by (a) the occasion of a public event and (b) the writer's conspicuous translation of that event into narrative.

I From Metaphysician to Journalist

With its emphasis on Hazlitt's embrace of the occasional, the particular, and the local, my discussion digresses from a recent critical return to Hazlitt's metaphysics. Prompted by Uttara Natarajan's provocative claim for the primacy of mind over sensory experience in Hazlitt's writing, there has been a renewed consideration of the 1805 *An Essay on the Principles of Human Action* and its influence on Hazlitt's later essays.[7] Significantly, the debate has centered on the dialectic in Hazlitt's writing between the metaphysical and the material, a phenomenon aptly encapsulated by Tim Milnes's contention that late in his career "Hazlitt remained epistemologically empiricist while appearing to be metaphysically idealist" (108). Qualifying Natarajan's contention that Hazlitt's early investment in a metaphysically unifying notion of imagination persists throughout his work, James Mulvihill, among others, has argued that "the self for Hazlitt is a constant dialectic of experience and abstraction" (33). While it is not my intention to add to this fruitful discussion with another reading of the *Essay*, I do believe it worthwhile to explore how that text prefigures the theatrical criticism's concern with identity's public dimension. On the one hand, the *Essay* seems, along the lines Natarajan suggests, to imagine an integral mind that refuses to subordinate itself to external stimuli:

> Personality does not arise either from the being this, or that, from the identity of the thinking being with itself at different times or at the same time, or still less from being unlike others, which is not necessary to it, but from the peculiar connection which subsists between the different faculties and perceptions of the same conscious being, constituted as man is, so that as the subject of his own reflection or consciousness the same things impressed on any of his faculties produce a quite different effect upon *him* from what they would do if they were impressed in the same way on any other being. (I.36)

Yet if for Natarajan this process ultimately confirms the primacy of mind in a Kantian way, a passage shortly further on in the *Essay* makes clear that the

1 From Metaphysician to Journalist

subject's awareness of its "peculiarity" can only emerge through *continual* interaction with others:

> It is by comparing the knowledge that I have of my own impressions, ideas, powers, &c. with my knowledge of the same or similar impressions, ideas, &c. in others, and with the still more imperfect conception that I form of what passes in their minds when this is supposed to be essentially different from what passes in my own, that I acquire the general notion of self. If I had no idea of what passes in the minds of others, or if my ideas of their feelings and perceptions were perfect representations, i.e. mere conscious repetitions of them, all proper personal distinction would be lost either in pure self-love, or in perfect universal sympathy. (I.37)

"Self" is a product of communicative action, in which social activity calls the mind's attention to its encounters with "the minds of others." Rather than providing raw material for the imagination's associative powers, sensory perception enables the social, which is to say linguistic, exchanges necessary for self-conception.[8] As experience becomes public, subject becomes self. Hazlitt writes in the later essay "Whether Genius is Conscious of its Powers?" that "no man is truly himself, but in the idea which others entertain of him" (12.117). Knowledge of that idea is produced by interaction, be it verbal conversation or the conversational exchange represented and facilitated by the printed page.

The relentless publicity necessary for the shaping of a lived, which is to say an experienced, self informs Hazlitt's review criticism at the level of both form and content.[9] For Hazlitt, the periodical essay is one link in a chain of ongoing conversation that transforms groups of individuals into communities. As a reviewer, he writes about those events most conducive to such identity-forming exchange. His theatrical reviewing, especially, displays a critical persona whose integrity is not predicated on a defended psychological isolation but rather on the unconcluded trajectories of personal engagement with others – trajectories most vividly represented in actors' performances.[10] This relation is a radical revision of both the Smithian notion of sympathy (which assumes two subjects whose identities have been individuated and then sutured by feelings of identification) and of the Wordsworthian egotistical imagination (which sees all things in itself).[11] For Hazlitt, the Wordsworthian subject in particular posits a discrete autonomy even as it continually reaches beyond itself. Wordsworth's poetry exhibits a relation to the external world that "rejects [objects or situations] as interfering with the workings of his own mind" and finally "sees all things in himself" (4.112). Hazlitt's reaction to the periodical culture I have described in Chapters 1 and 2 emerges from this revisionary philosophical position, and its influence is evident in his earliest journalistic writings.[12]

In 1812, Charles Lamb recommended Hazlitt to John Dyer Collier, foreign editor of the *Morning Chronicle*, as a parliamentary reporter. Hazlitt was a suitable candidate for the position formerly held by William "Memory" Woodfall because of Hazlitt's 1807 volume *Eloquence of the British Senate* and because he possessed, in the words of Lamb's reference letter, a "singular facility in retaining all conversations at which he has ever been present" (*Letters* 2.124). As I discuss in Chapter 1, parliamentary reporting was one of the central elements of the commercial press, a feature that worked with advertisements and other devices to attract commercially interested readers. Because theatrical criticism in newspapers developed along the same discursive lines as parliamentary reporting, with respect to both its position in the discourse of commercial news and its emphasis on providing readers with a sense of connection to a larger community, many theatrical critics began their careers as parliamentary reporters.[13] In six months, Hazlitt produced some seventy columns, moving from straightforward parliamentary reporting in November to political commentary in 1813 and eventually to the theatrical reviews that would earn him his lasting reputation. A brief return to an example of the *Morning Chronicle*'s parliamentary reporting offered in Chapter 1 will provide a sense of how Hazlitt's time as a parliamentary reporter shaped the development of his Romantic occasionalism:

> Mr. Abbott having then been conducted to the Chair in the usual manner, proceeded to address the House from it. He entertained a deep sense of the arduous duties which every person who filled that Chair was called upon to fulfill; and so long as he discharged these duties to the best of his judgment and ability, he hoped he should receive the support of the House. He begged leave to assure the House, that he was entirely devoted to its service. *(Hear, hear, hear!)* (*Morning Chronicle* November 25, 1812)

It is possible, though not certain, that Hazlitt composed this passage, or part of it, in late 1812. Whoever its author(s), the account's descriptive compression, its shifting perspective, and its dramatic structure are exemplary; these are all elements of what Hazlitt will later call the "familiar style," which becomes especially prominent in the review essays I will discuss at chapter's end.[14] Yet I recall these qualities not simply to argue that they manifest themselves explicitly in Hazlitt's later work. Rather, I would suggest more specifically that when Hazlitt's duties expand to include theatrical performances, he appropriates elements of reporterly language to situate his readers as imaginatively concurrent witnesses to the occasion of performance – to reproduce the sense of contemporaneity that parliamentary reporting required. Hazlitt was, all in all, a strictly parliamentary reporter for less than a year. But his time at the *Chronicle* began a lifelong familiarity with the industry's "rage for conveying information," with the importance of the widening readership that stoked its fires, and with the significance of the political arena as a stage for public self-fashioning (Hazlitt 16.221).[15]

Hazlitt knew well that newspapers both represented and facilitated the commercialization of Britain's theatrical experience and had elicited a reactionary anti-commercial discourse among many periodical reviewers. Continuing the critique of the press he began in his 1820 essay on "The Drama," Hazlitt asserted in an 1828 *Examiner* review of *The Beggar's Opera* that reaction to the French Revolution was in part to blame for this polarization: "In a word, the French Revolution has spoiled all, like a great stone thrown into a well, 'with a hollow and rueful rumble,' and left no two ideas in the public mind but those of high and low" (18.400). The split between "high" and "low" also structured a stark professional divide between early-nineteenth-century daily press writers, who were perceived as hacks, and gentlemanly contributors to newly ascendant review journals.[16] Yet Hazlitt is something of a transpontine figure, crossing boundaries between oppositional professional spheres, the competing discourses they produced, the diverse entertainments they considered, and the different readerships they imagined. Between 1812 and 1830, Hazlitt wrote for *The Morning Chronicle, The Times, The Champion, The Examiner, The Liberal, The London Magazine, The Edinburgh Magazine, The Edinburgh Review, The London Weekly Review, The Monthly Magazine,* and *The New Monthly Magazine*. He wrote for dailies, weeklies, and monthlies, for magazines, reviews, and newspapers. At some of these publications, such as the *Chronicle* and the *Examiner*, he held a regular position as theatrical critic. For others, he contributed articles on only a few occasions. Often he depended on work at one journal to secure him work at another, whose readership might only partly overlap with that of the first. In 1814, for example, Lady Catherine Mackintosh admired Hazlitt's articles on the fine arts in the *Champion* and was subsequently instrumental in helping him secure a spot as a contributor to the less radical *Edinburgh Review*, one of the most financially productive situations in his career. In part, Hazlitt's itinerancy was occasioned by the instability of the day's press institutions. Even as periodicals sought to distinguish themselves from one another, they disappeared quickly when they could not sustain a reading audience.[17] The emergence of new periodicals devoted to theater in the decade that spanned Hazlitt's most productive years was rivaled as a trend in periodical publishing only by the disappearance of many of those same publications. While much of the era's theatrical criticism is marked simultaneously by an attempt to transform widening theatergoing audiences into sustaining readerships and an antithetical insistence on distinguishing those readerships from the commercialized theatergoing audiences of which they were a part, Hazlitt's theatrical criticism contends with these discourses by substituting for the language of cultural distinction a language of personal theatrical experience.

Unlike other sometime journalists who, though they wrote for the press to supplement their incomes, could rely on annuities and pensions to maintain social status as poets or "men of letters" (Coleridge comes to mind), Hazlitt was a strictly professional writer.[18] Journalism provided both his central source of income and the field in which he achieved his public profile. Yet if intimate involvement with a variety of periodical publications necessitated that he develop a writing style different from the commercial newspaper's reports, the castigatory prose of Dutton, or the oracular machinations of Coleridge, it also enabled him to imagine anew the critic's role as cultural mediator for diverse communities of reception. David Bromwich has called Hazlitt's prose "extraordinarily varied" and "extraordinarily responsive" in its ability to mix familiar address with traditional eighteenth-century antithesis and aphorism (15): "Hazlitt carries on the inherited mode wherever its suits him, comfortably for any stretch of sentences, though as a rule he breaks it up before a paragraph is done" (15–16). For Bromwich, Hazlitt is the paradigm of a new kind of English critic whose intellectual rigor is balanced by the "willing imperfection of a man talking to you about what concerns him most" (16). Other scholars have described Hazlitt's prose as inherently dramatic, arguing that the quick shifts in perspective and tone Bromwich describes subvert the possibility of a unified subject-speaker. Jon Cook, for example, has claimed that Hazlitt's aphoristic style manifests a philosophical resistance to falsely authoritative, monological discourse.[19] Kevin Gilmartin goes further, suggesting that "Hazlitt's prose turned the negative energy of radical reform into a complex rhetorical problem to be worked out endlessly on the printed page" (*Print Politics* 231). But the protean qualities of Hazlitt's review criticism are as much an effect of the world of occasion within which he plied his journalistic trade, the world of a rapidly changing theater and its rapidly changing periodical press, as they are a stylistic embodiment of preexisting anti-egotistical philosophy. Hazlitt's criticism responds to the cultural tensions brought on by theater's commercialization – and the critical

1 From Metaphysician to Journalist

reaction against it – by portraying the critic as a subject whose daily cultural experience is determined by those tensions.[20]

While the daily news managed readers' experience in such a way that theater became viewed as one form of cultural exchange among many, Hazlitt's writing renders facile consumption of theater impossible even as it resists the narrowing impulse of elitist distinction. The eighteenth-century model of theatrical criticism can be understood, albeit simplistically, as the application of preexisting aesthetic categories to performed drama for a small coterie of readers. Hazlitt responds to the rise of commercial journalism by using the review to invent an ad hoc coterie interested in the lived experience of theater's reception. Such a discourse imagines the identities of both writer and reader to be in a state of perpetual flux. The result, though, is not the dissolution of an integral self, but rather recognition of how an individual's interaction with community provides a local context within, and a trajectory along which, personal and communal identity can cohere. This rhetorical mobility – a mobility fostered by Hazlitt's association with the Hunts' intergeneric and formally self-conscious *Examiner* – enables Hazlitt to attend in a unique way to the shifting nature of privacy and publicity and to the growing opposition between legitimate and illegitimate forms of theater. I do not claim that Hazlitt stands outside the early-nineteenth-century rise of middle-class philosophical criticism that Jon Klancher has described.[21] Following Kevin Gilmartin, in fact, I see Hazlitt's commitment to radical causes as "sublimated, and almost entirely translated to the printed page" (*Print Politics* 228).[22] But this is what makes Hazlitt a compelling figure. His position in the field of periodical publication required continual interaction with a variety of print genres, from commercial news to philosophical reviews, and his writing at times takes on and at times rejects the rhetorical elements of these genres in a manner unlike that found in any of his contemporaries. The openness of his style – his refusal to appropriate or reject wholesale the critical models available to him – renders Hazlitt's work a site of fruitful contention between various Romantic-period public discourses: radical, commercial, elite. Eschewing the drive for cultural distinction predicated on the conspicuous rejection of commercialism, Hazlitt marks himself as a critic whose potential audience is not limited to readers seeking to distinguish themselves from the consuming classes. He thus becomes one of the first, and last, theatrical critics to reach across a growing and institutionally sanctioned divide between high and mass culture, a divide nowhere more evident than in London's early-nineteenth-century theatrical world.[23] Engaging legitimate and illegitimate entertainments, providing philosophical argumentation and personal reflection, Hazlitt's review criticism is both the symptom of and the cure for this characteristic Romantic fracture. His theatrical reviews and the essays that develop from them become a model of cultural negotiation for readers, remaking with each instance of their reception the boundaries of Romantic-period public experience.

II Theatrical Critic

When he began writing theatrical reviews in late 1813, Hazlitt was a longtime theatergoer and an experienced reporter, aware of the efforts by commercial and periodical presses to organize the nation's theatrical experience. The preface to *A View of the English Stage*, written in 1818, reflected on Hazlitt's position at the center of the competitive field. Dismissed from the *Times* for being "too prolix on the subject of the Bourbons," he facetiously advises "any one who has an ambition to write, and to write *his best*, in the periodical press, to get if possible 'a situation' in the *Times* newspaper, the Editor of which is a man of business, and not of letters" (5.174). The italicization of *his best* suggests a certain disdain for commercially oriented professionals, men "of business, and not of letters," who cater their criticism to suit the tastes of a news-reading public. (Writing one's *best*, that is, is different from writing one's best.) Though less critical in the preface of his tenure at the *Chronicle*, Hazlitt describes how his reviewing style conflicted even there with his editor's expectations. Told to "give as favourable an account as I could" when reviewing Edmund Kean for the first time, Hazlitt "gave a true one":

> My opinions have been sometimes called singular: they are merely sincere. I say what I think: I think what I feel. I cannot help receiving certain impressions from things; and I have sufficient courage to declare (somewhat abruptly) what they are ... I do not make it a common practice, to think nothing of an actor or an author, because all the world have not pronounced in his favour, and after they have, to persist in condemning him, as proof not of imbecility and ill-nature, but of independence of taste and spirit. (5.175)

This defense organizes the practice of reviewing around "feeling," which in turn informs thought and opinion. "Independence" resides in the ability to communicate "impressions" without submitting to the prevailing opinions of peers, editor, or readers:

> I did not endeavor to persuade Mr. Perry that Mr. Kean was an actor that would not last, merely because he had not lasted; nor that Miss Stephens

knew nothing of singing, because she had a sweet voice. On the contrary, I did all I could to counteract the effect of these safe, not very sound, insinuations, and "screw the courage" of one principal organ of the public opinion "to the sticking place." I do not repent of having done so. (5.175)

Hazlitt emphasizes the *Chronicle*'s critical over its commercial function and sees the critic's role as a shepherd of public opinion rather than as a servant of its whims.[24] For this he runs the risk of biting the hand that feeds him: "I was ... placed out of the pale of theatrical orthodoxy, for not subscribing implicitly to all the articles of belief imposed upon my senses and understanding" (5.176). "The Drama, no. VII," published in 1820 in the *London Magazine* offers an even more forceful critique. There, Hazlitt attacks directly "the gentlemen-critics of the daily press" for having "no opinion of their own. They dare not boldly and distinctly declare their opinion of a new dramatic experiment, and the reason is, their convictions are not clear enough to warrant their placing any confidence in them, till they are confirmed by being put to a vote" (18.327). Authority, for Hazlitt, must come from the critic himself and not from an institutional or political affiliation.

Hazlitt's self-positioning in the periodical field is not fundamentally unlike that taken by anti-commercial critics like Thomas Dutton. However, despite his attacks on the commercial press, Hazlitt does not dismiss the newspaper's importance as a conduit for effective theatrical criticism. On the contrary, almost a third of his theatrical reviews appeared in either the *Morning Chronicle* or the *Times*. And the most significant institutional affiliation of his career, his position with the Hunts' *Examiner*, aligned him with a periodical that, though a weekly, appropriated the discourse of the commercial news both with its topicality and its printed form. Hazlitt's independence is as much a matter of style – a refusal to produce commercial criticism's "measured praise" of actors – as it is a refusal to submit to his editors' opinions on a given topic. By displaying the formation of the critic's subjective relation to public events, Hazlitt's prose resisted classification by readers as either an elite discourse of distinction or a commercial discourse of consumption.

A review from Hazlitt's first year as a London critic, which he chose to reprint in both the 1817 *The Round Table* and the 1818 *A View of the English Stage*, gives a fuller sense of his focus on the experiential dimension of theatrical reception. The analogy he uses to illustrate the appeal of Iago's character is revealing:

> We might ask those who think the character of Iago is not natural, why they go to see it performed – but from the interest it excites, the sharper edge which it sets on their curiosity and imagination? Why do we go to see tragedies in general? Why do we always read the accounts in the newspapers, of dreadful fires and shocking murders, but for the same reason? Why do so many persons frequent executions and trials; or why do the lower classes almost universally take delight in barbarous sports and cruelty to animals, but because there is a natural tendency in the mind to strong excitement, a desire to have its faculties roused and stimulated to the utmost? (5.213)

Theater, in other words, is sensational. But Hazlitt's attitude toward sensation differs from that exhibited by most journal writers of the time, who argue that sensational entertainments subvert theater's moral mission. In fact, Hazlitt does nothing less than render Shakespearean tragedy equivalent to newspaper reading as a stimulus for "strong excitement."[25] Iago, as performed spectacle, operates as an object of public fascination in the same way as reports of fire and murder. His actions on stage elicit the audience's voyeurism even as he exhibits an identical motivation on the level of his own character: he is both an object of and a subject constituted by sensational desire. Iago's character is "natural," though, because he is not only the focus of the audience's fascinations but also a representation of them:

> Whenever this principle [of excitement] is not under the restraint of humanity or the sense of moral obligation, there are no excesses to which it will not of itself give rise, without the assistance of any other motive, either of passion or self-interest. Iago is only an extreme instance of the kind; that is, of diseased intellectual activity, with an almost perfect indifference to moral good or evil, or rather with a preference of the latter, because it falls more in with his favorite propensity, gives greater zest to his thoughts and scope to his actions. (5.213)

Hazlitt here aligns cultural reception, both low (the reading of newspapers) and high (the spectatorship of Shakespearean drama), with the mind's "desire to have its faculties roused and stimulated to the utmost." The audience differs from Iago not in kind but in degree, for he is "only an extreme instance" of the same "intellectual activity" that impels their viewing. The review – first published in the *Examiner* – doubly implicates its reader as theatrical and news-seeking voyeur. Significantly, though, theater's sensationalism becomes a basis for criticism rather than an object of criticism's attack. Here Hazlitt nearly inverts the derision deployed by the young William Wordsworth in his *Preface* to *Lyrical Ballads* and by

Coleridge in *Biographia Literaria*, both of whom abjure theatrical sensationalism as a mind-numbing experience.

When Hazlitt considers the task of the professional reviewer in the preface to *A View of the English Stage*, he does not rail against theater's socially disruptive potential, as many of his contemporaries do. Rather, he begins by focusing on its positive public effects and the role that the actor takes in producing them:

> A good play, well acted, passes away a whole evening delightfully at a certain period of life, agreeably at all times; we read the account of it next morning with pleasure, and it generally furnishes one leading topic of conversation for the afternoon. The disputes on the merits or defects of the last new piece, or of a favourite performer, are as common, as frequently renewed, and carried on with as much eagerness and skill, as those on almost any other subject. (5.173)

In the case of performed drama, the audience's experience is mediated most effectively by the person of the actor. The public's conversational response is driven by an unspoken recognition that actors represent the audience's social condition, so that "while we are talking about them, we are thinking about ourselves" (5.173). In his 1817 *Examiner* article "On Actors and Acting," Hazlitt considers further the ways in which actors influence a viewer's daily life:

> We see ourselves at second-hand in them: they shew us all that we are, all that we wish to be, and all that we dread to be ... What brings the resemblance nearer is, that, as *they* imitate us, so we, in our turn, imitate them ... They teach us when to laugh and when to weep, when to love and when to hate, upon principle and with good grace! Wherever there is a playhouse, the world will not go amiss. (4.153)

Actors are the most significant element of performed theater, eliciting the "curiosity and interest" of the viewer, because they model particular experiences of intersubjective engagement (5.173). "Disputes on the merits or defects of the last new piece" constitute more than an exchange of opinion; they represent theatergoers' attempts to evaluate the relevance of the performance to their own modes of experience. Recalling in the *View*'s preface several stories he has "heard" about David Garrick, Hazlitt remarks that such "anecdotes" are worth remembering because they "shew his power over the human heart, and enable us to measure his genius with that of others by its effects" (5.174). Theatrical genius, that is, is measured by talk, and more specifically by talk that extends the power of a performance beyond its originating moment. Because the actors' "power over the human heart" is initially conveyed by a physical act, it needs the critic's pen to extend this social effect: "[T]he player's art is one that perishes with him, and leaves no traces of itself, but in the faint descriptions of the pen and pencil" (5.173). Between the evening passing away and the next day's conversation, the critic transforms those faint traces – a literal manuscript – into published text. Extending the reach of theatrical experience, Hazlitt is keenly aware of the transactional cultural space in which his reviews operate, particularly when writing for the dailies. Even the "detailed account of the stage" the *View* contains is taken from "criticisms which have appeared, with little interruption, during the last four years, in different newspapers" (5.174). This is to say that the book compresses a periodical construction of theatrical experience into one volume in an attempt to consolidate the impact of its constituent parts, providing a measure against which the performances of contemporary actors can be judged: "The knowledge of circumstances like these, serves to keep alive the memory of past excellence, and to stimulate future efforts" (5.174). The periodical reviewer is the conduit through which an evening's pastime helps constitute public experience in the larger, and longer, historical world.

What is at stake for Hazlitt in his theatrical criticism is not simply the reputation of dramatists or actors, or an assessment of representational styles, but an ongoing exploration of how theatrical criticism could extend theater's effects to a wider reading audience. For the theater critic, the review of a play differs from the review of other public events – say, parliamentary reporting – because it considers the actor as an experiential model. This of course demands attention on the critic's part to the conditions in which the actor's performance takes place, both in the moment of its execution and in its afterlife as it moves through the institutions of print criticism. Accordingly, Hazlitt denigrates stagecraft that obscures actors. In a late *Examiner* review of 1828, he laments the production values commercialization has begotten. In France, where unity of time and place predominate as dramaturgic principles, the scenery "is no object either of attraction or expense," so that "the excellence of the performance and the taste of the town keep pace with one another, and with the absence of show and extrinsic decoration" (18.409). In England, however, where spectacular effect is the dramatic standard,

> The scene travels, and our scene-shifters, scene painters, mechanists, and the whole theatrical *commiseriat* go along with it. The variety, the gaudiness, the expense is endless: to pay for the getting up such an immense apparatus, the

houses must be enlarged to hold a proportionable rabble of "barren spectators": the farther off they are thrown, the stronger must be the glare, the more astonishing the effect, and the play and the players (with all relish for wit or nature) dwindle into insignificance, and are lost in the blaze of a huge chandelier or the grin of a baboon. (18.409)

Commercialism produces a vicious circle in which massive effects elicit consumer desire for greater spectacles, in turn distancing viewers both physically and psychologically from engagement with the performance. Nor is commercialization's influence restricted to the play's scenic presentation. In an earlier review, published on February 24, 1814, in the *Chronicle*, Hazlitt comments on the "manner in which Shakespeare's plays have been generally altered, or rather mangled, by modern mechanists" (18.191). "[T]edious and misplaced extracts from other plays" added to *Richard III*, for example, only "make the character of Richard as odious and disgusting as possible," mimicking melodrama's oversimplified characterizations (18.192). Such alterations prevent the actor from representing the complex reactions that Shakespeare's plays demand: "We have taken the present opportunity to offer these remarks on the necessity of acting the plays of our great Bard, in spirit and substance, instead of burlesquing them, because we think the stage has acquired in Mr. Kean an actor capable of doing singular justice to many of his finest delineations of character" (18.194). Burlesquing assumes a commodity relation between modern performers and Shakespearean text: the play is raw material to be appropriated for inappropriate use, treated solely as a tool to satisfy audiences' desire for spectacle.[26] The critic, for Hazlitt, must sift through these obscurants to assess not simply the skill with which actors portray their dramatic roles but also their ability to enact particular *cases* – instances of experience that are relevant to contemporary audiences.

The primary measure of an actor's power is this ability to affect (and, in that way, effect) the critic. As Joseph Donohue has asserted, "the tenor of Hazlitt's reviews is wholly theatrical. His response is to the powerful immediate stimulus of the performance itself, and his position in the pit is one of close relationship to the audience" ("Hazlitt's Sense of the Dramatic" 715). In an 1814 *Champion* review of Eliza O'Neill, Hazlitt compares the rising actress to the great Sarah Siddons. Whereas in Siddons "passion was combined with lofty imagination and commanding intellect. Miss O'Neill owes everything to extreme sensibility" (18.196). O'Neill "gives herself up entirely to the impression of circumstances, is borne along the tide of passion, and absorbed in her sufferings. She realizes all that is suggested by the progress of the story, and answers the utmost expectation of the spectator, but she seldom goes beyond it. She does not lift the imagination out of itself" (18.196). By contrast, Siddons "seemed formed for scenes of terror and agony, and fit to contend with them," which is why "her acting left a weight upon the mind, and overpowered the faculties" (18.196). The measure of both actresses is the degree to which they elicit from the audience a parallel experience to that embodied on stage. The viewer's immediate response to the performer becomes the starting point of Hazlitt's evaluation, the beginning condition necessary for the critic's experiential mediation to occur. And that starting point opens new possibilities for the way theatrical experience can be valued. By rooting his favorable comparison of O'Neill with Siddons in the younger actress's ability to produce feeling in the viewer, Hazlitt recognizes the generative, if finally contained, qualities of "sensibility." While such an evaluation does, in the end, confirm G. J. Barker-Benfield's alignment of sensibility with a conventional and ultimately conservative figuration of female affect, Hazlitt's recognition of O'Neill's presentation on stage at least situates her as an agent whose acting has the capacity, if only seldom, to "go beyond" the expectation of the viewer. In Barker-Benfield's historical account, sensibility "signified revolution, promised freedom, threatened subversion, and became convention" (xvii). Yet even in its domesticated state, sensibility always retained the threat of breaking containment. While Hazlitt's certainly presents a variation of masculine judgment in his consideration of both actresses as "accomplished women," to employ Ann Bermingham's phrase ("Elegant Females" 507), his evaluation of O'Neill's sensible acting alongside Siddons's high tragic seriousness suggests a mode of theatrical experience that at least leaves open the possibility for female affect to challenge the expectation of the male spectator.[27]

Edmund Kean is the most significant actor in Hazlitt's theatrical criticism because, like O'Neill, his acting presents instances of how audiences might reimagine their own theatrical experience. Kean and Hazlitt emerged on the London theatrical scene at nearly the same moment. Both were products of a post–Old Price riots world in which theater's commercialism and its effect on audiences were constant subjects of dispute. Amid the varied and vehement reactions to Kean's controversial acting, Leigh Hunt's *Examiner* reviews are helpful in establishing how Kean propelled Hunt's shift toward experiential reviewing, paralleling Hazlitt's even more significant transformation as his own career lengthened. Upon Kean's release from prison in February 1815, Hunt went to see him in *Richard III* and was "disappointed" by the fact that Kean was "nothing but a first-rate actor of the ordinary, stagy class."[28] By 1818, however, Hunt had changed his opinion entirely, calling Kean's Othello "the masterpiece of the living stage." Hunt's later assessment considers the actor in a more complex fashion by connecting his "low and agitated affectation of quiet discourse" with the audience's awareness of his public persona offstage. "The actor's talent must be modified by his own character off the stage ... for we conjecture from anecdotes that are before the public, that Mr. Kean's temper is hasty, and his disposition excellent and generous; and it is of passion and natural generosity that *Othello*'s character is made up."[29] Kean's ability to present emotion to the audience, and indeed to instill emotion in them, is at least in part predicated on his presence as a sensational public figure in London society – his position as a subject of London's talk.

Hunt's changing opinion of Kean recognizes that Kean's performances and his public persona were prototypes of a new kind of theatrical experience that traditional criticism could not explain: urban, socially and sexually mobile, commercialized. And Hazlitt more than any of his contemporaries was attuned to this implication. As he commented in the *Examiner* in July 1814:

> There is no one within our remembrance, who has so completely foiled the critics as this celebrated actor: one sagacious person imagines that he must perform a part in a certain manner; another virtuoso chalks out a different path for him; and when the time comes, he does the whole off in a way, that neither of them had the least conception of, and which both of them are therefore very ready to condemn as entirely wrong. It was ever the trick of genius to be thus. We confess that Mr. Kean has thrown us out more than once. (5.212)

Kean's critical incorrigibility makes him a subject worth discussing. Hazlitt noted on more than one occasion, "Mr. Kean affords a never-failing source of observation and discussion" (5.211); he is "food for the critics" because "there is no end of the topics he affords for discussion – for praise and blame" (5.223). Representing in body the conflict between competing modes of theatrical experience that reviewers were trying to resolve, Kean was unreadable in any satisfactory way by most of them.

Like Hunt, Hazlitt responds to this critical impoverishment by devising a new mode of criticism in which the style of the review conspicuously mirrors Kean's ongoing occasionalism – his coming to terms with the changing occasions of dramatic situation. But where Hunt's strategy is to highlight the actor's socially representative function, Hazlitt goes further. Beginning with his earliest reviews, Hazlitt treats acting not only as the performance of a character's scripted lines, describing voice, body, and gesture, but also as the performer's display of an occasional mode of subjectivity – a way of relating to and choosing from among the multiple performative possibilities that a given text offers. Hazlitt's first theatrical assignment for the *Chronicle*, published in January 1814, is exemplary:

> The character of Shylock is that of a man brooding over one idea, that of its wrongs, and bent upon one unalterable purpose, that of revenge. In conveying a profound impression of this feeling, or in embodying the general conception of rigid and uncontroulable self-will, equally proof against every sentiment of humanity or prejudice of opinion, we have seen actors more successful than Mr. Kean; but in giving effect to the conflict of passions arising out of the contrasts of situation, in varied vehemence of declamation, in keenness of sarcasm, in the rapidity of his transitions from one tone and feeling to another, in propriety and novelty of action, presenting a succession of striking pictures, and giving perpetually fresh shocks of delight and surprise, it would be difficult to single out a competitor. (5.179)

Kean's ability to "give effect" in such a way that the audience is provided with "novelty" and a "succession of striking pictures" represents a departure from the more elegant, consistent style of legitimate actors like John Philip Kemble. By embodying a "conflict of passions" rather than a "profound impression" of a single "feeling," Kean's performance emphasizes the character's emotional and psychological occasionalism. The actor-subject is defined not by command of dramatic situations but by his rapidly changing responses to them. Remarkably, Hazlitt's style here reproduces the experience of Kean's acting, employing periodic sentences in its description of "other actors" but shifting once Kean's name is introduced into a hypotactic copia of theatrical effects – to the point of syntactic exhaustion.[30] On February 2, Hazlitt continued the analysis he had begun the previous week, offering in this instance a compressed and even more jolting stylistic representation of Kean's actions:

> His style of acting is, if we may use the expression, more significant, more pregnant with meaning, more varied and alive in every part, than any we have almost ever witnessed. The character never stands still; there is no vacant pause in the action; the eye is never silent. For depth and force of conception, we have seen actors whom we should prefer to Mr. Kean as Shylock; for brilliant and masterly execution, none. (5.180)

Moving from one feeling to another, and punctuating affective with physical mobility, Kean acts in such a way that *movement itself* becomes the subject of the audience's attention. This mobility is, in turn, replayed in Hazlitt's own prose. Scenes prompt the actor's process of subjective orientation toward the character he must embody, the resolution of which is continually deferred as one occasion develops from another in the play. This presentation creates in the critic – and in turn his readers – "shocks of delight and surprise" rather than a succession of coherent emotional states.

In an 1822 essay published in *Table Talk*, Hazlitt remarked on the necessity of seeing Kean's face to feel this multiply layered aspect of his performance:

> His face is the running comment on his acting, which reconciles the audience to it. Without that index to his mind, you are not prepared for the vehemence and suddenness of his gestures; his pauses are long, abrupt, and unaccountable, if not filled up by the expression; it is in the working of his face that you see the writing and coiling up of the passions before they make their serpent-spring; the lightning of his eye precedes the hoarse burst of thunder from his voice. (8.277)

Kean's acting represents a self-consciousness not found in earlier performers; his facial contortions render a "comment on his acting" even as he begins the presentation of another feeling.[31] As Hazlitt commented in an 1814 *Champion* review of Kean's Macbeth, which he called one of "the two finest things Mr. Kean has ever done," this style foregrounds the actor's human dimension, which in turn elicits the audience's emotional response:

> To enquire whether his manner in the latter scene was that of a king who commits a murder, or of a man who commits a murder to become a king, would be to "consider too curiously." But, as a lesson of common humanity, it was heart-rending. The hesitation, the bewildered look, the coming to himself when he sees his hands bloody; the manner in which his voice clung in his throat, and choked his utterance; his agony and tears, the force of nature overcome by passion – beggared description. It was a scene, which no one who saw it can ever efface from his recollection. (5.207)

The process of experience Kean models, his "agony and tears," his portrayal of "nature overcome by passion," displays the unpredictability and uncertainty of human psychological response – not unlike that which Hazlitt himself displays as he comments on how his ability to describe Kean is "beggared." Hazlitt's sentence bears the marks of this effect, as its compound subject oscillates between short pointed phrases ("The hesitation, the bewildered look ... his agony and tears") and longer descriptive clauses ("the coming to himself when he finds his hands bloody; the manner in which his voice clung in his throat"). The rhetorical tension this oscillation creates is released only by the deferred arrival of the sentence's verb, "beggared." Kean's constant physical and emotional movement, mirrored by Hazlitt's style, indicates not simply emotional range but also the difficulties that constitute an occasional subjectivity.

For Hazlitt, Kean's failures occur when his method of presentation calls *too much* attention to itself, becoming paradoxically egotistical even as it registers the power of situation to determine character.[32] "The fault of his acting was (if we may hazard the objection)," Hazlitt writes in the January 27, 1814, review, "an over-display of the resources of the art, which gave too much relief to the hard, impenetrable, dark groundwork of the character of Shylock" (5.179). The reason he lacks "dignified repose, and deep internal sentiment" is that he is a subject constituted by movement and social interaction (5.228). This is particularly true of Kean's portrayals of Othello. In a May 6, 1814 review of Kean in the part, Hazlitt comments that "there is even too much effect given, too many significant hints, too much appearance of study" in Kean's responses to the play's situations to allow his or the audience's natural immersion in them (5.184):

> Our highest conception of an actor is, that he shall assume the character once and for all, and be it throughout, and trust to this conscious sympathy for the effect produced. Mr. Kean's manner of acting is, on the contrary, rather a perpetual assumption of his part, always brilliant and successful, almost always true and natural, but yet always a distinct effort in every new situation, so that the actor does not seem entirely to forget himself, or to be so identified with the character ... But why do we try this actor by an ideal theory? Who is there that will stand the same test? It is, in fact, the last forlorn hope of criticism, for it shews we have nothing else to compare him with. (5.184)

Even as Hazlitt lingers on Kean's inability to reach the ideal standard, employing the vocabulary of a critical elite ("our highest conception"), he gives a potent picture of how Kean's limitations actually enable a new way of understanding, and writing about, an actor's representative function. "The last forlorn hope of criticism" is not simply to invent an ideal standard no actor can reach; it is, in a rhetorical move characteristic of Hazlitt's familiar style, self-consciously to break off from elitist criticism and comment on Kean's beggaring of evaluative categories. With a "distinct effort in every new situation," Kean struggles with the text. His "perpetual assumption of the part" indicates the impossibility of mastering the play's dramatic situations, enacting instead an ongoing dialectic between subject and cultural object that precludes both aristocratic ease and vulgar consumption.

Kean's controversial casuistry – his performed embodiment of a new kind of subject – is thrown into relief by Hazlitt's treatment of John Philip

Kemble. For Hazlitt, Kemble "is the most classical of actors. He is the only one of the moderns, who both in figure and action approaches the beauty and grandeur of the antique" (5.342). In a November 1814 review for the *Champion*, Hazlitt remarks that "the range of characters, in which Mr. Kemble shines, and is superior to every other actor, are those which consist in the development of some one sentiment or exclusive passion" (18.198). Whereas Kean attracts audiences with an ability to present, in a moment, a mass of contradictory feelings, Kemble's power resides in his mastery of the single emotion called for by each dramatic scene. Kemble's greatest excellence, though, is also his most glaring inadequacy in the contemporary historical moment. Often his pursuit of classical dignity underwhelms audiences, as Hazlitt comments in the May 16, 1816 *Examiner*: "Mr. Kemble sacrifices too much to decorum" because he is "chiefly afraid of being contaminated by too close an identity with the characters he represents" (5.303). Kemble's distance renders his performances, for all else they may be, less than natural: "He endeavors to raise Nature to the dignity of his own person and demeanor, and declines with a graceful smile and a waive of the hand, the ordinary services she might do him" (5.303). Kemble's neoclassical, eighteenth-century humanism denies the power of the external world (as it is represented on stage) to mold the subject in ways that are beyond its control. Kemble thus loses the power to represent modern theatergoers to themselves.[33]

The difference between Kemble and Kean is, from Hazlitt's perspective, nowhere more evident than in their contrasting performances of Shakespeare's Coriolanus. Hazlitt's *Examiner* review of Kemble's performance, published on December 15, 1816, famously describes (in terms taken from his *Characters of Shakespear's Plays*) the stakes of the drama: "The cause of the people is indeed but ill calculated as a subject for poetry ... the language of poetry naturally falls in with the language of power" (5.347). Juxtaposing the "imagination," which is "an aristocratical ... faculty" with the "understanding," which is "republican," Hazlitt finds Coriolanus decidedly in the camp of the former: "He is a conqueror and hero; he conquers other countries, and makes this a plea for enslaving his own" (5.348). The role suits Kemble perfectly because his aristocratic bearing enables a "lofty" presence on stage. By contrast,

> Mr. Kean's acting is not of the patrician order; he is one of the people, and what might be termed a *radical* performer. He can do all that may become a man "of our infirmity," "to relish all as sharply, passioned as we"; but he cannot play a God, or one who fancies himself a God, and who is sublime,

not in the strength of his own feelings, but in his contempt for those of others, and in his imaginary superiority to them. (18.290)[34]

Again, though, there is a critically generative dimension to Kean's failure. Because his lack of aristocratic pretension "evokes a tyranny which is provisional, precarious, half made up" (Moody, *Illegitimate Theatre* 129), it indicts the legitimate theatrical institutions that Kemble embodies as an actor and facilitates as a manager. Kemble communicates to theater's modern audience a beautiful remnant of a previous age – an enacted subjectivity with which they have little in common. Conversely, Kean's performance as Coriolanus fails because the role is an impossible one for an actor whose "want of grace and dignity," and whose dependence on the feelings of others, evokes the life of "the people."

Hazlitt's refusal to compare Kemble and Kean using the same standards exhibits his awareness that new forms of criticism are needed to attend to theater's changing social function. In a piece on Kemble's retirement, Hazlitt takes issue with critics who claim that Kemble has declined: "It is mere cant, to say that Mr. Kemble has quite fallen off of late – that he is not what he was: he may have fallen off in the opinion of some jealous admirers, because he is no longer in exclusive possession of the Stage: but in himself he has not fallen off a jot" (5.375). But Hazlitt's review of Kemble's King John, published a year before the actor's retirement, registers the personal effects of the Kean phenomenon: "We wish we had never seen Mr. Kean. He has destroyed the Kemble religion; and it is the religion in which we were brought up. Never again shall we behold Mr. Kemble with the same pleasure that we did, nor see Mr. Kean with the same pleasure that we have seen Mr. Kemble formerly" (5.345). Kean's acting, true to life as it is, does not compensate for the loss of a heroic presence on stage, so that "we feel the force and nature of Mr. Kean's acting, but then we feel the want of Mr. Kemble's person" (5.345). Kean renders his audiences ill at ease in their historical moment, bereft of the comforts of Kemble's paternal authority, because he conspicuously departs from the older performer's acting "according to the book of arithmetic; but no more" (5.346). Hazlitt, who argued time and again that the arts were not progressive, and who in fact explicitly cited the ephemeral nature of acting as the reason for its continued originality as an art, does not "wish we had never seen Kean" because Kean is a superior actor, but because Kean's acting is predicated on a recognition of historical loss, demanding from viewers the same post-revolutionary, post-legitimate self-consciousness he embodies. Hazlitt's defense of Kemble paradoxically demonstrates his belief in theater's ability to alter its modes of production both to reflect and to shape contemporary experience. Kemble has not declined, history has moved on without him – his performances remaining the same even as the audience's expectations of theater changed. Hazlitt's 1823 effusion in *Characteristics* confirms this: "It was ridiculous to set up Mr. Kean as a rival to Mr. Kemble. Whatever merits the first might have, they were of a totally different class, and could not possibly interfere with, much less injure those of his great predecessor. Mr. Kemble stood on his own ground, and he stood high on it" (9.181). The shift in public favor from Kemble to Kean signifies a more fundamental change in the understanding of what a "mental state" is, what a self is, and how that self is to be represented on stage. The critic must attend to this change, even as he recognizes the enduring technical excellence of Kemble's craft.

Kemble and Kean were not, of course, the only actors Hazlitt reviewed. But in Kean's acting Hazlitt recognized a crucial shift in theatrical experience during an increasingly abstracted age presided over by a commercial theatrical press. Kean's acting enabled, indeed necessitated, a new kind of criticism that represented the moment of critical reception as itself a historical act. Watching Kean, the critic's own subjectivity becomes a question considered rather than a certainty performed: as an act of self-fashioning it has no determinate end. This is why, despite Hazlitt's reverence for Sarah Siddons and his approval of other actors such as Eliza O'Neill, Kean is the hero of his career. If Kean's "conception is feeble" in one role and he "wants imagination" (5.271) in another, still he catalyzes the occasional selfhood Hazlitt sees as a vital response to the contemporary world.[35] What I am arguing, finally, is that because Kean responds to, and indeed embodies, the subjective uncertainty characterizing contemporary theatrical experience, Hazlitt learns from Kean to imagine an audience for theater that is similarly always in the process of formation.[36] Like Kean's "controversy," which reimagined the actor's relation to his audiences, Hazlitt's criticism resists the desire for a critical space protected from the way his readers experienced theater as part of their own lives. Hazlitt envisaged readers subject to the allure of commercial reporting but for whom elite criticism would present difficulties. His criticism constitutes its readership by emphasizing how actors, Kean especially, represented the same radical shifts in theatrical experience that their audiences – including readers like Keats – were encountering.

III The Essayist as Romantic Occasionalist

Before turning to Keats, I would like to explore the implications that Hazlitt's refiguration of theatrical experience has for his consideration of cultural experience beyond theater. I take two of his mid-career essays, "The Indian Jugglers" and "The Fight," as examples of a periodical criticism that charts a typical late Romantic-period collision between "high and low." In the 1819 essay "The Indian Jugglers," written at the height of his career as a theatrical critic and published in the *Examiner*, Hazlitt's newly configured theatrical experience becomes the basis for a self-conscious encounter with an illegitimate public entertainment. Whereas in Hazlitt's theatrical criticism the actor serves as a model of subjective negotiation for critic and reader, in "The Indian Jugglers" and "The Fight," the critic takes that role more explicitly on himself. In both essays, an athletic performance initiates a psychological reframing of the critic's imagined relation to the public world by positioning him discursively between a witnessed event and an audience of non-present readers. Stylistically, this dialectical procedure manifests itself in rapid shifts between detailed description and affective reaction. Hazlitt's speaker often lapses into colloquial musings even as his prose retains the compact descriptive quality of parliamentary reporting. The beginning of "The Indian Jugglers" provides an example: "Coming forward and seating himself on the ground in his white dress and tightened turban, the chief of the Indian Jugglers begins with tossing up two brass balls, which is what any of us could do, and concludes with keeping up four at the same time, which is what none of us could do to save our lives" (8.77). Even this single sentence displays a subtle oscillation between description and reaction, with no explicit interruption marking the shift between the two modes of writing. The rhetorical pattern drawn here intensifies as Hazlitt gives way to an extended reflection on the act of seeing itself: "To conceive of this effort of extra ordinary dexterity distracts the imagination, and makes admiration breathless. Yet it costs nothing to the performer, any more than if it were a mere mechanical deception" (8.78). As in Hazlitt's theatrical reviews, the critic attempts to understand not only the physical performance but also its enduring effect on his imagination. "Seeing the Indian jugglers," he continues, "makes me ashamed of myself. I ask what there is that I can do as well as this? Nothing. What have I been doing all my life?" Against the juggler's "instance of exact perfection," Hazlitt's writings become simply "abortions." "What errors, what ill-pieced transitions, what crooked reasons, what lame conclusions! How little is made out, and that little how ill!" (8.79).

III The Essayist as Romantic Occasionalist

Despite its seeming spontaneity, Hazlitt's exasperated outburst is highly deliberate, a rhetorical performance designed to illustrate a relation between intellectual and mechanical power that is inexpressible through the form of conventional report or review. As his expression of feeling departs from traditional modes of address, the essay's inadequacy becomes a paradoxical measure of the writer's communicative power. The critic's imaginative failure – his inability to succeed as a writer to the analogous degree of athletic perfection embodied by the juggler – elicits an uncontained emotion that registers perfectly, and negatively, the limitations of the form it implicitly transcends and explicitly derides. The outburst's colloquial character, its intimacy, and its intensity perform for the reader a depth of feeling beyond that which reporterly description can possibly convey. Not surprisingly, then, Hazlitt's spontaneous meditation ends when he begins to describe how his compositional method produces such fruitful lapses. When writing an essay, he asserts, "I endeavor to recollect all I have ever observed or thought upon a subject, and to express it as nearly as I can" (8.79). By transforming the initial perception from sensation into memory, recollection at once distances the witness from the moment of observation and enlarges that moment's experiential significance: to "recollect as nearly as I can" is to construct a mediated return to the immediate. Yet the review displays its "nearness" to the event by calling attention to its own incompleteness. The opening of "The Indian Jugglers" is a compact allegory of Hazlitt's position as a writer in a rapidly changing periodical field: perception and loss of the critical faculty are followed by the return of conscious reception, begetting a new form of criticism.

For Hazlitt, in other words, the critic composes in, and the review's form represents, the indescribable temporal and psychological gap between the occasion of observation and the occasion of expression. Further, review writing is the representation of a continually revised and textually performed negotiation between the different psychological orientations required by these discrete moments. The reviewer here is strikingly akin to the subject-actor that Kean represents on stage. A powerful external stimulus "distracts the imagination" from its critical office, divesting the viewer of the self-possession necessary to mitigate the flow of feeling and enable composition (8.78). Yet though the sensory experience must itself end for composition to begin, writing cannot be divorced from the initial moment of sensation or it will fail to engage the reader's imagination. Like Wordsworth's "spontaneous overflow of powerful feelings ... recollected in tranquility" (221), Hazlitt's composition registers the tension between the observer's immediacy of encounter and the writer's withdrawal into meditation. But unlike that great revisionary Wordsworth, who often elides scenes of writing with his speaker's meditation on the feelings that occasioned them, Hazlitt's writing displays the need for concentrated labor in the production, and indeed imagination, of imaginative expression. As a self-consciously periodical writer, Hazlitt's process of composition is performed *as compressed* – which is to say it is conspicuously *not* subsumed into a finished written form. Because reflection will only compromise the critic's authentic colloquial style, his withdrawal into the reflection that enables writing can therefore only be provisional: "I have also time on my hands to correct my opinions and polish my periods: but the one I cannot, and the other I will not do" (8.79). Here abstraction meets particularity: Hazlitt's critical subject situates himself joyfully between, and is enlivened by the incommensurability of, the world of ideas and the unwieldy material world to which his writing attends.

The tension between mechanical and intellectual power occasioned by Hazlitt's vision of the street performer structures "The Indian Jugglers." Compensation for the writer's imperfection is found when the witnessing "I" records the event as neither the event can record itself nor even as the standardized language of report can convey it. For Hazlitt, "no act terminating in itself constitutes greatness," because the act's public effect ends when the act is finished (8.85). The critic's response to the act, however, has the potential to extend the performance's occasion beyond the moment of first occurrence. For this reason, the critic must maintain contact with the experience he describes; otherwise, the review becomes an exercise in solipsistic abstraction:

> To throw a barley-corn through the eye of a needle, to multiply nine figures by nine in the memory, argues infinite dexterity of body and capacity of mind, but nothing comes of either. There is a surprising power at work, but the effects are not proportionate, or such as take hold of the imagination. To impress the idea of power on others, they must be made in some way to feel it. It must be communicated to their understandings in the shape of an increase of knowledge, or it must subdue and overawe them by subjecting their wills. (8.84–85)

Though the juggler's presentation of skill is a perfect one in mechanical terms, it is finite in time and space. Without the critic's witness – a response that conspicuously transcends formulaic expression – the event exists only as a momentary diversion. By contrast, greatness for Hazlitt is "great power, producing great effects," which is to say that greatness is public: "It is not enough that a man has great power in himself, he must shew it to all the world in a way that cannot be hid or gainsaid. He

III The Essayist as Romantic Occasionalist

must fill up a certain idea in the public mind" (8.84). Hazlitt's insistence on the public longevity of greatness is the political analog of his insistence on the necessity of interaction for the formation of personal identity. Like the ordinary man, the great man cannot exist unto himself: "[N]o man is truly great, who is great only in his life-time. The test of greatness is the page of history" (8.84). Hazlitt's distinction between power and greatness explains review criticism's social importance. In the temporal interstices between a perception's occurrence and its annihilation from the memory, the critic transforms fleeting acts into a text whose effects extend into his readers' life-world.

The dialectic between action and writing that frames "The Indian Jugglers" makes its final turn when Hazlitt quotes his own previously published elegy for the deceased handball "fives" player John Cavanagh. The "willing tribute to his memory" that Hazlitt pays is another abrupt shift in the essay, for it appears just as Hazlitt has argued for the primacy of intellectual over mechanical pursuits: "To return from this digression" (that is, from his consideration of greatness) "and conclude the Essay," Hazlitt explicitly remarks on the elegy's first publication without attributing it to himself: "[Cavanagh's] death was celebrated at the time in an article in the Examiner newspaper (Feb. 7, 1819)" (8.86). Because the unattributed elegy "falls in with my own way of considering such subjects, I shall here take leave to quote it" (8.86). Its extended and detailed description of Cavanagh's physical prowess raises his deeds to the status of art: "His blows were not undecided and ineffectual – lumbering like Mr. Wordsworth's epic poetry, nor wavering like Mr. Coleridge's lyric prose, nor short of the mark like Mr. Brougham's speeches, nor wide of it like Mr. Canning's wit, nor foul like the *Quarterly*, no[r] *let* balls like the *Edinburgh Review*. Cobbett and Junius together would have made a Cavanagh" (8.87). Thomas Talfourd argued that inclusion of the Cavanagh piece in "The Indian Jugglers" exemplified "the mass of personal feeling" that weakened Hazlitt as a philosopher and metaphysician: "He wrote elaborate essays to prove the superiority of physical qualifications to those of intellect – full of happy illustrations and striking instances ... *but all beside the mark*, proving nothing but that which required no proof – that corporeal strength and beauty are more speedily and more surely appreciated than the products of genius" (Talfourd 123). Hazlitt is, in Talfourd's view, so carried away by a fascination with physical beauty that he misses the worth of his own criticism, which he "nobly vindicated at other times, when he shows, and makes us feel, that 'words are the only things which last forever'" (123).[37] For Talfourd, the fault of "The Indian

Jugglers" is Hazlitt's failure to see that "the links of living sympathy ... [connecting] its author to distant times" are exemplified in "the very essay which would decry it" (123). Talfourd, though, carried away himself by Hazlitt's descriptive powers, misses the crucial truth that the elegy is a quotation. For when quoted within the context of the essay that is "The Indian Jugglers," the elegy's historical existence as a material text becomes its primary quality. The "willing tribute" it represents honors in the same moment both the beauty of Cavanagh the player and the power of the words that memorialize him – read, and written, once again.

Hazlitt's means of "ending" his consideration of intellectual labor's efficacy is to quote his own previously published valorization of a sporting hero's physical labor, a valorization accomplished by describing Cavanagh in the highest terms possible, as embodied language. This epitome of fleeting sporting elegance is the equal of "Cobbett and Junius together." The comparison of Cavanagh's "blows" with "Wordsworth's epic poetry," "Coleridge's lyric prose," "Brougham's speeches," and "Canning's wit" situates Hazlitt not merely as a spectator but as a reader who transforms bodily action into a cultural sign. "The Indian Jugglers" does not finally emphasize the triumph of one form of activity, intellectual or physical, over the other. Instead, it offers the critic's coming to awareness of their interdependence as an allegory for the cultural experience of the early-nineteenth-century reader. What Talfourd mistakes for a diverting sentimentalism we can understand as Hazlitt's resolute commitment to representing the vital interdependence of the mind that writes and the public world to which it speaks.

The occasionalist rhetoric of "The Indian Jugglers," which explicitly situates the critic as a commentator on and provider of occasional experience, develops in "The Fight" into a dramatic staging of the critic's role as the creator of a localized discursive community. First published in the *New Monthly Magazine* in 1822, "The Fight" narrates the life of a provisional public sphere occasioned by the most illegitimate of entertainments, a boxing match outside the city limits. Hazlitt depicts himself in the essay as one member of an audience bound together not simply by attendance at the fight, but by conversational interactions before and after. He is therefore a subject within the historical event he reports, a dual position that highlights the essay's production as a response to a particular occasion. Hazlitt's anticipations of and reactions to the spectacle are all, as such, occasions in themselves, worthy of attention because they register the fight's ability to "fill up a certain idea in the public mind." Again, this is not to say that description of the actual event itself carries no

III The Essayist as Romantic Occasionalist

weight in the review. On the contrary, it is, like the mechanical exploits detailed in "The Indian Jugglers," the central point to and from which the essay's rhetorical trajectories radiate. The portrayals of the combatants, the settings, and the action are all scrupulously detailed:

> The *swells* were parading in their white box-coats, the outer ring was cleared with some bruises on the heads and shins of the rustic assembly (for the *cockneys* had been distanced by the sixty-six miles); the time drew near, I had got a good stand; a bustle, a buzz, ran through the crowd, and from the opposite side entered Neate, between his second and bottle-holder. He rolled along, swathed in his loose great coat, his knock-knees bending under his huge bulk; and, with a modest cheerful air, threw his hat into the ring. (17.81)

This is a far cry from the self-deprecating annoyance of the *Theatrical Mince-Pie* reviewer, for whom the bustle of the crowd is little more than a hindrance to his own enjoyment of a West End play. Hazlitt's criticism makes no attempt to suppress the crowd's energy, instead raising their voyeurism to the level of Greek and Trojan soldiers watching "the modern Ajax" and "Diomed" in the *Iliad*'s mortal combat: "Who at that moment, big with a great event, did not draw his breath short – did not feel his heart throb?" (17.81).

Yet while it is certainly a new kind of report in which an illegitimate sporting battle takes on the qualities of a high cultural event, "The Fight" takes as its larger subject the spectators' collective experience and, further, the critic's role in communicating that experience to his own "spectators," that is, his readers. Mary Fairclough has argued that though "Hazlitt strives in 'The Fight' to make positive claims for the particular forms of sympathetic communication he wishes to advocate," he "still does not seem ready to celebrate unregulated communication" (208, 209). For Fairclough, that resistance registers in Hazlitt's emphasis on conversation over "the mail as a pure medium of communication" (209). Yet as with the translation of the Cavanagh elegy into print and then quotation in "The Indian Jugglers," the medium of "The Fight" – of the essay itself – reaches beyond the occasion of the conversations Hazlitt reports. Reports of conversational interactions make up more than half of the review. Like the descriptions of the fight, these portions of the essay bring into contact high and low culture by depicting the intersection of written and verbal communication. Each person Hazlitt encounters is figured as a member of the community occasioned by the fight and maintained by the critic's central conversational role. Hazlitt's desire to see the fight ("*Where there's a will, there's a way.* – I said so to myself") is matched only by his need to share the experience of that desire: "We are cold to others only when we are dull in ourselves. Give a man a topic in his head, a throb of pleasure in his heart, and he will be glad to share it with the first person he meets" (17.73). Tellingly, his conversation is not restricted to interactions with others – he talks even to himself. After debating with "Joe Toms" whether or not they could take one of the mail coaches to the fight, Hazlitt rushes off to Piccadilly:

> The mail coach stand was bare. 'They are all gone,' said I – 'this is always the way with me – in the instant I lose the future – if I had not stayed to pour out that last cup of tea, I should have been just in time' – and cursing my folly and ill-luck together, without inquiring at the coach-office whether the mails were gone or not, I walked on in despite. (17.73)

Encountering the Brentford stage along the road, Hazlitt's musings to himself take on the tenor of argumentation: "I argued (not unwisely) that even a Brentford coachman was better company than my own thoughts (such as they were just then), and at his invitation mounted the box with him. I immediately stated my case to him – namely, my quarrel with myself for missing the Bath and Bristol mail" (17.74).

This critical persona is a subject defined even internally by conversation. In a natural shift, then, Hazlitt's conversation extends easily both to the people he meets along the way and to the reader, so that the local community he imagines is bound together by the same conversational principle that informs his individual identity.[38] Informed by the coachman that the mails had not in fact left yet, he bemoans that "The Bath mail I had set my mind upon, and I had missed it, as I missed every thing else, by my own absurdity ... 'Sir,' said he of the Brentford, 'the Bath mail will be up presently, my brother-in law drives it, and I will engage to stop him if there is a place empty'" (17.74). Sliding between Hazlitt's imagined conversation with himself, his remarks to the coachman, quotations of the coachman, and descriptions of Hazlitt's own state of mind, the review positions the reader as an equal participant in the occasion of the critic's localized experience. This is to say that in "The Fight" there is little rhetorical distinction made between Hazlitt the fight goer and Hazlitt the review critic; direct observations to the reader repeatedly interrupt reported talk. The critic's written review becomes one element in a larger exchange that transcends the boundaries of print, enabling conversation to extend beyond the immediate moment of the fight's occurrence. Just as the essay shifts in its earlier phase between report and commentary, so here the critical voice marks both conversation *within* the essay's initial occasional horizon and written communication *beyond* that horizon. When Joe reports to Hazlitt that he'd gotten a free ride on the mail ("It's a pity I didn't meet with you; we could then have gone down for nothing. But *mum's the word.*"), Hazlitt's response to the request is not an apology to Joe, but an *apologia* before the reader, who is treated as the next member along the gossip chain: "It's the devil for any one to tell me a secret, for it's sure to come out in print. I do not care so much to gratify a friend, but the public ear is too great a temptation for me" (17.77).

And the shift goes both ways: from print to voice and, then, from voice to print, presenting what Kevin Gilmartin has called a dynamic interplay of occasion and publication that is "at once circular and open ended" (*William Hazlitt* 59). Listening admiringly to the conversation of a fellow barfly passing the night before the fight in a pub, Hazlitt remarks to the man: "I said, 'You read Cobbett, don't you? At least,' says I, 'you talk as well as he writes.' He seemed to doubt this. But I said, 'We have an hour to spare: if you'll get pen, ink, and paper, and keep on talking, I'll write down what you say; and if it doesn't make a capital Political Register, I'll forfeit my head'" (17.78). Though the man does not accept the offer, Hazlitt records the conversation that ensues:

> [He] told me soon afterwards, in the confidence of friendship, that "The circumstance which had given him nearly the greatest concern of his life, was Cribbs beating Jem [Belcher] after he had lost his eye by racket-playing." – The morning dawns; that dim but yet clear light appears, which weighs like solid bars of metal on the sleepless lids; the guests drop down from their chambers one by one – but it was too late to think of going to bed now (the clock was on the stroke of seven), we had nothing for it but to find a barbers. (17.78)

Again, the narrative shifts repeatedly between Hazlitt's quotation of the man – which, like a parliamentary report, retains the third person description despite its enclosure in quotation marks – and direct observations of the conversation as an event. Shortly after this passage, Hazlitt addresses his reading audience directly: "Reader, have you ever seen a fight?" Everything that follows takes on the characteristics of friendly conversation:

> The crowd was very great when we arrived on the spot; open carriages were coming up, with streamers flying and music playing, and the country-people were pouring in over hedge and ditch in all directions, to see their hero beat or be beaten. The odds were still on Gas, but only by about five to four. Gully had been down to try Neate, and had backed him considerably,

which was a damper to the sanguine confidence of the adverse party. About two hundred thousand pounds were pending. (17.79)

The paratactic clauses here strike a rhythm underscoring the critic's imaginative dialogue with the reader; conversational language authorizes the critic as experiential witness rather than simply as aesthetic evaluator. His nearness to both the original event and to the reader authorizes his description of the event's power, rendering the critical essay both a communication of, and initiator of, public experience.

On the way back to London, Hazlitt's role as facilitator of conversation extends the fight's impact beyond the short hour of its occurrence. Meeting some strangers who "appeared a little sly and sore" on the subject of the fight, Hazlitt questions them, "and it was not till after several hints dropped, and questions put, that it turned out that they had missed it" (17.84). Meeting others, he remarks that "some inquiry was made by the company about the fight, and I gave (as the reader may believe) an eloquent and animated description of it" (17.85). Hazlitt closes the essay by returning to his friend Joe Toms, who "called upon me the next day, to ask me if I did not think the fight was a complete thing? I said I thought it was. I hope he will relish my account of it" (17.86). The final word of the review is a postscript to the reader, who becomes something of a stand-in for Joe Toms himself. In "The Fight," then, the social function of criticism is reimagined as the formation of a local community of reception, achieved through Hazlitt's self-positioning as both speaker and writer, character and critic. The essay not only memorializes the discursive community brought into being by the fight, it also aims to perpetuate that community by situating readers as participants in a conversation completed, but not finished, by their presence as auditors.

In the essay's revision of review criticism's social function, conversation transforms an occasional event into an experience that alters the subjectivity of both critic and reader. The critic's response calls attention to its own, and its reader's, dependence on conversational interaction. Stanley Jones has commented on Hazlitt's "disinclination to pontificate, of his dislike of the egotistical; his views are commonly defined dramatically, on specific occasions, by opposition to those of others" (106). This is to say that, though Hazlitt was certainly a member of the class of philosophical critics Jon Klancher describes emerging in the early nineteenth century, his criticism authorizes itself not with philosophical rhetoric but rather through a performed affective reaction to the events he describes. He is more an "unsettling observer," to employ David

Bromwich's phrase, than a "resolute guide" (270). "The Indian Jugglers" performs this "unsettling" mode of criticism in Hazlitt's outburst of self-doubt and the extended meditation that follows, and "The Fight" stages it as an ongoing cultural conversation that, even as it transcends the boundaries of the written text, remains bound to an imagined locale whose center is the critic himself.[39]

Hazlitt's rhetorical mobility enabled him to be an effective critic of both legitimate and illegitimate entertainments. While many of his contemporaries quickly exhausted their vocabulary of derision on the spectacular events offered by London's illegitimate theaters, Hazlitt's focus on the cultural reception modeled by Kean's performances enabled a critical versatility that could encompass jugglers and pugilists as well as actors and actresses. The refashioning of Hamlet's statement as an epigraph for "The Fight," in which "the fight" replaces "the play" as "the thing wherein I'll catch the conscience of the king" – a rhetorical ploy duplicated by Hazlitt's subsequent inversion of Lady Macbeth ("in the instant I lose the future") – neatly brings legitimate and illegitimate modes of experience into contact and marks the critic as an agent who moves easily between the two worlds. Like the aim of Hazlitt's theatrical criticism, the essay's intent is to explore the ways that cultural experience engages "that trembling sensibility which is awake to every change and every modification of its ever varied impressions" ("Indian Jugglers" 8.82). There is something in Hazlitt's critical subjectivity akin to Walter Benjamin's storyteller, whose tale "bears the marks of the storyteller much as the earthen vessel bears the marks of the potter's hand" (159). Hazlitt parried the shocks that came with living in a world of expanding mass culture because he did not attempt to use criticism as a tool for a metaphysical overcoming of material life. Against the cloistered virtues of a clerisy preserving the nation's cultural tradition, or the commercialism of writers whose critical acumen was lost in pursuit of consumerist readerships, Hazlitt imagines the reporterly critic at large, bringing news of himself to the people. Doing so, Hazlitt not only charts the discursive territory between the cultural poles of high and low but also makes his subjective negotiations of that territory the focus of his criticism. And while later-nineteenth-century critics would find it increasingly difficult to follow him in reaching across divisions between different groups and classes of readers, Hazlitt's work continues to stand as an example of Romanticism's vital response to the emergence of mass culture.

Notes

1. All references to Hazlitt are to *The Complete Works of William Hazlitt*. Ed. P. P. Howe. 21 vols. (London: J. M. Dent, 1933). Cited by volume and page number.
2. "Our ancestors could write a tragedy two hundred years ago; they could write a comedy one hundred years ago; why cannot we do the same now?" (18.303).
3. With my emphasis on the ways in which Hazlitt's subjectivity displays a continual engagement with the occasions of lived experience, I diverge from Carl Schmitt's use of the term "romantic occasionalism" in *Political Romanticism*. Schmitt argues that "Romanticism is subjectified occasionalism. In other words, in the romantic, the romantic subject treats the world as an occasion and an opportunity for his romantic productivity" (17). Yet if that process does not mean "that the external world is negated" (98), still "every concrete point of the external world can be the 'elastic point': in other words, the beginning of the romantic novel, the *occasio* for the adventure, the point of departure for the fanciful game" (98). Romanticism for Schmitt resides almost entirely in "illusion" and "has no interest in really changing the world" (98). This subjugation of political consciousness to a radically imagined individuality is counter to my reading of Hazlitt's, and later Keats's, occasionalist engagements with history.
4. Hazlitt's methodology anticipates the commitment to the local and the personal that characterizes recent work in cultural history. Our own resistance to the master narratives of "public sphere" (Habermas, etc.) and "consumer revolution" (McKendrick, etc.) might, in this context, be considered to manifest some of the ideological characteristics of late-Romantic historiography.
5. My reading coincides with Kevin Gilmartin's emphasis on "Hazlitt's treatment of a potentially shared experience of life in London ... which offered perhaps the most compelling counterweight he could find to the feared post-war consummation of 'Legitimacy' that was his political nightmare" ("Hazlitt's Visionary London" 42).
6. For Hamilton, metaromantic *literary* texts are those "whose immanent unease rhetorically encourages translation into more effective means of discursive transmission, and, in so setting aside its traditional privileges, becomes a document of radicalism" (3). Hazlitt's *criticism* operates, I would argue, at once as an act of translation – Hazlitt's translation of the event into the discursive register of his criticism – and as an object of further translation by his readers. For a discussion of the ways in which Hazlitt imports Cockney vulgarism into his accounts of London as a critique of idealistic cosmopolitanism, see Jon Klancher's "Discriminations" (77–79).
7. Scholars have long emphasized the anti-egotistical aspects of the *Essay*, and specifically Hazlitt's assertion that the individual has as great an imaginative investment in other subjects as it does in its future self. See Bromwich 24–57. John Kinnaird connects the *Principles* to Hazlitt's development of "his sense of self as always in some mode or degree *intersubjective*, as existing and acting only

in tension with real or imagined otherness" (58). Tom Paulin likewise sees the *Principles* as the beginning of Hazlitt's exploration of the "social" imagination (34). For related discussions, see Mahoney, *The Logic of Passion* 74–75, and W. J. Bate, *John Keats* 255–59. By contrast, Natarajan sees the work as an elucidation of Hazlitt's belief in the power of the imaginative mind's unifying principle, arguing that "the creations of genius, equally as the exercise of 'disinterestedness' in the *Essay on the Principles of Human Action*, are enabled by a powerful self, an egotistical sublime that Hazlitt does not apologize for, but celebrates throughout his writing" (7). Natarajan posits that in missing this point, Hazlitt criticism has largely privileged "the 'pragmatic', the 'real', and the 'particular' at the expense of the theoretical and the abstract in Hazlitt's work" (9). While attempting to negotiate these divergent approaches, and sharing Natarajan's belief in Hazlitt's investment in "power, that is a theory not of self annihilation but of self affirmation" (9), I would claim finally that for Hazlitt the *practice* of abstraction – the witness to the mind abstracting principles from material experiences and testing them against material realities – becomes the focal point of his writing rather than an emphasis on abstraction itself. In this I follow Roy Park's cogent discussion of Hazlitt's commitment to concrete description and detail over the "abstraction" and "generality" of his age (2). See Park 1–6. For a discussion of the *Essay*'s recognition of "nominal abstraction" as a means to comprehending identity as ontological difference, see Mulvihill 33.

8. Hazlitt will develop this idea further in the *Lectures on English Philosophy*, where he criticizes the Baconian school for restricting the interpretation of the word "experience, confining it to a knowledge of things without us; whereas it in fact includes all knowledge relating to objects either within or out of the mind, of which we have any direct or positive evidence" (2.124).
9. The early roots of Hazlitt's notions of "intersubjectivity" (the term is John Kinnaird's) can be found in Hume's *A Treatise of Human Nature*, Book 2, Part 2, Section 5:

> We can form no wish, which has not a reference to society. A perfect solitude is, perhaps, the greatest punishment we can suffer ... Let all the powers and elements of nature conspire to serve and obey one man: Let the sun rise and set at his command; The sea and rivers roll as he pleases, and the earth furnish spontaneously whatever may be useful or agreeable to him: He will still be miserable, till you give him one person at least, with whom he may share his happiness, and whose esteem and friendship he may enjoy. (235)

10. In Jon Cook's formulation, "drama, for Hazlitt, is preeminently a social art, not just because it populates a stage and a theatre, but because it acts out a basic feature of the nature of social life itself" (xxvi).
11. In the opening section to *The Theory of Moral Sentiments*, for example, Smith writes that "as we have no immediate experience of what other men feel, we can have no idea of the manner in which they are affected, but by conceiving

what we ourselves should feel in the like situation" (3). Sympathy is the means by which the imagination imbues a spectating subject with feelings that, however they may be like those of the man whose experience he observes, are distinctly his own. Thus "it is by the imagination only that we can form any conception of what are his sensations" (3–4). For Hazlitt's assessment that Wordsworth "sees all things in himself," see "On Mr. Wordsworth's *Excursion*" in *The Round Table* (4.112).

12. Here I again echo Mary Fairclough's contention of Hazlitt's insistence on "individual autonomy," though in my account of Hazlitt's theatrical criticism he posits a critic – a writing subject – more open to the generative possibilities of intersubjective exchange (8).

13. The most obvious example of this professional connection is William Woodfall himself. See Bourne 219.

14. The "familiar style," Hazlitt argues in 1821, "utterly rejects not only all unmeaning pomp, but all low, cant phrases, and loose, unconnected, *slipshod* allusions. It is not to take the first word that offers, but the best word in common use; it is not to throw words together in any combinations we please, but to follow and avail ourselves of the true idiom of the language. To write a genuine familiar or truly English style is to write as any one would speak in common conversation, who had a thorough command and choice of words, or who could discourse with ease, force, and perspicuity, setting aside all pedantic and oratorical flourishes" (8.242). For a discussion of the "familiar style" as "heightened conversation," see Enright 119.

15. For a discussion of Hazlitt's time at the *Chronicle*, see Howe 145–54, Baker 191–97, and Stanley Jones 91–118. Baker calls the period "a most instructive apprenticeship" (195).

16. For a thorough accounting of this division, see Aspinall, "The Social Status of Journalists."

17. This fate was particularly common among the more radical journals sharing Hazlitt's politics. *The Black Dwarf*, which took parliamentary reform as its defining cause, failed in 1824 largely because, as Stanley Jones has put it, there was "no public devotedly attached to the cause," or more appropriately, to reading about the cause (249).

18. As Jon Cook states, "Hazlitt earned his living as a writer, and his living was precarious" (xxx). David Higgins has similarly described the ways in which Hazlitt's political commitments, and the familiar style that exemplified those commitments, cost Hazlitt both financially and personally (*Romantic Genius and the Literary Magazine* 102–26).

19. See esp. Cook xx–xxx. Cook argues that, for Hazlitt, "knowledge is … necessarily dramatic, born out of the thinker's commitment to a process of debate" (xx). Further, Hazlitt's "aphoristic style moves writing in the direction of the dramatic" (xxi).

20. Recent critics have emphasized the political dimensions of Hazlitt's work. John Whale's study claims, "Hazlitt's writings represent a conscientious attempt to test the efficacy of the sympathetic imagination against the

negative effects of the dominant ideology" (*Imagination Under Pressure* 110). Tom Paulin has improbably turned Hazlitt into something of an Irish revolutionary; see Paulin 142–70. Kevin Gilmartin has recently emphasized Hazlitt's political and aesthetic versatility both in his own time and as an object of historicist recovery (*William Hazlitt: Political Essayist*). My focus is more on Hazlitt's position in the expanding commercial and symbolic economies I describe in Chapters 1 and 2.

21. See Klancher, *Making of English Reading Audiences*, esp. 47–75.
22. John Whale similarly describes Hazlitt's "complex position as a polite essayist who is also a radical" ("Hazlitt on Burke" 465).
23. For a discussion of high and low theatrical culture in Romantic-period London, see Moody, *Illegitimate Theatre*, esp. 11–78.
24. Hazlitt criticizes newspaper commercialization at length in "The Periodical Press" (16.211).
25. Thomas DeQuincey will make a similar connection in his 1829 "On Murder Considered as One of the Fine Arts." See DeQuincey 9–124.
26. For a comprehensive study of Shakespearean burlesque in nineteenth-century Britain, see Schoch.
27. My contention, then, is that Hazlitt's mode of engagement with the actresses goes beyond "the complementary dynamic that by the later eighteenth century came to link the figures of the aestheticized accomplished woman and the aestheticizing gentleman connoisseur" (Bermingham, "Elegant Females" 507). Here I differ from, or at least offer a qualification to, Bermingham's assessment of "Hazlitt's acid invectives against the vulgarity of consumer culture and its corruption of taste as exemplified by women" ("Urbanity and the Spectacle of Art" 169).
28. "Theatrical Examiner" 193. *Examiner* (February 26, 1815). rpt. *Leigh Hunt's Dramatic Criticism* 112.
29. "Theatrical Examiner" 338. *Examiner* (October 4, 1818). rpt. *Leigh Hunt's Dramatic Criticism* 201–2.
30. Angela Esterhammer provides a similar example of how Byron's *Childe Harold* "mimics the real-time movement of improvisation, in which there is no going back to change or correct" (123).
31. Tracy Davis describes the importance of gaslight technology to understanding the politics of Kean's reception. Gaslight, which was introduced to Drury Lane in 1817, more than two years after Kean's debut, intensified for those seated in the inexpensive "pit" the actor's striking facial expressions. Inaccessible to those seated in more distant, and expensive, parts of the house, the phenomenon heightened the class divisions that marked Kean's controversial reception. See "Reading Shakespeare by Flashes of Lightning," esp. 933–35.
32. Keats will describe a related problem with regard to his idea of the "camelion poet." See *Letters* 1.386–88.
33. Joseph Donohue has argued that though Garrick, Kemble, and Kean "each had highly individual styles," their performances "held in common the

fundamental view that the essence of human nature is not in action, but in reaction" (*Dramatic Character* 222). But what distinguishes Kean from his predecessors is his integration of the *process* of reaction into the representation of dramatic moment.

34. Hazlitt alludes to Paul's description of Christ at Heb. 4:15: "For we have not an high priest which cannot be touched with the feeling of our infirmities; but was in all points tempted like as we are, yet without sin" (*King James Version*). The implication is that even as Kean becomes a kind of theatrical intercessor between the audience and the states of experience he represents, he maintains his position as "one of the people" to whom he speaks. Unlike Kemble, Kean as Hamlet or Macbeth still represents audiences themselves, to themselves.

35. Almost one-fifth of Hazlitt's theatrical reviews dealt with Kean, far more than any other actor. Perhaps more significantly, twelve of the first nineteen reviews that Hazlitt reprinted in *A View of the English Stage* focus on Kean, a fact to which he calls specific attention in the volume's preface. See Hazlitt 5.171, 174.

36. Joseph Donohue has remarked of Hazlitt that "if a philosophical consciousness emerges from Hazlitt's reviews, it is certainly an awareness that human failure must receive the most sympathetic and detailed inspection that can be brought to bear on it" (*Dramatic Character* 337).

37. Talfourd quotes from Hazlitt's "On Thought and Action" (Hazlitt 8.107).

38. As such the narrator/writer of "The Fight" shows himself as an effect of – and not just an author of – the Romantic "walking essay" Tim Fulford has recently described, which, signaling itself as a catalyst of coterie sociability, "valued companionable walking as an escape from the destructive effects" of the workaday world (191).

39. Insofar as the essay is a mediation of prize fighting for middle-class readers, as David Higgins has argued, it is also, perhaps more fundamentally, a meditation on the act of such mediation ("Englishness").

CHAPTER 5

Keats, Kean, and the Poetics of Interruption

I In Kean's Company

Just before Christmas 1817, John Keats wrote from Hampstead to his brothers George and Tom in Teignmouth, Devonshire. The two younger Keatses had left London to seek better environs for Tom, who would die from tuberculosis within a year. Left behind in the city to put the finishing touches on *Endymion*, John informs his brothers that he has busied himself with customary diversions: theater, reading, and dinners:

> I dined too (for I have been out too much lately) with Horace Smith & met his two Brothers with Hill & Kingston & one Du Bois, they only served to convince me, how superior humour is to wit in respect to enjoyment – These men say things which make one start, without making one feel, they are all alike; their manners are all alike; they all know fashionables; they have a mannerism in their very eating and drinking, in their mere handling a Decanter – They talked of Kean and his low company – Would I were with that company instead of yours said I to myself! I know such like acquaintances will never do for me. (*Letters* 1.192–3)

The letter derides the "mannerism" of Smith and his friends, members of the merchant class who aspired to cultural legitimacy through literary pursuits.[1] The diners' disdain for "Kean and his low company," an attempt to demonstrate distinguished taste, elicits from Keats a socially symbolic reversal in which Kean comes to stand for those qualities the men themselves lack.[2] I take this explicit alliance with Kean not only as an unapologetic embrace of a "low" social position against which critics commonly see Keats straining but also as an identification with the new modes of theatrical experience Kean embodied on the early-nineteenth-century London stage.[3] Kean's presence – in the theater and in London society – not only called attention to those low aspects of middle-class life that aspirants such as Smith, Hill, and Du Bois would have wanted to mask but also questioned the boundaries between private and public life that authorized such distinctions. The implications of Keats's emphatic desire to be of Kean's "company," then, are greater than a simple difference of opinion between dining fellows.[4]

Kean played a crucial role in shaping both Keats's attitudes toward his own social rank and his ideas about the changing nature of theatrical, and by extension all cultural, experience.[5] Educated to an understanding of Kean by Hazlitt's theatrical criticism, Keats's attention to the actor in letters and theatrical reviews in late 1817 and early 1818 coincided with and, I argue, occasioned his thoroughgoing revision of the poet's role as a cultural intermediary for readers. In response to the self-assured demeanor embodied by Smith, Hill, and DuBois, Keats imagines the poet continually engaged in the formation of an identity constituted by an encounter with the difficulties of lived history. The poems of early 1818, especially "On Sitting Down to Read King Lear Once Again" and "When I have fears that I may cease to be," revise contemporary notions of the literary because the poet speaks not only of but also from moments of doubt about his own authorial capacities. Far from simply representing a lower-class perspective defined against middle-class cultural experience, Keats posits his crisis as a standard of authenticity surpassing the "mannerism" of a would-be cultural elite. This in turn enables Keats to reconsider the imagination's relationship to the experience – the history – that both gives it rise and curtails its idealizing tendencies. What I will call Keats's "poetics of interruption" emerges from his theatrical experience at this time to reshape his conceptions of poetry's social function, a revision that finds its fullest manifestation in the odes.

The most obvious link between Kean's acting and Keats's ideas about poetry in late 1817 can be found in the same December letter, which continues more famously:

> Brown and Dilke walked with me & back from the Christmas pantomime. I had not a dispute but a disquisition with Dilke, on various subjects; several things dovetailed in my mind, & at once it struck me, what quality went to form a Man of Achievement especially in Literature & which Shakespeare possessed so enormously – I mean *Negative Capability*, that is when man is capable of being in uncertainties, Mysteries, doubts, without any irritable reaching after fact & reason. (*Letters* 1.193)

At the time Keats wrote the letter, which mentions Kean twice as well as *King Lear*, the libel trials of T. J. Wooler and William Hone, and Benjamin West's *Death on the Pale Horse*, he was also writing several theatrical reviews for the liberal periodical the *Champion*, the first of which

1 In Kean's Company

concerned Kean. That he and Dilke were returning from seeing a pantomime – the kind of production from which Kean derived his physical acting style – bolsters the connection between the moment of mental dovetailing and figurative stagecraft. As Nicholas Roe has demonstrated, Keats was also in these weeks reading the *Examiner*'s critique of the legitimate theater's attempts to "manage public opinion" by offering the actor David Fisher as a substitute for the "indisposed" Kean.[6] In this context, the letter that begins with Kean and ends with Keats's famous "negative capability" passage counters the contemporary, and persistent, view of Keats as a kind of perpetual social climber and represents a vital connection between Keats's theatrical experience and his poetry.

Keats has long been considered an exemplar of the upwardly mobile lower-class poet; even in his own lifetime, his work was invariably judged in relation to its author's humble beginnings. Citing Keats's repetitively enjambed lines, his salacious erotic detail, and his uneasy treatment of classical culture, *Blackwood's* "Cockney School" reviews attacked the 1817 *Poems* and the 1818 *Endymion* volumes as puerile, undisciplined, and immoral, establishing the critical vocabulary that would influence Keats criticism for two centuries.[7] In our own historical moment, Marjorie Levinson's *Keats's Life of Allegory* continues to provide the most thorough "historical-materialist" formulation of the poet's position outside the realm of elite culture.[8] For Levinson, the raw material of Keats's poetry, his life, is sadly deficient in content. Keats could not "draw from his everyday life, a monotonous struggle to get by and get ahead, for the interest, surprise, and suggestiveness which Byron and Shelley found in their large circumstances" (*Keats's Life of Allegory* 8). His was "a real life of substitute things," a life documented by poetry "which *signifies* – indeed fetishizes – its alienation from its representational objects and subjects, and, consequently, from its audience. This poetry is a discourse whose self possession is a function of its profound structural *dis*possession" (28). The paragon to which Keats futilely aspires in Levinson's reading is Wordsworth, whose statement of poetic intentions in the 1815 "Essay, Supplementary to the Preface" represents for Levinson the position of "a man so assured of his entitlement that he can trust his originality to be received as intelligible and valuable" (10).[9] By contrast, Keats is "a literary entrepreneur" (18), whose "lapses in good taste" (3) reveal "a man with nothing *but* words ... a man whose real deficit was one of substance" (235) and whose "terribly labored" poetry has "no immediate rhetorical situation" (35) because it is defined entirely by its "display of bad access and misappropriation" of culture (15).

At bottom, Levinson's conflation of cultural and social ambition does not distinguish between those attitudes and behaviors driven by attention to poetic models and those produced by economic need. To be sure, Keats was continually in financial straits, always seeking a situation that would enable him to devote his full energies to poetry. But by extending the realities of Keats's economic situation, of his very real "struggle to get by," rendering them "monstrous" and entirely constitutive of his cultural experience, Levinson minimizes the importance, indeed the existence, of an entire, varied, complicated, and fruitful life-world to which Keats had daily and immediate "access."[10] Nicholas Roe, among others, has contested such readings by emphasizing the progressive vitality of Keats's education at Enfield School and at Guy's Hospital, as well as the wide-ranging, urbane, and even cosmopolitan sociability of his friendships and cultural associations in London.[11] Reading this world as entirely and always painfully displaced from a fixed ideal of comfortable bourgeois subjectivity, though, Levinson sees a man who "sidestepped Chatterton's final solution" (i.e., suicide) only by sublimating ever-unsatisfied desires into the "contained badness" of his poetry (11). The more factitious the poem – the more the poem offers itself as a fetishized embodiment of literariness – the more energetic its desire to erase history's traumas.

Considered in light of Keats's relationship to London's theater and its attendant print culture, what Levinson sees as Keats's "alienation" reveals itself also – the two are not mutually exclusive – as his positive communication of a new mode of cultural experience altogether.[12] Keats did represent in his poetry a "new social phenomenon," and self-consciously so. But this self-consciousness is driven more by Keats's dissatisfaction with poetry as an expression of a "petty bourgeois" (as Levinson terms it) mastery of culture, nature, and history, than by masturbatory exhibitionism or a fraught display of "bad access." If Wordsworth's egotism represented, in both his life and his work, a literary parallel to the masterful authority displayed on the Covent Garden stage by John Philip Kemble, Edmund Kean embodied for Keats a refusal to seek cultural distinction by emulating that mastery. Kean nightly performed an agonistic encounter with Shakespeare and other legitimate drama, eliciting unprecedented enthusiasm from London's lower orders and unprecedented disdain from their upper- and middle-class counterparts. By enacting a similar refusal in his poetry, Keats began in 1818 to represent aesthetic experience as a continual, undecided negotiation that treated the high culture of art and the low culture of daily life with equal force and attention. Thus the unapologetically low experience of high culture – the encounter between low and high represented by Kean's acting and in Keats's poetry – claims for itself a unique authenticity because it resists conspicuously the mystifications upon which aristocratic or even middle-class ease is founded.

II Keats's Theatrical Experience

Insofar as they have been discussed at all, Keats's fascinations with theater have been recognized as influencing the dramatic structure and characterization of his poems.[13] For Bernice Slote, the first scholar to draw any connections between Keats's theatergoing and his poetry, Keats's most advanced appropriation of the dramatic occurs when he develops in the major lyrics a "dramatic voice [that] does not deny autobiographical relationships, but ... implies a subtler identification by idea and theme rather than by fact" (135). Slote here distils theater into drama, which in turn provides the formative structure of lyric complexity: "A dramatic quality in [Keats's] poetry is the use of contrasts and oppositions, but the energy of conflict is combined with the intensity of paradox" (32). Charles Rzepka develops this line of thinking when he argues that over the course of Keats's career, the poet seeks "to transform himself from a character or a persona represented in the theater of his own work" into a more self-conscious "stager," or presenter of poetic vision. Rzepka finds in Keats at his best "an essentially theatrical, which is to say self-distancing, point of view" (*The Self as Mind* 168). As Slote herself remarks, however, Keats's time in London's theaters would have provided him with more than an exposure to embodied dramatic principle. A regular theatergoer between 1815 and 1819, "Keats knew the underworld of crudities and half lights, as well as that of brilliance and dream" (Slote 53). The curious "Fragment of Castle-builder," written in 1818, provides a glimpse of Keats's experiences in this vein, and of how those experiences influenced his standards of cultural value. Itself a kind of proto-dramatic dialogue, the poem opens *in medias res*, with "Castle-builder" speaking:

CASTLE-BUILDER

In short, convince you that however wise
You may have grown from convent libraries,
I have, by many yards at least, been carding
A longer skein of wit in Convent Garden.

BERNADINE

A very Eden that same place must be!
Pray what demesne? Whose lordship's legacy?
What, have you convents in that Gothic Isle?
Pray, pardon me, I cannot help but smile –

CASTLE-BUILDER

Sir, Convent Garden is a monstrous beast;
From morning, four o'clock, to twelve at noon,
It swallows cabbages without a spoon,
And then, from twelve till two, this Eden made is
A promenade for cooks and ancient ladies;
And then for supper, 'stead of soup and poaches,
It swallows chairmen, damns, and hackney coaches.
In short, sir, 'tis a very place for monks,
For it containeth twenty thousand punks,
Which any man may number for his sport,
By following fat elbows up a court.[14]   (1–19)

The contrast here between the book learning of "convent libraries" and the "longer skein of wit" provided by "Convent Garden" is clear. Bernadine's notion of reading, an experience of cloistered privacy in which canonized tomes might be ruminated over, is replaced by Castle-builder's lighthearted reading of an unruly social text. Commerce, theater, prostitution ("punks") and the classless social whirl of the district create an enticing spectacle "which any man may number for his sport." The center of the "Gothic Isle" is not, as Bernadine fantasizes, an actual convent, but a "monstrous beast" of unbounded commercial, and sexual, energy and exchange.[15]

After Castle-builder's second short speech, the fragment breaks off into direct address by a speaker at line 20: "In such like nonsense would I pass an hour/With random friar, or rake upon his tour" (20–21). An extended reflection follows in which the speaker imagines a "gorgeous room" filled with sensual delights and various objects "upon the floor" (35). He enumerates them solely for the sake of seeing "what more my phantasy can win" (47): they include a "terrace . . . well bowered with oranges" (34),

A guitar-ribband – and a lady's glove
Beside a crumple-leaved tale of love;
A tambour frame, with Venus sleeping there,
All finish'd but some ringlets of her hair;
A viol, bow strings torn, cross-wise upon

II Keats's Theatrical Experience

> A glorious folio of Anacreon;
> A skull upon a mat of roses lying,
> Ink'd purple with a song concerning dying; (36–44)

In rhythm and ironic incisiveness, these are among Keats's most Byronic lines. The poem's speaker describes something of a cultural rag-and-bone shop filled with reproductions and fragments of the material past – one might think of it as a collection of what was left out when Porphyro "heap'd with glowing hand" the banquet of "delicates" for Madeline in *The Eve of St. Agnes* (1. 271). He jokingly mocks his interest in such things by contrasting it to a higher taste for classical antiquities:

> Greek busts and statuary have ever been
> Held by the finest spirits fitter far
> Than vase grotesque and Siamesian jar;
> Therefore 'tis sure a want of Attic taste,
> That I should rather love a Gothic waste
> Of eye-sight on cinque coloured potter's clay
> Than on the marble fairness of old Greece. (55–61)

The rhyme of "cross-wise-upon" with "Anacreon" (40–41) is followed by others of equal playfulness that evince what William Keach has called a Cockney "genial audacity" of rhyme, most notably the unstopped couplet that gives us "Attic taste,/That I should rather love a Gothic waste/of eyesight" (58–60).[16] With its scene of cultural detritus presented formally in this way, "Fragment of Castle-builder" not only implies a connection between the speaker's imaginative musings and "Convent Garden's" commercial and sexual carnival; it also explicitly contrasts theatrical experience with the fetishistic treatment of cultural artifacts. The speaker's self-conscious preference for a "grotesque and Siamesian jar" and his carefree lack of "Attic taste" contrast sharply with the earnest attitudes Keats is often argued to display toward classical culture in poems such as "On Seeing the Elgin Marbles" and "Ode on a Grecian Urn." Of course Keats did revere classical works of art. But the "Fragment" complicates the image of Keats as an unselfconscious fetishizer of Greek culture and suggests that theatrical world could produce a subject for whom display of upper-class taste was not a priority, and for whom poetry might not be tempted to the self-fetishization Levinson describes.[17] With continual attendance at London's theaters and imaginative considerations of his theatrical experience such as that found in the poem, Keats positioned himself at the center of an intense collision between artists and their audiences.

What does it mean, then, in late 1817, for Keats to imagine himself in Kean's "company"? Two factors must be considered. The first is Kean's ideological associations in Britain's theatrical culture and in British society at large. The second is Keats's understanding of those associations, as shaped by his theatrical experience, that is, by his attending and reading about Kean's performances. In 1817, a *Monthly Theatrical Reporter*'s review echoed the common derision of Kean I have already described, but also offered a more explicitly classed-based dismissal that stands as an almost direct inversion of Keats's sense of the actor during those same months.[18] After its evaluation of Kean's performance (the reviewer argued that the part of Romeo was "ill adapted to his personal and physical attributes"), the *Reporter* rejects popular opinion as a standard of critical judgment:

> [N]or does the great and general applause, which crowned his efforts on this occasion, in the least weaken or invalidate our argument ... Public opinion *may* be (and, to judge from Mr. Kean's reception, in this part, *is*) against us; but in matters of taste, every man has a right to his own private judgment. On this, as on every other occasion, we shall deliver our sentiments, with frankness and sincerity, uninfluenced by popular applause; unwarped by the tide and current of general report; u[n]biased by the dazzle and magic of a great name. The multitude, we know from long experience, and we have Shakespeare's authority to boot, are at all times caught by show and noise: but the practice of actual life; the regular course of human feeling and action, ought to be the critic's guide and clue, in judging of the complicated workings and effects of the passions, in their representation and depicture, on the stage.[19]

Kean's lot is with "the multitude," not with the critics, because his performances are based on the "dazzle and magic" that attracts audiences, rather than the "practice of actual life" as the critic sees it. Excoriated in numerous journals for his "pygmy body" and "weak voice," Kean's physical deficiencies carried the weight of a classed subjectivity that failed to measure up to the learned, sedate presence of Kemble and his imitators.

Keats went to see Kean perform on numerous occasions and would have been aware of the debates about Kean's affiliation with the lower orders of Drury Lane audiences. He refers to the actor at least seventeen times in his letters, beginning with the negative capability letter of December 1817 and continuing through late 1819 when Keats's and Charles Brown's tragedy *Otho the Great* was being considered at Drury Lane. On December 22, 1817 Keats comments to George and Tom that "I saw Kean return to the public in Richard III, & finely he did it" (*Letters* 1.191). In March 1818, he writes to Reynolds of attending the theater and being concerned about Kean's health, as "sickness – a fellow to whom I have a complete aversion" had been "seated ... between us at the Theatre – where I thought he look'd with a longing eye at poor Kean" (*Letters* 1.245). In December of that year, he describes going "the other evening to see Brutus a new Tragedy by Howard Payne, an American – Kean was excellent" (*Letters* 2.8). And in the spring of 1819, he complains, "[T]he weather in town was so stifling that I could not remain there though I wanted to see Kean in Hotspur" (*Letters* 2.71). Later in 1819, the references become more frequent, as Keats first composes *Otho* with Kean in mind and then worries about enlisting him to play the part of Ludolph. The most significant of these references comes in a letter to Benjamin Bailey on August 14, 1819: "One of my Ambitions is to make as great a revolution in dramatic writing as Kean has done in acting – another to upset the drawling of the blue stocking literary world – if in the course of a few years I do these two things I ought to die content" (*Letters* 2.139). Here again Keats explicitly allies himself with Kean, setting the two of them and their parallel cultural revolutions against the "drawling of the blue stocking literary world" – a feminized variation of the bourgeois life to which Keats is so often presumed to aspire.

III   Keats the Reviewer

The nature of the literary "revolution" Keats envisioned can be gleaned by revisiting briefly Hazlitt's long critical relationship with Kean, for it is principally through Hazlitt's reviews that Keats was educated to criticism of the theater.[20] The *Examiner*, along with the Whig *Morning Chronicle* and on occasion the liberal *Champion*, published the bulk of Hazlitt's reviews between 1814 and 1819. Keats's sustained exposure to these publications at Enfield and throughout the poet's early days as a member of the Hunt circle introduced him to a new way of thinking about theatrical performance.[21] In Kean, let us recall, Hazlitt found an actor who refigured the performer's relation to the dramatic – and specifically the Shakespearean – text. "The hesitation, the bewildered look, the coming to himself" Kean displays in Macbeth (Hazlitt 5.207) and the "rapidity of his transition from one tone and feeling to another" in Shylock represent Kean's finest quality: his ability to "[give] effect to the conflict of passions arising out of the contrasts of situation" (5.179). Because Kean's facial distortions serve as an "index to his mind" (8.277), indicating a self-consciousness of response as his character encounters one dramatic situation after another, Kean's "style of acting is ... more significant, more pregnant with meaning, more alive in every part, than any we have almost ever witnessed" (5.180). Paradoxically, it was Kean's conspicuous modernity that enabled him to represent these characters so compellingly; his symbolic presence on stage evoked the dangerous allegory of an offstage life, exposing the cultural fiction that patent-theaters dealt only in high culture. For Hazlitt, the illegitimate associations evoked by Kean's style rendered it impossible for him to play a patrician role such as Coriolanus; after all, his power as an actor was derived from a connection to the lower classes of theatergoers: "He is one of the people, and what might be termed a radical performer. He can do all that may become a man 'of our infirmity,' 'to relish all as sharply, passioned as we'" (18.290). Yet those same associations empowered his representation of other characters, because the "relish" with which he embodied them indicated the unapologetic approach of a new kind of urban, lower-class subject that took its authenticity not from elite learning but from lived experience.

Keats's own theatrical review of the actor, written for the *Champion* in December 1817, further elucidates the nature of Kean's influential performances. Asked by his friend John Hamilton Reynolds, the *Champion*'s regular theatrical critic, to take on reviewing duties while Reynolds was out of town, Keats produced three substantive reviews. The December 21, 1817 *Champion* contains his first, and for our purposes most significant, effort, entitled simply "Mr. Kean." Not surprisingly, this piece follows closely Hazlitt's understanding of the actor. Keats begins:

> "In our unimaginative days," – *Habeas Corpus'd* as we are, out of all wonder, uncertainty and fear; – in these fireside, delicate, gilded days, – these days of sickly safety and comfort, we feel very grateful to Mr. Kean for giving us some excitement by his old passion in one of the old plays. He is a relict of romance; – a Posthumous ray of chivalry, and always seems just arrived from the camp of Charlemagne.[22]

Keats values Kean's ability to contradict, with his "Posthumous ray of chivalry," the current age's belated cynicism. In a time of "sickly safety and comfort," he is a "relict of romance" because his imaginative embrace of each psychologically complex Shakespearean role is uncompromising: "In Richard he is his sword's dear cousin; in Hamlet his footing is germain to the platform. In Macbeth his eye laughs siege to scorn. In Othello he is welcome to Cyprus" (*HK* 227). Kean, and not Kemble, could seem to Keats "just arrived from the camp of Charlemagne," because the younger actor knew a world of experience entirely apart from Kemble's trained conventionality. Kean's style elaborated the distance between present reality and that imagined past, providing a modern experience of "romance" even as he showed that the age of romance could not finally be recovered.

Surprisingly, given Kean's reputation for having a weak voice, Keats fixes on "the music of elocution" as one of "his numerous excellencies." But Keats's meaning of "elocution" is not so much the sonorous quality of Kean's utterance as it is his ability to communicate with his voice an embodied experience of Shakespeare's poetry without presuming to sound the depths of the poet's language:

> The spiritual is felt when the very letters and points of charactered language show like the hieroglyphics of beauty; – the mysterious signs of an immortal freemasonry! "A thing to dream of, not to tell!" The sensual life of verse springs warm from the lips of Kean, and to one learned in Shakespearean hieroglyphics, – learned in the spiritual portion of those lines to which Kean adds sensual grandeur: his tongue must seem to have robbed "The Hybla bees, and left them honeyless." There is an indescribable gusto in his voice, by which we feel that the utterer is thinking of the past and the future, while speaking of the instant. (*HK* 229–30)

Kean's relation to the Shakespearean text is such that his enunciation of its "charactered language" conveys and even emphasizes to a knowing receiver the "spiritual portion" of the lines. Kean himself is not so much the master of those "mysterious signs" – the printed marks of the Shakespearean text that represent indescribable beauty – as he is a translator of their codes into the "sensuous life" of spoken verse.[23] To the critic, his acting marked an occasional and therefore transformative, if not always explicable, encounter with Shakespeare's language.

Keats's review parallels both conceptually and rhetorically Hazlitt's assessment of Shakespeare in his *Lectures on the English Poets*, which he gave at the Surrey Institution, and which Keats attended, between January and March of 1818:

> Shakespeare's language and versification are like the rest of him. He has a magic power over words: they come winged at his bidding; and seem to know their places. They are struck out at a heat, on the spur of the occasion, and have all the truth and vividness which arise from an actual impression of the objects. His epithets and single phrases are like sparkles, thrown off from an imagination, fired by the whirling rapidity of its own motion. His language is hieroglyphical. It translates thoughts into visual images. It abounds in sudden transitions and elliptical expressions.[24] (5.54–5)

For Hazlitt, Shakespeare's poetic excellence resides in his ability *to figure* continually and, as if, effortlessly. In the "sudden transitions and elliptical expressions," we find a "hieroglyphical" representation of experience that translates the endless "motion" of Shakespeare's imagining into particular "visual images" of figured language. In contrast to Chaucer's "consistent, but uniform" characters, this kind of particularity makes Shakespeare's creations "historical figures ... where every nerve and muscle is displayed in the struggle with others" (5.50, 51). In his copy of Hazlitt's *Characters of Shakespear's Plays*, a book published in the second half of 1817, Keats marked a passage in the "Lear" chapter that explicitly connects his assessment of Kean with Hazlitt's hieroglyphical reading of Shakespeare. After praising "the third act of Othello and the first three acts of Lear" as "Shakespear's greatest master-pieces in the logic of passion," Hazlitt remarks as follows:

> [T]hey contain the highest examples not only of the force of individual passion but of its dramatic vicissitudes and striking effects arising from the different circumstances and characters of the persons speaking. We see the ebb and flow of the feeling, its pauses and feverish starts, its impatience of opposition, its accumulating force when it has time to recollect itself, the manner in which it avails itself of every passing word or gesture, its haste to repel insinuation, the alternate contraction and dilation of the soul.

Underlining the indicated text and drawing a vertical mark next to the paragraph, Keats wrote in the margin: "This passage has to a great degree the hieroglyphic visioning" (*HK* 282).[25] Again, we see Hazlitt's emphasis, and Keats's seizing of that emphasis, on motion – an "ebb and flow" of a given feeling as it marks itself within the temporal unfolding of experience, the "availing" of "every passing word or gesture," the "alternate contraction and dilation of the soul." The connotative power of "has" is here typically Keatsian: does Hazlitt's passage "have," that is, possess, the "hieroglyphic visioning" itself? Or does it "have," that is, understand properly, the "hieroglyphic visioning" that is a property of Shakespeare's text? Keats's comment has the virtue of leaving both questions unresolved, imagining a relation between Hazlitt and his subject that is itself hieroglyphic – meaningful yet not reducible to conventional critical terms. This fruitful ambiguity realizes in an aphorism the relationship that Keats sees Kean enacting with respect to the performed Shakespearean text. As the vocabulary of Keats's marginal comment corroborates – his repetition of the word "hieroglyphic" in the marginalia and the review are surely not accidental – he was in late 1817 drawing coherent connections between Hazlitt and Kean and the way each engaged Shakespeare. Both were in this sense and at this time models for Keats, who the previous May had fancied Shakespeare "a Good Genius presiding over" him (*Letters* 1.142).[26]

Keats's use of the term "gusto" in the Kean review further indicates Hazlitt's influence. Hazlitt had defined "gusto" in an *Examiner* article of May 26, 1816, as "power and passion defining an object" (4.77). Keats relies on the phrase to indicate that he values the "passion" with which Kean engages Shakespeare's poetry. But Keats's "gusto," in contrast to Hazlitt's painterly ideal, is less a quality of definition than an intense emotional response to the object of the dramatic text. That the gusto is "indescribable," except by the feeling it imbues in the critic, confirms Kean's ability to represent in his own actions the very processes of theatrical reception that were common to his viewers. Kean stands in the same relation to Shakespeare's dramatic text as theatergoers do to Kean: as the cultural object of the "hieroglyphic" text promotes Kean's passion, so Kean's "indescribable" representation promotes the audience's passion. Keats's emphasis on indescribability echoes Hazlitt's own 1814 account, also published in the *Champion*, of how Kean's acting "beggared description" (5.207). Spectators "feel that the utterer is thinking," rather than perceiving his state of mind through traditional indicatory gestures and intonation. Though not in itself describable, the review suggests, the "gusto" in Kean's voice is perceivable in the new relation it enables between vocal instrument and printed text:

> Surely this intense power of anatomizing the passion of every syllable – of taking to himself the wings of verse, is the mean[s] by which he becomes a storm with such fiery decision; and by which, with a still deeper charm, he "does his spiriting gently." Other actors are continually thinking of their sum-total effect throughout a play. Kean delivers himself up to the instant feeling, without a shadow of a thought about any thing else. (*HK* 231)

Kean has no idea of what actors today would call a "through-line," the conception of a character's development that governs responses to situation throughout the play. Rather, his acting style brings forward the psychological complexities produced by each scene. By "anatomizing the passion of every syllable," Kean emphasizes for his viewers the "instant feeling" over the "sum-total effect" of the various states of mind he represents. Like the "hieroglyphic visioning" Keats notes in Hazlitt's text, Kean's "thinking of the past and the future" registers the subject's psychological position between dissolving and emerging moments, producing "feeling" at any given point.

Enacting a distinctly Hazlittean occasionalism in its final lines, Keats's review displays how Kean's "feeling" provides a corresponding experience for the critic: "Kean! Kean! have a carefulness of thy health, an in-nursed respect for thy own genius, a pity for us in these cold and enfeebling times. Cheer us a little in the failure of our days! for romance lives but in books, and the rainbow is robbed of its mystery!" (232). The curiously solicitous exhortation recalls Keats's earlier concern for the actor's well-being and reveals a deeply personal, even physical identification. But the review does not simply offer friendly caution, for it sets Kean as a heroic figure against a "cold and enfeebling time" when "the rainbow is robbed of its mystery!" Before a historically belated audience, Kean's acting not only imagines a moment of cultural encounter defined by feeling rather than intellectual mastery but also includes the viewer in the experience of that moment. In these contexts, Keats's *Champion* review takes on a Cockney political dimension similar to his expressed alliance with Kean in the negative capability letter. Given, too, that the *Examiner*'s pages in the weeks of Kean's "indisposition" were filled with discussion of the *Blackwood's* "Z" review of October 1817, Kean's political and social valences as a public figure would have been very much on Keats's mind as he was composing the letters and poems of late 1817 and early 1818.[27] In an era when theatrical experience was often cast by reviewers according to high versus low standards of distinction, the new kind of subject Kean embodied resisted such categorization and suggested, to Keats at least, the possibility of hope for poetry.

IV The Virtues of "Halfseeing"

Keats's theatrical experience, and his identification with Kean in particular, enabled him to revise radically his understanding of poetry's expressive capacities. In the weeks leading up to writing both the negative capability passage and the *Champion* reviews, Keats was repeatedly considering the issue in his letters. After the letters of November and December's writing on "Adam's dream," the "imaginative mind," and Shakespeare's disinterested compositional method, January and February 1818 bring Keats's first attendance at Hazlitt's lectures, several more visits to the London theaters, and the epistolary ruminations in which Keats begins to speak forcefully against "a certain Philosophy engendered in the whims of an Egoist." Writing on February 3 that he "will have no more of Wordsworth or Hunt in particular," he begins to apply to the idea of poetry the lessons he has learned from Kean against master narratives of the self:

> Every man has his speculations, but every man does not brood and peacock over them till he makes a false coinage and deceives himself – Many a man

IV The Virtues of "Halfseeing"

> can travel to the very bourne of Heaven, and yet want confidence to put down his halfseeing. Sancho will invent a Journey heavenward as well as any body. We hate poetry that has a palpable design on us – and if we do not agree, seems to put its hand in its breeches pocket. Poetry should be great & unobtrusive, a thing which enters into one's soul, and does not startle it or amaze it with itself but with its subject. (*Letters* 1.223–24)

For Keats, the anti-egotistical poet learns to "put down his halfseeing" – which is to say, to leave himself and his reader in half-knowledge – in such a way that a poem "does not startle . . . or amaze [the reader] with itself but with its subject." Poetry need not, indeed must not, be so conspicuous a demonstration of mastery over subject that its operation intrudes on the reader's establishing an individual relation to that subject. This attitude is strikingly second generation in Romantic terms, because it sets Wordsworth as the bearer of poetic tradition rather than as a rebel against it, and because it echoes Hazlitt's call for the valorization of concrete particulars over abstraction. Two weeks later, on February 19, Keats describes to Reynolds how the reception of poetry should likewise resist any "palpable design" a poem might have on its reader:

> I have an idea that a Man might pass a very pleasant life in this manner – let him on any certain day read a certain page of full Poesy or distilled Prose and let him wander with it, and muse upon it, and reflect from it, and bring home to it, and prophesy upon it, and dream upon it – untill it becomes stale – but when will it do so? Never – When Man has arrived at a certain ripeness in intellect any one grand and spiritual passage serves him as a starting post towards all "the two-and thirty Pallaces." (*Letters* 1.231)

In positing these operations for poetry, Keats is laying the groundwork for his expression later in the year of the "poetical Character" that "lives in gusto" and stands in contrast to the "wordsworthian or egotistical sublime" (*Letters* 1.387). But he is also, remarkably, rethinking the act of reading itself, reconceiving the reader's imaginative task as akin to poetic creation. It is a task characterized time and again by the properties Kean most palpably modeled: by a refusal of mastery, by rhetorical interruption, by the succession of one poetic figure after another.

These moments in the letters indicate a crucial shift in Keats's thinking in late 1817 and early 1818, what he calls in January a "change . . . in my intellect" (*Letters* 1.214), that is driven by his theatrical experience. At the time when Keats was considering Kean as a force on the stage, he made a first concerted effort to rework his conception of the poet's "imaginative Mind" and its relation to social and cultural experience. Kean's significance in these letters and in Keats's concurrent *Champion* article has been largely obscured by the overwhelming symbolic presence of Shakespeare. But if Shakespeare was the "presider" over this period, Kean was an attendant whose presence helped Keats imagine both a relationship with that presider and a new mode of poetic production and reception. Kean's method of communicating the mystery of Shakespearean "hieroglyphics" suggested to Keats that the depths of Shakespeare's genius need not be understood rationally to affect the receiving subject's identity. For Keats, poetry's ability to communicate halfseeing with "confidence" engenders musing, prophesying, and dreaming – in short, the passionate response first represented to him by the "indescribable gusto" of Kean's acting.

A poetry of halfseeing, which develops in Keats's later work into a more forceful poetics of interruption, puts the poet in a precarious position with respect to his audience. If "A Man's life of any worth is a *continual* allegory" (*Letters* 2.67; my emphasis), then the poet's language must represent a continually unresolved process. With the composition of the theatrical reviews and the letter of December 1817, though, the focus on cultural reception that Andrew Franta has called Keats's "review aesthetic" takes on a new dimension. Arguing that "Keats sees in the reviews a model for a poetic practice grounded in the unpredictability of reception" (78), Franta has stressed how poems such as "On First Looking Into Chapman's Homer" and "On Seeing the Elgin Marbles" both "capture an experience of a work of art" and "recommend the object that occasioned it" (94).[28] Two sonnets written at the beginning of 1818, however, emulate Kean's embodiment of an uncertain relation to the Shakespearean text by situating Keats as a reader overpowered by – not master of – the imagined objects he encounters. Nor is he even master of the experiences those encounters produce. The cultural experience of the speaker in both poems – "On Sitting Down to Read King Lear Once Again" and "When I have fears that I may cease to be" – is as much an occasion of identity formation as it is a self-conscious recommendation of certain practices of cultural reception. While similar in theme and tone to the earlier review sonnets, these poems, composed within seven days of each other in January 1818, emphasize more strongly the subjective ambiguity initiated by the occasions of cultural reception.[29]

"On Sitting Down to Read King Lear Once Again" is, like the "Chapman's Homer" sonnet, an occasional piece about Keats's reading of a literary text:

> O golden-tongued Romance, with serene lute!
> Fair plumed syren, queen of far-away!
> Leave melodizing on this wintry day,

IV The Virtues of "Halfseeing"

> Shut up thine olden pages, and be mute.
> Adieu! for, once again, the fierce dispute
> Betwixt damnation and impassion'd clay
> Must I burn through; once more humbly assay
> The bitter-sweet of this Shakespearean fruit.
> Chief Poet! and ye clouds of Albion,
> Begetters of our deep eternal theme!
> When through the old oak forest I am gone,
> Let me not wander in a barren dream:
> But, when I am consumed in the fire,
> Give me new phoenix wings to fly at my desire.

The poem endorses a generic hierarchy; Keats turns from composing his own "golden-tongued Romance" to reading Shakespeare's "fierce dispute/ Betwixt damnation and impassion'd clay" as a means of inspiring greater achievement. Yet the *Lear* sonnet demonstrates a shift not only in the speaker's relation to a canonized text but also in the poet's representation of that shift. Writing to George and Tom on the day after he composed the poem, Keats remarked:

> I think a little change has taken place in my intellect lately – I cannot bear to be uninterested or unemployed, I, who for so long a time, have been addicted to passiveness – Nothing is finer for the purposes of great productions, than a very gradual ripening of the intellectual powers – As an instance of this – observe – I sat down yesterday to read King Lear once again the thing appeared to demand the prologue of a Sonnet, I wrote it & began to read. (*Letters* 1.214)

In contrast to his discovery of something altogether new in Chapman's translation of Homer, this time Keats returns to a known text. Rather than a record of past reading as sublime discovery, expressed in "Chapman's Homer" by the phrase "*Then felt I* like some watcher of the skies" (my emphasis), the *Lear* sonnet, as a prologue, displays Keats's anticipation, his anxiety even, *before* he begins to read. While he knows Shakespeare's text and expects in some way the affective response it occasions, the speaker-reader's confidence that he can channel that response into productive literary labor is anything but secure. His invocation, to Shakespeare as the "Chief Poet!" and to "ye clouds of Albion," is a beseeching that he not be overwhelmed by the sublime experience of contact with *King Lear*'s "deep eternal theme," and that he be given "new phoenix wings to fly at my desire." Such uncertainty is, to Keats, a natural consequence of his ambition to be "among the English Poets" (*Letters* 1.394).

Significantly, Keats revised the three last words of the final line from his original "*to* my desire." The substitution of the preposition "at" for "to" is not minor, for it alters "desire" from an attainable object to an unlocated abstraction and suggests more forcefully the sense of flight as uncertain escape. To "fly to" a place is to follow a clear path to arrival; to "fly at" is to attempt with no surety of success. Yet the change also evokes an image of the poet flying "at," that is, "when" or "as" he desires – a sense only connotatively present in the original line's use of "to," as in "according to." By enabling the equal possibility of these readings, Keats's revision heightens the sense of affective tension that the poem ascribes to the reading experience. And the sonnet's rhyme scheme reinforces that, for Keats, the ability to communicate such tension without exposition or rhetorical distancing is a Shakespearean talent. With the apostrophe "Chief Poet!" at the beginning of line 9, the poem shifts from a typical Petrarchan octave (ABBAABBA) to a six-line Shakespearean conclusion (CDCDEE).[30] The poet's expectation that he will "assay/The bitter-sweet of this Shakespearean fruit" (7–8) not only signals a change in mode of address or feeling, it also occasions a transformation of the poetic form with which the poet represents himself. On the level of both form and content, then, the sonnet represents to its reader the transformative cultural experience of reading *King Lear* "once again," anticipating and in that act creating the poet's achievement even as it refuses to determine explicitly his uncertain position in the imagined future's literary history.

Keats's other January 1818 sonnet, "When I have fears that I may cease to be," manifests the widening implications of the representational mode Keats learned from Kean. As in the *Lear* sonnet, "When I have fears" presents a moment of crisis in which the speaker considers the consequences his current state of mind will have on future endeavors. Again, that present moment is constituted by its imagined significance in light of an anticipated future occurrence – in this case the poet's premature death. Here Keats is at his most "negatively capable" in the sense that the poem represents a Kean-like "instant feeling" of high uncertainty, expressed from the "when" – itself uncertain – of that uncertainty's occurrence:

> When I have fears that I may cease to be
> Before my pen has glean'd my teeming brain,
> Before high piled books, in charactry,
> Hold like rich garners the full ripen'd grain;
> When I behold, upon the night's starr'd face,
> Huge cloudy symbols of a high romance,
> And think that I may never live to trace

IV The Virtues of "Halfseeing"

> Their shadows, with the magic hand of chance;
> And when I feel, fair creature of an hour,
> That I shall never look upon thee more,
> Never have relish in the fairy power
> Of unreflecting love; – then on the shore
> Of the wide world I stand alone, and think
> Till love and fame to nothingness do sink.

Keats uses the Shakespearean form for the first time in this, his thirty-sixth sonnet. The three quatrains – beginning "When," "When," and "And when" – each represent and speak from a temporal moment, a *time when*, and an affective state, a sense of *being as*. Each relates the speaker's experience of an action unaccomplished, a potential unfulfilled. In the first quatrain, the "high pil'd books, in charactry" do not "Hold like rich garners the full ripen'd grain." In the second, the "Huge cloudy symbols of a high romance" remain untraced. And in the third, the "fair creature of an hour" is never looked upon more. The double connotation of "when" as moment and as state – and its repetition in all three quatrains – gathers and suspends the effect of each act of perception (the having of fears, the beholding of cloudy symbols, and the feeling of loss of the beloved) until the extended final couplet's expression of "instant feeling": standing alone "on the shore/Of the wide world" and thinking, without an object of thought.

In "When I have fears," the speaker does not reflect on past achievement or consider the promise of future accomplishment; instead, he speaks from a moment of uncertainty constituted by a future that has intruded on his plans, a moment in which to "think" is to stand paralyzed until "love and fame to nothingness do sink." Yet the poem itself enacts in the present (the reader's present) the poet's task – to produce for readers "charactry," figured language, that will enable them to reproduce his incomplete experience of reading the world's signs. What is most "theatrical" about the poem is what is most Shakespearean and most Kean-like about it: not Keats's removal to a "self-distancing point of view" (Rzepka, *The Self as Mind* 168), but his ability to represent individual subjectivity as a temporarily suspended relation between possibilities for self-realization.[31] The poem achieves its high tension because both speaker and reader know that such a suspension must, inevitably, give way to the rapid actuality of lived experience. The final six lines raise the poem's stakes by imagining love itself to be bound by the radical (un)certainty of the speaker's death. The intrusion of the final couplet into the third quatrain – that conspicuous and interruptive dash in the middle of line 12 – marks the poem's awakening to the imminence of its own end, a quickening of the quatrains' figurative wondering to premature closure. Here, at the end of Keats's first Shakespearean sonnet, we find a pattern that the later poems, and most vividly the odes, will follow in turn: not an imaginative transcendence of the physical world and an inevitable return to earth, as Jack Stillinger's influential readings have long taught us, but the realization that any act of imagining must always occur in time – and is therefore a product of the same historical condition that will occasion its extinction.[32]

Keats's poetic figuration of theatrical experience crystallizes in a new way in the poems of January 1818, which bear the marks of Kean's influence first because they render the poet a creature of unapologetic uncertainty, and second because the speaker communicates to the reader from within the experience of that uncertainty. Encountering both material and imagined objects – Shakespeare's text, the cloudy symbols of "high romance" – Keats refuses to present himself as a cultural master or even, like Wordsworth, as an already developed speaker reflecting back on growth that authorizes current speech. "Negative capability," so often described by Keatsians as a private mode of cultural production, is more properly understood here as a public mode of cultural reception. "When I have fears" depicts (in Keats) and encourages (in the reader) a scene of reception fraught with uncertainty and doubt, imagining a new kind of relation between the poet's "private" experience and the public to which he speaks. Like Kean, he is a teller of the "instant feeling," in which past experience and future potentiality intersect. The readers of the poems, like the Keatsian watcher of Kean, "feel that the utterer is thinking of the past and the future, while speaking of the instant" (*HK* 230). The "change" that "has taken place" in Keats's intellect at this historical point should not be attributed solely to the influence of Kean. But the change in his thinking about poetry's capacity to represent new forms of human experience bears a striking resemblance to Kean's public embodiment of a new performing subject.

V Keats, Interrupted

If Keats's 1818 sonnets display a kind of Kean-like halfseeing, his late lyric poems enact what I will call a "poetics of interruption" that takes Kean's rhetorical figurations on stage as a governing premise. Situating Keats's composition of *Lamia* in the context of larger conversations about historical interruption, I take the poem as a meditation on the relation between the theatricalized subject and its audience. In doing so, I aim to develop further my contention that Keats aligns himself with the cultural work of the Cockney Regency that Kean's acting represented on stage, as well as to move toward my concluding claim that even Keats's most "lyric" poems, the odes, manifest with their figural movements a theatrical mode of experience.[33] Turning first not to Keats but to Frances Burney's *The Wanderer*, which I present as both a political and a generic alternative to Keats's theatrical imaginings in *Lamia*, I argue that the 1814 novel is itself the product of a post-1809 theatrical age. Burney's representation of Elinor Joddrel's response to unrequited love, which manifests itself in Elinor's theatrical hysteria, displays theater as a degraded venue for the expression of feminine sensibility and, more fundamentally, as an ideologically suspect conceptual framework enabling that sensibility. This is a danger Keats will, writing *Lamia* in the same post-1809 context, invert both politically and formally.

Burney's novel presents, in short, a tale of theatrical experience's psychological damage. Intrepid foil to *The Wanderer*'s heroine Juliet Granville, Elinor Joddrel imagines her life and the lives of those around her to proceed along a theatrical plotline. Although the outcome of Elinor's romantic pursuit of the novel's chief male character, Albert Harleigh, is never certain, she is sure at least that its *structure* will be dramatic: "The second act of the comedy, tragedy, or farce, of my existence," she tells "Ellis" (the as-yet unrevealed Juliet), "is to be represented to-morrow. The first scene will be a conference between Ellis and Albert, in which Ellis will relate the history of Elinor" (Burney 161). Elinor's encapsulation of "history" within a theatrical "scene" here (itself within a novel) – her subordination of a personal developmental narrative to the vagaries of the dramatic genre – is telling. Flush with Wollstonecraftian ideals of personal and collective liberty, Elinor imagines a world free from the shackles of custom, rank, or religion, a world where agents act according to reason alone, even in matters of the heart.[34] Her "plan" is to claim Harleigh and "cast wholly aside the dainty common barriers, which shut out from female practice all that is elevated, or even natural" (157).

Given Elinor's attempted erasure of the lines between public and private, it is not surprising that she should choose a theatrical venue for her climactic act of self-scripting. Repeatedly spurned by Harleigh, whose heart belongs to the ever cryptic, mysterious, and intensely private Juliet, Elinor disguises herself as a motley deaf-mute and joins the expectant audience at Juliet's musical debut. Juliet, a refugee from revolutionary France who for political reasons cannot reveal her true identity and therefore cannot access the financial or cultural status – or the Englishness – to which she is heir, has been reduced to performing for money. As Juliet steps onto the stage, the sight of the crowd paralyzes her:

> [U]nused to being the object of tumultuous delight, the effect produced by such transports was the reverse of their intentions; and Ellis, ashamed, embarrassed, confused, lost the recollection, that custom demanded that she should postpone her acknowledgements till she arrived at her post. She stopt; but in raising her eyes, as she attempted to courtesy, she was struck with the sight of her deaf and dumb tormenter. (358)

The presence of the stranger, whom she suspects to be Elinor "come to perpetrate the bloody deed of suicide," so disconcerts Juliet that she is unable to perform; she preserves herself from prostituting her cultivated talents by conveniently fainting as Elinor casts off her motley attire:

> The large wrapping coat, the half mask, the slouched hat, and embroidered waistcoat, had rapidly been thrown aside, and Elinor appeared in deep mourning; her long hair, wholly unornamented, hanging loosely down her shoulders ... "Oh Harleigh! – adored Harleigh! – " she cried, as he flew to catch her desperate hand; – but he was not in time; for, in uttering his name, she plunged a dagger into her breast. (359)

The assemblage of voyeurs at Juliet's debut provides an audience for Elinor's performative casting off of costume, the means by which she reveals private hysteria and simultaneously shatters any pretensions to privacy that Juliet's benefit concert has. Elinor's hysterical body, "wholly unornamented," becomes an object of sensational attention; the confusion that ensues in the wake of her suicide attempt disconcerts everyone present. Ladies begin "hiding their faces, or running away," and men stand benumbed, "all eagerly crowding to the spot of this tremendous event, approaching rather as spectators of some public exhibition, than as actors in a scene of humanity" (359–60). In a scene straight out of Burke, the spectacle causes women to act ungracefully, and men not to act at all.

The strange temporality of the narrative voice in this passage produces in the reader an analogue for such powerlessness (I italicize the relevant terms): Elinor's clothes "*had been*" thrown aside; "she *cried, as* he flew to catch her desperate hand; – *but* he was not in time; *for, in* uttering his name, she *plunged* a dagger into her breast." It is only *after* we are told that Harleigh's intervention has failed that the reader becomes aware that, at the same moment of that failure – a moment opened up by the interruptive "but, he was not in time" – Elinor *has been* stabbing herself. If theater plants the seeds of civil disorder among the actors in Jane Austen's

Mansfield Park, in *The Wanderer* the actual moment of performance threatens to bring down more than the house.[35] Burney here casts Elinor as an embodiment of Enlightenment run amok. Luckily, from the novelist's perspective, that body – indeed the spirit of Enlightenment itself – is a finally corrigible one.

Though set "during the dire reign of the terrific Robespierre" (Burney 11), *The Wanderer* was published in 1814, the same year that the British counterrevolution reached its military apex with the Allied invasion of France, Napoleon's abdication, and his subsequent exile to Elba. Along with *Mansfield Park*, published just six weeks later, and Wordsworth's 1814 *The Excursion*, the novel comprises a vivid afterimage of the counterrevolutionary forces that had shaped 1790s Britain. Against Elinor's revolutionary fervor, Burney deploys both Juliet and Harleigh as agents of reclamation. In contrast to Elinor, Ellis/Juliet maintains a strict division between her public and private selves. "All public appeals," she insists, "are injurious to female fame" (143). And though Harleigh's attempt to interrupt Elinor's interruption at the performance is too late, his long Burkean discourses with Elinor temper her revolutionary enthusiasms throughout the latter half of the novel. Elinor's eventual reconversion to Christianity aligns her once again as a member of the authentic English community Juliet both courts and represents. In a more urgent (but also less vexed and less interesting) way than Austen, Burney deploys the novel's generic and stylistic conventions to diffuse the revolutionary energies theatrical experience threatens to occasion. In Burney's figuring, then, the interruption theater foments is momentary – an exception to the rule of a coherently narrated history.

Against this there is, of course, another 1814, which saw not only the publication of Burney's, Austen's, and Wordsworth's texts, but also – spurred by the consolidating sociability of Leigh Hunt's prison cell – witnessed Edmund Kean's London debut, Hazlitt's emergence as a theater critic for the *Morning Chronicle* and the *Examiner*, and the composition of Keats's earliest extant poems. Of course Hunt's time in prison, a sentence he received for libeling the Prince Regent in the pages of the *Examiner*, was an exercise in "transgressive social positioning," to employ Greg Kucich's phrase (246), but it was also an ongoing occasion for a sociability made possible by the interruption of Hunt's sentence. I use "interruption" in a dual sense here: to mark the prison sentence as an interruption in Hunt's career to be sure, but also to highlight Hunt's career as itself an interruption of the national hagiography that his original libel of the Prince Regent decried. That is, the sentence of 1813–1815 provided a generative interregnum both for Hunt himself *and* by becoming a sign of interruption around which others could convene resistance to the nation's presiding political narratives. As Kucich and others have shown, Hunt wrote in a sustained way throughout his incarceration, and his cell became a wayside locus for coterie activities that reinforced and extended the polemical social advocacies of the *Examiner*. Keats's sonnet "Written on the Day That Mr. Leigh Hunt Left Prison" (1815) is worth considering in this context, for it exemplifies Keats's Cockney political allegiances by explicitly dismissing the power structures that resulted in Hunt's imprisonment:

> Think you he nought but prison walls did see
> Till, so unwilling, thou unturn'dst the key?
> Ah, no! far happier, nobler was his fate!
> In Spenser's halls he strayed, and bowers fair,
> Culling enchanted flowers; and he flew
> With daring Milton, through the fields of air:
> To regions of his own his genius true
> Took happy flights. Who shall his fame impair
> When thou art dead, and all thy wretched crew? (6–14)

Keats attempts in the sonnet to provide an alternative history via the Cockney literary-political associations with which scholarship has made us familiar over the past two decades.[36] But the naïve attempt to apotheosize Hunt suggests that Keats had not yet learned fully what Hunt already knew, at least politically – that resistance must be bound to the very history the poem attempts to transcend, that the characteristic inversions of the Cockney school that Kucich, Jeffrey Cox, and others have described were just that – conspicuous counters to existing flows, interruptions and inversions that contended with the very languages they sought to resist. When considered in contrast, say, to the theatrical scene Burney imagines, Kean's public prominence modeled interruption – and Hazlitt's prose seized upon this model – as a means to rethink both personal and national identities. Interruption becomes a ground of representation rather than a sign of its impossibility – or, put more bluntly, interruption takes as a given the impossibility of representation as such. The point is not so much that post-1809 Regency marks an "age of interruption." The Regency marks, rather, an interruption in the very notion of "the age."

Educated to these possibilities by Kean's acting and Hazlitt's prose style, Keats would come to see interruption as a locus for particular kinds of political dreaming: witness *Isabella*, *The Eve of St. Agnes*, the *Hyperion*s, and, as I will argue, the "negatively capable" figurations the odes both represent and enact. I posit this speculation as a way of engaging our ongoing conversations about Romanticism's historiographical dimensions and its periodicity, and particularly (still) James Chandler's focus on late Romanticism as a moment when the notion of the "Spirit of the Age" comes to the fore – for Chandler, Waterloo opens the "Age of the Spirit of the Age" (*England in 1819* 105). I wish to qualify Chandler's point to suggest that interruption – as both a rhetorical and a temporal concept – can enhance our understanding of the Cockney politics that characterize late Romanticism's historical sense. Amid notions of progress and development, and even amid particular instantiations of decline that scholars such as Emily Rohrbach and Jonathan Sachs have argued characterize late Romantic historiographies, interruption posits a way to refuse the consolations that such narratives offer.[37]

Keats's *Lamia* offers a salutary counter to Burney's scene of interruption in *The Wanderer* and illustrates how the later Keats, theatricalized by Kean and Hazlitt, resists the kinds of historical triumphalism his earlier poem on Hunt displays. My aim is not to offer a reading of *Lamia* so much as it is to resituate the poem within the "poetics of interruption" that comes to constitute Keats's political and aesthetic commitments. Unlike Hunt's soaring consciousness in "Written on the Day," Lamia's spirit is ultimately bound to her body and its subjection to the historical circumstances in which she finds herself. The public, theatrical space of Lycius and Lamia's wedding recalls the theatrical scene of Elinor's attempted suicide in *The Wanderer*. Gender trouble occurs here, too, though in this instance its perpetrator is the cold Enlightenment Philosopher whose unstinting gaze unweaves Lamia's Gordian shape, rather than the object of the gaze herself:

> Then Lamia breath'd death breath; the sophist's eye,
> Like a sharp spear, went through her utterly,
> Keen, cruel, perceant, stinging: she, as well
> As her weak hand could any meaning tell,
> Motion'd him to be silent; vainly so,
> He look'd and look'd again a level – No!
> "A Serpent!" echoed he; no sooner said,
> Than with a frightful scream she vanished.   (2.299–306)

The nearly synaesthetic confusion of word and gesture is palpably Keatsian: "the sophist's eye" goes through Lamia "utterly" but also like "a sharp spear" even as her "weak hand" attempts to "tell" against that incursion. Under pressure too is the "Than" in "no sooner said,/Than" – which of course makes sense syntactically but also, following "sooner," evokes the temporal dimensions of its near-homophone "then." Courting representational impossibility as Keats's verse so often does, the formal consolations to interruption that Burney's novel offers are here nowhere to be found. We are left only Lycius's corpse as detritus of the battle – collateral damage in the contest between rainbow and seer:

> And Lycius's arms were empty of delight,
> As were his limbs of life, from that same night.
> On the high couch he lay! – his friends came round –
> Supported him – no pulse, or breath they found,
> And in its marriage robe, the heavy body wound. (2.307–11)

The dual connotation "wound" as both action and injury itself hearkens back to the poem's opening description of Hermes "Breathing upon the flowers his passion new/And wound with many a river to its head,/To find where this sweet nymph prepar'd her secret bed" (1.28–30), reminding us that from its outset the poem's idyll contains the seeds of a violation – or violations – which will never be healed. If for Burney the answer to – the consolation for – interruption is form, for Keats poetic form adheres to and instantiates in the reader the impossibility of such reclamation.

The issue here is not so much that interruption serves a different plot function in Keats's poem than it does in Burney's novel – nor that in Keats's text the allegiances tend toward the female in the public eye rather than against her. Rather, I wish to emphasize that where Burney's text closes off the possibilities interruption affords, Keats takes them as his poem's constitutive final (and, reading the text backward, entire) point. Against the grain of the "Upon a time" with which *Lamia* opens (1.1), the poem's ending theatrical scene offers only an abrupted narrative, an out-of-place heroic *triplet*, and a final image – "wound" for "wound" – that renders closure impossible. This is something different, I think, than the "linear contrariety" Greg Kucich finds in Keats's qualifications of progressive historiography; it is closer to how Mary Favret sees literature registering affect's "wayward power" (11). *Lamia* is, like all of Keats's late work, a willful anachronism that on the level of its own narrative and poetic form breaks, and breaks open, the possibility of developmental history and, what is more, writes from the fracture. What is at stake – vis-à-vis Burney – is therefore not merely the politics of a represented scene but nothing less than a recasting of literature's social and historical function and, further, the relation of Romantic "literary" figuration to the narrative investments of the "Enlightenment."[38]

Keats was composing *Lamia* at the same time as his play *Otho the Great*, in which he had envisioned Kean in the lead role of Ludolph. The poem also contains with its famous assertion that "Philosophy will/... unweave a rainbow" (2.234, 237) a striking allusion to Keats's assessment in his review that Kean counters the "rainbow" being "robbed of its mystery!" (232). Even as Keats is writing a narrative poem in heroic verse, theater is at the center of Cockney poetics. Julie Carlson has attended to the ways in which "the sociability of theater" (particularly for a critic such as Hazlitt), provides a kind of antidote, or at least a way of addressing, the fractures in both public and private life that the dissipation and disappointment of revolutionary ardor occasioned. But the fractures themselves are also generative, speaking to (and, it must be noted *from*) what is left over when narratives of development (or even decline) are interrupted ("Hazlitt and the Sociability of Theatre").[39] If we find in late Romanticism a resistance to the kinds of narrative closures Burney found consolatory, we might name that possibility as interruption: not a catastrophic rending of a temporal continuum such as those Chandler finds informing post-Waterloo writing, but a testimony – in form as well as content – against linear progressions of time, contiguousness of place, or wholeness of self. For Keats, such a rending generates a felt sense of the impossible as a new ground for speaking, writing, and living in the years after 1809, when Hunt was in prison, Kean on stage, and Hazlitt in the pit and at the press.

VI Keats's Theatrical Urn

Whereas Keats's earlier poems depict and enact interruptions, the odes are governed by – or even more fundamentally speak from – a state of interruption that recalls Kean's acting and Hazlitt's prose style. Rhetorically defined as they are by apostrophe, personification, and interrogative constructions, the odes not only eschew narrative in a way that might be called typically lyrical; they also perform figurally their interruption of (and paradoxical engagement with) narrative modes of understanding and expression.[40] We could turn to any of the odes to make the point – to the temporal inversions of the "Ode to Psyche," to the repetitive wonderings of "Ode to a Nightingale," perhaps most of all to the apostrophaic figurations of "To Autumn." I will conclude with a discussion of the self-correcting allegorical meditations of "Ode on a Grecian Urn," claiming the poem as a lyric instantiation of the interruptive poetics that are the formal result of, and analogue of, Keats's theatrical experience.

The narrative refusals *Lamia* highlights, and which the odes enact, can helpfully be seen in light of the concern with "smokeability" Keats expresses in his letter to the George Keatses on December 31, 1818. Taking as a point of departure Keats's comment that he can "now see through" Mary Tighe and James Beattie, poets who "once delighted me" (*Letters* 2.18), James Chandler has described how Hazlitt's association of poetry with arbitrary power inspired Keats's desire to avoid a "vulnerability to being grasped – *captured* – by a higher order intelligence" (400). In "Ode to Psyche," Chandler finds an homage to Keats's champion of this vision, an exemplar of empirical skepticism whose late arrival in antiquity inspires not simple faith but a return to belief after "superstition is explained and the political uses of superstition are exposed" (415). As an allegory of Keats's search for authoritative rhetorical complexity, "Psyche" allies its non-smokeability with Wordsworth's resistance to "enlightenment attempts to dissolve the soul into the mechanics of the body" (421). For Chandler, the alliance recalls Keats's praise of Shakespeare and has a distinctly gendered dimension: "the non-smokeable life is the allegorical life, and the most allegorical life is the most manly" (402). By early 1819, Chandler argues, negative capability has taken on a more forceful temper: the "capacity for selflessness" Keats lauded in late 1817 "has been recontextualized within a kind of self-conscious realism about power and predation" (402).

Chandler's reading emphasizes a forcefulness I have been arguing negative capability exhibits from its first expression in late 1817, a forcefulness modeled after Kean's energetic and sexually provocative self-fashionings on and off the London stage. The "self-conscious realism about power and predation" Chandler finds in the 1819 Keats need not be seen as a negation of the poet's uncertainty or doubt; nor should it be too easily aligned with a concept of masculine poetic authority. In fact, as my reading of *Lamia* suggests, Keats relies on a forceful and at times violent engagement with historical conditions to contest the notion of authorial mastery or progressive narratives. Put another way, the non-smokeable poet enacts a wondering response to the irreducibility of lived experience, a response that in turn occasions readerly wonder. Negative capability, that is, transforms the poet's "uncertainties, mysteries, doubts" into a figural representation of the mind's never-resting powers. In the odes especially, Keats reclaims poetry's authentic connection to human feeling, to what Chandler calls "soul," by representing occasions in which the poet's attempt to "smoke" the cultural and historical scenes that he encounters remains incomplete. The later poems enact an economy of reading between poet and reader that is rather more open (to alliance, to gratitude, to wonder) than Chandler's predatory self-defense would suggest. In the odes of 1819, in particular, Keats pushes soulful figuring to its limits. If *Lamia* dramatizes the poet's figural response to historical circumstance, the odes enact that labor in a personal way, rejoining the lyric engagement with history that *Lamia*'s interruptive conclusion signals. The odes' experimental stanzas and dynamic literariness reveal an ongoing dialectic between inherited forms and the poet's personal insistence on revitalizing those forms in what had become for poetry an impossible historical moment.[41] Turning now to "Ode on a Grecian Urn," I will discuss how the speaker's repeated attempts to engage the urn as an object that is both aesthetic (pushing us toward the universal) and historical (pushing us toward the particular and the material) echo the interruptive nature of Kean's acting and the dialectical oscillations of Hazlitt's occasional prose. Recent readings, most notably Jeffrey Cox's, have stressed the historicity of the poem's aesthetic project.[42] My aim, though, is to consider how "Ode on a Grecian Urn" attempts to convey more generally history's power to at once elicit and curtail the poet's imaginative practices of knowing the world. Rather than providing a new reading of an entirely familiar poem, I offer this discussion as an example of how reading Keats through the lens of his theatrical experience can help us advance historicism's insight that Romantic poetry not only refers to history but is a self-consciously performed historiographical action.

The question of history in "Ode on a Grecian Urn" is structured, of course, by a tension between the urn's presence as an object – a thing subject to history – and its significance as the object of the speaker's imaginative consideration. The series of paradoxical formulations that shape the poem's opening apostrophe – "Thou still unravish'd bride" (1), "foster-child of silence and slow time" (2), "Sylvan historian" (3) – evinces the urn's hybrid status and consequently the imaginative labor (an impossible labor) that would be necessary to make it refer to a particular historical reality. Even as the attributed conditions enable the urn to "express/A flowery tale more sweetly than our rhyme" (3–4), they position the urn as a found object, a thing whose materiality can be perceived only through an imagined, mythologized past. Like the hieroglyphs that appear in Keats's review of Kean, in his marginalia of Hazlitt's essay, and in Keats's *Hyperion*, the urn's material origins and even its imagined language come to us only as "remnants" whose meaning is "now lost," their "import gone" (*Hyperion* 1.281, 282). The urn never relinquishes this status despite the poem's vivid shifts in diction and tone: it is never of us or our moment and yet can never be of its own (because now unimaginable) time. In this vein, the speaker's search for a historical particularity to chasten his impulse toward abstraction can only be seen as rhetorical; the questions of stanzas 1 and 4 expect no answer. And yet because the urn's significance remains unclear, these questions establish the speaker's experience as particular, as lived, and therefore as historically bound.[43]

For many critics, beginning with Cleanth Brooks, the poem's too earnest grasping at an unreachable ideal asks that we distinguish the mature Keats from his immature speaker. In Brooks's estimation, the poem becomes something of a virtuoso mini-play: Keats's refusal to specify a historical urn invites us to read the ode as a "speech 'in character' and supported by dramatic context" (165). We can also recall Charles Rzepka's fashioning of a Keats who moves toward an "essentially theatrical, which is to say self-distancing, point of view" (*Self as Mind* 168). Even David Simpson, whose reading of the poem ultimately undercuts the notion of the poet's superiority to the speaker, posits that Keats's crafting of a fictionalized urn enables him provisionally "to distance his poetic persona from the speaker; to provide, in other words, the fixed level of metacommentary which enables the speaker's behavior to be seen in a critical, ironic light" (11). Against these positions I would argue that the poem asks its readers throughout its stanzas to avoid any assumption of such distance. Stanza 3, commonly seen as the climax of the initial attempt to establish the urn's negative historical relation to the speaker's present, provides a good place to develop my claim:

> Ah, happy, happy boughs! that cannot shed
>   Your leaves, nor ever bid the spring adieu;
> And, happy melodist, unwearied,
>   For ever piping songs for ever new;
> More happy love, more happy, happy love!
>   For ever warm and still to be enjoy'd,
>   For ever panting, and for ever young;
> All breathing human passion far above,
>   That leaves a heart high-sorrowful and cloy'd,
>   A burning forehead, and a parching tongue. (21–30)

With their pouncing repetition and self-conscious syntactical inversions – "All breathing human passion far above" strains even the most credulous ear as it strives to meet the demands of the stanza's end rhyme – the lines seem to exemplify the worst of Keatsian lyric excess. We need not rely solely on the self-alienation Levinson finds defining Keats's prosody to present this criticism. Indeed Brooks's "dramatic" reading of the poem runs into its most difficult stumbling block with stanza 3 (165): "I am not sure that this stanza can altogether be defended against the charge that it represents a falling-off from the delicate but firm precision of the early stanzas" (158). And Simpson's conception of "Romantic irony" relies as well on lines such as these to elicit an initial judgment that "the speaker's perspective is to be seen as limited" (10).

But if we grant that stanza 3 is less obviously figural than those that precede or follow, such a recognition need not be accompanied by the self-distancing of the poet from the speaker or, more dramatically in terms of each renewed encounter with the poem, of the reader from the poet. Stanza 4's explicit return to history and to the steadier diction of the interrogative "Who are these coming to the sacrifice?" (31) is often seen as a recuperation of the just-failed attempt to render the urn a timeless aesthetic object.[44] But in another sense, the poem needs no such recuperation, for it has never left history behind. The speaker's contention in stanza 3 that the urn places its figures far above "All breathing passion .../That leaves a heart high-sorrowful and cloy'd" (29–30) is tempered by the lines' negative formulations (*cannot* shed your leaves, *Nor ever* bid) and countered by their feverish rhythms: "More happy love! more happy happy love!/For ever warm and still to be enjoy'd,/For ever panting, and for ever young" (25–27). The "foster-child of silence and slow time," imagined from the outset to be incorrigible in the face of the present moment's reading of it, here occasions the reader's own pulse-quickening breath. As we imagine the urn depicting an eternal present, its "forever" is contrasted with the speaker's – and our own – inescapably temporal, figural, changing, breathing, voicing of the poem's words.[45] Thus the urn is, even before stanza 4's renewed search for historical particulars, "part of history," to employ Emily Sun's phrase (73), because the response it generates positions Keats as "a sufferer who participates in the suffering of others – and who calls upon the reader to do the same" (75). Remaining bound to the speaker's – and reader's – overwrought vocalizations, stanza 3's effort at idealization actually reintroduces readers to the reality of their own breathing lives. Not figural density, then, so much as human accessibility renders the lines aesthetically, and ethically, valuable – *because* they are in and of themselves easily "smoked." Like the incursion of the public that necessitates both Lamia's demise and *Lamia*'s conclusion, the speaker's simultaneous engagement with aesthetic making (the urn as imagined) and with lived experience (the lines as voiced) enables the awareness of finitude that the following stanzas will make explicit. Stanza 4 and its silent empty town, as well as stanza 5 and its vatic utterances, do not so much enact a return to a suppressed history as provide a differently figured rendering of the historical imagining that stanza 3 has already educed.

In its commitment to this kind of successive figuration, "Ode on a Grecian Urn" recalls for us not only Kean's figurative acting but also Paul de Man's notion of allegory in "The Rhetoric of Temporality." Refusing the "infinity of a totality" suggested by symbol, de Man's allegory unfolds conspicuously in time, figure upon figure necessitating the temporary refutation of the "empirical self" in favor of a self "that becomes like a sign in its attempt at differentiation and self-definition" (211). Theresa Kelley argues that the durative nature of allegory shapes as well the reader's sense of her or his own historical being: "Romantic figures that tend toward allegory emphasize the fact that their meaning is not organic, not simultaneously understood. Such figures encourage historical awareness among readers. Unlike symbols, whose meaning is supposed to be understood at first glance, allegories require a process of reading and reflection" (354–55). To claim a kind of consolidation, as Helen Vendler does, in which the more philosophically accomplished or self-assured formulations of the final stanza ("O Attic shape! Fair attitude! with brede/Of marble men and maidens overwrought" (41–42)) overcome previous attempts to grasp the urn's perfections is, from the perspective of allegory, beside the point.[46] Indeed the repetitions in these lines ("Attic . . . attitude," the alliteration in line 42) manifest that the practice of figurative continuation – a self-correction displayed in the poem's multiple shifts in address and tone – occurs at the level of phrasing as well. Keats's verse, like Kean's acting, cannot find the emblematic mode of expression it seeks on the level of either syntax or structure. And yet this lack becomes the means by which the poem occasions both poet's and reader's awareness of themselves as historical beings. The performed temporality of Keatsian allegory – which reaches its most vivid state in stanza 3 of "Ode on a Grecian Urn" – enlists the reader as a maker of the poem's ongoing historicity, an afterlife occasioned by readerly utterance. This is why allegory, in Theresa Kelley's words, "remains a capable figure, not because it asserts that referentiality or reality are all washed up, which it does not, but because its figural interventions can clear paths to help human reason make its way" (278). Taken together, the ode's five stanzas model poetic wondering as a way for "human reason to make its way" – albeit a grasping, interruptive, fragmented way – in an unreasonable world. The urn is a found object that, like the playtext to Kean or the theatrical performance to Hazlitt, cannot be possessed at all either historically or imaginatively: no summary conclusion of its meaning is possible. Yet as a material remnant of past imagining, it must elicit a human attempt to encounter its fading significances, to refigure its relevance.

And what then – the question is always before us – do we make of the final lines? Positing an emblematic end to the poem's fruitful if frustrating wondering, the final stanza enacts an encounter between poetry and lived experience that we can understand more (or less) clearly in light of Keats's affinity with Kean. If we consider "Ode on a Grecian Urn" as an allegorical poem, where allegory is a rhetorical unfolding in time of the speaker's self-alienation, it is an allegory that the urn's materiality must finally disrupt. In such a reading, the poem's final lines

> "Beauty is truth, truth beauty," – that is all
> Ye know on earth, and all ye need to know.[47]   (49–50)

stand out as an attempt to provide a closure that compensates for the urn's imagined inability to attend to the empirical world – or, put another way, for the speaker's failure to determine the urn's historical particularity. This double figuration (what we might, reversing de Man, call the irony of allegory) dramatizes the speaker's need to imagine a rhetorical if not a conceptual resting point for his ekphrasis.[48] If, in de Man's terms, "allegory exists entirely within an ideal time that is never here and now but always a past or an endless future" and this is the presiding mode of the poem, then the ode's final injunction undercuts that ideal time, embracing an irony that is "essentially the mode of the present" which "knows neither memory nor prefigurative duration" (226). Irony, then, is a refusal of allegory's idealized temporal movements – a forced return to the insistent now that curtails poetry's truth claims.

But my contention that the poem remains always conspicuously bound to the speaker's particular experience of the urn renders this reading insufficient as well. For irony too imagines, however contingently, a perspective outside the historical. As de Man comments, "Irony is a synchronic structure, where allegory appears as a successive mode capable of engendering duration as the illusion of a continuity that it knows to be illusionary. Yet the two modes, for all their profound distinctions in mood and structure, are the two faces of the same fundamental experience of time" ("Rhetoric of Temporality" 226). Simpson's ironic reading of the poem follows this logic. For Simpson, the injunction of lines 49–50 "itself contains a suppressed cyclic imperative, demanding re-reading and reconstruction in an attempt to justify the pseudo-finality of those lines" (12). To enable this imperative, though, Simpson must posit rhetorically differentiated positions: "the poet's" interjection in the famous final lines judges the "speaker's" earlier formulations as incomplete, only to be in turn ironized by the reader's recognition of the "pseudo-finality" of the poet's claim (Simpson 12). Here we have a Romantic "irony of irony," an irony that turns back on itself to reenlist its critical "metacomment" back into the poem's earnest "comment" (Simpson 22) – its genuine attempts to ascertain the urn's significance to the speaker. While Simpson's reading makes a great deal of sense, it is my contention that precisely because for Keats the poet must enact his own historicity, the ode refuses the split between poet and speaker Simpson theorizes. And we can find that refusal (a refusal to achieve either pure allegorizing or ironic critical distance) equally in "the poet's" authoritative injunction and in "the speaker's" earlier attempts to engage the urn.

How then might we reconcile the factitiousness of the poem's final words (" – that is all/Ye know on earth, and all ye need to know") with Keats's clearly heartfelt statement in his letter to Benjamin Bailey in late 1817 about "the holiness of the Heart's affections and the truth of Imagination – What the imagination seizes as Beauty must be truth" (*Letters* 1.183). One means to achieve a measure of reconciliation lies, I think, in the injunction's antique diction. Coming as it does as the last in a series of rhetorical attempts to make the urn *mean*, the conspicuous formality of the voice ("all *ye* know on earth") registers the work imagination must do to ventriloquize the urn. Emphasizing the urn's anachronism, its conspicuous pastness, this is the same kind of labor we've witnessed in the poem's early mythologizing, in the enthusiasms of stanza 3, in the interrogations of stanzas 1 and 4, and in the more assured addresses of stanzas 4 and 5.[49] Further, as a conspicuous remainder of the near-perfect chiasmus that precedes it, the phrase " – that is all/Ye know on earth, and all ye need to know" displays the inevitable intrusion of lived onto aesthetic experience, refusing to allow "Beauty is truth, truth beauty" to become an unqualified and therefore universal emblem. This curtailment of the ideal, part of what Theresa Kelley calls Keats's "contingent allegorical vision," borrows from both Kean's and Hazlitt's insistence on historical occasions and emblematizes lyric imagining's uneasy but necessary alliance with particular historical circumstance.[50] Rather than trying to "refuse himself, and his readers, the relief of absolute closure, at the very moment of suggesting one" (Simpson 13), Keats offers with the poem's final lines a closure that, as an outcome of the previous stanzas' boundedness to particular (and even bodily) experience, conspicuously *must* occur. This is not so much an ironic distancing as it is a performed subjection of poetic making to the lived experience of history, a rehearsal in an odal key of the same bitter interruption with which *Lamia* concludes. That is, while the epigraphic nature of the injunction highlights its "pseudo-finality" (Simpson 12), its position as an abrupt end to the poem's allegory of consciousness marks the experiential boundaries of that allegory, a figuration that must give way to our "earth," our world, the world of "future generations" imagined by the speaker through the urn's address. In stanza 5 as throughout the poem, Keats's ode refuses the "ideal time" necessary for pure allegorizing, positing rather that history's constant presence gives allegory its experiential urgency. To the degree that the poem courts the factitious all along, it also marks its status as a thing made by a singular human imagination. In this sense, the ode's speaker is, and always is, Keats.

Maintaining its connection to history throughout its rhetorical changes, "Ode on a Grecian Urn" enacts Keats's belief that any aesthetic strategy is bound to measure its own limits if it is to avoid the illusion of standing outside history. We need not distance "the poet" – Keats – from the Cockney excesses of stanza 3 any more than from the overly fine assertion that concludes the poem. What Robert Kaufman has termed the "constructivism" of Keats's late verse – a high formalism that critics have argued represents Keats's attempt to transcend history – actually presents us with a way of "thinking the historical" ("Everybody Hates Kant" 136).[51] If the object of history – urn or poem – cannot be mastered and fully known, still it can and must be imagined by red-blooded readers. Here Keats's warm and capable Keanian wondering parts company with the de Manian fantasy of infinite allegorical play even as it refuses the "freedom" born of an irony characterized by the "unwillingness of the mind to accept any stage in its progression as definitive" (220). Never forgetting that we cannot live in an alternatively imagined temporality, a rhetorical time both allegory and irony in their different ways assume, the speaker of the ode renders *every* stage of the mind's progression as definitive because the ability to abide, if only contingently, in any of them is the *sine qua non* of human experience. This is not to say that Keats attends at all times to historical particulars, or that he seeks a historical particularity from which to ironize his poem's allegorizing, but rather that his poems are allegories that see through themselves from the start, that know their imaginings are impermanent and yet imagine not in spite of but because of that knowledge. Scholars from de Man to Emily Rohrbach have argued that Keats's poetry imagines a horizon of expectation shaped by an impending future theorized but unknown.[52] But the ultimate unknown is also the ultimate known. Keats's "refusal to sublimate mortality as a social conspiracy," in Paul Fry's words (*Poet's Calling* 417), imagines the poet and by extension his reader as subjects always beholden to what will come – to that which will interrupt the current instant.[53] Like Kean they are figures in motion, figuring but able to abide in any given figure entirely as if it were the last, because it will not last. In this way, negative capability contends with the continual traumas visited upon us by an ever-changing life of allegory.

Keats's insistence on the final interruption that experience imposes on poetry provides a lesson of late Romanticism that we are still discovering. From it we can learn much about how to live in our own time, a time more spectacular, more urban, and more warlike even than the early nineteenth century. By attending with renewed vigor to the way that poetry's mystifying rhetorics reveal within themselves their historical origins – by adopting, if you will, a methodology that attends to poetic figuration as always subject to, and always a subject of, interruption – we might resist more fully our own moment's demand for intellectual, professional, and political certainties. Closer to home, we might chasten criticism's still prevalent desire to make poetry not only say something about the particularities of history but to make it primarily a historical object. Keats's ability – not merely to speak from moments of uncertainty, mystery, and doubt but also to occasion such moments in the reader – breaks in the starkest sense from the poetry of what he calls the "wordsworthian or egotistical sublime" (*Letters* 1.387). And the echo of that break resounds in the verse of the centuries that follow: in Barrett Browning's "I cannot teach my hand to hold my spirit so far off/from myself"; in Arnold's "darkling plain"; in Whitman's "Whoever you are holding me now in hand"; in the "watching strangers" of Bishop's "Questions of Travel"; in Stevens's "Death is the mother of beauty"; even and perhaps especially in Beckett's "Somehow nohow on." I would therefore in a polemical way reverse Jerome McGann's 1979 claim – a claim that still presides rightly over much criticism of Romantic poetry – that we must understand the specific "human limits which history imposes" on the Romantic poets' attempts to transcend their moment if we are to understand their achievement ("Keats and the Historical Method" 1027). Of course this remains true. But in our belated and critical hour, we would also do well to attend more fully (as Chandler and Hamilton and Kelley have done) to how, specifically, the Romantics' rhetorical figurations affirm from the outset the uncertainty of any attempt at transcendence – understanding how Romantic poetry made, and continues to make, history.

Theatrical experience in all its variety is a way into Romantic poetry rather than a way out, for like the literary work it engendered, Britain's early-nineteenth-century theatrical world shows us an open human response to the incongruities of history's events and occasions. One thinks back not only to Edmund Kean but to the *Times* reader making sense of the day's events, to the intrepid *Theatrical Mince Pie* reviewer jostled by his fellow audience members, to Hazlitt's intentful loitering along the margins of a great boxing match. Keats's refusal to see history as a solvable riddle and his accompanying insistence on keeping allegory real confirms Paul Hamilton's claim that Keats resists the aesthetic recuperations provided by "the ironies of poetic self criticism" (112). Courting but refusing such recuperation, the concluding lines of "Ode on a Grecian Urn" mark the reader's subjection to the same historical realities that have shaped the speaker's figuring throughout the poem, realities that will "waste" the current generation. This knowledge saves the poem from the illusion of imagination's infinite "freedom," reclaiming feeling as the means by which we grasp our human finitude.[54] The ode's striking fidelity to its own figures, its refusal to seek an aesthetic solution to history's – to death's – irrefutable presence, performs at once poetry's limit and its highest ethical function. Another way of putting this is that for Keats, poetry's task is to seek out and display language's final inability to erase the traumas history imposes. What a halfseeing, interruptive poetics – what a theatrical poetics – meant for Keats, and what it asks of us as readers still working in the "now" that Romanticism first imagined, is neither that we take history's remnants as objects to be possessed, nor that we take poetry's signs for inexplicable wonders. Rather, like the actor Kean on stage, like the critic Hazlitt in the pit, like the poet Keats in the theatrical city and in the world, these poems insist that we wonder at their signs without seeking to master them, even as we embrace the "instant feelings" they occasion – wondering ourselves, in the same act, into a new kind of life.

Notes

1. Horatio "Horace" Smith (1779–1849) was educated at a school in Chigwell. Unlike his brother, who became a solicitor, he went to work in a merchant's counting house. Distracted from his profession by the lures of London's theatrical and literary life, he wrote a poem "lamenting the decay of public taste as evidenced in the neglect of the plays of Richard Cumberland." *Dictionary of National Biography (DNB)*, eds. Sir Leslie Stephen and Sir Sidney Lee, 22 vols. (Oxford: Oxford University Press, 1921–1922. rpt. 1959–1960), 18.461. Cumberland subsequently took Smith as his literary protégé. Thomas Hill (1760–1840) was born in Lancaster but went to London at an early age, "where for many years he carried on an extensive business as a dry-salter at Queenhithe" (*DNB* 9.875). An avid book collector, he eventually became part owner of the

Monthly Mirror. And Edward DuBois (1774–1850) was the home-educated son of a London merchant who "adopted literature as his profession" (*DNB* 6.78). DuBois contributed to a variety of periodicals, eventually serving as editor of the *Monthly Mirror* under Hill's ownership.

2. In *Keats and Embarrassment*, Christopher Ricks points to a similar "fine comic inversion of the social situation" when Keats, in an 1820 letter to Dilke, expresses dislike for "the hauteur of Lord Chesterfield" (Ricks 77, 76) by commenting that he "would not bathe in the same River with lord C. though I had the upper hand of the stream" (*Letters* 2.272).

3. There is a long tradition of criticism that considers Keats's poetry as evidence of his transcending circumstance. See, for example, Trilling, as well as W. J. Bate, and Vendler.

4. Several contemporary definitions of "company" are helpful. "Com'pany. [*Compagnie*, F]: an Assembly of People; a Society, or Body Corporate; a small Body of Foot commanded by a Captain; also Conversation, Fellowship." Nathan Bailey, *An Universal English Dictionary* (London: R. Ware, 1775). Keats owned an edition of this dictionary. See *The Keats Circle: Letters and Papers*, ed. Hyder Edward Rollins, vol. 1 (Cambridge, MA: Harvard University Press, 1965), 122. "Com'pany. *n.s.* [*compagnie*, French; either from *con* and *pagus*, one of the same town; or *con* and *panis*, one that eats of the same mess.] . . . 5. A number of persons united for the execution or performance of any thing; a band." Samuel Johnson, *A Dictionary of the English Language* (New York: Arno, 1979; London: W. Strahan, 1755).

5. For an account of Keats's political alliance with Kean that in many respects parallels my own, see John Kandl's "Plebian Gusto, Negative Capability, and the Low Company of 'Mr. Kean:' Keats' Dramatic Review for the *Champion* (21 December 1817)." Gillian Russell more recently provides another account of Keats's alliance with Kean, and Keats's experience of "theatre as a site of sociability . . . which interacted with the theatricality of the other literary publics in which he was participating" ("Keats, Popular Culture, and the Sociability of Theatre" 208).

6. Nicholas Roe, *John Keats and the Culture of Dissent* 237–39. Roe focuses on the *Examiner* articles as "indicative of the immediate backgrounds to Keats's intellectual and imaginative life" at the time, remarking suggestively that "it is notable too that Keats mentions a dinner at which Edmund Kean was discussed immediately before he tells his brothers how the idea of negative capability had 'struck' him" (238–39).

7. For the original *Blackwood's Edinburgh Magazine* reviews, see *The Romantics Reviewed*, ed. Donald H. Reiman, *Shelley, Keats, and the London Radical Writers*, part C, vol. I, 80–96.

8. Levinson remarks that "the basic method of this book might be described as post-structuralist; its governing ideology, historical-materialist" (33). For other developments of Levinson's approach, see Elizabeth Jones's discussion of Keats's "suburbanism" and "desire for middle-class status" in "Keats in the Suburbs" (23), as well as Daniel Watkins's materialist claim that Keats sought

"to create imaginative worlds free of all struggle and conflict" (*Keats's Poetry and the Politics of the Imagination* 104).

9. Wordsworth writes in the *Essay* "that every Author, as far as he is great and at the same time *original*, has had the task of *creating* the taste by which he is to be enjoyed." *William Wordsworth: The Oxford Authors*, ed. Stephen Gill, 657–58. Appropriating Wordsworth as Levinson does is a problematic gesture, as more recent scholars have argued. For example, Lucy Newlyn has noted that "at the time Wordsworth wrote his 'Essay Supplementary to the Preface,' he was acutely anxious about his reception, and had no reason to suppose that hostility would give way to admiration" among either reviewers or the larger reading public. *Reading, Writing, and Romanticism: The Anxiety of Reception* 176. Among other discussions of Wordsworth's uncertainty about his cultural and professional position, see Charles Rzepka, "A Gift that Complicates Employ: Poetry and Poverty in 'Resolution and Independence,'" 225–47; and Mark Schoenfield, *The Professional Wordsworth: Law, Labor, and the Poet's Contract* 94–138.

10. As Tilottama Rajan notes, Levinson's critique is more closely allied with high formalism then she allows, for it "does not so much contest the figuration of Keats as reproduce it negatively, as the sign of incapacity and social failure" (334).

11. Nicholas Roe, *John Keats and the Culture of Dissent* as well as Roe, *John Keats: A New Life* (esp. 19–157).

12. I here rely on and revise Donald Reiman's claim that Keats was at the head of a "third generation" of British Romantic poets, born after the French Revolution, who were "scions of the mobile middle classes." Donald H. Reiman, "Keats and the Third Generation" 111.

13. Harry Beaudry's *The English Theatre and John Keats* is the singular exception to this silence. Beaudry details plays in repertory at the time Keats would have been attending London theaters and describes the various theatrical writings of the Keats circle, including reviews and plays by Keats, John Hamilton Reynolds, Leigh Hunt, and Charles Dilke. A number of mid-twentieth-century critics recognized in the later poetry what M. R. Ridley called a "strong dramatic instinct, that sense indeed of 'theatre'" complicating Keats's lyricism. *Keats's Craftsmanship: A Study in Poetic Development* 69. W. J. Bate noted "a successful intrusion of the dramatic" in the odes: in "Ode on a Grecian Urn" and "Ode to a Nightingale," especially, Bate contends, "we are dealing with a miniature drama" of the speaker's attempt "to identify himself with an object that can lift himself beyond a world of flux." See Bate, "Keats's Style: Evolution Toward Qualities of Permanent Value" 227.

14. All references are to John Keats, *The Complete Poems*, ed. Jack Stillinger (Cambridge, MA: Belknap, 1978). "Co(n)vent Garden" is, of course, the center of London's West End theater district, and the name of one of two Theatres Royal in Keats's London, the other being Drury Lane Theatre. Keats's transmutation of "Covent" into "Convent" connotes profanation

and may also license a vulgar pun similar to that which Byron makes with his instance that "*Cant* is so much stronger than *Cunt*" (*Letters and Journals* 5.232). For a discussion of Byron's wordplay, see Christopher Ricks, *Allusion to the Poets* 152–53.

15. For a discussion of the ways in which market growth transformed traditional modes of public contact into a continually negotiated "problematic of exchange," see Jean-Christophe Agnew.

16. There is a considerable body of scholarship that arranges the terms of the original *Blackwood's* attacks along a continuum of "development," in which Keats progresses from his juvenile association with Leigh Hunt toward a refiguration of poetry's expressive capacities. In this view, represented most powerfully by the mid-century criticism of W. J. Bate, Keats demonstrates a stylistic overcoming; poems become the evidence of a heroic attempt to construct a "life of sensations" despite the difficulty of the poet's lived conditions. What attracts scholars to Keats is, for Bate, an "achievement so compelling when, at the same time, so little is apparently given at the start" (*John Keats* 2). Thomas McFarland has argued that Keats assumes imaginative "masks," enabling him to figure the disappointments of his real life into poetry. By "transform[ing] his negative circumstances" into "a visage that could be readily accepted by the reading public of his time," Keats demonstrates for McFarland a version of Romantic "genius." *The Masks of Keats: The Endeavor of a Poet* (227, 3). For William Keach, Keats's "genial audacity" of rhyme signals to the reader the poet's formal flexibility, "as well as an indication that he is letting himself be surprised by what turns up next" (191). That Keats was still employing the technique well into 1818 suggests that his "development" away from the Cockney style – and social position – was not so neat as earlier scholars contend.

17. In "History, Existence, and 'To Autumn,'" Paul Fry makes the crucial point that although Keats deliberately moved away from the Cockney style displayed in his early poems, "it hardly follows that he specifically wanted them to be more servile to the canons of the ruling class" (216). This is to say that the traditional opposition between the Cockneyism of the early poetry and the maturity of the later poetry dovetails too readily into a critique of Keats's class aspirations. Both Nicholas Roe and Jeffrey Cox have provided historically grounded arguments for reconsidering Keats's relationship to classical culture as a sophisticated "Cockney classicism" rather than as evidence of youthful naiveté. See Roe, *John Keats and the Culture of Dissent* 60–71 and Cox, *Poetry and Politics in the Cockney School* (Cambridge: Cambridge University Press, 1998) 146–86.

18. Charles Lamb saw around the time of Kean's debut the emergence of a new "race of actors" for whom "less study is found necessary than was formerly judged to be requisite" (*Works* 151). Rather than coherent representation, this "new acting" was driven by a "coquetting between the performer and the public" that appealed to theatergoers' desire for sensation (152).

19. *Monthly Theatrical Reporter* 5 (February 1815): 192.

20. Harry Beaudry was the first to explore in any depth Keats's theatrical reading of Hazlitt (Beaudry 124–31).
21. In his *Recollections of Writers*, Charles Cowden Clarke comments that "Leigh Hunt's Examiner – which my father took in, and I used to lend to Keats – no doubt laid the foundation of his love of civil and religious liberty" (124). For a discussion of the *Examiner*'s significance in Keats's schooling, see Roe 27–50. Jeffrey Cox notes similarly the importance of the periodical in maintaining and publicly representing the Hunt circle: "The *Examiner* is, in a sense, the textual home of the group, setting forth common ideological positions and publishing the verse of the circle's members" (*Poetry and Politics* 7). See also Keats's 1817 letter to Reynolds, in which he refers to reading the *Morning Chronicle* (*Letters* 1.190).
22. John Keats, *The Poetical Works and Other Writings of John Keats: Hampstead Edition*, ed. H. Buxton Forman, vol. 5 (New York: Scribner, 1939), 227. Subsequently in the text, abbreviated as *HK*. Two weeks later, in the January 4, 1818, issue of the *Champion*, Keats's two additional reviews were published: "On 'Retribution, or The Chieftain's Daughter'" and "On 'Don Giovanni,' a Pantomime." The *Hampstead Keats* attributes to Keats a fourth review, published in the December 28, 1817 *Champion* concerning "On Kean in 'Richard Duke of York.'" See *HK* 233–46. The review was actually written by Reynolds. For a discussion of the misattribution, see Slote 86–96 and Leonidas Jones "Keats's Theatrical Reviews in the *Champion*," *Keats-Shelley Journal* 3 (Winter 1954): 55–65. Without question, Hazlitt's subjective reviewing style was a model for these brief essays. Slote remarks that following Hazlitt, the reviews "are personal reaction, comment, talk, and they do not attempt much objective analysis" (88). Kenneth Muir sees them as "obvious imitations of Hazlitt" (141). W. J. Bate's more positive view claims that Keats prepared for his assignment by reading Hazlitt's theatrical criticism, and that the first review especially is "written with the rapid verve, the darting impressionism, of Hazlitt's manner" (*John Keats* 236), and David Bromwich remarks that the Kean review "contained a sentence easily mistakable for one of Hazlitt's" (367). What Keats found in Hazlitt, though, was not just stylistic flair, but also recognition of theatrical performance's power to shape the viewer's notions of experience.
23. The most appropriate *Oxford English Dictionary* definition for Keats's nineteenth-century use of "hieroglyphic" would seem to be "A picture standing for a word or notion, esp. one symbolizing something which it does not directly figure (like many of the Egyptian hieroglyphs); hence, a figure, a device, or sign, having some hidden meaning; a secret or enigmatical symbol, an emblem; a hieroglyph." *Oxford English Dictionary* (5.273).
24. Much has been made of Hazlitt's influence on Keats, beginning with Thorpe's "Keats and Hazlitt" in 1947. But note that Hazlitt's lecture occurs one month after Keats's review of Kean was published. Keats missed the first lecture and was late for the second. See his letter of January 23, 1818 (*Letters* 1.214). Regarding the lectures, David Bromwich offers a tellingly theatrical

assessment: "[W]hen Keats attended Hazlitt's lectures . . . he went not to hear criticism but Hazlitt" (14).
25. For Keats's marginalia and markings throughout his copy of the volume, see *HK* 280–86. W. J. Bate also records Keats's observation in *John Keats* 262. For the passage in Hazlitt, see 4.259.
26. In *Shakespearean Constitutions: Politics, Theater, Criticism 1730–1830*, Jonathan Bate has described how "Shakespeare was constituted" in various and conflicting ways through Romantic-period caricature, criticism, parody, and performance. This is to say that the "Shakespeare" imagined by Hazlitt or Kean would have carried particular political and class associations that appealed to Keats. Kathryn Prince argues that theatrical periodicals were "the most significant means by which Shakespeare was disseminated to the nineteenth-century working classes" (17).
27. See, for example, the famous response to "Z" in *Examiner* 516 (Sunday, November 16, 1817), in which Hunt rails, "the anonymous Author of the above atrocious attempt to destroy the personal character of the Editor of this Paper, is again called upon to avow himself: which he cannot fail to do, unless to an utter disregard of all *Truth* and Decency, he adds the height of Meanness and Cowardice" (729).
28. Franta's work is helpful in providing literary reviewing as an institutional context for Keats's refiguration of poetry's social function. But the most important form of review, the type of review Keats read most frequently, was the theatrical review. More specifically, Hazlitt's reviews of Kean encouraged Keats to see in the moment of cultural reception a transformative experience that itself becomes the subject of the actor's, or, for Keats, the poet's, representation. This is to say that Keats's notion of poetry's "recommendatory function" is different from that of the typical literary review Franta describes. For related discussions of review culture's effects on literary production in the Romantic period, see Newlyn 173–223 and Kathryn Sutherland "'Events . . . Have Made Us a World of Readers': Reader Relations 1780–1839" (24–36).
29. See Jeffrey Cox's related assertion that "Keats's verse is overwhelmingly occasional" (*Poetry and Politics* 89).
30. Randall McLeod was the first to suggest this insight to me. See "Un-Editing Shakespeare" 29–33.
31. Here I recall but diverge from treatments of Keats as inhabiting a state of suspension as unfulfillment. See, for example, Brendan Corcoran's discussion of Keats's "perpetually suspended dying" (347). Robert Mitchell describes Romantic "suspended animation" more positively as "a vitality that liberate[s] sensation from its usual subordination to action" (113). In my reading, such suspension is predicated on the expectation of a future departure from that state – figurally as well as affectively or actually.
32. See Stillinger's introduction to his edition of Keats's *Complete Poems* for a distilled instance of this reading.

33. Here I follow Mary Favret's insights – focused in her case on the nature of "wartime" – about the way certain kinds of affect, one may say affect altogether, is made possible by historical interruption. See Favret 9–22.
34. For a cogent discussion of Wollstonecraft's indictment of female "hypocrite modesty," see Crafton 277–99. See Guest for an account of how in Wollstonecraft "sensibility acquires a radical edge, a political inflection" that is resistant to just the kinds of strictures Burney places on it in her novel (301). For a related discussion, see Burgess, "Courting Ruin."
35. Several discussions of Austen's concerns with theatricality complicate this point, arguing persuasively that even as *Mansfield Park* exhibits trepidation about theater's power, the novel also registers theater's ability to illuminate and expose true character. See Penny Gay's *Jane Austen and the Theatre* (98–122) as well as Paula Byrne's identically titled study (149–209).
36. See, among others, Dart, Cox, Kandl, and Roe.
37. Emily Rohrbach, "Reading the Heart, Reading the World"; Jonathan Sachs, "The Time of Decline."
38. Here Dan Edelstein's contention that we need to recognize "The Enlightenment" as itself a commitment to narrative is helpful in considering how Romantic lyric figuration resists progressive notions of individual or collective national experience by swerving from and undercutting its own narrative trajectories (13–18).
39. Alexander Regier offers a related discussion of how Keats's letters manifest "a linguistic predicament of brokenness" (119).
40. For a discussion of Keats's "partly quizzing, partly prospective" (310) tone and of the "interrogative mode" Keats employs throughout his poems, see Susan Wolfson's *The Questioning Presence*. The *Romantic Praxis* volume *"Ode on a Grecian Urn": Hypercanonicity and Pedagogy*, edited by James O'Rourke, contains several reflections, including Wolfson's own, on the poem's exemplary status as an act of figuration in Keats's oeuvre and in literary history.
41. For a discussion of Keats's development of the ode stanza and its conspicuous indebtedness to the sonnet tradition, see Mulrooney, "Keats's 'Dull Rhymes' and the Making of the Ode Stanza."
42. See *Poetry and Politics in the Cockney School* 147–86. Cox situates the poem as responding to "a very real commercialized classicism" by attempting to "recreate in fiction the 'aura'" of an object infused with classically erotic associations (150). Courting a truth that is "didactic" and even "pornographic," Keats's urn refutes in a Cockney way the contemporary politics of Britain's imperial, masculinist triumphalism. Cox neatly summarizes his argument: "Keats's *Ode on a Grecian Urn* – with its Catullan wordplay, its erotic classicism, its sympathy with the Ariadnes and Emma Hamiltons of the world – is part of the Cockney school's attempt to define the classic as the pagan, the passionate, and the politically radical" (185). See also Nicholas Roe's discussion of the poem's "unillusioned response to revolutions which had found in pagan antiquity a powerful inspiration for the renovation of the modern world" (*Keats and the Culture of Dissent* 85–87).

43. Jerome McGann argues that the poem's fictionalized drive toward historical particularity "asks its readers to try to visualize, in a concrete way, the urn of the poet's imaginings" (*The Beauty of Inflections* 44). Emphasis on this drive has informed a number of historically concerned readings, most notably Cox's. See Cox's discussion of McGann in *Poetry and Politics in the Cockney School* (148–49).

44. James Kee, who sees the poem as a Heideggerean unfolding of a "happening of truth" that culminates in the speaker's final "letting be" of the urn (39, 40), attributes the shift in tone to stanza 4's recovery of historical forgetfulness: "Without question, the tone of the poem changes when the speaker is . . . led to recollect human passion and sorrow" (36). More recently, Emily Sun argues from a psychoanalytic perspective that stanza 4 marks a crucial turn in the "failure of the apostrophaic gesture" (75), reintroducing the speaker to the traumatic world stanza 3 has attempted to transcend. See esp. 72–73.

45. Citing Keats's pun about the "rougueglyphics in Moors almanack" (*Letters* 2.247), Garret Stewart makes an astute observation that parallels my emphasis on the sound quality of the verses here: "This tossed off joke, in part about the fugitive phonetic element in alphabetic characters, often dissonant and mischievous (the fusing *g* sounds), maps directly onto Keats's most considered views of how meanings emerge on both glyphic and phonic levels of signification" (137). Stewart also notes how Keats "saw this literary instinct at work in the Shakespearean actor Edmund Kean" (137–38).

46. Noting that "the language of the close of 'Urn' cannot be entirely assimilated to the language used earlier in the ode, and this is a flaw" (145), Vendler sees the final stanza enacting a more rigorous and manly philosophical approach: "Attempting to allow the perplexed brain full freedom in this ode, Keats becomes in this last stanza the nineteenth-century intellectual man who is acquainted with archeological terms and literary genres" (146).

47. Stillinger's edition follows Keats's *1820* volume in enclosing "Beauty is truth, truth beauty" in quotations. There are of course multiple variants of the lines, the chief difference being that earlier versions, including the transcriptions by Charles Brown and George Keats and the poem's original publication in the *Annals of the Fine Arts*, omit the quotation marks around the phrase. For a substantive account of these differences, see Cox, *Keats's Poetry and Prose* 461; as well as Allott, *The Poems of John Keats* 537–38. My reading does not so much seek to answer the long-standing question of who speaks the phrase, or the lines, as it suggests that the question is itself part of the poem's fundamental effect.

48. Here I would resist Brooks's insistence that the poem's final injunction must be "dramatically prepared for" by not striking the reader as "a bewildering break in tone, he must not be too much disturbed to have the element of paradox latent in the poem emphasized, even in those parts of the poem which have none of the energetic crackle and wit with which he usually associated paradox" (154, 155). In my view, the injunction's abrupt appearance confirms both its own limitation as a way of imagining the urn and the related

"limited" authenticity of the previous stanzas that have conditioned the speaker to accept the necessity of such a conclusion.
49. For a discussion of the poem's movement from apostrophe to prosopopoeia, see Emily Sun (73–74).
50. See Kelley's claim, "By placing the urn's story of beauty and truth within the humanizing lens of pathos, Keats rejects the pure allegory of fixed, emblematic objects in favor of a less pure, contingent allegorical vision" (*Reinventing Allegory* 170). Jeffery Cox similarly notes that Keats's "truth is not some absolute ... but the contingent ideological positions that one constructs as one seeks" a way of explaining human experience that does not rely on the consolations of religion (183).
51. Kaufman employs the term "constructivism" in "Negatively Capable Dialectics." See especially 370–71. In his discussion of Blake, Kaufman argues against the critical opposition between history's movements and form's monumentalization because form is itself an historical act: "far from having its unruly heteronomy whipped into shape by the abstract force of formal discipline, the material (or materiality) gets to count as material in the first place by virtue of its relationship to an act – provisional though it be – of framing, an act of form" ("Everybody Hates Kant" 135).
52. See de Man's "Introduction to the Poetry of John Keats" and Rohrbach's "Reading the Heart, Reading the World."
53. Here Keats's meditation in the letters on "circumstances" comes to mind: "Circumstances are like Clouds continually gathering and bursting – While we are laughing the seed of some trouble is put into <he> the wide arable land of events – while we are laughing it sprouts i[t] grows and suddenly bears a poison fruit which we must pluck – Even so we have leisure to reason on the misfortunes of our friends; our own touch us too nearly for words" (*LJK* 2.79).
54. De Man describes Baudelaire's fashioning of an "ironic mind" characterized by "an endless process that leads to no synthesis. The positive name he gives to the infinity of this process is freedom" ("Rhetoric of Temporality" 220). I apply "freedom" here to the kind of temporal imagining de Man finds in both allegory and irony.

Bibliography

"Advertisements." *Quarterly Review* 97 (June & September 1855): 183–225.
"The Advertising System." *Edinburgh Review* 155 (February 1843): 2–43.
Agnew, Jean-Christophe. "Coming Up for Air: Consumer Culture in Historical Perspective." *Consumption and the World of Goods*. Eds. John Brewer and Ray Porter. London and New York: Routledge, 1993. 19–39.
  Worlds Apart: The Market and the Theater in Anglo-American Thought, 1550–1750. Cambridge: Cambridge University Press, 1986.
Altick, Richard. *The English Common Reader: A Social History of the Mass Reading Public, 1800–1900*. Columbus: Ohio State University Press, 1957.
  The Shows of London. Cambridge, MA: Belknap, 1978.
Anderson, Benedict. *Imagined Communities: Reflections on the Origin and Spread of Nationalism*. New York: Verso, 1983.
Aspinall, Arthur. *Politics and the Press, c. 1780–1850*. London: Home & Van Thal, 1949.
  "The Social Status of Journalists at the Beginning of the Nineteenth Century." *The Review of English Studies* 21.81 (January 1945): 216–32.
Asquith, Ivon. "Advertising and the Press in the Late Eighteenth and Early Nineteenth Centuries: James Perry and the *Morning Chronicle* 1790–1821." *The Historical Journal* 18.4 (1975): 703–24.
Austen, Jane. *Mansfield Park*. Ed. John Lucas. Oxford: Oxford University Press, 1975.
Baer, Marc. *Theatre and Disorder in Late Georgian London*. Oxford: Clarendon, 1992.
Bailey, Nathan. *An Universal English Dictionary*. London: R. Ware, 1775.
Baker, Herschel. *William Hazlitt*. Cambridge, MA: Belknap, 1962.
Barker, Hannah. *Newspapers, Politics, and Public Opinion in Eighteenth-Century England*. Oxford: Clarendon, 1998.
Barker-Benfield, G. J. *The Culture of Sensibility: Sex and Society in Eighteenth-Century Britain*. Chicago: University of Chicago Press, 1992.
Bate, Jonathan. "Keats's Two *Hyperion*s and the Problem of Milton." *Romantic Revisions*. Eds. Robert Brinkley and Keith Hanley. Cambridge: Cambridge University Press, 1992. 321–38.
  Shakespearean Constitutions: Politics, Theatre, Criticism 1730–1830. Oxford: Clarendon, 1989.

Bate, Walter Jackson. *John Keats*. Cambridge, MA: Belknap, 1963.
  "Keats's Style: Evolution Toward Qualities of Permanent Value," *The Major English Romantic Poets*. Eds. Clarence D. Thorpe, Carlos Baker, and Bennett Weaver. Carbondale: Southern Illinois University Press, 1957.
Beaudry, Harry R. *The English Theatre and John Keats*. Salzburg: Salzburg Studies in English Literature, 1973.
Behrendt, Stephen C., ed. *Romanticism, Radicalism, and the Press*. Detroit: Wayne State University Press, 1997.
Benjamin, Walter. *Illuminations*. Ed. Hannah Arendt. Trans. Harry Zohn. New York: Schocken, 1968.
Bewell, Alan. "The Political Implication of Keats's Classicist Aesthetics." *Studies in Romanticism* 25.2 (Summer 1986): 220–29.
Bermingham, Ann. "Urbanity and the Spectacle of Art." *Romantic Metropolis: The Urban Scene of British Culture, 1780–1840*. Eds. James Chandler and Kevin Gilmartin. Cambridge: Cambridge University Press, 2005. 151–76.
  "Elegant Females and Gentleman Connoisseurs: The Commerce in Culture and Self-image in Eighteenth-century England." *The Consumption of Culture 1600–1800: Image, Object, Text*. Eds. Ann Bermingham and John Brewer. London and New York: Routledge, 1995. 489–513.
  and John Brewer, eds., *The Consumption of Culture 1600–1800: Image, Object, Text*. London and New York: Routledge, 1995.
The Bible: Authorized King James Version. Eds. Robert Carroll and Stephen Prickett. Oxford: Oxford University Press, 2008.
Black, Jeremy. *The English Press in the Eighteenth Century*. Philadelphia: University of Pennsylvania Press, 1987.
Bloom, Harold. "The Internalization of Quest Romance." *Romanticism and Consciousness*. Ed. Harold Bloom. New York: Norton, 1970. 3–24.
  The Visionary Company: A Reading of English Romantic Poetry. Rev. Edition. Ithaca: Cornell University Press, 1971.
Blunden, Edmund. *Leigh Hunt's "Examiner" Examined*. New York: Archon, 1967.
Bohstedt, John. *Riots and Community Politics in England and Wales, 1790–1810*. Cambridge, MA: Harvard University Press, 1983.
Bolton, Betsy. *Women, Nationalism and the Romantic Stage: Theatre and Politics in Britain, 1780–1800*. Cambridge: Cambridge University Press, 2001.
Bourdieu, Pierre. *Distinction: A Social Critique of the Judgment of Taste*. Trans. Richard Nice. Cambridge, MA: Harvard University Press, 1984.
  The Field of Cultural Production: Essays on Art and Literature. Ed. Randal Johnson. New York: Columbia University Press, 1993.
  The Rules of Art: Genesis and Structure of the Literary Field. Trans. Susan Emanuel. Stanford: Stanford University Press, 1996.
Bourne, H. R. Fox. *English Newspapers: Chapters in the History of Journalism*. Vol. 1. New York: Russell & Russell, 1966. 1887.
Bratton, Jacky. "The Celebrity of Edmund Kean: An Institutional Story." *Theatre and Celebrity in Britain, 1660–2000*. Eds. Mary Luckhurst and Jane Moody. New York: Palgrave, 2006. 90–106.

New Readings in Theatre History. Cambridge: Cambridge University Press, 2003.

Brewer, John. "'The Most Polite Age and the Most Vicious': Attitudes towards Culture as Commodity, 1660–1800." *The Consumption of Culture 1600–1800: Image, Object, Text.* Eds. Ann Bermingham and John Brewer. London and New York: Routledge, 1995. 341–61.

Bromwich, David. *Hazlitt: The Mind of a Critic.* Oxford: Oxford University Press, 1983.

Brooks, Cleanth. *The Well-Wrought Urn: Studies in the Structure of Poetry.* New York: Harvest/HBJ, 1947.

Burgess, Miranda J. "Bearing Witness: Law, Labor and the Gender of Privacy in the 1720s." *Modern Philology* 98.3 (2001): 393–422.

——— "'Courting Ruin:' The Economic Romances of Frances Burney." *Novel: A Forum on Fiction* 28.2 (Winter 1995): 131–55.

Burke, Edmund. *Reflections on the Revolution in France.* Ed. Conor Cruise O'Brien. New York: Penguin, 1968.

Burney, Frances. *The Wanderer; or, Female Difficulties.* Eds. Margaret Anne Doody, Robert L. Mack, and Peter Sabor. Oxford: Oxford University Press, 1991.

Burroughs, Catherine B. *Closet Stages: Joanna Baillie and the Theater Theory of British Romantic Women Writers.* Philadelphia: University of Pennsylvania Press, 1997.

——— ed. *Women in British Romantic Theatre: Drama, Performance, and Society, 1790–1840.* Cambridge: Cambridge University Press, 2000.

Burwick, Frederick. *Playing to the Crowd: London Popular Theatre, 1780–1830.* New York: Palgrave Macmillan, 2011.

——— *Romantic Drama: Acting and Reacting.* Cambridge: Cambridge University Press, 2009.

Byrne, Paula. *Jane Austen and the Theatre.* London: Hambledon and London, 2002.

Calhoun, Craig, ed. *Habermas and the Public Sphere.* Cambridge, MA: MIT Press, 1992.

Campbell, Colin. *The Romantic Ethic and the Spirit of Modern Consumerism.* Oxford: Blackwell, 1987.

——— "Understanding Traditional and Modern Patterns of Consumption in Eighteenth-Century England: A Character-Action Approach." *Consumption and the World of Goods.* Eds. John Brewer and Roy Porter. London and New York: Routledge, 1993. 39–57.

Caputo, Nicoletta. "Theatrical Periodicals and the Ethics of Theatre in the Romantic Age." *The Romantic Stage: A Many-Sided Mirror.* Eds. Lilla Maria Crisafulli and Fabio Liberto. Amsterdam: Rodopi, 2014. 43–56.

Carlson, Julie A. "Hazlitt and the Sociability of Theatre." *Romantic Sociability: Social Networks and Literary Culture in Britain 1770–1840.* Eds. Gillian Russell and Clara Tuite. Cambridge: Cambridge University Press, 2002. 145–65.

In the Theatre of Romanticism: Coleridge, Nationalism, Women. Cambridge: Cambridge University Press, 1994.
Carlyle, Thomas. "Signs of the Times." *Edinburgh Review* (June 1829): 439–59.
The Censor. London [biweekly], 1828–1829.
The Champion. London [weekly], 1814–1822.
Chandler, James. *England in 1819.* Chicago: University of Chicago Press, 1998.
  "Hallam, Tennyson, and the Poetry of Sensation: Aestheticist Allegories of a Counter-Public Sphere." *Studies in Romanticism* 33.4 (Winter 1994): 527–37.
Chandler, James and Kevin Gilmartin, eds. *Romantic Metropolis: The Urban Scene of British Culture, 1780–1840.* Cambridge: Cambridge University Press, 2005.
Christensen, Jerome. *Lord Byron's Strength: Romantic Writing and Commercial Society.* Baltimore: Johns Hopkins University Press, 1995.
  Romanticism at the End of History. Baltimore: Johns Hopkins University Press, 2000.
Christie, Ian. *Stress and Stability in Late Eighteenth-Century Britain.* Oxford: Clarendon, 1984.
Cibber, Colley. *The Plays of Colley Cibber.* Ed. Rodney L. Hayley. Vol. 1. New York: Garland, 1980.
Clarke, Charles Cowden and Mary Cowden. *Recollections of Writers.* Fontwell: Centaur, 1969.
Clive, John. *Scotch Reviewers: The Edinburgh Review, 1802–1815.* Cambridge, MA: Harvard University Press, 1957.
Coleridge, Samuel Taylor. *Biographia Literaria. The Collected Works of Samuel Taylor Coleridge.* Eds. Walter Jackson Bate and James Engell. Vol 1. Princeton: Princeton University Press, 1985.
  Table Talk. The Collected Works of Samuel Taylor Coleridge. Ed. Carl Woodring. Vol. 14, Part 2. Princeton: Princeton University Press, 1990.
Colley, Linda. *Britons: Forging the Nation 1707–1837.* New Haven: Yale University Press, 1992.
The Columbine and Weekly Review. London [weekly], 1829–1830.
Complete Defence of Kean Against the Unmanly Attacks of The Times. London: W. Mason, 1825.
Cook, Jon. Introduction. *William Hazlitt: Selected Writings.* Ed. Jon Cook. Oxford: Oxford University Press, 1992.
Corcoran, Brendan. "Keats's Death: Towards a Posthumous Poetics." *Studies in Romanticism* 48.2 (Summer 2009): 321–48.
The Covent Garden Theatrical Gazette. London [daily], 1816.
Cox, Jeffrey. *Poetry and Politics in the Cockney School: Keats, Shelley, Hunt and their Circle.* Cambridge: Cambridge University Press, 1998.
  "Re-viewing Romantic Drama." *Literature Compass* 1.1 (2004): http://dx.doi.org/10.1111/j.1741–4113.2004.00096.x; January 14, 2015.
Cox versus Kean: Fairburn's Edition of the Trial between Robert Albion Cox, Esq. and Edmund Kean, Defendant for Criminal Conversation with the Plaintiff's Wife. London: Fairburn, 1825.

Cranfield, G. A. *The Press and Society: From Caxton to Northcliffe*. London: Longman, 1978.
Crafton, Lisa Plummer. "'Insipid Decency': Modesty and Female Sexuality in Wollstonecraft." *European Romantic Review* 11.3 (Summer 2000): 277–99.
Crisafulli, Lilla Maria and Fabio Liberto, eds. *The Romantic Stage: A Many-Sided Mirror*. Amsterdam: Rodopi, 2014.
Crochunis, Thomas C. "British Women Playwrights Around 1800: New Paradigms and Recoveries." Introduction to special issue of *Romanticism on the Net* 12 (1998): www.erudit.org/revue/ron/1998/v/n12/index.html; January 14, 2015.
  "Edmund Kean's 'Radical' Acting." Paper delivered at the Association for Theatre in Higher Education Conference. Chicago, IL, July 1994.
  "Women and Dramatic Writing in the British Romantic Era." *Literature Compass* 1 (2004): 1–14: www.literature-compass.com/viewpoint.asp; January 14, 2015.
The Daily Advertiser [London]: February 26, 1730.
The Daily Courant [London]: March 11, 1702, October 8, 1708.
The Daily Universal Register (later *The Times*) [London]: January 1, 1785, January 4, 1785.
Davis, Tracy C. "'Reading Shakespeare by Flashes of Lightning:' Challenging the Foundations of Romantic Acting Theory." *ELH* 62 (1995): 933–54.
Davis, Tracy C. and Thomas Postlewait, eds. *Theatricality*. Cambridge: Cambridge University Press, 2004.
Defoe, Daniel. *Defoe's Review: Reproduced from the Original Editions*. Vol. 1. New York: Columbia University Press, 1938.
De Man, Paul. "Introduction to the Poetry of John Keats." *Critical Writings, 1953–1978*. Ed. Lindsay Waters. Minneapolis: University Minnesota Press, 1989.
  "The Rhetoric of Temporality." *Blindness and Insight: Essays in the Rhetoric of Contemporary Criticism*. Minneapolis: University of Minnesota Press, 1983. 187–228.
DeQuincey, Thomas. *The Collected Writings of Thomas DeQuincey*. Ed. David Masson. Vol. XIII. *Tales and Prose Phantasies*. New York: AMS, 1968; Edinburgh: Adam and Charles Black, 1890.
Dictionary of National Biography. Eds. Sir Leslie Stephen and Sir Sidney Lee. 22 vols. Oxford: Oxford University Press, 1921–22. rpt. 1959–60.
Donohue, Joseph W., Jr. *Dramatic Character in the English Romantic Age*. Princeton: Princeton University Press, 1970.
  "Hazlitt's Sense of the Dramatic: Actor as Tragic Character." *Studies in English Literature* 5.4 (1965): 705–21.
  Theatre in the Age of Kean. Totowa, NJ: Rowman & Littlefield, 1975.
The Drama; A Daily Register of Histrionic Performances on the Dublin Stage. Dublin [daily], 1821.
The Drama; or, Theatrical Pocket Magazine. London [monthly], 1821–1825.
The Dramatic Censor. London [weekly], 1800–1801.

The Dramatic Censor; or, Critical and Biographical Illustration of the British Stage. London [monthly], 1811.
The Dramatic Correspondent, and Amateur's Place Book. London [weekly], 1828–1829.
The Dramatic Magazine. London [monthly], 1829–1831.
The Dramatic Observer and Musical Review. London [daily], 1823.
Eagleton, Terry. *The Function of Criticism: From* The Spectator *to Post-Structuralism.* London: Verso, 1984.
Eberle-Sinatra, Michael. *Leigh Hunt and the London Literary Scene: A Reception History of His Major Works, 1805–1828.* New York: Routledge, 2005.
Edelstein, Dan. *The Enlightenment: A Genealogy.* Chicago: University of Chicago Press, 2010.
Edinburgh Dramatic Review. Edinburgh [daily], 1824–1825.
Edinburgh Dramatic Tete-a-Tete. Edinburgh [daily], 1828.
Eger, Elizabeth, Charlotte Grant, Clíona Ó Gallchoir, and Penny Warburton, eds. *Women, Writing, and the Public Sphere, 1700–1830.* Cambridge: Cambridge University Press, 2001.
Ellis, Aytoun. *The Penny Universities: A History of the Coffee-houses.* London: Secker and Warburg, 1956.
Enright, Nancy. "William Hazlitt and His 'Familiar Style.'" *Essays on the Essay: Redefining the Genre.* Ed. Alexander J. Butrym. Athens: University of Georgia Press, 1989.
Esterhammer, Angela. *Romanticism and Improvisation, 1750–1850.* Cambridge: Cambridge University Press, 2009.
The Examiner. London [weekly], 1808–1836.
Faflak, Joel. "Romantic Psychoanalysis: Keats, Identity, and '(The Fall of) Hyperion.'" *Lessons of Romanticism.* Eds. Thomas Pfau and Robert Gleckner. Durham, NC: Duke University Press, 1998. 304–27.
Favret, Mary. *War at a Distance: Romanticism and the Making of Modern Wartime.* Princeton: Princeton University Press, 2009.
Fay, Elizabeth. "Mary Robinson: On Trial in the Public Court." *Studies in Romanticism* 45.3 (Fall 2006): 397–23.
Franta, Andrew. *Romanticism and the Rise of the Mass Public.* Cambridge: Cambridge University Press, 2007.
Fraser, Nancy. "Rethinking the Public Sphere: A Contribution to the Critique of Actually Existing Democracy." *Habermas and the Public Sphere.* Ed. Craig Calhoun. Cambridge, MA: MIT Press, 1992. 109–42.
Fry, Paul. "History, Existence, and 'To Autumn,'" *Studies in Romanticism* 25.2 (Summer 1986): 211–19.
  The Poet's Calling in the English Ode. New Haven: Yale University Press, 1980.
Fulford, Tim. *Romantic Poetry and Literary Coteries: The Dialect of the Tribe.* New York: Palgrave Macmillan, 2015.
Gamer, Michael. "Authors in Effect: Lewis, Scott and the Gothic Drama." *ELH* 66.4 (1999): 831–61.

"A Matter of Turf: Romanticism, Hippodrama, and Legitimate Satire." *Nineteenth-Century Contexts* 28.4 (2006): 305–34.

Romanticism and the Gothic: Genre, Reception and Canon Formation. Cambridge: Cambridge University Press, 2000.

Gamer, Michael and Terry F. Robinson, "Mary Robinson and the Dramatic Art of the Comeback." *Studies in Romanticism* 48.2 (Summer 2009): 219–56.

Ganzel, Dewey. "Patent Wrongs and Patent Theatres: Drama and the Law in the Early Nineteenth Century," *PMLA* 76 (1961): 384–896.

Gay, Penny. *Jane Austen and the Theatre*. Cambridge: Cambridge University Press, 2002.

Gentleman, Francis. *The Dramatic Censor, or Critical Companion*. London: J. Bell, 1770.

The Genuine Theatrical Observer [Dublin], daily, 1823.

Gilmartin, Kevin. "Hazlitt's Visionary London." *Repossessing the Romantic Past*. Eds. Heather Glen and Paul Hamilton. Cambridge: Cambridge University Press, 2006. 40–62.

Print Politics: The Press and Radical Opposition in Early-Nineteenth Century England. Cambridge: Cambridge University Press, 1996.

William Hazlitt: Political Essayist. Oxford: Oxford University Press, 2015.

Gonda, Caroline. "Misses, Murderesses and Magdalens: Women in the Public Eye." Eds. Elizabeth Eger, Charlotte Grant, Clíona Ó Gallchior, and Penny Warburton. Cambridge: Cambridge University Press, 2001. 53–71.

Goodman, Kevis. *Georgic Modernity and British Romanticism: Poetry and the Mediation of History*. Cambridge: Cambridge University Press, 2004.

Gowen, David Robert. *Studies in the History and Function of the British Theatre Playbill and Programme, 1564–1914*. Diss. St. Catherine's College, Oxford, 1998.

Gray, Charles Harold. *Theatrical Criticism in London to 1795*. New York: Columbia University Press, 1931.

Guest, Harriet. *Small Change: Women, Learning, Patriotism 1750–1810*. Chicago: University of Chicago Press, 2000.

Habermas, Jurgen. *The Structural Transformation of the Public Sphere: An Inquiry into a Category of Bourgeois Society*. Trans. Thomas Burger with Frederick Lawrence. Cambridge, MA: MIT Press, 1989.

Hadley, Elaine. *Melodramatic Tactics: Theatricalized Dissent in the English Marketplace, 1800–1885*. Stanford: Stanford University Press, 1995.

Hamilton, Paul. *Metaromanticism: Aesthetics, Literature, Theory*. Chicago: University of Chicago Press, 2003.

Hanson, Frank Burton. *London Theatre Audiences of the Nineteenth Century*. Diss. Yale University, 1953.

The Harlequin. London [weekly], 1829.

Harris, Michael. "The Structure, Ownership, and Control of the Press, 1620–1780." *Newspaper History: From the Seventeenth Century to the Present Day*. Eds. George Boyce, James Curran, and Pauline Wingate. London: Constable, 1978. 82–97.

Hawkins, F. W. *The Life of Edmund Kean.* London: Tinsley Bros., 1869.
Hays, Michael and Anastasia Nikolopoulou, eds. *Melodrama: The Cultural Emergence of a Genre.* New York: Palgrave Macmillan, 1999.
Hazlitt, William. *The Complete Works of William Hazlitt.* 21 vols. Ed. P. P. Howe after the edition of A. R. Waller and Arnold Glover. New York: AMS Press, 1967.
Hessell, Nikki. *Literary Authors, Parliamentary Reporters: Johnson, Coleridge, Hazlitt, Dickens.* Cambridge: Cambridge University Press, 2012.
——— "The Opposite of News: Rethinking the 1800 *Lyrical Ballads* and the Mass Media." *Studies in Romanticism* 45.3 (Fall 2003): 331–55.
Higgins, David. "Englishness, Effeminacy, and the *New Monthly Magazine*: Hazlitt's 'The Fight' in Context." *Romanticism* 10 (2004).
——— *Romantic Genius and the Literary Magazine.* New York: Routledge, 2005.
Hill, Aaron and William People. *The Prompter: A Theatrical Paper, 1734–1736.* Eds. William W. Appleton and Kalman A. Burnim. New York: Benjamin Blom, 1966.
Hillebrand, Harold Newcomb. *Edmund Kean.* New York: Columbia University Press, 1933.
Hindle, Wilfred. *The Morning Post 1772–1937: Portrait of a Newspaper.* London: Routledge, 1937.
The History of The Times. Vol. 1. *The Thunderer in the Making 1785–1841.* New York: Macmillan, 1935.
Hogan, Charles Beecher, *The London Stage, 1776–1800: A Critical Introduction.* Carbondale, IL: Southern Illinois University Press, 1968.
——— ed. *The London Stage 1660–1800.* Part 5, Vol. 3. *1776–1800.* Carbondale: Southern Illinois University Press, 1968.
Holland, Peter. "'Some of you might have seen him': Laurence Olivier's Celebrity." *Theatre and Celebrity in Britain, 1660–2000.* Eds. Mary Luckhurst and Jane Moody. New York: Palgrave, 2006. 214–32.
Howe, P. P. *The Life of William Hazlitt.* New York: George H. Doran, 1923.
The Hull Dramatic Censor. Hull [weekly], 1826–1827.
Hume, David. *A Treatise of Human Nature.* Eds. David Fate Norton and Mary J. Norton. Oxford: Oxford University Press, 2000.
Hunt, Leigh. *The Autobiography of Leigh Hunt.* 2 vols. New York: AMS Press, 1965.
——— *Leigh Hunt's Dramatic Criticism, 1808–1831.* Eds. Lawrence Huston Houtchens and Carolyn Washburn Houtchens. New York: Columbia University Press, 1949.
——— "Prospectus." *Examiner* 1.1 (June 3, 1808): 6–8.
——— *The Selected Writings of Leigh Hunt.* Vol. 1: *Periodical Essays, 1805–14.* Eds. Greg Kucich and Jeffrey N. Cox. London: Pickering and Chatto, 2003.
Hunt, Lynn. *Politics, Culture, and Class in the French Revolution.* Berkeley and Los Angeles: University of California Press, 1984.
The Independent Theatrical Observer. Dublin [daily], 1822.
The Irish Dramatic Censor. Dublin [monthly?], 1811–1812.

Jacobus, Mary. "Intimate Connections: Scandalous Memoirs and Epistolary Indiscretion." *Women, Writing, and the Public Sphere, 1700–1830*. Eds. Elizabeth Eger, Charlotte Grant, Clíona Ó Gallchior, and Penny Warburton. Cambridge: Cambridge University Press, 2001. 274–89.
Jeffrey, Francis. "The State and Prospects of Europe," *Edinburgh Review* 45 (April 1814): 1–40.
Jewett, William. *Fatal Autonomy: Romantic Drama and the Rhetoric of Agency*. Ithaca: Cornell University Press, 1997.
Johnson, Samuel. *A Dictionary of the English Language*. New York: Arno, 1979; London: W. Strahan, 1755.
   The Yale Edition of the Works of Samuel Johnson. Vol. 2: *The Idler and The Adventurer*. Eds. W. J. Bate, John M. Bullitt, and L. F. Powell. New Haven: Yale University Press, 1963.
   The Yale Edition of the Works of Samuel Johnson. Vol. 6: *Poems*. Ed. E. L. McAdam, Jr. with George Milne. New Haven: Yale University Press, 1964.
Jones, Elizabeth. "Keats in the Suburbs." *Keats-Shelley Journal* 45 (1996): 23–43.
Jones, Leonidas. "Keats's Theatrical Reviews in the *Champion*." *Keats-Shelley Journal* 3 (Winter 1954): 55–65.
Jones, Stanley. *Hazlitt: A Life*. Oxford: Clarendon, 1989.
Kahan, Jeffrey. *The Cult of Kean*. Aldershot: Asghate, 2006.
Kandl, John. "Plebian Gusto, Negative Capability, and the Low Company of 'Mr. Kean': Keats' Dramatic Review for the *Champion* (21 December 1817)," *Nineteenth-Century Prose* 28.2 (2001): 130–41.
Kaufman, Robert. "Everybody Hates Kant: Blakean Formalism and the Symmetries of Laura Moriarty." *Modern Language Quarterly* 61.1 (2000): 131–55.
   "Negatively Capable Dialectics: Keats, Vendler, Adorno, and the Theory of the Avant-Garde." *Critical Inquiry* 27.2 (2001): 354–84.
Keach, William. "Cockney Couplets: Keats and the Politics of Style." *Studies in Romanticism* 25.2 (Summer 1986): 182–96.
Kean Vindicated, or the Truth Discovered with his Flattering Reception on Monday Evening. London: Reed. 1825.
Keats, John. *Complete Poems*. Ed. Jack Stillinger. Cambridge, MA: Belknap, 1978.
   Keats's Poetry and Prose. Ed. Jeffrey N. Cox. New York: Norton, 2009.
   The Letters of John Keats. Ed. Hyder Edward Rollins. 2 vols. Cambridge, MA: Harvard University Press, 1958.
   The Poems of John Keats. Ed. Miriam Allott. New York: Norton, 1970.
   The Poetical Works and Other Writings of John Keats. The Hampstead Edition. Ed. H. Buxton Forman. Revised Maurice Buxton Forman. Vol. 5. New York: Charles Scribner's Sons, 1939.
Kee, James. "Addressing the 'Cold Pastoral': Word, Image, and the Drama of Romantic Selfhood in Keats's 'Ode on a Grecian Urn.'" *Interfaces* 18 (2000): 33–42.

Kelley, Theresa. *Reinventing Allegory.* Cambridge: Cambridge University Press, 1997.
Kinnaird, John. *William Hazlitt: Critic of Power.* New York: Columbia University Press, 1978.
Klancher, Jon P. "Discriminations, or Romantic cosmopolitanisms in London." *Romantic Metropolis: The Urban Scene of British Culture, 1780–1840.* Eds. James Chandler and Kevin Gilmartin. Cambridge: Cambridge University Press, 2005. 65–82.
  Introduction. "Romanticism and its Publics." *Studies in Romanticism* 25.2 (Summer 1986): 523–25.
  The Making of English Reading Audiences, 1790–1832. Madison: University of Wisconsin Press, 1987.
  "Romantic Criticism and the Meanings of the French Revolution." *Studies in Romanticism* 28 (Fall 1989): 463–91.
Klein, Lawrence E. "Politeness for Plebes: Consumption and Social Identity in Early Eighteenth-Century England." *Consumption and the World of Goods.* Eds. John Brewer and Ray Porter. London and New York: Routledge, 1993. 362–82.
Korobkin, Laura Hanft. *Criminal Conversations: Sentimentality and Nineteenth Century Legal Stories of Adultery.* New York: Columbia University Press, 1998.
Kruger, Loren. *The National Stage: Theatre and Cultural Legitimation in England, France, and America.* Chicago: University of Chicago Press, 1992.
Kucich, Greg. "'The Wit in the Dungeon': Leigh Hunt and the Insolent Politics of Cockney Coteries." *European Romantic Review* 10 (1999): 242–53.
Kucich, Greg and Jeffery N. Cox. "Introduction." *The Selected Writings of Leigh Hunt.* Vol. 1. *Political Essays, 1805–1814.* Eds. Greg Kucich and Jeffrey N. Cox. London: Pickering and Chatto, 2003. xxix–liii.
Lamb, Charles and Mary. *The Letters of Charles and Mary Lamb.* Ed. E. V. Lucas. 3 vols. New York: AMS, 1968; London: Methuen, 1935.
  The Works of Charles and Mary Lamb. Ed. E. V. Lucas. 5 vols. *Miscellaneous Prose 1798–1834.* New York: AMS, 1968; London: Methuen, 1903.
Latham, Sean and Robert Scholes, "The Rise of Periodical Studies," *PMLA* 121.2 (March 2006): 517–31.
Levinson, Marjorie. *Keats's Life of Allegory: The Origins of a Style.* Oxford: Blackwell, 1988.
  The Romantic Fragment Poem: A Critique of Form. Chapel Hill: Universtiy of North Carolina Press, 1986.
Lillywhite, Bryant. *London Coffee Houses.* London: Allen and Unwin, 1963.
Lincoln Dramatic Censor. Lincoln [weekly], 1809.
Liu, Alan. "The Power of Formalism: The New Historicism." *ELH* 56.4 (Winter 1989): 721–71.
Loftis, John. *Sheridan and the Drama of Georgian England.* Cambridge, MA: Harvard University Press, 1977.

Lynch, James J., *Box, Pit and Gallery: Stage and Society in Johnson's London*. Berkeley and Los Angeles: University of California Press, 1953.
Mackintosh, James. "A Speech in Defence of Jean Peltier, Accused of a Libel on the First Consul of France." *The Miscellaneous Works of the Right Honourable Sir James Mackintosh*. Boston: Phillips, Sampson & Company: 1854. 484–504.
Magnuson, Paul. *Reading Public Romanticism*. Princeton: Princeton University Press, 1998.
Mahoney, John L. *The Logic of Passion: The Literary Criticism of William Hazlitt*. New York: Fordham University Press, 1981.
Mander, Raymond and Joe Mitchenson. *The Theatres of London*. Illus. Timothy Birdsall. London: Rupert Hart Davis, 1961.
Mason, Nicholas. "Building Brand Byron: Early Nineteenth-Century Advertising and the Marketing of *Childe Harold's Pilgrimage*." *Modern Language Quarterly* 63.4 (2002): 411–40.
Maurer, Shawn Lisa. *Proposing Men: Dialectics of Gender and Class in Eighteenth-Century English Periodical*. Stanford: Stanford University Press, 1998.
Mayer, David, III. *Harlequin in His Element: The English Pantomime, 1806–1836*. Cambridge, MA: Harvard University Press, 1969.
McCann, Andrew. *Cultural Politics in the 1790s: Literature, Radicalism, and the Public Sphere*. New York: St. Martin's, 1999.
McFarland, Thomas. *The Masks of Keats: The Endeavor of a Poet*. Oxford: Oxford University Press, 2000.
McGann, Jerome J. *The Beauty of Inflections: Literary Investigations in Historical Method and Theory*. Oxford: Clarendon, 1985.
 "Keats and the Historical Method in Literary Criticism." *Modern Language Notes* 94.5 (1979): 988–1032.
 The Romantic Ideology. Chicago: University of Chicago Press, 1983.
 Towards a Literature of Knowledge. Chicago: University of Chicago Press, 1989.
McKendrick, Neil. "The Consumer Revolution of Eighteenth-Century England." *The Birth of a Consumer Society: The Commercialization of Eighteenth-Century Society*. Eds. Neil McKendrick, John Brewer, and J. H. Plumb. Bloomington: Indiana University Press, 1982.
McKeon, Michael. *The Secret History of Domesticity: Public, Private, and the Division of Knowledge*. Baltimore: The Johns Hopkins University Press, 2005.
McLeod, Randall. "Un-Editing Shakespeare." *SubStance* 33.4 (1982): 26–55.
Milnes, Tim. "'Darkening Knowledge:' Hazlitt and Bentham on the Limits of Empiricism." *Metaphysical Hazlitt: Bicentenary Essays*. Eds. Uttara Natarajan, Tom Paulin, and Duncan Wu. London: Routledge, 2005. 125–36.
Mitchell, Robert. "Suspended Animation, Slow Time, and the Politics of Trance." *PMLA* 126.1 (2011) 107–22.
Mole, Tom. *Byron's Romantic Celebrity: Industrial Culture and the Hermeneutic of Intimacy*. New York: Palgrave Macmillan, 2007.
The Monthly Theatrical Reporter. London [monthly], 1814–1815.
The Monthly Theatrical Review. London [monthly], 1829.

Moody, Jane. "'Fine wore, legitimate!': Towards a Theatrical History of Romanticism." *Texas Studies in Language and Literature* 38.3/4 (1996): 223–44.
Illegitimate Theatre in London, 1770–1840. Cambridge: Cambridge University Press, 2000.
"Romantic Shakespeare." *The Cambridge Companion to Shakespeare on Stage*. Eds. Stanley Wells and Sarah Stanton. Cambridge: Cambridge University Press, 2002. 37–57.
"The Silence of the New Historicism: A Mutinous Echo from 1830." *Nineteenth Century Theatre*. 22.2 (1996): 61–89.
"The Theatrical Revolution, 1776–1843." *The Cambridge History of British Theatre:* Vol. 2: *1660–1800*. Ed. Joseph Donohue. Cambridge: Cambridge University Press, 2008. 199–215.
Morison, Stanley. *The English Newspaper: Some Account of the Physical Development of Journals Printed in London Between 1622 & the Present Day*. Cambridge: Cambridge University Press, 1932.
The Morning Chronicle [London]: May 3, 1792, November 25, 1812, December 2, 1812.
Muir, Kenneth. "Keats and Hazlitt." *John Keats: A Reassessment*. Ed. Kenneth Muir. Liverpool: Liverpool University Press, 1969.
Mulrooney, Jonathan. "Keats's 'Dull Rhymes' and the Making of the Ode Stanza." *Literature Compass* 5.1 (2008).
"Reading Theatre 1730–1830." *The Cambridge Companion to British Theatre 1730–1830*. Eds. Jane Moody and Daniel O'Quinn. Cambridge: Cambridge University Press, 2007. 249–60.
Mulvihill, James. "Hazlitt and the Idea of Identity." *Metaphysical Hazlitt: Bicentenary Essays*. Eds. Uttara Natarajan, Tom Paulin, and Duncan Wu. London: Routledge, 2005. 30–42.
The Museum, or Record of Literature (June 1822).
Natarajan, Uttara. *Hazlitt and the Reach of Sense: Criticism, Morals, and the Metaphysics of Power*. Oxford: Clarendon, 1999.
Tom Paulin, and Duncan Wu, eds. *Metaphysical Hazlitt: Bicentenary Essays*. London: Routledge, 2005.
The National Omnibus; and Entertaining Advertiser. London [bi-weekly], 1831–1833.
Negt, Oskar and Alexander Kluge. *Public Sphere and Experience: Toward an Analysis of the Bourgeois and Proletarian Public Sphere*. Trans. Peter Labanyi, Jamie Owen Daniel, and Assenka Oksiloff. Minneapolis: University of Minnesota Press, 1993.
Newey, Vincent. "Keats, History, and the Poets." *Keats and History*. Ed. Nicholas Roe. Cambridge: Cambridge University Press, 1995.
Newlyn, Lucy. *Reading, Writing, and Romanticism: The Anxiety of Reception*. Oxford: Oxford University Press, 2000.
"Newspaper Press." *The Westminster Review* 10.19 (January 1829): 216–37.
"Newspapers." *The Westminster Review* 1.3 (July 1824): 194–212.

Nichols, John. *Literary Anecdotes of the Eighteenth Century*. 2nd ed., Vol. 1. London: Nichols, Son & Bentley, 1812.

Nicoll, Allardyce. *The Garrick Stage: Theatres and Audiences in the Eighteenth Century*. Athens: University of Georgia Press, 1980.

— *A History of English Drama 1660–1900*. Vol. 3. *Late Eighteenth Century Drama, 1750–1800*. Cambridge: Cambridge University Press, 1966.

Nuss, Melynda. *Distance, Theatre, and the Public Voice, 1750–1850*. New York: Palgrave Macmillan, 2012.

O'Neill, Michael. "'When this warm scribe my hand': Writing and History in 'Hyperion' and 'The Fall of Hyperion.'" *Keats and History*. Ed. Nicholas Roe. Cambridge: Cambridge University Press, 1995. 143–64.

The Opera Glass. London [monthly], 1829–1830.

O'Quinn, Daniel. *Entertaining Crises in the Atlantic Imperium, 1770–1790*. Baltimore: Johns Hopkins University Press, 2011.

— *Staging Governance: Theatrical Imperialism in London 1770–1800*. Baltimore: Johns Hopkins University Press, 2005.

The Original Theatrical Observer. Dublin [daily], 1821.

O'Rourke, James, ed. *'Ode on a Grecian Urn': Hypercanonicity and Pedagogy*. Romantic Praxis Series (2003): www.rc.umd.edu/praxis/grecianurn/; January 14, 2015

Oxberry's Theatrical Inquisitor; or, Monthly Mirror of the Drama. London [monthly], 1828.

Oxford English Dictionary. Eds. James A. H. Murray, Henry Bradley, W. A. Craigie, and C. T. Onions. Oxford: Clarendon, 1970.

Park, Roy. *Hazlitt and the Spirit of the Age*. Oxford: Clarendon, 1971.

Parker, Mark. *Literary Magazines and British Romanticism*. Cambridge: Cambridge University Press, 2000.

Pascoe, Judith. *Romantic Theatricality: Gender, Poetry, and Spectatorship*. Ithaca: Cornell University Press, 1997.

— *The Sarah Siddons Audiofiles: Romanticism and the Lost Voice*. Ann Arbor: University of Michigan Press, 2013.

Paulin, Tom. *The Day-Star of Liberty: William Hazlitt's Radical Style*. London: Faber and Faber, 1998.

Playfair, Giles. *The Flash of Lightning: A Portrait of Edmund Kean*. London: William Kimber, 1983.

Plotz, John. *The Crowd: British Literature and Public Politics*. Berkeley: University of California Press, 2000.

Plumly, Stanley. *Posthumous Keats: A Personal Biography*. New York: Norton, 2008.

Plymouth Theatrical Spy. Plymouth [weekly], 1828.

The Poetic Epistles of Edmund, with Notes, Illustrations, and Reflections. London: Effingham Wilson, 1825.

Pope, Alexander. *The Poems of Alexander Pope: A Reduced Version of the Twickenham Text*. Ed. John Butt. New Haven: Yale University Press, 1966.

Pratt, Kathryn. "'Dark Catastrophe of Passion': The 'Indian' as Human Commodity in Nineteenth-Century British Theatrical Culture." *Studies in Romanticism* 41.4 (Winter 2002): 605–26.

Prince, Kathryn. *Shakespeare in the Victorian Periodicals*. New York: Routledge, 2008.

Purinton, Marjean. *Romantic Ideology Unmasked: The Mentally Constructed Tyrannies in Dramas of William Wordsworth, Lord Byron, Percy Shelley, and Joanna Baillie*. Newark: University of Delaware Press, 1994.

Rajan, Tilottama. "Keats, Poetry, and 'The Absence of the Work.'" *Modern Philology* 95.3 (1998): 334–51.

Rea, Robert. *The English Press in Politics*. Lincoln: University of Nebraska Press, 1963.

Regier, Alexander. *Fracture and Fragmentation in British Romanticism*. Cambridge: Cambridge University Press, 2010.

Reiman, Donald H. "Keats and the Third Generation." *The Persistence of Poetry*. Eds. Robert M. Ryan and Ronald A. Sharp. Amherst: University of Massachusetts Press, 1998. 109–19.

  ed. *The Romantics Reviewed: Contemporary Reviews of British Romantic Writers*. Part C. Vol. 1. *Shelley, Keats, and the London Radical Writers*. New York: Garland, 1972.

Remarks on the Causes of the Dispute between the Public and Managers of the Theatre Royal, Covent Garden, by John Bull. London: John Fairburn, 1809.

Reynolds, Paige. "Modernist Periodicals." *A History of Modernist Poetry*. Eds. Alex Davis and Lee Jenkins. Cambridge: Cambridge University Press, 2015. 118–38.

Richardson, Alan. *A Mental Theater: Poetic Drama and Consciousness in the Romantic Age*. University Park: Pennsylvania State University Press, 1988.

Ricks, Christopher. *Allusion to the Poets*. Oxford: Oxford University Press, 2002.

Keats and Embarrassment. Oxford: Clarendon, 1984.

Ridley, M. R. *Keats's Craftsmanship: A Study in Poetic Development*. Oxford: Clarendon, 1933.

Roach, Joseph. "Public Intimacy: The Prior History of 'It.'" *Theatre and Celebrity in Britain, 1660–2000*. Eds. Mary Luckhurst and Jane Moody. New York: Palgrave, 2006. 15–30.

Robbins, Bruce, ed. *The Phantom Public Sphere*. Minneapolis: University of Minnesota Press, 1993.

Robinson, Terry F. "National Theatre in Transition: The London Patent Theatre Fires of 1808–1809 and the Old Price Riots." *BRANCH: Britain, Representation and Nineteenth-Century History*. Ed. Dino Franco Felluga. July 14, 2017: www.branchcollective.org/?ps_articles=terry-f-robinson-national-theatre-in-transition-the-london-patent-theatre-fires-of-1808-1809-and-the-old-price-riots.

Roe, Nicholas. *Fiery Heart: The First Life of Leigh Hunt*. London: Pimlico, 2005.

John Keats: A New Life. New Haven: Yale University Press, 2012.

John Keats and the Culture of Dissent. Oxford: Oxford University Press, 1997.

Rohrbach, Emily. "Reading the Heart, Reading the World: Keats's Historiographical Aesthetic." *European Romantic Review* 25.3 (June 2014): 275–88.

Rollins, Hyder Edward. *The Keats Circle: Letters and Papers*. 2 vols. Cambridge, MA: Harvard University Press, 1965.

Russell, Gillian. "'Announcing each day the performances': Playbills, Ephemerality, and Romantic Period Media/Theater History." *Studies in Romanticism* 54 (Summer 2015): 241–68.

"Keats, Popular Culture, and the Sociability of Theatre." *Romanticism and Popular Culture in Britain and Ireland*. Eds. Philip Connell and Nigel Leask. Cambridge: Cambridge University Press, 2009. 194–213.

"Playing at Revolution: The Politics of the O.P. Riots of 1809," *Theatre Notebook* 44 (1990): 16–26.

"Theatre." *An Oxford Companion to the Romantic Age*. Eds. Iain McCalman et al. Oxford: Oxford University Press, 1999.

The Theatres of War: Performance, Politics and Society, 1793–1815. Oxford: Clarendon, 1995.

Women, Sociability and Theatre in Georgian London. Cambridge: Cambridge University Press, 2007.

Russell, Gillian and Clara Tuite, eds. *Romantic Sociability: Social Networks and Literary Culture in Britain 1770–1840*. Cambridge: Cambridge University Press, 2002.

Rzepka, Charles J. "A Gift That Complicates Employ: Poetry and Poverty in 'Resolution and Independence.'" *Studies in Romanticism* 28.2 (Summer 1989): 225–47.

The Self as Mind: Vision and Identity in Wordsworth, Coleridge, and Keats. Cambridge, MA: Harvard University Press, 1986.

Sachs, Jonathan. "The Time of Decline." *European Romantic Review* 22.3 (June 2011): 305–12.

Schaffer, Simon. "The Consuming Flame: Electrical Showman and Tory Mystics in the World of Goods." *Consumption and the World of Goods*. Eds. John Brewer and Ray Porter. London and New York: Routledge, 1993. 489–526.

Schmitt, Carl. *Political Romanticism*. Trans. Guy Oakes. Cambridge, MA: MIT Press, 1986.

Schoch, Richard. *Not Shakespeare: Bardolatry and Burlesque in the Nineteenth Century*. Cambridge: Cambridge University Press, 2002.

Schoenfield, Mark. *British Periodicals and Romantic Identity: The "Lower Literary Empire."* New York: Palgrave Macmillan, 2009.

The Professional Wordsworth: Law, Labor, and the Poet's Contract. Athens: University of Georgia Press, 1996.

Scott, Joan Wallach. *Gender and the Politics of History*. rev. edition. New York: Columbia University Press, 1999.

Scrivener, Michael. *Poetry and Reform: Periodical Verse from the English Democratic Press*. Detroit: Wayne State University Press, 1992.

Secrets Worth Knowing: Suppressed Letters, Cox v. Kean. London: T. Reed, 1825.
Shakespeare, William. *Othello*. Ed. E. A. J. Honigmann. London: Arden, 1996.
Sherwin, Paul. "'Dying into Life': Keats's Struggle with Milton in *Hyperion.*" *PMLA* 93.3 (1978): 383–95.
Simpson, David. *Irony and Authority in Romantic Poetry*. London: Macmillan, 1979.
Simpson, Michael. *Closet Performances: Political Exhibition and Prohibition in the Dramas of Byron and Shelley*. Stanford: Stanford University Press, 1998.
Siskin, Clifford. *The Work of Writing: Literature and Social Change in Britain, 1700–1830*. Baltimore: Johns Hopkins University Press, 1998.
Slote, Bernice. *Keats and the Dramatic Principle*. Lincoln: University of Nebraska Press, 1958.
Smith, Adam. *The Theory of Moral Sentiments*. Amherst, NY: Prometheus, 2000.
The Stage; or, Theatrical Inquisitor. London [monthly], 1828–1829.
The Stage; or, Theatrical Touchstone. London [biweekly], 1805.
Stewart, Garrett. "Keats and Language." *The Cambridge Companion to Keats*. Ed. Susan Wolfson. Cambridge: Cambridge University Press, 2001. 135–51.
Stone, Laurence. *Road to Divorce: England, 1530–1987*. Oxford: Oxford University Press, 1990.
Strachan, John. *Advertising and Satirical Culture in the Romantic Period*. Cambridge: Cambridge University Press, 2007.
Stratman, Carl J. *Britain's Theatrical Periodicals, 1720–1967*. New York: New York Public Library, 1972.
Straub, Katrina. *Sexual Suspects: Eighteenth-Century Players and Sexual Ideology*. Princeton: Princeton University Press, 1992.
Stuart, Daniel. "Anecdotes of Public Newspapers." *Gentleman's Magazine* (July 1838): 23–27.
Styles, John. *The Dress of the People: Everyday Fashion in Eighteenth-Century England*. New Haven: Yale University Press, 2007.
Sun, Emily. "Facing Keats with Winnicott: On a New Therapeutics of Poetry." *Studies in Romanticism* 46.1 (Spring 2007): 57–75.
Sutherland, James. *The Restoration Newspaper and Its Development*. Cambridge: Cambridge University Press, 1986.
Sutherland, Kathryn. "'Events … Have Made Us a World of Readers': Reader Relations 1780–1839." *The Penguin History of Literature*. vol. 5. *The Romantic Period*. Ed. David B. Pirie. New York: Penguin, 1995.
Talfourd, Thomas Noon. *Critical and Miscellaneous Writings*. Boston: Phillips, Sampson, and Company, 1854.
The Tatler. Ed. Donald Bond. Vol. 2. Oxford: Clarendon, 1987.
Taylor, George. *The French Revolution and the London Stage, 1789–1805*. Cambridge: Cambridge University Press, 2000.
Thalia's Tablet and Melpomene's Memorandum Book. London [weekly], 1821.
The Theatrical Examiner. London [daily], 1823–1831.
The Theatrical Gazette. London [daily], 1815.
The Theatrical Inquisitor; or, Literary Mirror. London [monthly], 1812–1820.

The Theatrical Looker-On. Birmingham [weekly], 1822–1823.
The Theatrical Mince Pie. London [weekly], 1825.
The Theatrical Mirror; or Daily Bills of the Performances. London [daily], 1827.
The Theatrical Observer. Dublin [daily], 1821 (later *Original Theatrical Observer*, 1821–1822).
The Theatrical Observer. Dublin [daily], 1821–1822 (later *Nolan's Theatrical Observer*, 1822–1825).
The Theatrical Observer: and Daily Bill of the Play. London [daily], 1821–1876.
The Theatrical Recorder. London [monthly], 1805.
The Theatrical Repertory, or Weekly Rosciad. London [weekly], 1801–1802.
The Theatrical Review. Bath [weekly], 1822–1824.
The Theatrical Rod! London [weekly], 1831.
The Thespian Sentinel; or Theatrical Vademecum. London [daily], 1825.
Thomas, Peter D. G. "The Beginning of Parliamentary Reporting in Newspapers, 1768–1774." *English Historical Review* 74 (October 1959): 623–36.
Thompson, E. P. *The Making of the English Working Class.* New York: Vintage, 1963.
—— "The Moral Economy of the English Crowd in the Eighteenth Century." *Past & Present* 50 (1971): 76–136.
—— "Patrician Society, Plebian Culture." *Journal of Social History* 7.4 (1974): 382–405.
Thorpe, Clarence D. "Keats and Hazlitt: A Record of Personal Relationship and Critical Estimate." *PMLA* 62 (1947): 487–502.
The Times. [London]: August 19, 1789, August 3, 1795, September 30, 1806, October 7, 1806, August 29, 1809, August 30, 1809, September 4, 1809, January 15, 1829.
The Townsman, Addressed to the Inhabitants of Manchester on Theatricals. Manchester [weekly, tri-weekly], 1803–1805.
Trilling, Lionel. "The Poet as Hero: Keats in His Letters." *The Opposing Self.* New York: Viking, 1955. 3–49.
Vendler, Helen. *The Odes of John Keats.* Cambridge, MA: Belknap, 1983.
Walker, R. B. "Advertising in London Newspapers, 1650–1750." *Business History* 15.2 (July 1973): 112–30.
Wanko, Cheryl. "'Fans' and the Eighteenth-century English Stage." *Romanticism and Celebrity Culture, 1750–1850.* Ed. Tom Mole. Cambridge: Cambridge University Press, 2009. 209–26.
Watkins, Daniel. *Keats's Poetry and the Politics of the Imagination.* Toronto: Associated University Presses, 1989.
—— *A Materialist Critique of English Romantic Drama.* Gainesville: University of Florida Press, 1993.
Watt, Ian. *The Rise of the Novel: Studies in Defoe, Richardson and Fielding.* Berkeley and Los Angeles: University of California Press, 1957.
The Weekly Dramatic Register, A Concise History of the London Stage. London [weekly], 1825–1827.
"Weekly Newspapers." *The Westminster Review* 10.20 (April 1829): 466–80.

Werkmeister, Lucyle. *The London Daily Press: 1772–1792*. Lincoln: University of Nebraska Press, 1963.
Whale, John. "Hazlitt on Burke: The Ambivalent Position of a Radical Essayist." *Studies in Romanticism* 25.4 (Winter 1986): 465–81.
Imagination Under Pressure, 1789–1832. Cambridge: Cambridge University Press, 2000.
Wheatley, Kim, ed. *Romantic Periodicals and Print Culture*. New York: Routledge, 2003.
Williams, Raymond. *Culture and Society: 1780–1950*. New York: Columbia University Press, 1983; 1958.
The Long Revolution. New York: Penguin, 1961.
"The Press and Popular Culture: An Historical Perspective." *Newspaper History: From the Seventeenth Century to the Present Day*. Eds. George Boyce, James Curran, and Pauline Wingate. London: Constable, 1978. 41–50.
Wilson, Kathleen. "The Good, the Bad, and the Impotent: Imperialism and the Politics of Identity in Georgian England." *The Consumption of Culture 1600–1800: Image, Object, Text*. Eds. Ann Bermingham and John Brewer. London and New York: Routledge, 1995. 237–62.
The Sense of the People: Politics, Culture and Imperialism in England, 1715–1785. Cambridge: Cambridge University Press, 1995.
The Wind-Up; or, Candor versus The Times. London, 1825.
Wolfson, Susan. *The Questioning Presence: Wordsworth, Keats, and the Interrogative Mode in Romantic Poetry*. Ithaca: Cornell University Press, 1986.
Woods, Leigh. "Edmund Kean, New Plays, and Critics of Acting." *Nineteenth Century Theatre* 20.2 (1992): 77–100.
Wordsworth, William and Samuel Coleridge. *Lyrical Ballads 1798 and 1800*. Eds. Michael Gamer and Dahlia Porter. Peterborough, ONT: Broadview, 2008.
Worrall, David. *The Politics of Romantic Theatricality: The Road to the Stage, 1787–1832*. New York: Palgrave, 2007.
Theatric Revolution: Drama, Censorship, and Romantic Period Subcultures 1773–1832. Oxford: Oxford University Press, 2006.
Wu, Duncan. *William Hazlitt: The First Modern Man*. Oxford: Oxford University Press, 2008.

Index

Act of 1752, 60
acting
  Garrick's style of, 61, 189
  Gentleman's criticism of drama's potential effect on, 66
  Hazlitt on, 169–70
  Kean's style of, 109, 110, 112, 120, 121, 122, 124, 139, 143, 145, 146, 148, 170, 171, 189, 192, 195, 199, 200, 201, 206, 214, 217, 222
actors
  audience's experience mediated through, 165
  audience's knowledge of private life of, 123
  benefit performances for, 55, 61
  critics' starting point with performance of, 168
  ethnic and class demographic changes and, 15
  Garrick's Drury Lane changes affecting, 61
  gaslight's impact on audience experience of, 149, 189
  Hazlitt on, 154, 165–66, 167–68, 169, 176
  human dimension of, 171
  Hunt on independence of critics and relationships with, 92
  Lamb on emergence of new race of, 230
  monthly theatrical periodicals' biographies of, 75
  positive public effects of theater and, 165
  relationship between private and public life of, 119, 144, 146
  reviews of. *See* theatrical criticism; theatrical reviews
  social exchange between spectators and, 61
  stage as primary avenue for celebrity of, 120
  star status mentioned in reviews of, 44
  visibility of face of, for audiences, 171
Addison, Joseph, 28
advertisements
  as selling point to readers, 34
  booksellers and, 54
  commercialization of newspapers and, 29, 32, 34
  culture linked with, 46
  daily newspapers and, 30, 31
  daily theatrical periodicals with, 67
  difficulty differentiating reviews from, 36
  Examiner's lack of, 60, 94
  examples of, 34–36
  first household product in, 54
  front-page placement of, 32, 34, 36
  local history of manners reflected in, 34, 36
  multiple strains of information with, 31
  personal and commercial in, 54
  personal exchange in, 35
  playbills as, 69
  range of content of, 32
  range of varied content alongside, 30, 46
  reading habits attracted and shaped by, 34
  reporters' voice in, 45
  review size compared with size of, 37
  reviews published near, 46
  rhetorical divide between reports and, 45
  satire and, 54
  sensationalist details in, 45–46, 115
  shift in form and number of, 34, 36, 37, 88
  size and page area of, 36
  standard pattern of direct address and description in, 35
  theater as both reported event and, 28
  theater's presence in newspapers through, 25
  Times' iconography for, 37
  timing of traditional publishing process of, 31
advertisers (periodicals), 28, 29
advertising, 31–37
  disparate kinds of information mixed with, 119
  newspaper revenue from, 25, 27, 51
  newspapers' seamless metonymy of actual events and, 28
  press as social institution and, 50
  professionalizing of reviews and, 43
  readers' idea of "Britain" shaped by, 27
  readers' perceptions of theater as public experience in, 10
  theater's presence in newspapers through, 24
  widespread use of public signs in, 3–5

Index

Agnew, Jean-Christophe, 16, 230
allegory
   de Man's notion of, 222, 223, 225
   Hazlitt's "Indian Jugglers" and, 177, 180
   Keats's "Ode on a Grecian Urn" and, 222, 223, 224, 225
   Keats's "Ode to Psyche" and, 218
   Keats's "Ode on a Grecian Urn" and, 235
Altick, Robert, 76
Allott, Miriam, 234
Anderson, Benedict, 27, 48
Arnold, Matthew, 226
As You Like It (Shakespeare), 128
Aspinall, Arthur, 50, 188
Asquith, Ivon, 34
associationist literary strategies, 46
audiences. *See also* readers
   actor's face's visibility to, 171
   actor's private life known to, 123
   actors and experience of, 168
   architectural changes separating stage events from, 61, 62
   class interaction in, 63, 64, 65
   commentary as "critical companion" to, 66
   commercialization of theatrical experience and, 168
   construction of, 116
   critics' interaction with, 58
   galleries and, 62
   gaslight's impact on experience of, 149, 189
   Gentleman's criticism of drama's potential effect on, 66
   Hazlitt on actors' relationship to, 154
   Hazlitt's criticisim and, 152
   Kean's address to, after disturbances, 135, 141
   Kean's controversy and reactions of, 143–44
   Kean's trial's impact on reactions of, 133, 134, 136, 140
   new performance types and, 60
   newspapers' creation of, 27–28
   Old Price riots (1809) and, 65
   playbill periodicals used by, 70
   playbill periodicals' description of, 72
   playbills and, 69
   protests predating 1809 Old Price riots by, 100
   riots against pricing and seating changes by. *See* Old Price (O. P.) riots (1809)
   saving and binding of playbill periodicals by, 73
   sensationalist content desired by, 77, 146
   sense of theatrical history in playbill periodicals and, 73
   social exchange between actors and, 61
   social importance of theaters and, 100
   theater as ideal public space and, 65
   theater as inherited right and, 62, 63, 64, 65
   theater changes challenging old codes of behavior for, 62
   theater producers' relationship with, 77
   theatrical criticism standards negotiated through direct contact with, 66
   theatrical periodicals' endeavor to refine taste of, 99
Audley, Mervyn (Lord Audley), 148
Austen, Jane, 54, 212, 213, 233

Baer, Marc, 100
Bailey, Benjamin, 199, 224
Baker, Herschel, 188
Barker, Hannah, 25, 26, 27, 50, 51
Barker-Benfield, G. J., 168
Barnes, Thomas, 111, 130, 146
Bate, Jonathan, 117, 149, 232
Bate, W. J. [Walter Jackson], 187, 228, 229, 230, 231, 232
Baudelaire, Charles, 235
Beatrice role, Shakespeare, 96
Beattie, James, 218
Beaudry, Harry, 229, 231
Beckett, Samuel, 226
Beggar's Opera, The (Gay), 66, 159
Behrendt, Stephen, 59
Bell, John, 54
Benedick role, Shakespeare, 96
benefit performances, for actors, 55, 61
Benjamin, Walter, 16, 185
Bermingham, Ann, 5, 16, 99, 116, 168, 189
Biographia Literaria (Coleridge), 121, 165
Bishop, Elizabeth, 226
Black, Jeremy, 50, 52
Blackwood's Magazine, 193, 204, 230
Bloom, Harold, 16
Blunden, Edmund, 106
Bohstedt, John, 100
Bolton, Betsey, 17
booksellers
   ad size and placement and, 54
   periodicals sold by, 35, 76, 103
Booth, Junius Brutus, 71
Bourdieu, Pierre, 9, 19, 103
Bourne, H. R. Fox, 51, 93, 188
Bratton, Jacky, 15, 19, 111, 113, 130, 148
Brewer, John, 5, 6
Britain, newspapers' shaping of readers' idea of, 27
Bromwich, David, 160, 185, 186, 231
Brooks, Cleanth, 220, 234
Brougham, Henry, 179, 180

Brown, Charles, 192, 198, 234
Browning, Elizabeth Barrett, 226
Brutus (Payne), 89, 199
Burke, Edmund, 2, 26, 212
burlesque, 167
burletta, 60, 70
Burgess, Miranda, 147, 233
Burney, Frances, 13, 211–16, 217, 233
Burwick, Frederick, 15, 19
Byron, George Gordon (Lord Byron), 14, 17, 19, 146, 151, 189, 193, 230
Byrne, Paula, 233

Campbell, Colin, 16, 53
Canning, George, 179, 180
Caputo, Nicoletta, 99
caricatures
    Cruikshank's portrayal of Kean and Mrs. Cox in Kean's dressing room in, 125
    Drury Lane's commercial reliance on Kean shown in, 125, 128
    Kean trial and, 110, 125
    Kean's portrayal in theater costume in, 125
    support for Kean in, 128
Carlile, Richard, 56, 78, 144
Carlson, Julie, 7, 9, 154, 217
Cavanagh, John, 179, 180, 181
Censor, The, 103
censorship
    Byron's work and, 19
    press and, 51
Champion, The
    Hazlitt's reviews in, 159, 167, 171, 173, 199
    Kean reviewed in, 122, 123, 192, 231
    Keats's reviews in, 13, 192, 200, 203, 204, 205, 231
Chandler, James, 7, 47, 51, 153–54, 215, 217, 218, 226
Characteristics (Hazlitt), 175
Characters of Shakespear's Plays (Hazlitt), 152, 173, 202
Charles I, King of England, 51
Charles II, King of England, 60
Chatham, John Pitt, 2nd Earl of, *Times* letter of, 38, 39, 42, 55
Chaucer, Geoffrey, 202
Chesterfield, George Stanhope, 6th Earl of, 228
Childe Harold (Byron), 189
Christensen, Jerome, 2, 51, 151
Christie, Ian, 100
Chronicle. See Morning Chronicle, The
Cibber, Colley, 150
Clarke, Charles Cowden, 1, 231
class relations
    audience interaction and, 63

Kean's controversy and, 112, 116, 143–44
theater and, 2
theater riots and, 63, 64, 65, 100
theatergoers' divergent interests and, 111
theatrical experience and, 135
classical culture, and Keats's poetry, 193, 197, 230, 233
Clive, John, 52
Cobbett, William, 48, 56, 78, 144, 179, 180, 183
Cockney culture
    Blackwood's reviews and, 193
    Hazlitt's reviews and, 186
    Hunt and Keats associated with, 12, 93
    influence of, 9
    Kean's acting style and, 110, 211
    Keats's poetry and, 13, 197, 214, 225, 230, 233
    Keats's review of Kean and, 204
    late Romanticism's historical sense and, 215
    London's theatrical world and, 98
    sociability and intellectual work hand-in-hand in, x
    sociability of theater and, 217
    suburbs' role in construction of, 19
coffee houses, 53, 101
    daily newspaper growth and, 29
    Lamb on joys of, 23
Coleridge, Hartley Nelson, 54
Coleridge, Samuel Taylor, 160
    anti-Jacobin political philosophy in plays of, 8
    Biographia Literaria of, 121, 165
    Cavanagh's style compared with, 179, 180
    fears about social tensions and possible revolution and, 26
    Kean's acting style and, 109, 121
    Lyrical Ballads of, 8, 50
    prose style of, 160
    theatrical sensationalism and, 165
Colley, Linda, 49, 51
Collier, John Dyer, 158
Colman, George, the younger, 105
Columbine (pantomime character), 105
Columbine and Weekly Review, The, 88, 90, 105
Comédie-Française, Paris, 61
commercialization of newspapers
    ads and, 29, 32, 34
    early morning publication of, 32
    free-press narrative and, 58
    Hazlitt's response to, 152, 154, 155, 161, 163, 189
    morning newspapers and, 29
    new class of readers and new form and, 30
    partisan politics involvement and, 50
    readers and, 152, 153
    timing of traditional publishing process and, 31
    traditional narratives of newspapers in public life challenged by, 29

commercialization of theatrical experience
    audiences and, 168
    critics' resistance to, 60
    Hazlitt on, 159, 166–67
    Kean's controversy and impact of, 112
    newspapers and, 159, 160
    theatrical periodicals' views on, 66
    transition to, 65
Complete Defence of Kean against the Unmanly Attacks of "The Times" (pamphlet), 151
constructivism, 225
consumer culture
    Hazlitt's invectives against, 189
    individual identity in, 110
consumer revolution, 5, 52, 186
consumption
    coffee houses and daily newspaper expansion related to, 29
    newspapers' daily ritual of, 29, 47, 52
Conversations of James Northcote (Hazlitt), 156
Cook, Jon, 160, 187, 188
Cooke, George Frederick, 43, 44
Corcoran, Brendan, 232
Coriolanus role, Shakespeare, 123, 173, 200
"Court of King's Bench turn'd into a Cock pit, The" (caricature), 125
Covent Garden Theatre, London
    competition and changes for audiences' experiences in, 61
    free admission for reviewers at, 43
    Keats's "Fragment of Castle-builder" and, 195, 196, 197
    Keats's pun on name of, 229
    Kemble's management of, 143
    Kemble's performances at, 194
    newspaper publication of playbills of, 69, 76
    obligations of theater managers at, 64
    Old Price riots (1809) and, 6, 44, 63, 64, 65, 101
    renovations and rebuilding of, 3, 61
    reviews of performances at, 46, 83, 84, 143
    theater patent held by, 60
    theatrical dailies and, 69
    Times theatrical ads for, 36
    weekly theatrical magazines and, 76
Covent Garden Theatrical Gazette, The, 67, 71, 73, 102
Cowper, William, 50
Cox v. Kean. See Kean's trial
Cox versus Kean (Fairburn), 114, 116–18, 119
Cox, Charlotte
    caricatures' portrayal of, 125, 127, 128
    Kean's relationship with, 110
    love letters of, 114, 117, 118, 131–33, 134, 139, 142
Cox, Jeffrey, 11, 18, 106, 214, 219, 230, 231, 232, 233, 235

Cox, Robert Albion, 11, 110, 114
criminal conversation (crim con) trials, 115, 116
Crafton, Lisa, 233
Critic, The (Sheridan), 58
Critical Essays on the Performers of the London Theatre (Hunt), 95
Critical Review, 52
criticism. *See* theatrical criticism
critics
    anti-commercial rhetoric of, 60, 159
    approaches to reviewing Kean by, 110
    conflicts between "high" and "low" spheres of, 159, 204
    Hazlitt on role of, 160, 165, 167
    Hazlitt's attacks on, 163
    Hunt on independence of, 92, 93
    Hunt's satiric set of rules and key phrases for, 92–93
    Johnson on, 101
    masculine judgment of actresses and, 168
    parliamentary reporters' background as, 158
    performers as starting point for, 168
    readers as companions to, 57, 58
    role as cultural mediator, 160
    self-parody of, 57–58
    social function of, 98, 152
    theatergoers guided by, 75
Crochunis, Thomas, 18, 121, 148
Cruikshank, George, 125, 128
cultural experience
    commercialism's creation of, 98
    critic's experience of cultural tensions and, 161
    daily newspapers' portrayal of theater and, 37, 62
    Examiner's reimagining of, 95, 97, 98
    Hazlitt's refiguration of theatrical experience and, 176
    theatrical criticism and reimagining of, 7
    theatrical sociability and, 17
cultural negotiation, Hazlitt's model for, 154, 162
cultural values
    appropriation of Shakespeare's words and, 117
    Kean's trial coverage and, 111, 113, 129
culture
    ads linked with, 46
    critics and rethinking of our positions in, 10
    nation at war and military and political spectacle in, 2
    Romantic period and conceptions about, 5
    theater's role at center of, 59
Cumberland, Richard, 227
Cure for the Heart-Ache, A (Morton), 83–84

Daily Advertiser, The, 28
Daily Courant, The, 28, 29, 52

Index

daily newspapers, 21–49
  advertising revenue for, 25, 27
  balance of useful and entertaining matter in, 30
  circulation of, 28
  claim of unique focus on some aspect of public culture by, 30
  coffee houses and increased demand for, 29
  combined discourses of range of content in, 30
  competition from Sunday newspapers and, 30
  daily ritual of consumption and, 29, 47, 52
  format and content changes from tax on, 52
  free-press narrative and, 29
  government subsidies and, 25, 51
  Hunt on problems with criticism in, 91
  interplay of objectivity and sensationalism in, 46
  Kean's trial coverage in, 129, 130
  new class of readers and commercial interests of, 30
  objectivity and attention to detail in, 40
  political commentary in, 40
  political content of, 91
  publishing trends and, 30
  range of varied content in, 30, 46
  readers' relation to public life through, 23, 31
  Register's innovation of early morning publication of, 32
  reviews in, 59
  rhetorical divide between reports and advertisements in, 45
  sensationalist details in, 45–46
  social force in Romantic period of, 24
  theatrical criticism in, 24
  theatrical experience portrayed in, 37
  vision of multiple strains of information in, 31
  Wellington's and Chatham's dispatches in, 55
  working class and growth of, 29
daily theatrical periodicals, 66, *See also* theatrical periodicals
  ads in, 67
  anti-commercial rhetoric of, 82
  audience behavior described in, 72
  audience-making strategies of, 66, 67, 69, 130
  defense of ideal theatrical tradition by, 75
  descriptive analysis in, 71–72
  distribution of, 103
  emergence of, 67
  growth of theatrical consumerism and, 77
  Hazlitt's writing for, 159
  intracity rivalries among, 102
  Kean's controversy and, 112
  Kean's trial coverage and, 130
  newspaper criticism similar to, 75
  playbill reproductions in, 68, 69, 70
  public's perception of plays in, 70, 71, 72
  reading habits of newspaper audiences and, 71
  self-promotion of, 67
  style of, 69
  theatrical history in, 73
  weekly and monthly theatrical periodicals compared with, 75
  weekly and monthly theatrical periodicals' criticism of, 74
  weekly theatrical periodicals' use of criticism from, 76
Daily Universal Register, The, 30, 51
Dart, Gregory, 12, 19, 93, 233
Davis, Tracy, 19, 120, 124, 147, 148, 149, 189
de Man, Paul, 222, 223, 225, 235
de Vries, Jan, 16
Death on the Pale Horse (West), 192
Defoe, Daniel, 28, 106
democracy, press as agent of, 25, 26
DeQuincey, Thomas, 189
descriptive analysis, in playbill periodicals, 71–72
Dibdin, Charles, 104
Dilke, Charles Wentworth, 192, 193, 228, 229
Donohue, Joseph, 147, 167, 189, 190
Drama, or Theatrical Pocket Magazine, The, 75, 147
"Drama, The" (Hazlitt), 152–53, 159
Drama, The (periodical), 68
Dramatic Censor, or Critical Companion, The (Gentleman), 66
Dramatic Censor, The
  anti-commercial commentary in, 11, 77, 78
  Dutton's departure from, 105
  moralistic critique to transform public opinion in, 83–84, 90
  Morton's play review in, 83–84
  Opera Glass's review style compared with, 89
  other newspapers' reviews criticized in, 79
  philosophy of, 79
  reviews in, 101
  size of, 76
Dramatic Correspondent, and Amateur's Place Book, The, 76, 87
Dramatic Magazine, The, 75
Dramatic Observer and Musical Review, The, 102
Drury Lane Theatre, London
  audience protests (1775) at, 100
  commercial reliance on Kean by, 128
  competition and changes for audiences' experiences in, 61
  critic on audiences at, 58
  critic on commercial aspect of play choices at, 74
  delineation between stage and house in, 61
  Garrick's changes at, 61

gaslight's impact on audience experience
at, 189
Kean and audiences at, 198
Kean's controversy and, 110, 113
Kean's performances at, 11, 109, 113, 120, 124,
128, 133–35, 142, 198
Keats and, 1
Loutherbourg's innovations at, 61
newspaper publication of playbills of,
69, 76
renovations and rebuilding of, 3, 61
representative public sphere aspect of, 134
reviews of performances at, 58, 74, 80, 113, 120,
124, 133–35, 142
theater patent held by, 60
theatrical dailies and, 69
visual representations of Kean at, 125
weekly theatrical magazines and, 76
Drury-Lane Company, 36
Du Bois, Edward, 191
Dublin
audience protests in, 100
theatrical periodicals in, 68, 69
Dutton, Thomas
anti-commercial commentary of, 11, 77, 78, 87,
89, 163
Coleridge's style compared with, 160, 163
critical attitude toward audience reaction in
reviews of, 86
degraded state of public mind described by, 84
Hunt's style compared with, 96
moralistic critique to transform public opinion
by, 83–84
Opera Glass's style of review compared with, 89
other newspapers' reviews criticized by, 79–80
prose style of, 78
Suspicious Husband review on audience taste
from, 84–86
theater's moral dimension and, 88
theatrical experience and, 77

Eberle-Sinatra, Michael, 18, 95, 106
Edelstein, Dan, 233
Edinburgh Dramatic Review, 68, 102
Edinburgh Dramatic Tete-a-tete, The, 102
Edinburgh Magazine, The, 159
Edinburgh Review, 27, 48, 52, 55, 106, 159, 179
Edinburgh, theatrical periodicals in, 69, 102
editors
competition from Sunday newspapers and, 30
Hazlitt's parliamentary reports and, 55
mantra of "facilitate–record–abridge" for, 32
melodramatic tactics to hold readers' attention
used by, 46
readers' theatrical experience and, 79

rhetoric of reporting and, 39
theatrical history in theatrical periodicals
and, 102
Times' editorial voice and, 40
weekly theatrical periodicals and, 76
widening readerships and, 27
Elliston, Richard, 96, 117, 135, 136
Ellis, Aytoun, 53
Eloquence of the British Senate (Hazlitt), 158
English Reform Bill (1832), 2
Enright, Nancy, 188
"Essay, Supplementary to the Preface"
(Wordsworth), 193
Essay on Man, An (Pope), 54
*Essay on the Principles of Human Action,
An* (Hazlitt), 156
Esterhammer, Angela, 189
Eve of St. Agnes, The (Keats), 13, 197, 214
Examiner, The, 91–99
ad-free approach of, 60, 94
Blackwood's debate covered in, 204
circulation of, 106
commercial daily press's influence on, 94
founding of, 91
Hazlitt's article on actors and acting in, 165
Hazlitt's essays in, 169, 176, 179, 203
Hazlitt's reviews in, 97, 152, 159, 161, 163, 164,
166, 173, 199, 213
Hunt's libelling of Prince Regent in, 213
Hunt's reviews in, 96, 97, 168–69
Hunt's success in Cockney Moment and, 93
Hunt's theatrical criticism approach in, 95
independence in theatrical criticism and, 92,
93, 97
Keats's reading of criticism in, 193, 199, 231
major sections of, 94, 95
occasional modes of theatrical reviewing in, 11,
60, 155
philosophy of, 91, 93
primary role of theater in public experience
and, 95
reviewer-reader relationship and, 96
social advocacies of, 214
textual layout of, 94, 95
theater criticism as major component of, 94
uniqueness of, among London periodicals, 94
view of theater presented in, 60, 63
Excursion, The (Wordsworth), 213

Fairburn, John, 114, 116–18, 119, 125, 128, 130
Fairclough, Mary, 100, 155, 181, 188
Favret, Mary, 216, 233
Fay, Elizabeth, 115, 116, 148
"Fight, The" (Hazlitt), 13, 19, 155, 156, 176,
180–84, 185

Index

Fisher, David, 193
Fitzgiggio riots (1763), London, 100
Flying-Post or Post-Master, The, 52
"Fragment of Castle-builder" (Keats), 195–97
France, lighting and scenery technology in, 61, 166
Franklin, Andrew, 104
Franta, Andrew, 206, 232
Fraser, Nancy, 16, 147
"Free Admission, The" (Hazlitt), 156
free press
   as distinctly English virtue, 25
   commercial discourse of information and exchange and, 58
   continuing influence of concept of, 51
   daily newspaper reading and, 29
   Mackintosh's speech on Peltier and, 25
   newspapers and ideology of, 25–28
French Revolution, 9, 26, 51, 125
   Burke on, 2
   Hazlitt on, 152
   Hunt on, 106, 159
   reports and ads with sensationalist details of, 45
   theatrical tastes of public affected by, 1
Fry, Paul, 225, 230
Fulford, Tim, 190

Gamer, Michael, 8, 11, 19, 55, 115, 148
Garrick, David, 61, 65, 77, 109, 120, 165, 189
gaslight technology, and audience experience, 149, 189
Gay, John, 66, 159
Gay, Penny, 233
gender
   actresses' female affect challenging expectation of male spectators and, 168
   criminal conversation trials and, 115
   Kean's controversy and, 112, 116
   Kean's trial and, 12, 111
   Kean's trial caricature and, 125
   Robinson's criminal conversation trial and, 115
   separation between domestic and public spheres and, 149
   theatrical experience and, 11, 135
Gentleman, Francis, 66
Genuine Theatrical Observer, The, 102
George IV, King of England (earlier Prince of Wales, Prince Regent)
   Hunt's libelling of, 94, 213
   Mary Robinson's relationship with, 148
Gilmartin, Kevin, ix, 7, 16, 24, 48, 186, 189
Gonda, Caroline, 149
Goodman, Kevis, 50
Gowen, David, 70

Gray, Charles Harold, 101
Guardian, The, 65
Guest, Harriet, 6, 12, 16, 110, 233

Habermas, Jurgen, 16, 53, 147
Hadley, Elaine, 65, 100
Hamilton, Paul, 155, 226, 227
Hamlet (Shakespeare), 118
Hamlet role, Shakespeare, 123, 190, 200
handbills, 102
Harlequin (pantomime character), 105
Harlequin, The (periodical), 88, 90, 105
"Hart-Leap Well" (Wordsworth), 19
Hawkins, F.W., 149
Haymarket Theatre, London, 36
Hazlitt, William, 25, 152–85
   actors as focus of reviews of, 154, 165–66, 167, 169, 176
   commercialization of newspapers and, 152, 154, 155, 161, 163, 185
   commercialization of theatrical experience and, 159, 166–67
   critics attacked by, 163
   critics' role and, 150, 165, 167
   critics' social function and, 152
   "Drama" of, 152–53
   Essay on the Principles of Human Action of, 156
   essays of, 12, 152–53, 155, 156
   Examiner essays of, 169, 179, 203
   Examiner reviews of, 97, 152, 159, 161, 163, 164, 165, 166, 173, 199, 213
   familiar style of, 158, 172
   "Fight" of, 13, 19, 155, 156, 176, 180–84, 185
   focus on experiential dimension of theatrical reception by, 163
   independence of, 163
   "Indian Jugglers" of, 13, 155, 156, 176–80, 181, 185
   journalism as central source of income and professional profile for, 160
   Kean reviewed by, 120, 153, 155, 159, 162, 163, 168–75, 199–200, 232
   Kean's case and, 114
   Keats influenced by, 155, 203, 210, 214, 217, 223, 231, 232
   Lectures on English Philosophy of, 187
   Lectures on the English Poets of, 13, 152, 201
   methodology of, 186
   new mode of criticism devised by, 169
   new model of cultural negotiation in criticism of, 154, 162
   newspapers' rage for conveying information and, 29
   "On Actors and Acting" of, 154, 165
   parliamentary reporting of, 12, 41, 55, 155, 158–59, 176

political commentary by, 158
radical causes and, 161
range of publications publishing writing of, 159, 160, 163
range of work published by, 152
range of writing by, 12
reviews of, 12, 13, 153, 157, 158, 162–75
Romantic casuistry in criticism of, 154
Shakespeare's assessment by, 201–2
shifts between detailed description and affective reaction used by, 176
Spirit of the Age of, 153
split between "high" and "low" spheres noted by, 159, 181
standardized narrative discourse of, 55
style of, 152, 154, 160–61, 162–63, 169, 217
theatrical criticism approach of, 155, 160, 161, 166
theatrical experience reconfigured by, 155, 176
varied and responsive prose of, 160
View of the English Stage of, 152, 162, 163, 165, 190
Henry IV, Part 1 (Shakespeare), Hotspur role, 199
Henry VIII role, Shakespeare, 120
Hessell, Nikki, 50, 55
Higgins, David, 188, 190
Hill, Aaron, 101
Hill, Thomas, 191, 192, 227
Hillebrand, Harold Newcomb, 84
Hindle, Wilfred, 84
historical-materialist approach, and Keats's poetry, 193
history, in "Ode on a Grecian Urn," 219, 225, 227
Hoadley, Benjamin, 84–86
Hogan, Charles Beecher, 68, 99, 105
Holcroft, Thomas, 75
Holland, Peter, 124
Homer, Keats's poem on reading, 206, 207
Hone, William, 23, 192
Hotspur role, Shakespeare, 199
Hull Dramatic Censor, The, 90
Humber, Alice, 130, 131
Hunt, John, 11, 60, 67, 91, 92, 93, 94, 95, 152, 161, 163
Hunt, Leigh
commercial commitments of theatrical press and, 91
criticism of, 154
Examiner reviews of, 96, 97, 168–69, 232
Examiner weekly paper of, 11, 60, 63, 67, 93, 95, 111, 152, 163, 231
Examiner's ad-free approach and, 94
Examiner's founding by, 91
Examiner's philosophy and, 91, 93
Hazlitt's criticism published by, 163
Hazlitt's theater criticism and, 99
imprisonment for libel by, 94, 213–14
independence in theatrical criticism and, 92
Keats association with, 230
Keats's poem on imprisonment of, 214, 215
Keats's thinking influenced by, 199, 204
News theatrical reviews of, 91, 92, 93, 95
occasional modes of theatrical reviewing by, 11, 155
playbill periodicals and, 69, 70
review illustrating approach of, 96
reviewer-reader relationship and, 96
reviewing strategy of, 169
satiric set of rules and key phrases for theater critics from, 92–93
significance as a theater critic, 97
style of, 95
theatrical criticism approach of, 95
Hunt, Lynn, 47
Hyperion poems (Keats), 214, 219

Iago role, Shakespeare, 163, 164
illegitimate theater, 2, 77, 97, 109, 137, 161, 162, 176, 180, 185
Independent Theatrical Observer, The, 102
"Indian Jugglers, The" (Hazlitt), 13, 155, 156, 176–80, 181, 185
Ireland, playbill periodicals in, 69
Irish Dramatic Censor, The, 79
Isabella (Keats), 13, 214

Jacobus, Mary, 6, 133
Jeffrey, Francis, 48
Jewett, William, 17
Joddrel, Elinor, 211
Johnson, Samuel, 41, 54, 65, 66, 77, 96, 101
Jones, Elizabeth, 228
Jones, Stanley, 184, 188
Jones, Leonidas, 231

Kahan, Jeffrey, 124
Kandl, John, 228, 233
Kaufman, Robert, 225, 235
Keach, William, 197, 230
Kean, Edmund, 109–46
acting style of, 109, 110, 112, 120, 121, 122, 124, 139, 143, 145, 146, 148, 170, 171, 189, 192, 195, 199, 200, 201, 206, 214, 217, 222
appearances in London society as extensions of roles of, 120
celebrity and fame of, 111, 113, 116, 140, 141, 145, 146, 148
character development by, 203

Kean, Edmund (cont.)
  Charlotte Cox's relationship with, 110
  fame and celebrity of, 121, 135
  Hazlitt on, 121, 167
  institutional forces affecting late career of, 111
  Keats and low company of, 191, 198
  Keats influenced by, 192, 208
  Keats's alliance with, 199, 228
  Keats's attendance at performances of, 198–99
  Keats's ideas about poetry and acting of, 192
  Keats's reference to, in letters, 198–99
  Kemble's acting compared with, 112, 121, 170, 173, 175
  love letters of, 114, 117, 118, 131–33, 134, 139, 142
  low aspects of middle-class life and, 191
  masculine authority of, 124
  methodical intent behind spontaneous style of, 149
  mode of self-representation of, 123
  performances as exercises in self-publicity for, 121
  reasons behind controversial aspects of, 112
  return to the stage and press coverage of, 111, 145–46
  Shakespearean roles of. *See* Kean's roles
  split between "high" and "low" spheres and, 195
  success of, 109
  theatrical revolution of, 146, 149
  visual representations of, 125–29, 150
  voice of, 120
"Keen-ish Sport in Cox's Court!!: or Symptoms of Crim.Con. in Drury Lane" (caricature), 114, 125
Kean's controversy, 109
  class and gender knowledge and, 112
  Kean Vindicated pamphlet on, 144–45
  Kean's acting affected by, 124, 143
  Kean's address to audience about disturbances over, 135
  Kean's identity and, 115
  Kean's status after return to the stage and, 145–46
  new generation of O. P. and, 143
  range of press reactions to, 113
  range of print reactions to, 112
  relationship between private and public life in, 112, 114, 119, 129, 133, 134, 135, 138, 140, 141, 144, 145, 146
  Shakespeare re-imagining and, 112
  theatrical experience and, 110, 111, 113, 114, 120, 136, 137, 138, 145, 146
  use of term, 110
Kean's reviews, 120, *See also* Kean's roles
  audiences' construction of, 116
  character development noted in, 203
  class relations and, 143–44
  construction of, 116
  embodiment of characters' psychological states noted in, 121
  Hazlitt and, 120, 121, 153, 155, 162, 168–75, 199–200, 232
  Hunt's *Examiner* and, 168–69
  Kean's celebrity's influence on, 121
  Kean's mode of self-representation and, 123
  Kean's return to the stage and, 145
  Kean's small stature and weak voice noted in, 121, 198, 201
  Keats and, 200–1
  public opinion cited in, 143
  relation between voice and printed text noted in, 203
  reviewers' approach to, 110
  sensation and acting style noted in, 122
  sensation in performances noted in, 122
  supporters of Kean's approach in, 122
  Times' use of two reviewers for single performance in, 136
Kean's roles, 199
  Coriolanus, 123, 173, 200
  Hamlet, 123, 190, 200
  Henry VIII, 120
  Hotspur, 199
  Kemble's Coriolanus compared with, 173
  Lear, 117, 118
  Macbeth, 117, 123, 136, 171, 190, 199, 200
  Othello, 122, 134, 147, 169, 172, 200
  Richard II, 121
  Richard III, 1, 122, 125, 133, 140, 145, 150, 168, 198
  Romeo, 198
  Shylock, 1, 120, 122, 170, 172, 199
  Timon of Athens, 124
Kean's trial
  anti-Kean publicity surrounding, 118
  audiences in plays affected by, 133, 134, 136, 140
  caricature on Kean's portrayal in, 125
  caricature on newspapers' treatment of, 128
  conflation of trial and performance in coverage of, 133
  criminal conversation (seduction) aspect of, 115
  criticism of *Times*' coverage of, 112, 119, 138, 141–43, 144–45
  critics' reactions to, 112
  daily newspapers' coverage of, 129
  damages sought in, 115
  Fairburn's publication on, 114, 116–18, 119
  Humber's cross-examination in, 130

Kean's address to audience about, 135, 141
Kean's defense in, 115, 134, 135
Kean's theatricality and treatment of, 127
love letters in, 114, 117, 131–33
press's shaping of social and cultural values and, 113
public reaction to, 110, 113
publications on, 114, 118
range of responses to, 119
reader-as-eyewitness technique in coverage of, 130
return to the stage after, 111, 145
sexual morality debate and, 111, 112, 116, 118, 130, 141
shifts between report and commentary in coverage of, 131
Theatrical Observer's coverage of, 137–41, 143
Times' coverage of, 111, 129–37
Times' initial support in, 111
Kean Vindicated, or the Truth Discovered with his Flattering Reception on Monday Evening (pamphlet), 144–45
Keats, George, 191, 198, 207, 218, 234
Keats, John, 25, 191–227
  alliance with Kean of, 199, 228
  as both actor and audience member, 1
  classical culture in poems of, 193, 197, 230, 233
  Cockney style of, 230, 233
  embrace of a "low" social position by, 191
  encounter between "low" and "high" in poetry of, 195
  Eve of St. Agnes of, 13, 197, 214
  "Fragment of Castle-builder" of, 195–97
  Hazlitt's influence on, 155, 203, 210, 214, 217, 223, 231, 232
  historical-materialist approach to, 193
  humble background cited in criticism of, 193
  Isabella of, 13, 214
  Kean and his low company and, 191, 198
  Kean references in letters of, 198–99
  Kean reviews of, 200–1
  Kean's acting and ideas about poetry of, 192
  Kean's case and, 114
  Kean's influence on, 192, 208
  Kean's performances seen by, 198–99
  Lamia of, 13, 210, 211, 215–17, 218, 219, 221, 224
  love of theater of, 1
  negative capability and, 13, 192, 193, 198, 204, 210, 218, 226
  occasionalism and, 186
  "Ode on a Grecian Urn" of, 13, 197, 217, 219–26
  "Ode to a Nightingale" of, 217, 229

"Ode to Psyche" of, 217, 218
ode stanza development by, 233
"On First Looking into Chapman's Homer" of, 206, 207
"On Sitting Down to Read King Lear Once Again" of, 206–8
Otho the Great of, 198, 199, 217
poet as cultural intermediary for readers and, 192
poetics of interruption of, 192, 206, 210, 215, 217
poetry of halfseeing of, 206
reviews of, 192, 199–204
shift in thinking related to theatrical experience of, 205
smokeability and, 218
social mobility and, 193
split between "high" and "low" spheres noted by, 194, 195
state of suspension as unfulfillment in, 232
theatrical experience of, 1, 193, 195–99, 219
"To Autumn" of, 217
understanding of poetry by, 204–5
"When I have fears that I may cease to be" of, 208–10
"Written on the Day That Mr. Leigh Hunt Left Prison" of, 214, 215
Keats, Tom, 191, 198, 207
Kee, James, 234
Kelley riot (1747), Dublin, 100
Kelley, Theresa, 222, 224, 226, 235
Kemble, John Philip, 120
  acting style of, 112, 120, 173, 174, 175, 200
  Covent Garden management by, 63, 143, 174
  Hazlitt on, 120, 173
  Kean's acting compared with, 112, 121, 170, 173, 175, 200
  Keats on, 200
  Old Price riots (1809) and, 63
  reviews of, 36
  rhetorical mastery of, 109
  Shakespearean roles of. *See* Kemble's roles
Kemble's roles
  Coriolanus, 173
  hallmarks of, 146
  Kean's Coriolanus compared with, 173
  King John, 174
  Macbeth, 63
Kenilworth (play), 86
King John role, Shakespeare, 174
King Lear (Shakespeare), 114
  Kean's Lear role in, 117, 118
  Keats's poem on reading, 192, 206–8
King's Theatre, Haymarket, London, 36
King's Theatre, Pantheon, London, 36

Kingston, John, 191
Kinnaird, John, 186, 187
Klancher, Jon, 10, 16, 24, 48, 55, 104, 106, 161, 184, 186, 189
Klein, Lawrence, 110
Kluge, Alexander, 16
Korobkin, Laura, 148
Kruger, Loren, 16
Kucich, Greg, 11, 106, 213, 214, 216

Lamb, Charles, 154
  attachment to the *Times* of, 23–24, 27, 47, 48
  Hazlitt recommendation from, 158
  new race of actors and, 230
  private experience of solitary readers and, 124
Lamia (Keats), 13, 210, 211, 215–17, 218, 219, 221, 224
Latham, Sean, 6
Lear role, Shakespeare, 117, 118
Lectures on English Philosophy (Hazlitt), 187
Lectures on the English Comic Writers (Hazlitt), 152
Lectures on the English Poets (Hazlitt), 13, 152, 201
Letters to Imlay (Wollstonecraft), 133
Levinson, Marjorie, 193–94, 197, 220, 228
Lewis, Matthew "Monk," 105
Liber Amoris (Hazlitt), 156
Liberal, The, 159
Licensing Act (1737), 60
lighting technology, 61, 62
Lillywhite, Brian, 53
Lincoln Dramatic Censor, 80
Literary Anecdotes of the Eighteenth Century (Nichols), 41
Liu, Alan, 47
London
  ethnic and class demographic changes in, 15
  number of daily newspapers in, first decade of nineteenth century, 28
  range of theatrical periodicals in, 102
  theater as central public experience in, 1, 3
  theater riots in. *See* Old Price (O. P.) riots (1809)
London Magazine, The, 152, 159, 163
London Post, The, 52
London Weekly Review, The, 159
Loutherbourg, Philip de, 61
Lynch, James, 99
lyric poetry
  as paradigmatic Romantic genre, 7
  newspaper's "teeming presentness" and, 50
  textual mediation of theater and, 14
Lyrical Ballads (Coleridge and Wordsworth), 8, 50

Macbeth (Shakespeare), 1, 44, 128, 185
Macbeth role, Shakespeare, 1, 44, 128, 190, 200
  Kean and, 117, 123, 136, 171, 199
  Kemble and, 63
Mackintosh, James, 25–26
Mackintosh, Lady Catherine, 159
Magnuson, Paul, 15
Mahoney, John L., 187
managers
  sensationalist content desired by audiences and, 77
  theater as ideal public space and, 65
Mansfield Park (Austen), 54, 212
Mason, Nicholas, 151
Maturin, Charles, 121
Maurer, Shawn, 149
McFarland, Thomas, 230
McGann, Jerome, 15, 18, 226, 234
McKendrick, Neil, 5, 52
McKeon, Michael, 150
McLeod, Randall, 233
melodrama, 17, 60, 70, 74, 167
melodramatic tactics, of newspapers, 46
Merchant of Venice (Shakespeare), 1, 120, 122, 170, 172, 199
middle class
  Hazlitt's "The Fight" and, 190
  Kean's performances and, 194
  Keats's poetry and cultural experience of, 192
  newspaper readership and, 48
  philosophical criticism and, 161
  review culture and, 49
military affairs, *Times*' coverage of, 38–39, 46
military culture
  Burney's *Wanderer* and, 213
  social effects of performance in national theaters and, 2
Milnes, Tim, 156
Mince Pie. *See* Theatrical Mince Pie
Mitchell, Robert, 232
Mole, Tom, 99, 149
Monthly Magazine, The, 75, 159
Monthly Mirror, The, 75, 228
Monthly Review, The, 52, 75
monthly theatrical periodicals, 66, *See also* theatrical periodicals
  anti-commercial rhetoric of, 77, 79, 82
  audience-making strategies of, 66, 75
  daily theatrical periodicals compared with, 75
  daily theatrical periodicals criticized by, 74
  Hazlitt's writing for, 159
  magazine format mimicked by, 75
  playbill periodicals' evocative power compared with, 73
  popularity of, 75

range of content of, 75
role of, 76
similarities to general publications by, 75
Monthly Theatrical Reporter, The, 105, 147, 230
Monthly Theatrical Review, The, 75
Moody, Jane, 2, 15, 18, 19, 60, 97, 112, 125, 146, 148, 149, 174, 189
moral standards
　Kean's controversy invoking, 130
　Kean's trial and, 111, 112, 116, 118, 141
　theatrical criticism and, 67, 74, 80, 82, 83–84, 85, 88, 90, 95, 96
Morning Chronicle, The
　ads, both personal and commercial in, 54
　consumer revolution and, 52
　focus of, 30
　Hazlitt on his reviewing style in, 162–63
　Hazlitt's parliamentary reporting in, 155, 158, 159
　Hazlitt's reviews in, 152, 159, 163, 167, 170, 199, 213
　Kean reviewed in, 170
　Kean's controversy reporting in, 113, 139
　Keats's reading of, 231
　Old Price riots mentioned in review in, 44
　parliamentary reporting in, 40, 41
　placement, form, and number of ads in, 37
　professionalizing of theatrical reporting in, 43
　shift in form and number of ads in, 34, 36
　typical front page of, 32
Morning Herald, 80
morning newspapers
　ads in, 32
　circulation of, 28
　commercial aims of, 29
　Hazlitt on rage for conveying information in, 29
　parliamentary reports in, 31
　reports of public events in, 37
Morning Post, The, 30, 34, 36, 41, 52
Morton, Thomas, 83–84
Much Ado About Nothing (Shakespeare), 96
Muir, Kenneth, 231
Mulvihill, James, 156, 187

Natarajan, Uttara, 156–57
National Omnibus, and Entertaining Advertiser, The, 76
negative capability, and Keats, 13, 192, 193, 198, 204, 210, 218, 226
Negt, Oscar, 16
new historicism, 7
New Monthly Magazine, The, 159, 180
Newlyn, Lucy, 229, 232
news stories. *See* reports

News, The, 91, 92, 93, 94, 95
newspapers
　advertising in. *See* advertisements; advertising
　advertising revenue for, 25, 27, 51
　associationist strategies in, 46
　audience-making strategies of, 159
　balance of useful and entertaining matter in, 30
　booksellers' founding of, 54
　both local experiences and global events presented in, 28
　caricature on Kean's treatment in, 128
　commercialization of. *See* commercialization of newspapers
　commercialization of theatrical experience and, 159, 160
　creation of audience by, 27–28
　criminal conversation trials in, 115
　daily ritual of consumption and, 29, 47, 52
　daily theatrical periodicals' criticism similar to, 75
　daily theatrical periodicals' emulation of, 67
　dating ranges in one issue of, 48
　difficulty differentiating ads from reviews in, 36
　distinction between interpretive journals and commercial aspect of, 28
　distribution of, 50
　editorial voice of, 39
　favors and patronage system in, 36
　free press ideology and, 25–28
　front-page placement of ads and other content in, 32, 36
　Hazlitt on coverage of, 153
　Hazlitt's writing for range of, 159, 163
　illusion of immediacy in, 28
　information age in Romantic period and, 28
　interplay of objectivity and sensationalism in, 46
　Kean reviews in, 109
　Kean trial coverage in, 110
　Kean's celebrity and, 121
　Lamb's attachment to, 23–24
　mantra of "facilitate–record–abridge" for, 32
　melodramatic tactics of, 46
　narration of public events as purpose of, 31, 37
　narrative sensation as approach for news stories in, 45
　Old Price riots (1809) coverage in, 44, 62, 63, 65, 101
　parliamentary reporting and, 158
　partisan lines in reporting Kean court case in, 113
　pleasure of reading of, 23

newspapers (cont.)
  poetry and, 50
  post as institution and, 23
  public discussions initiated by, 25
  public life and social role of, 24, 29, 48
  public opinion and, 25, 27, 111
  publicity and, 37, 42, 45, 142
  publishing trends and, 30
  rage for conveying information of, 159
  ramifications of generic blurring of discourses in, 47
  readerly expectations and desires shaping, 27
  readers' consumerist desires and, 47
  readers' engagement in theatrical culture and, 24
  readers' idea of "Britain" shaped by, 27
  readers' relation to public life through, 23, 51
  reporting as central part of textual form of, 37
  rhetoric structuring audience response in, 39
  seamless metonymy of actual and potential events in, 28
  sensationalist details in, 45–46, 115, 164
  sense of contemporaneity in, 47
  shift in form and number of ads in, 34, 36, 37, 88
  social effects of, 27
  social function of, 47
  task of making audience for, 27
  theater attendance as newsworthy event for, 121
  theatrical criticism in, 80, 163
  theatrical experience and changing forms of textual publicity in, 37
  theatrical periodicals on criticism published by, 79–82
  theatrical periodicals' anti-commercial rhetoric on, 66, 79
  theatrical periodicals' borrowings from, 71
  timing of traditional newspaper publishing process and, 31
  translation of events and performance into objects of readerly attention by, 6
  variety of content in, 37
  widening readerships and changes in, 27
  writing style of, 160
Nichols, John, 41
Nicoll, Allardyce, 61
Nolan's Theatrical Observer, 102
Noverre, Jean-Georges, 100
Nuss, Melynda, 15, 19

O. P. riots. *See* Old Price (O. P.) riots
O. P.ers
  goal of later generation of, 143
  Kean opposition by, 143

Observer. *See Theatrical Observer, The* (London)
occasional modes of theatrical reviewing, 11, 60, 155
occasional publications, and Kean's controversy, 143, 144–45
occasionalism
  Hazlitt's model of cultural negotiation and, 155
  Hazlitt's parliamentary reporting's shaping of, 158
  Hazlitt's review rhetoric and, 180
  Keats and, 186, 203
  theater as catalyst for, 153
  use of term, 153
occasionalism, use of term, 186
"Ode on a Grecian Urn" (Keats), 13, 197, 217, 219–26
"Ode to a Nightingale" (Keats), 217, 229
"Ode to Psyche" (Keats), 217, 218
Old Price (O. P.) riots (1809), 62–65
  background to, 62, 65
  causes of, 63
  eighteenth-century riots compared with, 63
  Hunt in the *Examiner* on, 63
  mediation of theater via print to reading audiences and, 65
  new generation of O. P.ers after, 143
  newspaper coverage of, 44, 62, 63, 95, 101
  pamphleteer on cause of, 64
  press reaction to, 62
  print responses to, 65
  proliferation of theatrical periodicals after, 24, 44
  prostitution and sexual activity in darkened boxes and, 64
  settlement in, 63
  theater press and impact of, 6
  theatrical periodicals' coverage of, 101
Olivier, Laurence, 124
"On Actors and Acting" (Hazlitt), 154, 165
"On First Looking into Chapman's Homer" (Keats), 206, 207
"On Londoners and Country People" (Hazlitt), 156
"On Seeing the Elgin Marbles" (Keats), 197, 206
"On Sitting Down to Read King Lear Once Again" (Keats), 192, 206–8
"On the Feeling of Immortality in Youth" (Hazlitt), 156
"On Thought and Action" (Hazlitt), 190
O'Neill, Eliza, 167, 168, 175
Opera Glass, The, 76, 104
  audience for, 90
  format and content of, 88, 90, 105
  review style of, 89
O'Quinn, Daniel, 2, 17, 19

Original Theatrical Observer, The, 102
O'Rourke, James, 233
Orwell, George, 93
Othello (Shakespeare), 150, 163, 164, 202
Othello role, Shakespeare, 122, 134, 147, 169, 172, 200
Otho the Great (Keats and Brown), 198, 199, 217
Oxberry's Theatrical Inquisitor, 76

pantomime, 60, 71, 72, 80, 84, 105, 193
papers. *See* newspapers
Park, Roy, 187
Parker, Mark, 56
Parliament
  importance of, 40
  Licensing Act of 1737 and, 60
  printing regulation and, 52
  theater as alternative representative assembly to, 58
parliamentary reform, 25, 26, 188
parliamentary reporting, 30
  Daily Universal Register's new approach to, 32
  early morning publication cycle and, 32
  forerunner to the theatrical reviews in, 40, 43
  Hazlitt and, 12, 41, 55, 155, 158–59, 176
  Hazlitt's occasionalism shaped by, 158
  informational narratives in, 40
  language of, 42
  Morning Chronicle's daily description of debates in, 40
  Morning Chronicle's focus on, 30
  narrative style of, 130, 183
  notion of publicness in, 43
  objective style in, 42, 93
  sense of contemporaneity in, 159
  special importance of, 40
  specialization and multiple reports in, 41
  theater critics' background in, 158
  theater's presence in newspapers through, 25
  theatrical reporting compared with, 166
  traditional approaches to, 31
  typical narrative report in, 41–42
  Woodfall's revolutionary approach to, 40–41
Parry, John Orlando, 3–5
Pascoe, Judith, 15, 17
patent theaters, 15, *See also* Covent Garden Theatre, London; Drury Lane Theatre, London
  architectural changes in, 61
  competition and changes for audiences' experiences in, 61
  cultural domain of, 60
  establishment of, 60
  Kean trial debates and social role of, 120

Kean's career and, 111
Kean's controversy and, 113
riots in eighteenth century at, 62
weekly theatrical periodicals on performances at, 76
Paulin, Tom, 187, 189
Payne, Howard, 89, 199
Peltier, Jean, 25, 26
performance
  commitment to objective and detailed reporting of, 43
  Hazlitt and critic's reaction to, 154
  Hunt circle and Keats's thinking about, 199
  reshaping imagination of personal identity by, 120
  Romantic casuistry in critic's response to, 154
  theatrical experience beyond time of, 11
periodicals. *See also* theatrical periodicals *and specific titles*
  authors as cultural intermediary between readers and public events, 28
  distinction between commercial and interpretive publications in, 28, 52
  Hazlitt and, 157
  Hazlitt's criticism and, 155
  historical overview of development of, 51
  Kean's celebrity and, 116
  political commentary in, 40
  range of subjects in, 28
  rapid growth and diversification of, 28
Perry, James, 34, 36, 37, 43, 162
Pizarro (Sheridan), 58, 105
play reviews. *See* theatrical criticism; theatrical reviews
playbill periodicals
  audience behavior described in, 72
  audience use of, 70
  audience-making strategies of, 69
  commentary accompanying playbills in, 71
  cultural hierarchy of drama and genres represented in, 71
  descriptive analysis in, 71
  first appearance of, 69
  impact of aesthetic judgments in, 73
  public's perception of plays in, 70, 71, 72
  saving and binding of, 73
  theatrical history in, 73
  Theatrical Observer format in, 69
  wide distribution of, 69
playbills
  as advertisements, 69
  cultural hierarchy of drama and genres represented in, 70
  daily theatrical periodicals' reproduction of, 68, 69, 70

playbills (cont.)
  distribution through commercial channels of, 68
  informational mission of, 70
  new technologies for production of, 15
  newspaper publication of, 69, 76
  posting restrictions on, 68
  public's perception of plays in, 70
  publicity from smaller handbill forms of, 102
  size and contents of, 68
Playfair, Giles, 147
Plotz, John, 100
Plymouth Theatrical Spy, The, 76, 80
pocket magazines, 102
poet, as cultural intermediary for readers, 192
Poetic Epistles of Edmund, The (book), 118–19
poetry
  halfseeing with confidence and, 206
  Kean's ability to communicate embodied experience of Shakespeare's, 201, 203
  Kean's acting and Keats's ideas about, 192, 193
  Kean's celebrity and understanding of, 113
  Keats's understanding of, 204–5
  newspaper reading compared with reading of, 24
  newspaper's "teeming presentness" and, 50
  periodicals with, 75, 87
  reading aloud and experience of, 24
  relation to external world in, 157
  social function of, 192, 232
  Sunday newspapers with, 30
political allegiance
  critic authority and, 163
  Kean and, 214, 215
political assembly, theater as, 61
political commentary
  daily newspapers and, 30, 31, 40, 47, 91
  front-page placement of, 32
  Hazlitt and, 158
  newspapers' combined discourses of range of content with, 30
  readers' desire for, 31, 47
  theater's presence in newspapers through, 25
political culture
  newspaper advertising revenues and emergence of, 25
  social effects of performance in national theaters and, 2
political philosophy, Coleridge's plays and, 8
Political Register, 48
politics
  newspaper commercialism and involvement in, 50
  theatrical experience and, 135, 153
"Politics and the English Language" (Orwell), 93

Pope, Alexander, 54, 85
popular opinion, and critical judgment, 198
Post (newspaper). *See Morning Post*
Post Boy, The, 52
Post Man, The, 52
post, and newspapers, 23
Posterman, The (Parry), 3–5
Pratt, Kathryn, 150
Preface to Lyrical Ballads (Wordsworth), 2, 84, 165
press. *See also* newspapers
  as agent of democracy, 25, 26
  belief in stabilizing effect of, 26
  Byron's death and focus on Kean in, 151
  censorship limiting development of, 51
  commercialization of. *See* commercialization of newspapers
  favors and patronage system in, 36
  freedom of. *See* free press
  government regulation of, 52
  information age in Romantic period and, 28
  Kean trial coverage in, 110
  news and commodity and transformation of, 53
  parliamentary reporting as central element of, 158
  positive public view of, 25
  social and cultural values shaped by, 113
  social function of, 50
Prince Regent (later George IV), Hunt's libelling of, 94, 213
Prince, Kathryn, 232
privacy
  Hazlitt's response to, 161
  Kean's controversy and notion of, 145
Prompter, The, 101
prostitution, and Old Price riots (1809), 64
public events
  authors as cultural intermediary between readers and, 28
  critic's subjective relation to, 163
  Hazlitt's essays and, 156
  newspaper reports on, 37
  newspapers' purpose as narration of, 31, 37
  Old Price riots (1809) as, 63
  reviewers on performances as, 43, 44
public life
  commercialization of newspapers, 29
  Hazlitt's reconception of, 154
  modes of expression and intersubjectivity included in, 16
  new genre of periodicals affecting, 27
  newspaper as social force in, 24, 29, 48
  newspapers and readers' relation to, 23
  Romantic period and conceptions about, 5
  separation between domestic and, 149

public opinion
  critic's role in shepherding, 163
  Kean's controversy and, 111, 134, 141, 143, 198
  Kean's trial and, 111
  newspapers' articulation of, 25, 27
  periodicals' transformation of, 83–84
  press's role in shaping, 112
  theater's attempts to manage, 193
  Times' claim to represent, 130, 134, 138, 142, 143
public space of theater, 15, 65, 109, 125
publicity
  Byron and, 146
  Garrick and, 120
  Hazlitt's response to, 161
  Hazlitt's review criticism and, 157
  Kean's fame and, 112, 120, 140, 149
  Kean's performances as exercises in self-publicity, 121
  Kean's trial and, 11, 110, 114, 118, 119, 125, 129, 137, 143, 145, 146
  newspapers as conduits of, 37, 142
  Old Price riots (1809) and, 44
  playbills and, 4, 102
  professional reporting and, 42
  Robinson's criminal conversation trial and, 115
  women's writing and, 147
Purinton, Marjean, 17

Quarterly Review, The, 35, 55, 179

radical causes, and Hazlitt, 161
radical periodicals, 24, 27, 66, 188
radical writers, 56, 78, 93, 144, 189
Rajan, Tilottama, 229
Rea, Robert, 50
readers. *See also* audiences
  ads for attracting, 34
  advance knowledge of plays in playbill periodicals and, 70, 71, 72
  as companions to critics, 57, 58
  authors as cultural intermediary between public events and, 28
  changing forms of textual publicity and, 37
  commercialization of newspapers and fracturing of, 152, 153
  consumerist desire for, 47
  critics' social function and, 152
  cultural practice of reading and writing for theatrical periodicals and, 58
  daily newspapers' commercial interests and, 30
  daily ritual of consumption by, 29, 47
  daily theatrical periodicals and, 71
  disappearance of periodicals not able to sustain, 159
  editorial voice and, 39

Hazlitt's model of cultural negotiation for, 154, 162
illusion of immediacy in newspapers and, 28
increase in number of, 53
melodramatic tactics to hold attention of, 46
newspapers shaped by expectations and desires of, 27
newspapers' creation of audience of, 27–28
newspapers' facilitation of interactions with public world by, 31
newspapers' rhetoric structuring response of, 39
poet's role as cultural intermediary for, 192
reactions to *Times*' attacks on Kean by, 129
reader-as-eyewitness technique in coverage and, 130
relation to public life through newspapers of, 23
reporting method alterations from increases in, 27
reports and advertisements with similar focuses on, 45
rhetoric of reporting and, 39
saving and binding of playbill periodicals by, 73
sensationalist details in reports and ads and, 45
sense of connection to a larger community and, 158
sense of theatrical history in playbill periodicals and, 73
theatrical periodicals' shaping of theatrical experience of, 59
theatrical periodicals' strategies for attracting and keeping, 66, 67, 69, 75, 76, 130, 158
theatrical press as part of daily experience of, 3
timing of traditional publishing process of, 31
reading
  Keats's anticipation of beginning, 207
  Keats's rethinking act of, 205
reading aloud, and experience of poetry, 24
Reflections on the Revolution in France (Burke), 2
Regier, Alexander, 233
Reiman, Donald, 228, 229
Remarks on the Causes of the Dispute (pamphlet), 64, 65, 101
reporting
  commercialization of newspapers and, 29
  consumer desire for daily dose of public world and, 30
  daily newspapers' vision of multiple strains of information with, 31
  disparate kinds of information mixed with, 87, 119
  Hazlitt's use of language from, 158

reporting (cont.)
    Hazlitt's view of readers and, 175
    Kean's controversy and, 136
    notion of publicness in, 43
    parliamentary. *See* parliamentary reporting
    readers' idea of "Britain" shaped by, 27
    readers' perceptions of theater as public experience in, 10
    readership increases and alterations in methods of, 27
    standardized objective style in, 42
    theater's presence in newspapers through, 24
    theatrical review construction similar to, 72
reports
    as central part of textual form, 37
    immediate connection to readers' everyday lives sought in, 45
    newspapers' seamless metonymy of potential events and, 28
    range of content and sources in, 30, 37, 46
    rhetorical divide between advertisements and, 45
    sensationalist details in, 45–46, 115
    theater as both advertisement and, 28
Restoration, 51, 60
reviewers. *See* critics
reviews. *See* Kean's reviews; theatrical reviews
revolution
    French Revolution and English fears of, 26
    Keats "Ode on a Grecian Urn" as response to, 233
    theatrical tastes of public affected by, 1, 3
Reynolds, John Hamilton, 54, 91, 198, 200, 205, 229, 231
Reynolds, Paige, 7
Richard II role, Shakespeare, 121
Richard III (Shakespeare), 167
Richard III role, Shakespeare, 1, 43–44, 71–72, 122, 125, 133, 140, 145, 150, 168, 198
Richardson, Alan, 17
Ricks, Christopher, 228, 230
Ridley, M.R., 229
riots. *See also* Old Price (O. P.) riots (1809)
    in eighteenth century, 62
Roach, Joseph, 123
Robinson, Mary, 55, 115–16
Robinson, Terry, 11, 55, 115, 148
Roe, Nicholas, 19, 106, 193, 194, 228, 229, 230, 233
Rohrbach, Emily, 215, 225, 233, 235
Romantic occasionalism. *See* occasionalism
Romantic period
    daily newspaper as social force in, 24
    Hazlitt's influence on, 152, 155
    high and low theater culture in, 189
    new genre of periodical publication emerging in, 27
    newly powerful media and information age in, 28
    political and material aspects of theatrical revolution during, 2
    public circulation of texts during, 15
    Shakespeare's interpretions in, 232
    theater as central public experience in, 1, 3
    theatrical experience in, 119
Romantic sociability, 2
Romanticism, and mass culture, 185
Romeo and Juliet (Shakespeare), 118, 125
Romeo role, Shakespeare, 198
Rose, George, 50
Round Table, The (Hazlitt), 152, 163
Russell, Gillian, 2, 11, 15, 16, 17, 19, 58, 99, 102, 147, 228
Rzepka, Charles, 195, 220, 229

Sachs, Jonathan, 215, 233
satire, 54, 119, 128
scenery technology, 61, 62, 166–67
Schaffer, Simon, 101, 147
Schmitt, Carl, 186
Schoenfield, Mark, 16, 96, 229
Scholes, Robert, 7
Scrivener, Michael, 50
Schoch, Richard, 189
Scott, Joan, 148
sensation, and Kean's acting style, 122
sensationalism
    interplay of objectivity and, 46
    newspaper examples of, in reports and ads, 45–46, 115, 164
    reviews and, 46
    theater and, 164, 230
Shakespeare, William
    anti-Kean publicity about Kean's fitness for roles in, 118
    anti-Kean publicity from his misappropriation of, 118
    commercialism in theater and, 112, 137
    Cox v. Kean debate's impact on changing understanding of, 120
    criminalization of through cultural appropriation of words and symbolic figure of, 117
    Fairburn volume's epigraph from, 114, 118
    Hazlitt on alterations of, 167
    Hazlitt's assessment of, 201–2
    Kean's ability to communicate embodied experience of, 199, 201, 203
    Kean's acting style and re-imaging of, 112

Kean's commercial associations and popular reception of, 125, 137
Kean's court case's impact on, 117
Keats on, 202, 206
letters between Kean and Mrs. Cox with quotations from, 118
notion of the theater and, 1
patent theaters' rights to, 60
Romantic period's approach to, 232
working-class access to, via theatrical periodicals, 232
Shakespeare's plays
  As You Like It, 128
  Coriolanus, 123, 173, 200
  Hamlet, 118, 123, 185, 190, 200
  Henry IV, Part 1, Hotspur role, 199
  Henry VIII, 120
  King John, 174
  King Lear, 114, 117, 118, 192, 206–8
  Macbeth, 1, 44, 63, 117, 123, 128, 136, 171, 185, 190, 199, 200
  Merchant of Venice, 1, 120, 122, 170, 172, 199
  Much Ado About Nothing, 96
  Othello, 122, 134, 147, 150, 163, 164, 169, 172, 200, 202
  Richard II, 121
  Richard III, 1, 43–44, 71–72, 122, 125, 133, 140, 167, 168, 198
  Romeo and Juliet, 118, 125, 198
  Timon of Athens, 124
Shakespearean roles
  Beatrice and Benedick, 96
  Iago, 163, 164
  Kean-Kemble comparison for, 112, 173, 200
Shakespearean roles of Kean, 1, 109, 123, 124, 199
  Coriolanus, 123, 173, 200
  Hamlet, 123, 190, 200
  Henry VIII, 120
  Hotspur, 199
  Kemble compared with, 173, 200
  Lear, 117, 118
  Macbeth, 117, 123, 136, 171, 190, 199, 200
  Othello, 122, 134, 147, 169, 172, 200
  Richard II, 121
  Richard III, 1, 122, 125, 133, 140, 145, 150, 168, 198
  Romeo, 198
  Shylock, 1, 120, 122, 170, 172, 199
  Timon of Athens, 124
Shakespearean roles of Kemble
  Coriolanus, 173
  hallmarks of, 146
  Kean compared with, 173
  King John, 174
  Macbeth, 63

Shelley, Percy Bysshe, 14, 17, 106, 193
Sheridan, Richard Brinsley, 50, 58, 105
Sheridan, Thomas, 43
Shylock role, Shakespeare, 1, 120, 122, 170, 172, 199
Siddons, Sarah, 36, 120, 167, 168, 175
Simpson, David, 220, 221, 223
Simpson, Michael, 17
Siskin, Clifford, 53
Slote, Bernice, 195, 231
Smith, Adam, 157, 187–88
Smith, Horace, 191, 192, 227
Smock Alley Theatre, Dublin, 100
social exchange, between spectators and actors, 61
social function
  criticism and, 152, 184
  critics and, 98
  newspapers and, 47
  poetry and, 192, 232
  press and, 50
  theater and, 49, 74, 79, 109, 174
social imaginary, newspaper and post in, 23
social mobility, and Keats, 193
social order, and theater rioters, 62
social position
  critics and, 93
  Hunt's libelling of Prince Regent and, 213
  Keats and, 191, 230
  theatrical dailies and, 77
Spectator, The, 65
"Speech in Defence of Jean Peltier, A" (Mackintosh), 25
Spirit of the Age, The (Hazlitt), 153
Stage, or Theatrical Inquisitor, The, 103
Stage, or Theatrical Touchstone, The, 103
Steele, Richard, 28, 59, 65
Stevens, Wallace, 226
Stewart, Garret, 234
Stillinger, Jack, 210, 229, 232, 234
Stone, Laurence, 148
Strachan, John, 46, 51
Straub, Kristina, 17
Stuart, Daniel, 34
subsidies, and daily newspapers, 25, 51
Sun, Emily, 221, 234, 235
Sunday newspapers. *See also* newspapers
  circulation of, 28
  competition from range of content in, 30
  demand for daily newspapers and sales of, 53
Suspicious Husband, The (Hoadley), 84–86
Sutherland, Kathryn, 232

Table Talk (Hazlitt), 152, 171
Talfourd, Thomas, 179, 180, 190

Tatler, The, 52, 65, 70
Thalia's Tablet and Melpomene's Memorandum Book, 87, 88
theater
   alternative representative assembly aspect of, 58
   anti-commercial rhetoric on decline of, 59
   as both commodity and institution, 14
   attendance at as newsworthy event, 121
   binary separation of literature and performance in, 1
   both as advertisement and as reported event, 28
   catalyst for occasionalism by, 153
   central public experience of, 1, 3
   criticism and eighteenth-century changes in, 65
   daily newspapers and, 21–49
   daily theatrical criticism as defender of traditions of, 75
   emergence of periodical culture devoted to, 59
   English brand of sociable behavior and, 1
   French Revolution's impact on public's taste in, 2
   Kean's trial as sign of decline of, 111
   local history of manners reflected in, 37
   playgoing conventions in, 57
   political assembly aspect of, 61
   positive public effects of, 165
   public experience and, 60, 95
   public space of, 15, 65, 109, 125
   relationship between audiences and theatrical producers in, 77
   seen as inherited right, 62, 63, 64, 65
   sensationalist aspects of, 164, 230
   social function of, 49, 74, 79, 109, 174
   social importance of, 100
   theater critics' view of, 77
   theater time in experience of, 11
   theatrical periodicals' safeguarding of integrity of, 73
   theatrical press and wider reach of, 3
   universe of experience held together by notion of, 1
theater critics. *See* critics
theater managers
   ethnic and class demographic changes and, 15
   Old Price riots (1809) due to changes by, 63, 64, 65
   theater changes and profit concerns of, 63
theater time, 11
theaters. *See also* Covent Garden Theatre, London; Drury Lane Theatre, London
   architectural changes in, 61
   benefit performances for actors in, 55, 61
   commercial aspect of play choices at, 74
   competition and changes for audiences' experiences in, 61
   delineation between stage and house in, 61
   free admission for reviewers in, 43
   gaslight's impact on audience experience in, 149, 189
   Hazlitt's closeness to life in, 154
   legislation spurring proliferation of, 60
   notion of public function of, 61
   Old Price riots and *See* Old Price (O. P.) riots (1809)
   patents granted to, 60
   playbills issued by, 68
   publicity for, 119
   representative public sphere aspect of, 134
   riots in eighteenth century in, 62
   social exchange between spectators and actors in, 61
Theatre, The (Steele), 59, 65
theatrical criticism. *See also* reviews
   as cultural practice, 58
   audience's "critical companion" in, 66
   audience-making strategies and, 143, 160
   critics of newspapers' theatrical reports as, 80
   cultural experienced reimagined and, 7
   daily press's transmission of, 24
   defense of ideal theatrical tradition by, 75
   eighteenth-century changes in playhouses and, 65
   Hazlitt's approach to, 155, 160, 161, 166
   Hazlitt's body of work crucial in, 152
   Hazlitt's new mode of, 169
   Hunt on best approach in, 95
   mantra of "facilitate–record–abridge" for, 32
   moral mission of, 80, 82
   moral standards of, 83–84, 85, 88, 90, 95, 96
   Morning Chronicle's professionalizing of, 43
   neo-classical aesthetic standards in, 66
   newspaper as conduit for, 163
   other types of reviews compared with, 166
   parliamentary reporting as forerunner to, 40, 43
   performance seen as a public event in, 44
   popular opinion as standard in, 198
   Romantic casuistry in, 154
   social function of, 152, 184
   standards negotiated through direct contact with audiences in, 66
   Steele's early work in, 65
   theatrical experience at intersection of public and private worlds and, 58
theatrical culture
   high and low, in Romantic period, 189

Index 273

Kean's controversy and, 145
patent legitimacy and, 15
rethinking Romantic authorship and, 8
sociability venues and, 18
textual forms of newspapers and readers' engagement in, 24
Theatrical Examiner, The, 69–70, 71
theatrical experience
  actors' mediation of, 165
  changing forms of textual publicity and, 37
  commercialization of. *See* commercialization of theatrical experience
  daily newspapers' portrayal of, 37
  factors in eighteenth century change in, 60
  Hazlitt's refiguration of, 152, 155, 176
  Hazlitt's reviews and, 162
  interaction with fellow Londoners and, 58
  intersection of public and private worlds in, 58
  Kean's acting and, 124, 138, 175
  Kean's celebrity and, 136
  Kean's controversy and, 110, 111, 113, 114, 120, 137, 138, 145, 146
  Kean's new model of, 191, 192
  Kean's performances and his public persona as prototypes of new kind of, 169
  Keats and, 195–99, 219
  Keats's love of theater and, 1
  Keats's poetics of interruption and, 192
  Keats's poetry and, 193
  Keats's shift in thinking related to, 205
  meaning and use of term, 6
  new models of interaction in, 77
  performers as starting point for, 168
  political and material aspects of, 2
  Romantic poetry and, 226
  Romantic sociability and, 2
  separation of theater as literature and as performance versus, 1
  theater's print artefcts and, 6
  theatrical periodicals' endeavor to create ideal, 99
Theatrical Gazette, 69
Theatrical Inquisitor, The, 75, 147
Theatrical Looker-On, The, 86
Theatrical Mince Pie, The, 57, 58, 86, 87, 89, 90, 93, 181, 227
Theatrical Mirror, The, 102
Theatrical Observer, The (Dublin), 102
Theatrical Observer, The (Edinburgh), 102
Theatrical Observer, The (London), 74, 119
  audience-making strategy of, 143
  criticism of *Times*' Kean trial coverage by, 138, 141–43
  Kean court case in, 137–41

Kean's status after return to the stage and, 145, 146
reviews in, 72
success of playbill format of, 69
theatrical reporting focus of, 68, 73
weekly digest of, 76
theatrical periodicals, 65–90, *See also* daily theatrical periodicals, monthly theatrical periodicals; weekly theatrical periodicals; *and specific titles*
  anti-commercial commentary in, 59, 87
  anti-commercial rhetoric of, 66, 67
  audience-making strategies of, 66, 67, 69, 75, 76, 130, 158
  contradictory aims of criticism in, 82
  cultural practice of reading and writing for, 58
  early examples of, 65–66
  emergence of, 59, 160
  Hazlitt's innovation in, 152
  Hazlitt's reaction to culture of, 157
  Hazlitt's writing for, 159
  impact of aesthetic judgments in, 73
  Kean reviewed in, 109, 110
  middle-class review culture and, 49
  moral critique presented by, 67, 74
  new models of interaction and, 77
  newspaper criticism as focus of, 79–82
  occasional modes of theatrical reviewing in, 11, 60, 155
  Old Price riots (1809) and proliferation of, 24, 44
  Old Price riots (1809) coverage in, 65, 101
  publication frequency and size, look, and feel of, 59
  range of publication formats of, 59
  readers' theatrical experience shaped by, 59
  safeguarding theater's integrity by, 73
  Steele's early work with, 65
  style of, 69
  sustained growth in number of, 59
  translation of events and performance into objects of readerly attention by, 6
theatrical press, 57–99, *See also* theatrical periodicals
  Byron's death and focus on Kean in, 151
  daily experience of readers and, 3
  Examiner's uniqueness in, 94
  expansion of range of theater audiences and, 3
  Hazlitt's transformation of, 155
  Hunt on commercial commitments of, 91
  Hunt on independence in theatrical criticism in, 92, 93
  Hunt's satiric set of rules and key phrases for critics in, 92–93
  Kean's controversy in, 111

theatrical press (cont.)
   Kean's public figure shaped by, 120
   Kean's status after return to the stage and, 145–46
   Kean's trial coverage and, 111, 130
   Old Price riots' impact on, 6
   pocket magazines and, 102
   Romantic poetics shaped by, 7
   shift in theatrical experience and, 175
   translation of events and performance into objects of readerly attention by, 6
Theatrical Recorder, The, 75
Theatrical Repertory, or Weekly Rosciad, The, 76
Theatrical Review, The (Bath), 77, 81, 103
theatrical reviews. *See also* Kean's reviews
   ad size compared with size of, 37
   advertisements published near, 46
   commitment to objective and detailed reporting of, 43
   comprehensiveness and size of, 36–37
   difficulty differentiating ads from, 36
   favors and patronage system in, 36
   free admission for reviewers and, 43
   Hazlitt on writing of, 177
   imbalance between reporterly detail and aesthetic evaluation in, 43–44
   Kean's trial coverage in newspapers similar to, 139
   notion of publicness in, 43
   objectivity of, 36, 44
   parliamentary reporting as forerunner to, 40, 43
   reviewer independence in, 43
   sensationalist details in, 46
   star status mentioned in, 44
theatrical revolution
   Kean and, 146, 149
   political and material aspects of, 2
Theatrical Rod!, The, 78
Thespian Sentinel, The, 73, 102
Thompson, E. P., 62, 100
Tighe, Mary, 218
Times, The, 32
   ad placement in, 32, 36, 45, 46, 72
   associationist strategies in, 46
   caricature Kean's treatment in, 128
   circulation of, 106
   commercial interests and, 30
   commercialized theatrical culture and, 146
   conflation of trial and performance in trial coverage of, 133
   consumer revolution and, 52
   cultural criticism and commercial exchange in, 137
   dating ranges in one issue of, 55
   defense of Kean court case coverage by, 135–37
   distinction between private and public spheres of experience and, 140
   editorial voice of, 39
   French Revolution reporting in, 45
   Hazlitt's dismissal from, 162
   Hazlitt's reviews in, 159, 163
   Kean court case in, 111–12, 113, 117, 118, 129–37, 138, 227
   Kean's fame and reviews in, 111
   Kean's love letters published in, 131–33, 139, 142
   Kean's new brand of celebrity and, 146
   Kean's reviews and responses in, 133–37
   Kean's status as object in, 121
   Lamb's attachment to, 23–24, 47
   military affairs coverage of, 38–39, 46
   military affairs letters from Wellington and Chatham in, 38–39
   narrative sensation as approach for news stories in, 45
   notions of privacy and, 138
   objectivity of, 44, 111, 136, 137
   Old Price riots mentioned in review in, 44
   opinions on reports and events in, 39
   other publications' criticism of Kean coverage by, 112, 119, 138, 141–43, 144–45
   parliamentary reporting in, 41
   power of, in Kean's trial reporting, 142
   public opinion shaped by, 111, 130, 138, 142, 143
   range of information in, 39, 46
   reader-as-eyewitness technique used by, 130
   reading practices encouraged by, 60
   reviews in, 46, 111, 130
   rhetoric structuring audience response in, 39
   shift in form and number of ads in, 36, 37
   shifts between report and commentary in trial coverage of, 131
   techniques of sensation employed by, 25
   theater ad iconography in, 37
   theatrical criticism approach of, 43–44
   Theatrical Observer's criticism of Kean trial coverage by, 138, 141–43
   theatrical review comprehensiveness and size in, 36–37
   typical front page of, 32
Thorpe, Clarence, 231
Timon of Athens role, Shakespeare, 124
"To Autumn" (Keats), 217
Townsman, The, 86
Trilling, Lionel, 228

Veblen, Thorstein, 53
Vendler, Helen, 222, 228, 234

View of the English Stage, A (Hazlitt), 152, 162, 163, 165, 190

Wales, Prince of (later George IV), and Mary Robinson's relationship, 148
Walker, R.B., 54
Walter, John, 29, 30, 31–32, 34
Wanderer, The (Burney), 13, 211–16
Wanko, Cheryl, 64
Watkins, Daniel, 17, 228
Watt, Ian, 56
Weekly Dramatic Register, The, 76
Weekly Review of the Affairs of France, 28
weekly theatrical periodicals, 66, *See also* theatrical periodicals
  anti-commercial rhetoric of, 77, 78, 79, 80, 82
  audience-making strategies of, 66, 76
  complexity of content of, 76
  daily theatrical periodicals compared with, 75
  daily theatrical periodicals criticized by, 74
  distribution of, 76
  format and content of, 76
  Hazlitt's writing for, 159
  playbill periodicals' evocative power compared with, 73
  primary textual component of, 76
Wellington, Arthur Wellesley, 1st Duke of, *Times* letter of, 38, 39, 42, 55
Werkmeister, Lucyle, 50
West, Benjamin, 192
Westminster Review, The, 29, 30, 53
Whale, John, 188, 189
Wheatley, Kim, 16
"When I have fears that I may cease to be" (Keats), 192, 206, 208–10
"Whether Genius is Conscious of its Powers?" (Hazlitt), 157
Whitman, Walt, 226
Wilkes, John, 25
Williams, Raymond, 40, 53
Wilson, Kathleen, 5, 28, 112
Wind-Up; or, Candour versus The Times, The, 151
Wolfson, Susan, 233
Wollstonecraft, Mary, 133, 211, 233
Wolves Club (Kean fan club), 121, 141
women. *See* gender
  criminal conversation and, 115
Woodfall, William "Memory," 40–41, 42, 43, 158, 188
Woods, Leigh, 110, 121
Wooler, T.J., 192
Wordsworth, William, 210, 213
  as bearer of poetic tradition, 205
  Cavanagh's style compared with, 180
  egotism of, 194
  epic poetry of, 179, 180
  Excursion of, 213
  "Hart-Leap Well" of, 19
  initial moment of sensation and, 177
  Keats on, 204, 205
  Keats's "Ode to Psyche" and, 218
  Lamb's letter to, 23, 24
  Preface to Lyrical Ballads of, 2, 84, 165
  public taste for spectacle and, 2, 84
  relation to external world in poetry of, 157
  statement of poetic intentions of, 193
  theatrical sensationalism and, 165
working class
  British Romanticism and, 14
  daily newspapers' growth and, 29
  theatrical periodicals' dissemination of Shakespeare to, 232
Worrall, David, 15, 17
Wren, Christopher, 61
"Written on the Day That Mr. Leigh Hunt Left Prison" (Keats), 214, 215
Wu, Duncan, 55

CAMBRIDGE STUDIES IN ROMANTICISM

General Editor
JAMES CHANDLER, *University of Chicago*

1. *Romantic Correspondence: Women, Politics and the Fiction of Letters*
   MARY A. FAVRET
2. *British Romantic Writers and the East: Anxieties of Empire*
   NIGEL LEASK
3. *Poetry as an Occupation and an Art in Britain, 1760–1830*
   PETER MURPHY
4. *Edmund Burke's Aesthetic Ideology: Language, Gender and Political Economy in Revolution*
   TOM FURNISS
5. *In the Theatre of Romanticism: Coleridge, Nationalism, Women*
   JULIE A. CARLSON
6. *Keats, Narrative and Audience*
   ANDREW BENNETT
7. *Romance and Revolution: Shelley and the Politics of a Genre*
   DAVID DUFF
8. *Literature, Education, and Romanticism: Reading as Social Practice, 1780–1832*
   ALAN RICHARDSON
9. *Women Writing about Money: Women's Fiction in England, 1790–1820*
   EDWARD COPELAND
10. *Shelley and the Revolution in Taste: The Body and the Natural World*
    TIMOTHY MORTON
11. *William Cobbett: The Politics of Style*
    LEONORA NATTRASS
12. *The Rise of Supernatural Fiction, 1762–1800*
    E. J. CLERY
13. *Women Travel Writers and the Language of Aesthetics, 1716–1818*
    ELIZABETH A. BOHLS
14. *Napoleon and English Romanticism*
    SIMON BAINBRIDGE
15. *Romantic Vagrancy: Wordsworth and the Simulation of Freedom*
    CELESTE LANGAN
16. *Wordsworth and the Geologists*
    JOHN WYATT
17. *Wordsworth's Pope: A Study in Literary Historiography*
    ROBERT J. GRIFFIN

18. *The Politics of Sensibility: Race, Gender and Commerce in the Sentimental Novel*
    MARKMAN ELLIS
19. *Reading Daughters' Fictions, 1709–1834: Novels and Society from Manley to Edgeworth*
    CAROLINE GONDA
20. *Romantic Identities: Varieties of Subjectivity, 1774–1830*
    ANDREA K. HENDERSON
21. *Print Politics: The Press and Radical Opposition: in Early Nineteenth-Century England*
    KEVIN GILMARTIN
22. *Reinventing Allegory*
    THERESA M. KELLEY
23. *British Satire and the Politics of Style, 1789–1832*
    GARY DYER
24. *The Romantic Reformation: Religious Politics in English Literature, 1789–1824*
    ROBERT M. RYAN
25. *De Quincey's Romanticism: Canonical Minority and the Forms of Transmission*
    MARGARET RUSSETT
26. *Coleridge on Dreaming: Romanticism, Dreams and the Medical Imagination*
    JENNIFER FORD
27. *Romantic Imperialism: Universal Empire and the Culture of Modernity*
    SAREE MAKDISI
28. *Ideology and Utopia in the Poetry of William Blake*
    NICHOLAS M. WILLIAMS
29. *Sexual Politics and the Romantic Author*
    SONIA HOFKOSH
30. *Lyric and Labour in the Romantic Tradition*
    ANNE JANOWITZ
31. *Poetry and Politics in the Cockney School: Keats, Shelley, Hunt and their Circle*
    JEFFREY N. COX
32. *Rousseau, Robespierre and English Romanticism*
    GREGORY DART
33. *Contesting the Gothic: Fiction, Genre and Cultural Conflict, 1764–1832*
    JAMES WATT
34. *Romanticism, Aesthetics, and Nationalism*
    DAVID ARAM KAISER
35. *Romantic Poets and the Culture of Posterity*
    ANDREW BENNETT
36. *The Crisis of Literature in the 1790s: Print Culture and the Public Sphere*
    PAUL KEEN
37. *Romantic Atheism: Poetry and Freethought, 1780–1830*
    MARTIN PRIESTMAN

38. *Romanticism and Slave Narratives: Transatlantic Testimonies*
    HELEN THOMAS
39. *Imagination under Pressure, 1789–1832: Aesthetics, Politics, and Utility*
    JOHN WHALE
40. *Romanticism and the Gothic: Genre, Reception, and Canon Formation, 1790–1820*
    MICHAEL GAMER
41. *Romanticism and the Human Sciences: Poetry, Population, and the Discourse of the Species*
    MAUREEN N. MCLANE
42. *The Poetics of Spice: Romantic Consumerism and the Exotic*
    TIMOTHY MORTON
43. *British Fiction and the Production of Social Order, 1740–1830*
    MIRANDA J. BURGESS
44. *Women Writers and the English Nation in the 1790s*
    ANGELA KEANE
45. *Literary Magazines and British Romanticism*
    MARK PARKER
46. *Women, Nationalism and the Romantic Stage: Theatre and Politics in Britain, 1780–1800*
    BETSY BOLTON
47. *British Romanticism and the Science of the Mind*
    ALAN RICHARDSON
48. *The Anti-Jacobin Novel: British Conservatism and the French Revolution*
    M. O. GRENBY
49. *Romantic Austen: Sexual Politics and the Literary Canon*
    CLARA TUITE
50. *Byron and Romanticism*
    JEROME MCGANN and JAMES SODERHOLM
51. *The Romantic National Tale and the Question of Ireland*
    INA FERRIS
52. *Byron, Poetics and History*
    JANE STABLER
53. *Religion, Toleration, and British Writing, 1790–1830*
    MARK CANUEL
54. *Fatal Women of Romanticism*
    ADRIANA CRACIUN
55. *Knowledge and Indifference in English Romantic Prose*
    TIM MILNES
56. *Mary Wollstonecraft and the Feminist Imagination*
    BARBARA TAYLOR
57. *Romanticism, Maternity and the Body Politic*
    JULIE KIPP

58. *Romanticism and Animal Rights*
    DAVID PERKINS
59. *Georgic Modernity and British Romanticism: Poetry and the Mediation of History*
    KEVIS GOODMAN
60. *Literature, Science and Exploration in the Romantic Era: Bodies of Knowledge*
    TIMOTHY FULFORD, DEBBIE LEE, and PETER J. KITSON
61. *Romantic Colonization and British Anti-Slavery*
    DEIRDRE COLEMAN
62. *Anger, Revolution, and Romanticism*
    ANDREW M. STAUFFER
63. *Shelley and the Revolutionary Sublime*
    CIAN DUFFY
64. *Fictions and Fakes: Forging Romantic Authenticity, 1760–1845*
    MARGARET RUSSETT
65. *Early Romanticism and Religious Dissent*
    DANIEL E. WHITE
66. *The Invention of Evening: Perception and Time in Romantic Poetry*
    CHRISTOPHER R. MILLER
67. *Wordsworth's Philosophic Song*
    SIMON JARVIS
68. *Romanticism and the Rise of the Mass Public*
    ANDREW FRANTA
69. *Writing against Revolution: Literary Conservatism in Britain, 1790–1832*
    KEVIN GILMARTIN
70. *Women, Sociability and Theatre in Georgian London*
    GILLIAN RUSSELL
71. *The Lake Poets and Professional Identity*
    BRIAN GOLDBERG
72. *Wordsworth Writing*
    ANDREW BENNETT
73. *Science and Sensation in Romantic Poetry*
    NOEL JACKSON
74. *Advertising and Satirical Culture in the Romantic Period*
    JOHN STRACHAN
75. *Romanticism and the Painful Pleasures of Modern Life*
    ANDREA K. HENDERSON
76. *Balladeering, Minstrelsy, and the Making of British Romantic Poetry*
    MAUREEN N. MCLANE
77. *Romanticism and Improvisation, 1750–1850*
    ANGELA ESTERHAMMER
78. *Scotland and the Fictions of Geography: North Britain, 1760–1830*
    PENNY FIELDING

79. *Wordsworth, Commodification and Social Concern: The Poetics of Modernity*
    DAVID SIMPSON
80. *Sentimental Masculinity and the Rise of History, 1790–1890*
    MIKE GOODE
81. *Fracture and Fragmentation in British Romanticism*
    ALEXANDER REGIER
82. *Romanticism and Music Culture in Britain, 1770–1840: Virtue and Virtuosity*
    GILLEN D'ARCY WOOD
83. *The Truth about Romanticism: Pragmatism and Idealism in Keats, Shelley, Coleridge*
    TIM MILNES
84. *Blake's Gifts: Poetry and the Politics of Exchange*
    SARAH HAGGARTY
85. *Real Money and Romanticism*
    MATTHEW ROWLINSON
86. *Sentimental Literature and Anglo-Scottish Identity, 1745–1820*
    JULIET SHIELDS
87. *Romantic Tragedies: The Dark Employments of Wordsworth, Coleridge, and Shelley*
    REEVE PARKER
88. *Blake, Sexuality and Bourgeois Politeness*
    SUSAN MATTHEWS
89. *Idleness, Contemplation and the Aesthetic*
    RICHARD ADELMAN
90. *Shelley's Visual Imagination*
    NANCY MOORE GOSLEE
91. *A Cultural History of the Irish Novel, 1790–1829*
    CLAIRE CONNOLLY
92. *Literature, Commerce, and the Spectacle of Modernity, 1750–1800*
    PAUL KEEN
93. *Romanticism and Childhood: The Infantilization of British Literary Culture*
    ANN WEIRDA ROWLAND
94. *Metropolitan Art and Literature, 1810–1840: Cockney Adventures*
    GREGORY DART
95. *Wordsworth and the Enlightenment Idea of Pleasure*
    ROWAN BOYSON
96. *John Clare and Community*
    JOHN GOODRIDGE
97. *The Romantic Crowd*
    MARY FAIRCLOUGH
98. *Romantic Women Writers, Revolution and Prophecy*
    ORIANNE SMITH
99. *Britain, France and the Gothic, 1764–1820*
    ANGELA WRIGHT

100. *Transfiguring the Arts and Sciences*
    JON KLANCHER
101. *Shelley and the Apprehension of Life*
    ROSS WILSON
102. *Poetics of Character: Transatlantic Encounters 1700–1900*
    SUSAN MANNING
103. *Romanticism and Caricature*
    IAN HAYWOOD
104. *The Late Poetry of the Lake Poets: Romanticism Revised*
    TIM FULFORD
105. *Forging Romantic China: Sino-British Cultural Exchange 1760–1840*
    PETER J. KITSON
106. *Coleridge and the Philosophy of Poetic Form*
    EWAN JAMES JONES
107. *Romanticism in the Shadow of War: Literary Culture in the Napoleonic War Years*
    JEFFREY N. COX
108. *Slavery and the Politics of Place: Representing the Colonial Caribbean, 1770–1833*
    ELIZABETH A. BOHLS
109. *The Orient and the Young Romantics*
    ANDREW WARREN
110. *Lord Byron and Scandalous Celebrity*
    CLARA TUITE
111. *Radical Orientalism: Rights, Reform, and Romanticism*
    GERARD COHEN-VRIGNAUD
112. *Print, Publicity, and Popular Radicalism in the 1790s*
    JON MEE
113. *Wordsworth and the Art of Philosophical Travel*
    MARK OFFORD
114. *Romanticism, Self-Canonization, and the Business of Poetry*
    MICHAEL GAMER
115. *Women Wanderers and the Writing of Mobility, 1784–1814*
    INGRID HORROCKS
116. *Eighteen Hundred and Eleven: Poetry, Protest and Economic Crisis*
    E. J. CLERY
117. *Urbanization and English Romantic Poetry*
    STEPHEN TEDESCHI
118. *The Poetics of Decline in British Romanticism*
    JONATHAN SACHS
119. *The Caribbean and the Medical Imagination, 1764–1834: Slavery, Disease and Colonial Modernity*
    EMILY SENIOR
120. *Science, Form, and the Problem of Induction in British Romanticism*
    DAHLIA PORTER

121. *Wordsworth and the Poetics of Air*
    THOMAS H. FORD
122. *Romantic Art in Practice: Cultural Work and the Sister Arts, 1760–1820*
    THORA BRYLOWE
123. *European Literatures in Britain, 1815–1832: Romantic Translations*
    DIEGO SIGALIA
124. *Romanticism and Theatrical Experience: Kean, Hazlitt and Keats in the Age of Theatrical News*
    JONATHAN MULROONEY
125. *The Romantic Tavern: Literature and Conviviality in the Age of Revolution*
    IAN NEWMAN